ultimates

ROBERT CUMMINGS NEVILLE

ultimates

PHILOSOPHICAL THEOLOGY

VOLUME ONE

State University of New York Press

Cover art: *Ultimates* by Beth Neville
Graphite pencil and colored pens on Bristol board paper, 10"x10", January, 2013

Published by
STATE UNIVERSITY OF NEW YORK PRESS, ALBANY

© 2013 State University of New York

All rights reserved

Printed in the United States of America

No part of this book may be used or reproduced in any manner whatsoever without written permission. No part of this book may be stored in a retrieval system or transmitted in any form or by any means including electronic, electrostatic, magnetic tape, mechanical, photocopying, recording, or otherwise without the prior permission in writing of the publisher.

For information, contact
STATE UNIVERSITY OF NEW YORK PRESS, ALBANY, NY
www.sunypress.edu

Production, Laurie Searl
Marketing, Kate McDonnell

Library of Congress Cataloging-in-Publication Data

Neville, Robert C.
  Ultimates : philosophical theology / Robert Cummings Neville.
    pages cm
  "Volume one."
  Includes bibliographical references and index.
  ISBN 978-1-4384-4883-1 (hardcover : alk. paper)
  ISBN 978-1-4384-4884-8 (paperback : alk. paper)
  1. Philosophical theology. 2. Philosophy and religion. I. Title.
  BL51.N446 2013
  210—dc23   2013003405

10 9 8 7 6 5 4 3 2 1

for Wesley J. Wildman

The art on the cover of this volume is by Beth Neville, my wife, who has provided art for many of my SUNY Press books. She has my great thanks. Its symbolic meaning gives visual expression to the thesis that there are five ultimates. The central yellow square represents the ultimate ontological act of creation from which all determinate things come, as all lines go out from it. Any determinate thing has four ultimate cosmological traits: form, components formed, location in an existential field, and value-identity, represented by the sides of the central square. All things are mixtures of these four cosmological ultimates, represented by the many lines and angles that intersect in the colored pencil drawing. The formal composition suggests ontological stability, which is part of the argument of the volume. But the visibility of the individually drawn lines in the colored patches and the fact that the formal composition is not quite exact suggest the singularity and exceptionalism of each thing, another part of the argument. Understanding the book helps to see the cover art in its depth.

Contents

Cross References	xiii
Preface	xv
Acknowledgments	xxv
Introduction	1
I. The Hypothesis	1
II. Defining Religion	4
III. Identifying Religion in Public Discourse	9
IV. Distinguishing Marks of *Philosophical Theology*	12

Part I
Ultimates Defined

Part I. Preliminary Remarks	25

Chapter One
Sacred Canopies	29
I. A Theory of Sacred Canopies	29
II. Finite/Infinite Contrasts	33
III. World-Defining Human Problems	34
IV. Truth in Sacred Canopies	42

Chapter Two
Reference, Reduction, Philosophy, and Metaphysics	45
I. The Presupposition of Real Reference	45
II. The Scientific Bracketing of Real Reference	49

III. Philosophy's Control for Reductionism　52
　　　IV. Metaphysics Explained and Defended　55

CHAPTER THREE
Symbolic Engagement　63
　　　I. Interpretation as Engagement　63
　　　II. The Pragmatic Heritage　68
　　　III. Iconic, Indexical, and Conventional Reference in
　　　　　Extension and Intention　70
　　　IV. Engaging Finite/Infinite Contrasts　73

CHAPTER FOUR
Worldviews　81
　　　I. Orientation and Worldviews: The Sacred/Mundane
　　　　　Continuum　81
　　　II. The Transcendence/Intimacy Continuum　84
　　　III. The Sophistication/Popular Culture Continuum　87
　　　IV. The Existential Continua: Sharing,
　　　　　Comprehensiveness, Intensity　91

Part I. Summary Implications　95

PART II
Ultimates Symbolized

Part II. Preliminary Remarks　101

CHAPTER FIVE
Ultimate Reality and Ultimate Concern　105
　　　I. Ultimate and Proximate Concerns　105
　　　II. Ultimacy and Dialectic　109
　　　III. Ultimate Concern as a Function of True Ultimacy　113
　　　IV. Tensions along the Worldview Continua　118

CHAPTER SIX
Toward Transcendent Symbols of Ultimacy　121
　　　I. Scale　121
　　　II. Idolatry　124
　　　III. Explanation: Metaphysics　127
　　　IV. Experience　131

Chapter Seven
Toward Intimate Symbols of Ultimacy   135
  I. Nature's Depths   135
  II. The Uncanny Familiar   138
  III. Human Meaning   141
  IV. Human Correction   146

Chapter Eight
Ultimacy in Theological Framing: Ontology and Narrative   149
  I. Narrative of the Divine   149
  II. Narrative of the People   153
  III. The Symbolic Falsehood of All Narratives   155
  IV. Living with Broken Narratives and Humanized Transcendents   158

Part II. Summary Implications   163

Part III
Ultimates Demonstrated

Part III. Preliminary Remarks   169

Chapter Nine
The Metaphysics of Ontological Ultimacy   173
  I. Ultimate Reality, Being, and the Problem of the One and the Many   173
  II. Whether Being Is One or Many   176
  III. Whether Being Is Analogical or Univocal   180
  IV. Whether Being Is Determinate or Indeterminate   184

Chapter Ten
The Metaphysics of Cosmological Ultimacy   193
  I. Determinateness as Harmony: Essential and Conditional Components   193
  II. Transcendental Elements of Harmony: Form and Components   197
  III. Transcendental Elements of Harmony: Existential Location   202
  IV. Transcendental Elements of Harmony: Achieved Value-Identity   204

Chapter Eleven
Proof of an Ultimate Ontological Creative Act   211
    I. Radical Contingency and the Ontological Context of Mutual Relevance   212
    II. Proof of an Ontological Creative Act   215
    III. The Determinate World as the End of the Act   218
    IV. Abyss in the Act: Symmetry of the Concept versus Asymmetry of What Is Conceived   221

Chapter Twelve
The Ontological Ultimate: An Act of Creation   227
    I. The Nature of the Ultimate Act as Created   227
    II. The Eternity of Creation   232
    III. Time and Eternity in the Three Modes of Time   235
    IV. Eternity as Ontological and Cosmological Ultimate Reality   241

Part III. Summary Implications   245

Part IV
Ultimates Known

Part IV. Preliminary Remarks   251

Chapter Thirteen
What Can Be Known about Ultimacy   253
    I. The Ultimate as Modeled: God, Consciousness, Emergence   253
    II. Ultimacy and the Transcendentals: Form, Components, Existential Location, Value-Identity   262
    III. Eternity and the Divine Life   266
    IV. Ultimacy in Extension and Intension   269

Chapter Fourteen
What Cannot Be Known about Ultimacy   273
    I. The Ultimate Has No Intrinsic Nature apart from Creation   273
    II. The Ultimate and Other Possible Worlds   276
    III. The Ultimate Is Not a Person   279
    IV. The Ultimate and Intelligibility   282

CHAPTER FIFTEEN
Symbolic Engagement as Praying the Ultimate — 287
    I. Theological Understanding as a Sign — 287
    II. Multiple Symbols along the Sophistication/
        Popular Religion, Transcendence/Intimacy, and
        Sacred/Mundane Continua — 290
    III. Systematic Thinking for Controlling Symbols — 293
    IV. Thinking the Ultimate — 297

CHAPTER SIXTEEN
Mystical Engagement — 301
    I. The Path of Meditation: Nondualism — 303
    II. The Path of Contemplation: Suchness — 306
    III. The Path of the Mystical Abyss — 309
    IV. The Path of Love — 312

Part IV. Summary Implications — 319

Notes — 325
Bibliography — 343
Index — 357

Cross References

As a systematic work, the three volumes of *Philosophical Theology* involve much cross-referencing among its parts. Although each of the volumes has a primary title—*Ultimates, Existence, Religion*, the cross-references are to the volumes by number. Cross-references are in footnotes on the occasion where commentary is required; otherwise they are in the lines of the text. The general rubric for cross-referencing is this. Cross-references will always be in *italics* and this means that they refer to volumes of *Philosophical Theology*; the first Roman numeral refers to the volume. If the reference is to a chapter, the volume number will be given first, followed by a comma, then the chapter number in Arabic, and perhaps if needed a comma followed by a section number in lower-case Roman numerals. So, "Volume two, Chapter three, Section IV" would be *II, 3, iv*. If the reference is to a part of a volume, the Roman volume number is first, followed by a comma and "pt" for part and an Arabic numeral for the number of the part. So, "Volume two, Part III" would be *II, pt 3*. Often a part is referred to as a whole; but if the reference is to the "preliminary remarks" or the "summary implications," which are always keyed to parts, not chapters, then the referent to the part would be followed by a comma and "pr" and/or "si." So, "volume three, part 4, preliminary remarks and summary implications" would be *III, pt 4, pr, si*. If reference is made to a part or chapter without an indication of volume number, the assumption is that the volume is the one in which the reference is made. The text spells out units of the three volumes when it discusses them directly.

Preface

This preface introduces a three-volume systematic project in philosophical theology, a scale of reflection uncommon today and in need of some prefatory explanation. The overall topic of the project is "theology" in the sense of dealing with first-order issues in religion, to use the increasingly common word for intellectual construction and analysis in all religious traditions. Such first-order issues include but are not limited to the nature of ultimate reality, the defining predicaments of human life, the ecstatic fulfillments embraced within religion, the elusive beauty of existence itself, and authenticity of personal and communal religious living. The overall genre of reflection is philosophy, with the caveat that philosophy includes or makes use of any discipline that might bear helpfully upon the topic; more will be said here about philosophy (*III, preface*). The overall perspective of the reflection embraces first-order experiences and religious revelations as much as possible but denies to any the authority to trump alternatives without themselves being subject to critical examination This project does not give trumping authority to any special committed religious location. Hence this project creates an intellectual roadway between confessional theology that does assume some kind of trumping authority for a revelation, tradition, or community and so-called objective religious studies that avoids the questions of truth about first-order theological issues. Those questions of truth are among the ultimately most important to be asked and the business of philosophical theology is to ask them.

For an inquiry to presuppose a committed religious location inevitably turns those who occupy different committed locations, or none, into outsiders. The outsiders' response to a theology argued from within such a committed location at best is curiosity about how "others" do it and more likely is plain neglect. The result is failure to summon a public within which everyone who might be interested in the outcome of first-order religious inquiry is invited to participate. Surely a theology of first-order religious issues needs to render itself vulnerable to anyone who might have something to contribute or a critical word of correction. Therefore, thinking from the location of a confessional commitment makes outsiders precisely of those who might be the most important conversation partners.

Equally problematic for first-order religious inquiry is thinking from the location of the particular commitment that no religious commitments can be true, as happens with many scholars identifying themselves with the scientific study of religion. Almost inevitably this means that the first-order religious issues are never addressed in detail if at all. So the stakes are very high for developing a sophisticated, systematic, and thoroughly vulnerable theology of first-order religious issues that is not hampered by these prior commitments. The aim of these volumes is to do precisely this.

The strategy of *Philosophical Theology* is to employ philosophy to set an ongoing critical construction of categories, vulnerable to correction by philosophical argument as well as by empirical evidence from religion and other domains, which provide for a deep, integrated, and relatively comprehensive understanding of first-order religious issues.[1] Through the philosophical categories and arguments, inquiries will be conducted into the nature of ultimacy, the human predicaments as well as ecstatic fulfillments that define the ultimate meanings of the human condition, and what is worthy or deleterious in religious life. The aim is to produce an understanding of these first-order theological issues in rich empirical detail with good cases for what is true about the main topics and for how these truths can guide life in its religious dimensions. Hence, this is a *philosophical* theology.

These volumes extend into theological areas a philosophical system that has been worked out in its core tenets and developed in many directions besides religion.[2] The philosophical system supports itself in the spectrum of contemporary and classical philosophical positions and is vulnerable to correction by them, including postmodern philosophies that are hostile to system. The public for the philosophy as developed here for theological issues includes thinkers who come from any religious or secular tradition with ideas to contribute to the first-order theological issues or to the second and higher order issues of analysis and methodology. The public also includes thinkers from any of the philosophical, literary, scientific, and practical disciplines who might be interested in the arguments necessary to make cases for claims about the first-order issues.[3] Although philosophy is out of favor with contemporary confessional theologians in many religious traditions, this has not always been so. In fact, in most traditions philosophy has not been distinguished from theology of the systematic sort and many of the greatest thinkers about first-order religious issues have been known also as philosophers (I, 2, iv).

That this theology is so philosophical might well be alienating to some theologians who identify themselves with a confessional commitment to a particular religious location, especially those who view that commitment as providing premises from which theological claims should follow and without which argument is impossible. Many academicians, theologians, and journalists in America today assume that "theology" is restricted to those with such confessional commitments, despite the fact that the term also has a much broader denotation. Ironically, confessional theologians would make outsiders of those who will not operate within their premises, turning their own theology into an insider enterprise. From the perspective of those whose commitment to a religious location entails that the location provides premises that are the ground rules for theology, *Philosophical Theology* is an outsider enterprise.

Despite this exclusion of *Philosophical Theology* from the circle of a confessional commitment, the project here still should have things to say about the first-order issues in any religious location, claims that at least in principle are not biased by a commitment that functions as an unchallengeable premise. This project should serve the theological interests of Buddhists, Christians, Confucians, Daoists, Hindus, Jews, and Muslims just as much as the work of their own confessional theologians, and with an openness to comparison and correction that provides a broad and somewhat tested context. As explained in the Introduction, *Philosophical Theology* respects and interprets the revelatory claims of the religions it studies without treating them as unchallengeable premises. Thus *Philosophical Theology* speaks *to* and *for* the religious locations it studies but not *from* any of them in the sense of presupposing their truth.

No one escapes historical and social locatedness, however, and I have grown old becoming increasingly individuated in my religious and intellectual contexts.[4] These historical particularities cause distortions in this project that will be as apparent as they are inevitable. Nevertheless, the structure of the project sets itself up to be vulnerable to correction as the distortions are pointed out. The methodological discussions work hard to expose and correct for bias. No bias exists here that comes from explicit commitment to a theological position as an unchallengeable premise from which the rest follows, even if there are implicit commitments that function as hidden premises until they are exposed and questioned. This said, the intent of *Philosophical Theology* is to speak to and for anyone concerned with religion and its first-order issues, in any religion or combination of them.

The three volumes begun here present a systematic philosophical theology, and so are subtitled *Philosophical Theology One, Two,* and *Three,* with the respective titles *Ultimates, Existence,* and *Religion.* The volumes collectively and the system as a whole are referred to simply as *Philosophical Theology.* This trilogy is prefaced by my *On the Scope and Truth of Theology: Theology as Symbolic Engagement,* which serves as an elaborate introduction to the kind of philosophical theology exhibited here, especially the epistemological and methodological issues involved.

Among other things, *Philosophical Theology* addresses first-order questions of truth, authenticity, and value in the topics of theology and religion. And among those other things, it also addresses the higher-order questions that bear upon making its cases about the first-order questions. These include philosophical questions, as well as issues in the literary, artistic, practical, historical, social scientific, and natural scientific approaches to religion, both substantive and methodological. *Philosophical Theology* thus needs to develop and justify, so far as possible, a theory of religion in order to make its cases for first-order claims. All the disciplines and approaches helpful or necessary for a theory of religion are internal to *Philosophical Theology*, which therefore has no neat professional boundaries.[5]

This *Philosophical Theology* might also be called a systematic "philosophy of religion," if "philosophy of religion" can be allowed to address first-order questions, such as the nature of ultimate reality. In its classic eighteenth- and nineteenth-century forms, Western philosophy of religion did indeed address these first-order questions. John Locke's *The Reasonableness of Christianity*, David Hume's *Dialogues concerning Natural Religion*, and the whole of G.W.F. Hegel's system are classic philosophies of religion in the sense that they dealt with religion's questions, including first-order ones.

These classic philosophies of religion, however, have been criticized as Christian theology in disguise and the criticism is largely accurate. Locke and Hume took religion to be mainly Christianity (or Christian deism) and showed little awareness of or concern for other religions. Even Baruch Spinoza's *A Theological-Political Treatise*, though authored by a "God-intoxicated Jew," construed religion in ways dominated by European attempts to define it relative to the wars of religion, which were primarily conflicts within Christianity. Hegel's *Philosophy of Religion* for its day was astonishingly erudite concerning world religions. Hegel understood, as perhaps only Leibniz had before him among modern Western philosophers, that a case for Christianity can be made only by giving all the other religions their due, which Hegel attempted to do. Without claiming that the concern to justify Christianity was more important than many other motives in the development of Hegel's philosophy, nevertheless it is true that Hegel organized his analysis of world religions according to how they lead up to and are fulfilled by his version of Christianity. So this classic tradition of philosophy of religion that did deal with first-order religious questions has been largely discredited as covert Christian theology. The Christian theological background is not even covert in the kind of philosophy of religion in an analytical mode expressed in the work of Alvin Plantinga and his colleagues in "Reformed epistemology."

"Philosophy of religion" in our time names many projects that are not always connected. Analytic philosophy of religion, including Plantinga's, treats religious topics with a *method* of philosophical analysis rather than with a developed system of philosophy such as the one guiding *Philosophical Theology*. Some analytic philosophy of religion deriving from Wittgenstein, such as that of D.Z. Phillips, is plainly apologetic for Christianity, arguing that religious forms of life are beyond criticism. Rarely is analytic philosophy of religion systematically erudite about world religions and their comparison. Keith Ward is an outstanding exception because of the comparative base of his systematic theology.[6] In recent years, however, the term *philosophical theology* has been applied to a family of analytical philosophies that treat Christian theological topics, usually in an apologetic way.[7] *Philosophical Theology* rejects Christian apologetics, and any other kind of religious apologetics, as justification for its positions, although of course it needs to analyze apologetic theologies. It also has a much more expansive sense of philosophy than is to be found in analytic philosophy. But insofar as analytic philosophical theology is philosophical reflection on theological issues, with attention to all the other approaches to religion that might be relevant to understanding and dealing with first-order theological issues, the analytic sense of the phrase is acceptable to the project of *Philosophical Theology*, which of course is no more Christian than Confucian.

A special note needs to be taken of the revival of pragmatism within certain quarters of analytical philosophy that has strong bearing on second- and higher-order issues pertaining to theology and religion. In a perceptively edited volume, Nancy K. Frankenberry has shown how the philosophies of Donald Davidson, Richard Rorty, and most especially Robert Brandom bear upon the understanding of the nature of religious belief.[8] The philosophy in *Philosophical Theology* develops out of classical pragmatism (and process philosophy, Confucian philosophy, Platonism, and other important roots) and so is closely related to the re-inscription of pragmatic themes within the projects of analytical philosophy.[9] The analytic pragmatic discussion assembled by Frankenberry emphasizes the role of belief in religion (with a counterweight in a chapter by Catherine M. Bell) in a way that abstracts it from religious practice and engagement with religious things, which *Philosophical Theology* tries not to do. Perhaps this is an inevitable limitation of a certain kind of analytic philosophy that believes philosophy should analyze language and belief, not the life in which beliefs direct and shape encounters.[10] Moreover, the authors in this analytical pragmatic discussion take belief in "superhuman agents" to be necessary to or definitive of religion, which *Philosophical Theology* rejects (*III, 1, i, ii*). The authors in Frankenberry's volume also are allergic to philosophical cosmology and metaphysics, and to notions of the sacred, for reasons having to do with previous attempts to define and characterize religion exclusively in those terms; but that allergy should not blind the discussion to what might be contributed by those approaches.[11] The value in the analytic pragmatic discussion is its elaboration of the ways in which practices of thinking, guided by norms of practice rather than "logical implication" alone, organize the meaning of religious beliefs. *Philosophical Theology* offers ample supplementation of this good point by analyses of actual religious engagements shaped by beliefs. The most important contributor in the analytical pragmatic discussion so far, most likely, is Robert Brandom (*I, 3, ii*).[12]

Perhaps the most active kind of philosophy of religion today in America is that having to do with comparisons among religions and theological traditions. The comparative theology associated with Francis X. Clooney, S.J., is an exciting, growing, intellectual movement.[13] It demonstrates that "theology" is not a title owned by Christianity. But it is hesitant about systematic attempts to answer first-order questions from a comparative base. *Philosophical Theology* is more direct in declaring its independence from confessional locations that might claim uncriticizable authority.

Wesley J. Wildman calls his work, which in many respects is similar to the project here, "religious philosophy" to avoid both the stigma of much contemporary philosophy of religion in bracketing out first-order questions and the stigma of much contemporary theology in being confessional, mainly Christian.[14] The limitation of his neologism is that it does not connote the commitment to first-order issues that he makes in fact, and it does not indicate that his substantive "philosophy" includes within it the sciences and other approaches to religion necessary to make first-order theological cases, which he also in fact intends and signifies by describing "religious philosophy" as "multidisciplinary."

So "philosophical theology" seems the most appropriate title for this project. Because of its orientation to first-order issues, it is theology. Because it does not decide those issues on a confessional base but is required to make cases for them, it aims to include the disciplines necessary for making those cases. Because the first-order issues arise in all the great religions, and the cases for them need to acknowledge the competition where it is found, *Philosophical Theology* assumes and employs a public of comparative theology, including "secular theologies." The primary genre of *Philosophical Theology Three* can be called "philosophy of religion" because its main topic is religion as such (*III, preface*); in this sense, philosophy of religion is a proper part of philosophical theology and as such is philosophy that deals with first-order religious questions.

"Philosophical theology" is a descriptive phrase with something of its own history. Some have argued that it was a title invented for Paul Tillich when he moved to Harvard University. It was an apt title for him at the time, distinguishing him from biblical theologians such as Rudolf Bultmann, although he knew and used the Bible extensively with the critical methods of his time. The title also distinguished him from confessional theologians such as Karl Barth, although Tillich thought of himself, like Barth, to be operating within the Christian "theological circle." In a general sense, *Philosophical Theology* follows Tillich in this with major changes. The "theological circle" needs to include all (or at least as many as possible) claims to revelation and authority, not only Christian ones, properly adjudicated of course. And the approach to scriptures of various traditions, as well as practices, liturgies, and institutions, should include all the methodological perspectives of religious studies, including now those of evolutionary biology and cognitive science. This expansion of the theological circle follows the trajectory initiated by Tillich.[15] An important intermediate position in this expansion is Christopher Morse's *Not Every Spirit: A Dogmatics of Christian Disbelief*. While resolutely remaining in the Christian theological circle, he subjects a great many of the classical theological loci to the plausibility conditions of the twenty-first century. He does not go so far, however, as actually to place all the major traditions on an equal evidential basis although he comes very close to doing so with the considerations of secular modernity.

Philosophical Theology is *systematic* in at least three senses. First, it aims to have a coherent formal structure that exhibits something of the connection of the topics. Formal systematic structure need not be propositional, such as that of Thomas Aquinas or Karl Barth, although those are good examples of formal structures. This project is structurally systematic because it is shaped around a metaphysical hypothesis and a theory of religion, interpreted philosophically so as to aim at comprehensiveness and interconnection. Of course it falls short of true comprehensiveness—what could that mean regarding religion?—but it is responsible to that ideal.

Second, *Philosophical Theology* aims to treat its topics from the most important relevant angles and is systematic in that sense. Determining which are the relevant angles is part of the systematic problem and attaining leverage from those angles often involves creating categories, modes of argument, and connections with various disciplines that are somewhat original with the philosophical theology. This is to say, philosophical theology needs its formal structure in order to take responsibility for that on which it stands when it inquires from the angles it believes to be relevant. "Standing on something" for inquiry is a misleading metaphor. Rather inquiry is like scrambling for balance on a log careening down the rapids of a river. One of the principal senses in which this systematic theology is philosophical is that philosophy is required to enable the poise to make the critical connections with needed disciplines, levels of analysis, and theoretical constructions.

The third sense in which *Philosophical Theology* is systematic, deriving from the first two, is that it aims to exhibit its subject matter consistently, coherently, applicably, and adequately, so as to come into one view. These systematic criteria were elucidated by Alfred North Whitehead in the first chapter of *Process and Reality*. More to the point here, however, is the notion of "exhibition."[16] Charles Peirce taught that the first step in any reflection or "musement" is the "abduction" of an hypothesis that explains or describes the subject matter under investigation.[17] This imaginative exercise does not follow any logical rule, said Peirce, but is more like a guess. The abductive process begins wildly and vaguely but works through stages of clarification and precision so as finally to reach a stage where one can make predictive inferences from it and test those predictions in experience. The result of abduction is a grand hypothesis that "exhibits" the structures, characters, textures, and values of its subject matter, allowing them to be grasped. Whether that hypothesis is true, beyond its persuasiveness in exhibiting its subject matter, is a matter for further testing.

Philosophical Theology is primarily exhibitive, aiming to work through some of the main theological and philosophical complexities of ultimate reality, religion, and related topics so as to present them as a consistent, coherent, adequate, and applicable view. Many arguments are to be found within it, putatively justifying this or that category or interpretation. These arguments are crucial elements in exhibiting the structure, characters, textures, and values in philosophical theology's subject matter. Hopefully, they will make the system persuasive as a complex hypothesis filled with subhypotheses. Nevertheless, the real testing of the system in experience is something outside the system itself and is only rarely attempted in these volumes. With this in mind, an argument can be given, resonant with Peirce, that the outcome of a long run of tests of a theology is not simply a certificate of successful testing but rather a cumulative exhibition of understanding in which many things have come to make sense. Perhaps the rhetoric of "inquiry" into the solution of problems of theological understanding gives way in the end to the rhetoric of understanding itself, *Verstehen*.[18] To the extent this is so, the arguments internal to the exhibition of this theological hypothesis are among the tests that evaluate the hypothesis.[19] The exhibitive character of *Philosophical Theology* calls for the frequent summaries and reiterations of the main themes in these volumes that serve to recall and reorient the discussion at hand to the basic hypothesis whose range is being exhibited.

A work such as *Philosophical Theology* that aims to address a public that includes thinkers from all religious traditions and many modes of inquiry relevant to religion faces a practical problem of citation. When can basic concepts be assumed to be common property and when should they be given explication with citations of debate and critical inquiry? Written in English, *Philosophical Theology* can suppose that most readers would have a fairly deep background knowledge of Judaism and Christianity so that, for instance, it would be patronizing to inform the reader that there are two biblical "testaments," the Old Testament or Hebrew Bible and the New Testament, with citation of scholarly discussions of their differences. It cannot suppose that this same audience would have comparable familiarity with the internal structure of the Vedas, however. Because of my background, the discussions of Western monotheisms are likely to be more discriminating than discussions of other religions, save perhaps Confucianism. As a long-time Confucian, I think of many of the relevant issues in Confucian terms without remembering that those terms are unfamiliar, certainly not second nature, to many of the English speaking readers. At some basic level, no way exists for getting around this historical particularity.

The working principle of citation, however, is this. Readers' knowledge of world religions can be presupposed at the level of good encyclopedia articles. Thus common notions such as Brahman, sharia, dependent co-origination (*pratitya samutpada*), Dao, and filial piety can be used without scholarly citation, although the text here needs to define how they are used. All of these notions and others in common educated religious knowledge are subject to debate by experts, however, and these debates need to be cited when the debates themselves are relevant to the argument here. Often this is the case when the point being made is that a tradition has many different ways of interpreting its central symbols and notions. Citation is also necessary when the argument here deliberately follows a particular line of interpretation. Citation is all the more important when second order issues of methodology and justification are at stake. I beg pardon when citation of the obvious is offensive to some and when failure to cite leaves others baffled.

Acknowledgments

I wish to thank members of the doctoral seminar in Advanced Systematic Theology at Boston University in fall 2010 for their careful reading and commentary on a draft of this volume. They include Joshua Hasler, Anne Hillman, Sungrae Kim, Divine Mungre, Lancelot Watson, and Lawrence Whitney. In fall 2012 students in another doctoral seminar also commented helpfully on the manuscript in a later draft. They include Kenneth Armentrout, Seth Waltemyer, Adnan Rehman, Chanhong Kim, Toar Hutagalong, and Jaehu Jang; Xinjun Liu, visiting from China, and my faculty colleague M. Thomas Thangaraj participated in the seminar and contributed to the revisions, especially the latter. Because this work as a whole is the culmination of nearly six decades of my education, I am indebted to all the people who have formed and corrected me from high school onward; many of these people are thanked explicitly in the prefaces to my other books and the preface to Volume Three discusses people particularly helpful in my learning about the history of religions. I have learned from and been shaped enormously by colleagues in the faculties of institutions where I have worked and taught, including Yale University, Fordham University, The Hastings Center, the State University of New York College at Purchase, the State University of New York at Stony Brook, and Boston University. I have been nurtured deeply by four ongoing discussion and research groups with which I have been involved for decades: The New Haven Theological Discussion Group, The American Theological Society, The Boston Theological Society, and The Highlands Institute for American Religious and Theological Thought (now calling itself the Institute for American Religious and Theological Thought). Seven friends and colleagues have tracked the argument here and read some or all of the manuscript with helpful comments: John H. Berthrong (to whom my *Ritual and Deference* is dedicated), Richard Peters, Christian Polke, Robert S. Corrington, Wesley J. Wildman, Nikolas Zanetti, and Jay Schulkin. Because of all these people, but especially these last seven and my wife, Elizabeth E. Neville, *Philosophical Theology* is the product of a long and splendid collaboration for whose virtues all may take credit and for whose faults I alone am is responsible even after all these years.

All quotations from the Hebrew and Christian Bibles, unless otherwise noted, are from the New Revised Standard Version, copyrighted in 1989 by the Division of Christian Education of the National Council of the Churches of Christ in the United States of America. Credits for all other citations are in the bibliography.

Philosophical Theology One is dedicated to Wesley J. Wildman who has brought the author incomparable intellectual companionship and collaboration for many years at Boston University. He is a friend on many levels: religious interests and affiliations, philosophical enthusiasms, institutional commitments, the sharing of students and courses, family involvements, personal and emotional support, and tender care for the soul. But most relevant for *Philosophical Theology* is the fact that his creative and critical mind and his endless patience have tuned this work at every point, for which my gratitude knows no bounds. Even our disagreements are in tune.

I am deeply grateful to my friends at SUNY Press, especially Nancy Ellegate, my long-time editor, Laurie Searl, production editor, and Kate McDonnell, marketing manager. They and others at the Press have made it a rare treasure in the field of academic publishing. After many years, I feel part of the SUNY Press family and am very proud of this.

Introduction

1. THE HYPOTHESIS

The complex metaphysical hypothesis to be elaborated throughout the volumes of *Philosophical Theology* is that the ultimate reality of the world consists in its being created in all its spatiotemporal complexity by an ontological act of creation. Everything determinate in any way is part of the world so created. The ontological creative act is a making and its only nature comes in the determinate character of what it makes. Apart from creating the world, the ontological creative act is indeterminate, that is, nothing, not something rather than nothing nor something rather than something else. Without creating, the act is not an act.

This ontological act cannot be modeled in any literal sense because a model supposes some isomorphism with what it models, and the creative act as such has no form to model save in its terminus (*I, 13, i*). Making cannot be modeled except in what it makes, which of course prescinds from the making itself. But human cultures have taken familiar elements within the world and transformed them so as to serve as tentative or "broken" symbols of that ontological creative act.[1]

Three such models are vastly influential, each with many variants. One is to turn conceptions of human personhood (of which there are many) into concepts of gods or God (of which there are many). A second is to turn the experiences of consciousness in relation to objects of consciousness (of which there are many kinds) into concepts of absolute consciousness, mind, Shiva, Buddha-mind, mystical union, Brahman, or the like.[2] The third is to turn familiar instances of spontaneous emergence, as in budding trees, maturing people, gushing springs, and many forms of spontaneous decision and creativity into sophisticated models of the Dao, yin/yang transformations, and the like.[3] Although nearly all major cultures use versions of all three, the first, the model of God or gods, characterizes the dominant rhetorical symbology of West Asian monotheisms, paganism, and some South Asian communities. (All cultures have symbols of supernatural agents, but not all cultures ascribe anything like ultimacy to them.) The model of consciousness characterizes many South Asian religions, often in relation to the god model. The model of emergence, especially spontaneous emergence, characterizes East Asian religions, although with a popular cosmology populated by gods and with a strong Buddhist "consciousness" motif affecting some ideas of emergence. The conception of ultimate reality as the ontological act of creation that results in the world as its terminus thus excludes theism, consciousness-oriented Brahmanism and Buddhism, and emergentist notions such as the Dao as literal renditions of ultimate reality (*I, 13-14,* especially *I, 13, i*). Any approach to characterizing ultimate reality in determinate terms requires mediation through a theory of religious symbolism that sets conditions under which the determinate symbols do and do not apply.

Philosophical Theology thus is not a theism that takes the symbolic rhetoric of God as the basic or controlling rhetorical center, only as one possible rhetorical center under the qualifications of broken symbolism. "Divine" symbolism is on a rough par with "consciousness" and "emergentist" symbolism, although we need to bear in mind that there are many variations as well as combinations in all these symbol systems. Therefore, the aim of *Philosophical Theology* is not primarily a defense of or elaboration of a theory of God (or divinity or other cognates), but rather a defense and elaboration of a theory of ultimate reality as the ontological act of creating a radically contingent cosmos. It defends the symbolic validity of God-language under certain hermeneutical restrictions. But it also defends the roughly equal validity of consciousness-motifs and spontaneous emergentist-motifs under parallel hermeneutical restrictions.

As a result, the appropriation of this philosophical theology for confessional purposes needs to accept the theory of symbolism that breaks the literal reference of the symbols and shows how they still can convey what is valid under certain conditions (*I, 3*). Personal theism is not literally true, nor is Brahmanical or Buddhist consciousness language, nor spontaneous emergentist symbolism. At the same time, we can say that they are validly employed as symbols of the ultimate reality of the ontological act of creation, each in its own place and under appropriate restrictions. These valid employments are crucial for the guiding symbology of religious communities. This apophatic point of *Philosophical Theology* has long been recognized in all major world religions.

The principal hypothesis of *Philosophical Theology* argues for the ultimate reality of an ontological act of creation through an analysis of determinateness (*I, pt 3*). To be a part of the world, any part of the world, any part of any world, is to be determinate. Determinateness is the most basic and universal characteristic of what it is to be. Therefore, the transcendental traits of determinateness are ultimate conditions of the world and of the ultimate ontological act of creation as creating a determinate world. In contrast to the radical contingency of all determinate things on the ontological act of creation, which can be called "ontological ultimacy," or the "ontological ultimate reality," the transcendental traits of determinateness per se can be described as "cosmological ultimates." The hypothesis here is that there are four cosmological ultimates.

As these three volumes argue and illustrate, any determinate thing is a harmony of components and therefore has a form or pattern by which the components are together (I, 10; II, pt 1, pr; III, 4, ii). Form is an ultimate condition of determinateness. Relative to human life, form is particularly problematic in the shape of future possibilities. Future possibilities often offer alternatives for actualization and, to the extent that human beings have some control over which alternatives are actualized, they are under obligation to choose the better. Form, it will be argued, bears value; hence anything with form has a value (II, 1; III, 9). The ultimate reality of form thus translates into the human (and, because ultimate, religious) boundary condition of lying under obligation.

Having components, a determinate thing has a harmony that comports itself in certain ways toward its components; often this is a trivial matter—things just integrate their components according to their forms. But for us human beings, often alternate ways exist of comporting ourselves toward our components, and these ways have to do with how, if at all, we human beings come to wholeness (II, 2). The forms of life so often involve covering over deep human contradictions. The ultimate reality of having components thus translates into the human religious condition of needing to seek wholeness, however that is identified. The need for wholeness is an ultimate boundary condition of human life.

Because any determinate thing is determinate with respect to other things it exists in an existential field with them and has an existential location.[4] To be related to other things with respect to which it is determinate is a cosmological ultimate condition of any determinate thing. From a human perspective this means that relating to others as others, not simply as functions of one's own experience but as external related others, is an ultimate boundary condition of human life (II, 3).

Any determinate thing has the value of establishing its components in its pattern in its existential location. The thing's value includes both the value embraced within its harmony and the values that it has caused or affected in other things that are embraced within their harmonies; the former will be analyzed (II, 4) as "subjective value-identity and the latter as "objective value-identity." This claim, of course, presupposes the possibility of elaborating and defending a theory of value that has to do with form relative to components in an existential location, and such a theory is defended here (II, 1; III, 9). The thesis amounts to saying that anything that has an actual identity has an actual value. Its ultimate identity is its value, although the value is always borne by the identity achieved with *this form* of *these components here*. For human beings, the meaningfulness of life depends on achieved value-identity. Achieving a value-identity is an ultimate boundary condition of human life that comes simply from the fact that human beings are determinate.

Thus, the four cosmological ultimate realities that come from determinateness itself, and are relevant to human life, are: form/value/obligation, components/comportment/wholeness, existential location/relation/otherness, and value-identity/achievement/meaning.

These five ultimate realities—one ontological ultimate and four cosmological ultimates—are real ultimate conditions that every human being in every culture must face. As will be argued in detail, as long as human beings have semiotic systems that allow them to interpret conditions for human life, they have the religious problems of interpreting and comporting themselves toward the five ultimate conditions. All that is required is a semiotic system complex enough to register nests of causes or conditions, causal series and the causes of the series, forms within forms, degrees of wholeness, levels of engagement of others, and proximate and more encompassing meaningfulness.

Religion thus is a universal human reality so long as people have elementary semiotic systems. Religions differ by virtue of the differences in their cultural or semiotic systems. Each cultural semiotic system has virtues and vices of relevance and articulateness about these conditions, and so the religious cultures of the world are by no means the same. But they all are different cultural ways of addressing the same ultimate realities: radical contingency, form, components, existential location, and cumulative value-identity. This is the hypothesis that will be elaborated and defended throughout *Philosophical Theology*.

The analysis of religious cultures or traditions to be given here is more closely allied with the "genealogical" approach of looking backward from a religious situation, an approach associated with postmodern studies, than with the more customary "branching" approach, as Talal Asad calls it, that starts from a religion's "beginning" and works forward.[5] Thus, although traditional names such as Buddhism, Christianity, Confucianism, Daoism, Hinduism, Islam, and Judaism (to name large living Axial Age religions in alphabetical order) will be used as convenient indices, any concrete religious situation exhibits a mix of these and their internal variations, compounded by ideas and practices from other domains of experience (*III, 3, 4*).[6]

II. DEFINING RELIGION

For purposes of orientation at the beginning of *Philosophical Theology*, the following is a working definition of religion to be elaborated and justified through the volumes. *Religion is human engagement of ultimacy expressed in cognitive articulations, existential responses to ultimacy that give ultimate definition to the individual and community, and patterns of life and ritual in the face of ultimacy.*[7]

Ultimacy is a notion that Paul Tillich began to develop with both ontological and existential or anthropological categories.[8] He associated ultimate reality with being-itself, and in turn with God as the Ground of Being (following Thomas Aquinas and others in this). He defined ultimate reality existentially as the object of ultimate concern. He also pointed out that many aspects of experience not ordinarily associated with religion, such as art and mental health, have dimensions of ultimacy that call for theological interpretation.[9] Although *Philosophical Theology* extends the notion of ultimacy far beyond Tillich's use, for instance enlarging his existentialist notion of ultimate concern to include cognitive and social elements of orientation, Tillich's ideas are seminal.[10] He surely was right that theology requires a metaphysical moment in which ultimate reality is articulated as such, not merely as what is symbolized in a religion's sacred canopy.

The conceptualization of "religion" that comes with this approach is perhaps the greatest innovation of *Philosophical Theology*, although of course no idea is without antecedents. As mentioned, religion is not to be identified in truly concrete ways with religious traditions such as Buddhism, Christianity, Confucianism, Daoism, Hinduism, Islam, and Judaism. Rather, religion is to be identified concretely with the ways by which human beings have engaged ultimate realities and seek to do so today. *Philosophical Theology* argues on philosophical grounds that there are indeed ultimate realities and ultimate dimensions of experience, and that people have responded to them, still do so, and will need to do so in the future, just as they respond to the realities of their climate, the geography of their habitats, and their social and personal situations. The responses to ultimacy vary by differences in culture and history, just as do the responses to climate, geography, and social and personal situations.

Defining religion as symbolically formed engagement with ultimacy decisively distinguishes *Philosophical Theology* from approaches such as that of Mark C. Taylor that is so close in many ways, not the least of which is the shared heritage of Tillich. Taylor develops an extremely rich conception of what here is called symbolic engagement, often parallel to the weave of threads detailed below. He describes how symbolic engagements are constructive ways of feeling, thinking, and acting that both give integrative meaning to life and also disrupt those meanings. His definition is as follows:

> Religion is an emergent, complex, adaptive network of symbols, myths, and rituals that, on the one hand, figure schemata of feeling, thinking, and acting in ways that lend life meaning and purpose and, on the other, disrupt, dislocate, and disfigure every stabilizing structure.[11]

What is remarkable from the standpoint of *Philosophical Theology* is that religion in Taylor's definition has nothing to do with the objects symbolized or mythologized, with that to which feeling, thinking, and action are schematized. It is as if there was nothing that calls forth the religious response as a source of meaning. This is all the more remarkable because Taylor's definition recognizes the critical disruptive power of reality to dislocate the human responses to ultimacy as the ground of meaning and purpose, thus falsifying, or at least problematizing, the religious symbolic systems.

People respond to a great many things all at once. To distinguish religion from politics, social organization, economic efforts, and a host of other things falling under traditional scholarly labels is difficult if scholars look for religion as a "phenomenon." But religion is not a phenomenon alongside others, such as social or artistic phenomena (nor are these other domains of experience "phenomena" in any easily defined sense). Attempts to define religion (or religions) as if it were a phenomenon invariably fall prey to accusations, usually valid, that the scholar has imported preconceived categories into the definition, usually reflecting a particular cultural or religious bias. Rather, religion should be defined philosophically as those elements in the human engagement of the world (which has very many different kinds of things in it) that relate to ultimacy. This strategy looks arbitrary from the standpoint of phenomenologists and historians of religion who believe they have identified religion through observation alone. But what really is arbitrary is their labeling of their observations as religious. The philosophic definition, by contrast, is stipulative and guides inquiry as an hypothesis about how to think about religion. Its merit can only be shown in the fruitfulness of inquiry carried out under its guidance. *Philosophical Theology Three* is about the issues in defining religion.

Defining religion in terms of the engagement of ultimacy is an *hypothesis*, which signals that the whole of *Philosophical Theology* is empirical. Thinkers attempting to be scientific object to this claim because of its use of philosophy, especially metaphysics, within the hypothesis. Their assumption, indeed their a priori postulation, is that "empirical" means justifying hypotheses within the reductionistic framework of some science, a point these volumes discuss from many angles (*III, 1*). In all the social and biological sciences, however, part of what this means is that the first-order claims of religion are bracketed out of the discussion: *that* people believe certain things about ultimate realities can be admitted to study, and perhaps *why* they do so can be understood in terms of evolutionary forces, neurological and psychological mechanisms, social forces, and secular utility in general. But whether the beliefs are justified as beliefs, and under what circumstances, is ruled out of most so-called "empirical" studies in the sciences. Indeed, religion is often defined as belief in supernatural agents or as beliefs about sacred liminal objects or places, and for the most part scientists themselves believe these beliefs are false. But rarely if ever are proper experiments or empirical studies proposed that take those religious beliefs seriously, that ask what they might mean in a religious context and inquire into their truthfulness. On the contrary, it is assumed usually that they simply are false and, always, that they cannot be studied empirically. So the a priori postulations of most scientific reductionisms in the study of religion are radically non-empirical. Of course, we learn a great deal from these scientific approaches. But they are tainted in powerful ways by their non-empirical assumptions. Belief in general is less important than these approaches suppose; engagement is the more concrete center of religion.

Philosophical Theology insists that a fair consideration of the truth of religious beliefs be included in inquiry about religion and employs metaphysics to make this happen. Metaphysical hypotheses are empirical in their own way (*I, 3; I, 9. i*). They are not empirical in the same ways that scientific hypotheses are, which can be defined in terms of controlled experiments or other short-term ways of sifting evidence, because metaphysical hypotheses need to determine the very conditions for defining evidence. But they are empirical nevertheless. Integrated with other ways of studying religion, the metaphysical approach to understanding ultimacy provides controls for assessing the truth claims of religion as understood in the philosophy of symbolic engagement (*I, 1, 2, 3*).

With this definitional approach to the study of religion, it is easy to see why the identification of religion with named religions is problematic: that identification requires the endless qualification of multiple kinds of Buddhism, Islam, etc., of crossover influences from one tradition to another, and of ways in which each generation redefines its heritage. Therefore, the principal locus for the study of religion should not be with the past "founders and founding events" as if they have a straight-line heritage. Rather, it should be with the present "religious situation."[12] Of course that analysis should penetrate as deeply into the past roots as is possible with texts, archeological information, anthropological studies, and evolutionary biological findings. The religious situation now is extremely diverse geographically, culturally, politically, artistically, and in a great many other ways. Different positions within the religious situation have resources for engaging ultimacy that are diverse and their needs to integrate ultimate engagements with the other domains of their lives require different sacred worldviews and religious practices. Given these differences, no one "religion" such as Buddhism can possibly be true for all. "A religion" in this sense is a great abstraction from the many concrete ways people in the present religious situation can best and most viably engage ultimacy. The discourse of "religious pluralism" (and "exclusivism" and "inclusivism") is a phantom play with abstractions from real engagements with ultimacy at the diverse locations within the religious situation. Those locations are to be understood far more concretely by examining the histories of how diverse religious traditions have come down to be present resources for engaging ultimate matters. Those histories can embrace all the traditions that can be appropriated at a given location, however they are named, with their own internal twists and turns, with crossovers, with modifications by geopolitical events such as the rise and fall of empires, acknowledging differences of class and communicative connections with other parts of the religious situation, and a thousand other empirically identifiable factors, including the religious contributions of secular or "anti-religious" movements that still involve the engagement of ultimacy.

A further motivation for imagining religion through a philosophical definition and concrete historical analyses of a rich polyglot multicultural background for different locations within the religious situation comes from a new historical program of analysis put forward by certain postmodern historians, particularly Daniel Boyarin and Thomas Sizgorich. They look to understand how Judaism, Christianity, and Islam came to be separated from one another in the first millennium of the Common Era. Examining cultural witnesses, they find that people we now identify as belonging to separate "religions" often lived together, intermarried, worked together, did business together, and worshipped together, at least in overlapping institutions, and that there were many competing communities within and around Judaism, Christianity, and Islam. But certain people wanted to create differences and separations, and to "police the boundaries" of the different religions. These police often were people who themselves were marginal to the ways of daily life, such as monks, people in religious hierarchies, or political leaders. Their attempts to create the boundaries sometimes took the form of advocating narratives of violence in the past, often violence between political units, such as tribes, but represented as a conflict between separate religions.[13] For instance, the Christian Chrysostom, a significant policeman of boundaries, published eight orations "Against Jews" the purpose of which was to persuade Christians to stop going to the Jewish synagogues to worship and otherwise thinking of themselves as Jews as well as Christians; his sermons promulgated the narratives of Jewish persecution of Jesus and the early Church.[14] Jewish and Muslim boundary policemen made similar arguments. Thus, the exclusivist identity of the religions came to be formed by those narratives of conflict, which in historical fact were only a small part of the story. Narrative is nearly always a story of conflict and opposition, and so the very use of narrative served to create divisions. In our own time we have seen this strategy at work in the destruction of the fairly integrated and harmonious society of Yugoslavia by the Serbian appeal to narratives of fourteenth century battles between Orthodox (Serbian) Christians against Muslims (Bosnians), and of twentieth-century battles between Roman Catholic Nazis (Croatians) and Serbs. The narratives of violence have been used to create religious "identities" with boundaries and thus to promote hostility where peace had been more possible.

Philosophical Theology takes a circumscribed view of the use of narrative in religion and a somewhat negative view of the concern for putting theology to the service of "religious identity." In the contemporary religious situation, a person or community in a particular location might vest itself in a religious label, such as Kashmir Shaivism or Christianity. In concrete reality, however, it engages ultimate matters with a complex set of symbolic and practical resources that draw on a history that is vastly more inclusive than would be indicated by the label. The true religious identity of the person or community is the concrete set of resources by means of which it engages ultimate matters in its context, not the identity that comes from a label. One of the functions of theology is to help people gain practical access to those concrete ways of engaging ultimacy, drawing on many traditional and other resources.

III. IDENTIFYING RELIGION IN PUBLIC DISCOURSE

One of the distinct *disadvantages* of organizing theological inquiry around a philosophical definition of religion is that people "know" what religion is from their own experience and from its treatment in the popular press and what they "know" does not conform cleanly to the philosophical categories. North American public discussions at the present time tend to identify religion with evangelical or even fundamentalist Protestant and conservative Roman Catholic Christianity. This identification is supported on the one hand by the extreme conservatives, who reject moderate or liberal Christianity and all other religions as viable religion, and on the other hand by secularists, who want to see religion in its worst light, according to their views.[15] In fundamentalist Iran (at least in 2012), the government press "knows" that true religion is only of the fundamentalist sort and the more moderate and liberal pretentions to Islam are secularism in disguise.

The phenomena identified as religious from different perspectives are extremely confusing and sometimes the media can be forgiven for perpetuating stereotypes. One of the distinct *advantages* of a philosophical approach to the identification of religion, however, is that it can provide some guidance for sorting through the various respects in which phenomena can be classified as religious. Obviously, phenomena identified as religious, such as the martyrdom of the terrorists who bombed the World Trade Center on September 11, 2001, contain elements that are political, economic, psychological, and theatrical, and yet they were sacrifices of themselves and their thousands of victims for the purposes of God as they understood them. The philosophical theory helps identify elements of religion in such phenomena and distinguish respects in which those phenomena are religious and respects in which they are not. The respects that bear on ultimacy (in the ontological and cosmological senses) are religious, even when the bearing is indirect.

A distinction is to be drawn between three senses of religious engagement: authentic, distorted, and quasi-religious.

Authentic religion is all those engagements of the ultimate realities just discussed, the ontological and cosmological ultimates. These symbolic engagements are organized in various ways and need not be comprehensive in dealing with all of the ultimates. A complicating factor in identifying putative religious phenomena is that the symbols involved often are not intended literally and sometimes have to be broken if they are construed that way. Furthermore, some symbols can be employed with much greater truth than others, and some common symbols are false or misleading, all this in ways that are explored extensively in these volumes. The symbologies of different religious traditions can be mutually contradictory, at least on the surface, even when they engage the same ultimate. For instance, Buddhists seek wholeness through a variety of strategies of denying the reality of the self, whereas Hindus have a variety of strategies for locating the true self on a deep ontological plane, and Muslims see wholeness in a self perfectly individuated before Allah. Buddhists, Hindus, and Muslims can all authentically engage the ultimate reality of having components of life to which a person must be comported properly in order to be whole, however. The important point about identifying authentic religion is that it be the real ultimates that are engaged, so far as this can be discerned.

Distorted religion might well engage the ultimates authentically in some respects but also seriously treat certain non-ultimate things as if they were ultimate. This leads to giving ultimate commitments and energies to non-ultimate things. Worse, it leads to distorting engagement of the ultimate realities. Fundamentalisms, for instance, have been thoroughly studied as global religious movements of the last century. One of the most sophisticated studies defines fundamentalism as referring *"to a discernible pattern of religious militance by which self-styled 'true believers' attempt to arrest the erosion of religious identity, fortify the borders of the religious community, and create viable alternatives to secular institutions and behaviors."*[16] Arresting the erosion of religious identity, fortifying community borders, and creating alternative religious institutions and behaviors is not necessarily a betrayal of engagements of truly ultimate realities, and in fact can be undertaken in the service of those ultimate realities. But they are not ultimate activities and their purposes deal with proximate realities. When they are undertaken with religious militance they often lead to distortions of ultimate realities. For instance, part of human ultimacy is facing choices among possibilities that have different value, which puts people under obligation. Properly to address the ultimacy of being under obligation is to understand the possibilities as well as can be done. Fundamentalisms often lead people into denial about what can otherwise be known, as in the case of the denial of biological evolution or in the projective imputation of evil motives to others. Any religious engagement that is in denial about what can otherwise be known is to that extent compromised in its authenticity. Similarly, fundamentalisms can define personal wholeness in very narrow terms that relate to quick martyrdom, denying the rich complexity of components that make up a life and that need to be addressed. Fundamentalisms can be so exclusivistic as to deny their need to care for others, demonizing those outside the group. Fundamentalisms often reduce the meaning of life to a defensive operation of protecting a specific religious culture instead of all the aspects of relations to environment, history, and personal achievements that cultures need to include. Fundamentalisms can be so resentful of what they take to be the forces causing the erosion of their religious identity that they abandon the overwhelming sense of gratitude owed to the ontological creation of the world. All of these issues will be discussed in *Philosophical Theology Two* and *Three*. Distorted religion is when the engagement of non-ultimate things as ultimate distorts the engagement of the real ultimates. Many Christians, Jews, and Muslims are dedicated to justice and care for all people, not only those within their in-group, but make an exception for gay, lesbian, and transgender people: This exception is a distortion of their otherwise authentic engagement of others in their existential field. Racism and ethnic hatred are common distortions in many religions. When religious individuals or communities become defined more by the distortions than by the authentic aspects of their engagements, as is the case with fundamentalisms, they become distorted religious people and communities.

Quasi-religions are those that organize ultimate concerns around objects that are not ultimate and that do not seriously engage the ultimate realities.[17] Marxism, humanism, and nationalism can be quasi-religions because they can arouse ultimate commitments but explicitly deny the reality of what is argued here are the genuine ultimates. John E. Smith says that the generic meaning of religion is a diagnosis of a flaw in human existence considered in the light of what is taken to be ultimate, and the quest for a deliverer or delivering knowledge that can remedy the flaw.[18] Quasi-religions provide diagnoses of flaws and recommend restorative measures, but substitute ideals of human measures and their limitations. "Quasi-religions" is a complicated category to use because all of those movements might merely deny traditional religious language about the ultimates but in fact have their own symbols of ultimacy that have great virtues. All three of those movements have had strains that provided symbols of the utmost gratitude toward existence, vigorous treatments of lying under obligation, serious programs for the pursuit of wholeness, generous commitments to helping others and the environment, and effective ways of articulating ultimate meaning for life. But they also have had strains that have flattened engagements with any of these ultimates through anger and resentment toward "traditional religions." To the extent these and other movements organize ultimate concern and have symbols that in their own ways engage the ontological and cosmological ultimates, they are authentic religions. To the extent they organize ultimate concern in religious ways but without engaging the ultimates, they are quasi-religions

These points about the discrimination of authentic, distorted, and quasi-ways of engaging ultimate realities, or proximate realities as ultimate, indicate the force of the emphasis in *Philosophical Theology* on engagement. As *Philosophical Theology Two* argues in detail, the immediacy of religion for most people is twofold. On the one hand, the ultimate conditions of life cause predicaments such that human life is ordinarily broken or wounded and needs something religious to fix it (*II, pt 2*). Human beings are under obligation but so often fail. People should be whole but usually are personally broken. People should engage others in their existential field with care for the values those others bear, but usually let selfishness or fears distort that engagement. People look for meaning in life but find absurdity. Gratitude for the creation of the radically contingent universe is compromised by the knowledge that everyone suffers and dies. On the other hand, human life within these conditions also opens onto many experience of ecstatic fulfillment, and these experiences are sometimes a bit oblivious as to how the people stand with respect to the predicaments (*II, pt 3*). As if something glimpsed from the corner of the eye, a strange, elusive beauty pervades things that overlays and penetrates their terrors. "Beauty" may be too soft and particular a word for this qualitative feel of ultimate reality, meaning, and value; yet it is known to poets and many other religious people. These are existential realities that everyone faces, understanding them in the terms of some religious culture or other or searching for some other understanding.

The practice of religion, thematized mainly in *Philosophical Theology Three*, is extremely important, and understanding it probably is sufficient for understanding most religious people in their religious situation. But behind it, underneath it, permeating it, is the existential dimension in which each person faces the ultimate realities as they constitutes the ultimate conditions for human life. The raw immediacy of brokenness, and religion's responses to this, as studied in *Philosophical Theology Two*, and the ecstatic states of ultimate religious fulfillment, are preliminary to the more theoretical and organized sense of religion.

IV. DISTINGUISHING MARKS OF *Philosophical Theology*

Four principal points distinguish this *Philosophical Theology* from more common approaches to theology in the contemporary world and serve to justify the imagination of religion, and theology's place within it, just sketched. These are as follow: its metaphysical pragmatism, with sidebars on value and logic; its shift from doctrines to engagements, with a sidebar on revelation; its shift from viewing religions as comprised of socially constructed categories to viewing religion as a universal part of human nature with socially constructed variants; its emphasis on the breakdown of sacred canopies.

METAPHYSICAL PRAGMATISM

The first distinctive point is that *Philosophical Theology* elaborates a philosophical approach, metaphysical pragmatism, which is out of the current academic mainstream in Western philosophy. The main themes of metaphysical pragmatism, however, are right in the center of the millennia-long Confucian tradition and somewhat ambivalently located with regard to traditions of Indian philosophy. The many arguments to come will unfold the nature of this form of metaphysical pragmatism. But an important rationale for it can be expressed here so as to orient the kind of philosophy it is relative to competitors. One of the chief marks of pragmatism is its realism with regard to value. The following historical observation indicates the significance of this.

Value. Western philosophy since the early modern period has been concerned to understand what reality might be such that the world can be interpreted accurately in the mathematical forms of modern science. This is to say, mathematical science can interpret the world in certain respects, and these respects allow of astonishing generalization. But what about the other respects in which mathematics cannot interpret the world, particularly the respects in which nature, communities, cultures, and people are valuable? That they bear value is obvious to anyone who has made a mistake about the value of something and the values of things have been represented copiously in imaginative literature and poetry. No one tells this tale better than Alfred North Whitehead in *Science and the Modern World*, particularly the chapter on romanticism.

The principal project to which Western philosophy is heir since the romantic period is the squaring of scientific knowledge with what we know experientially about value, overcoming the fact/value distinction that seems to be essential to mathematical science. Early modern philosophy made an understandable but disastrous mistake. Most of the important philosophers inferred from the fact that nature could be interpreted mathematically in certain respects to the conclusion that nature really is nothing more than what mathematical science says it is—that there are no other respects, such as those bearing value. Mathematical science says that nature is a set of facts expressed in terms of mathematical relations and explanatory principles and assumes that, if nature is also valuable in various respects, this cannot be known (because knowledge is only in the form of mathematical science). Some philosophers struggled to account for why values seem so important when there is no natural base for them in the factual qualities of reality. Others, such as Leibniz, did attempt to account for value in real things in terms of "density of being" consisting of complexity and simplicity. This was developed with great brilliance by Whitehead who understood what was at stake in reconciling the fact-picture of the world presented by mathematical science with the value-picture by which people live. His conception of actual occasions, a variant of Leibniz's theory of monads, showed how things are appreciated as valuable in terms of categories of vagueness, triviality, narrowness, and width, categories further developed in *Philosophical Theology*.[19] But Whitehead's analysis of actual occasions applies only to what he calls the "genetic division" of actual things as they come to be. He also recognized that the world of actual occasions needs to be analyzed with what he called "morphological" or "coordinate division," which is the respect in which mathematical science interprets the world. With respect to morphological division, Whitehead had nothing to contribute regarding value. The result is that we are left with the problem of understanding how form itself, that which expresses morphological or coordinate division in Whitehead's sense and can be articulated mathematically, can bear value.

A dispute between Plato and Aristotle reveals how deep this problem is. Plato had the ideal of developing a science based on mathematics, both geometry and algebraic "ratios" (the two "likely stories" of the creation of the world in the Timaeas). The mathematics of his time was far too simple for him to be successful. He delivered a famous "Lecture on the Good," the text of which has been lost but which was reported to have been confusingly mathematical. If we can extrapolate from Plato's Philebus, a very late dialogue, he was trying to find mathematical ways of expressing balance, proportion, and harmony as the values that orient life. His problem was to find mathematical ways of showing how things harmonize with others to form new things, how components of a harmony change according to their positions in the harmony, how things that are harmonies are conditioned by the things around them so that changes in the environment change their value, and so forth. The "value" of something needs to find expression in the "ratios" of these kinds of relations. Value, Plato hoped, could be expressed in relations among quantities, or ratios.

Logic. Aristotle, by contrast, had the ideal of a logic of qualities, properties, or classes, as expressed in his theory of form as a hierarchy of genera and species. His logic was about arguments relating qualities: if a, then b; a, therefore b. The history of Western logic has descended from Aristotle, not Plato, most likely for the good reason that Plato could not work out the mathematics expressing value in nature or elsewhere. But the result is that logic is still about relations among qualities or properties. This is true of all the modern logics and semantic theories that use propositional functions such as $f(x)$. The "f" is a property or quality, not a ratio as it must be to indicate something as valuable.

Insofar as contemporary philosophy employs logic based on propositional functions, it assumes that real things are objects with properties, not harmonies with internal and external relations that constitute their values. Such logic generates great excitement and its history from Frege to the present time is full of many discoveries; in fact, it has generated a sense of philosophy as "making discoveries," that is, the elaboration of logical relations and the solving of logical problems. And yet, insofar as a main task of contemporary Western philosophy is to be able to articulate value in nature relative to the kinds of things science knows, such logic stands in the way of inquiry. For all its internal intrigue, "properties of objects logic" prevents the articulation of value and restricts articulation to qualities or properties that are facts.

For this reason, the philosophy in *Philosophical Theology* sidesteps most of the developments in formal logic and analytic philosophy, knowing that any inference from the nature of the logical language to its references in nature will exclude the values in the things referred to. Instead, the pragmatic philosophy developed here always treats logic as a means to the end of articulating reality in its value-bearing complexity.[20] Philosophical language needs to be periphrastic, not intending to be only iconic in the senses to be discussed in Chapter 3, Section III, but rather intending to indicate the values in the things referred to through verbal, non-mathematic, descriptions of their ratios. The most important feedback in inquiry is not from the structure of the signs involved but from the realities referred to in the engagement, resisting attempts to evaluate them wrongly.

Ironically, Charles Sanders Peirce, the founder of pragmatism and the inspiration behind the theory of symbolic engagement developed here, is credited along with Frege with the invention of much of modern logic. Yet his own phenomenology employing the categories of Firstness, Secondness, and Thirdness expresses a relational theory of what it is to be determinate: he might have sponsored a different approach to logic through the kinds of ratios Plato had in mind. But he did not, and his own theory of value followed Aristotle's and Hegel's in attributing value to the fulfillment or concreteness of actualizing form. The proper mathematizing of value is an intellectual project yet to be undertaken seriously. Given that lack, *Philosophical Theology* shall talk about value in relational terms but without mathematical formulation that might be related to the "factual" mathematics of late modern science.

FROM DOCTRINE TO ENGAGEMENT

The second distinguishing mark of *Philosophical Theology* is that it shifts the locus of theological truth from doctrines to interpretive engagements. From this it also shifts the public for theology from the theologian's own religious community to a public consisting of anyone with an interest in the outcome of the inquiry. Both of these derive from an epistemology of "symbolic engagement" (I, 3). Whereas much theology has thought that truth and falsity resides in doctrines, expressed formally or as commentary, the position here is that doctrines by themselves are neither true nor false. Only when they are asserted in an interpretive act of some sort (many sorts exist) might they be true or false. Doctrines that are asserted and are true in one context might be false in another, or when asserted by different people or for different purposes. The locus of the question of truth in theology, for *Philosophical Theology*, is in how interpreters engage reality with theological symbols, not alone in properties of the doctrines themselves.

An important consequence of shifting the topic of theological truth from doctrines to engagement is that the boundaries of religious communities that might be defined by doctrinal affiliation are blurred, if not wholly relativized. The connections relevant to trace in understanding concrete engagements might weave in and out of community involvements, or even cultural systems. Hence the second-order analytical and methodological inquiries relevant to symbolic engagements of ultimacy are not defined by the culture of a religious community except in contingent ways. The public for which the theology is written thus shifts from the author's given religious community alone to the congeries of intellectual and other publics consisting of anyone who has an interest in the theological topics. Such an indefinitely bounded public determines the scope of accountability for the theology. An implication of the shift in publics is a further shift from the exclusive trumping priority of revelatory claims to a complicated, multilayered, contextual, making of cases.[21]

Revelation. Because *Philosophical Theology* exhibits a pervasive theme of resistance to confessional theology, an introductory word about revelation is appropriate here, premature although it is in a systematic sense. Revelation here is interpreted as the acquisition and use in symbolic engagement of symbols that allow some aspect of ultimate reality to be engaged that could not be accessed by the other symbols at hand, thus revealing something new. Lacking the requisite symbols, something about ultimacy is hidden until the symbols are acquired and appropriately deployed. Sometimes the distinction has been made between general revelation and special revelation. General revelation is what is revealed through common (or perhaps elite) reason, whereas special revelation comes in the events or specific historical contexts in which the new revelatory signs arise and are deployed in symbolic engagement. Human reason itself has a history, however, and general "revelatory" notions such as the contingency of the world arose in specific contexts, for instance during the Axial Age when people learned signs for signifying "the world" and other signs for signifying "universal causation." From an historical point of view, taking into account the evolution of human semiotic systems, all revelation is special; with many revelatory signs, it is impossible to name and place their revelatory origins. Whether claims to revelation are true does not depend on the authority of a putative revealer but on whether they actually reveal something, which sometimes is hard to determine. Religion is always particular, in senses to be explored, and so is based on traditions that have authoritative weight, although the assessment of that weight goes beyond revelatory claims themselves.

One of the connotations of revelation is that first-order ultimate realities are the objects of revelation and, in some sense, reveal themselves. Admitting (1) the historical cultural contexts in which revelatory signs arise, (2) the genius of the poetic symbolic founders, and (3) the clarifying work of interpretive traditions, ultimate reality is simply what it is and, when encountered, calls forth the symbols by which it might be engaged. Some traditions symbolize this by saying that the ultimate is a god who sends the words, or causes the events around which interpretive words gather. But that need not be the only revelatory form. The revelations of the legendary Buddha were not sent by a higher power. Yet the Buddha was wrestling with ultimate issues that demanded what was, for him in his context, some novel forms of engagement. A persistent theme of *Philosophical Theology* is that theology arises in response to realities bluntly encountered and that it is corrected and pushed the better to engage those realities. Any symbolic engagement of ultimacy reveals it in some respect, to the extent that it is true. And we have always been in the "middle" of engaging ultimate matters, never without some symbols that point in ultimate directions even when they display their inadequacy.

Perhaps even more surprising from the perspective of confessional views of revelation is that *Philosophical Theology* defends the view that the center of ultimacy (the ultimate reality of ultimate realities, the ground of the ultimate dimensions of things in experience) is an ontological creative act that creates all determinate things (I, pt 3). This ontological act is wholly arbitrary in the sense that it has no determinate antecedents, conditions, or necessities. The world thus is radically contingent and wholly arbitrary as such, however, much rational and causal connections exist within it. This revelatory insight finds symbolic expression in many traditions and is registered in symbolic engagement with shock, surprise, awe, terror, despair, and a peculiar gratitude, perhaps even love. The complexity of the insight is that the positive apprehension of radically contingent existence is revealed only in a dark contrast with some version of the counter-factual grasp of what would exist without the ontological creative act—absolutely nothing. That we are in the middle of our lives' processes rests on nothing other than the absolutely arbitrary act of creation.

Thus, the central revelation is in full accord with what some theologians, especially the Christian Karl Barth of recent memory, call the pure and full grace of God. Our lives are nothing but God's grace, to use the monotheistic symbols. Thus, even our theological existence as symbolically engaged with ultimacy is the product of free, unmotivated grace. Little is more shocking and surprising, awesome, terrifying, despairing, gratifying, and loving, than religious existence, the symbolic engagement of first-order ultimacy. An important way of understanding Barth's criticism of "religion" is to see it as an attack on those forms of religion and theology that seek to explain a reason or motivation for existence, thus denying its wholly gracious revealed character.[22] Religion in the bad sense, for Barth, involves making *claims* for revelation, whereas the better theological interest is in locating the actuality of revelation in concrete symbolic engagements.[23]

From Religions to Religion

The third main distinguishing component of *Philosophical Theology* is that the orientation framing *Philosophical Theology* is shifted from foundational socially constructed categories (perhaps attributed to revelation or the social sciences) to approaches to religion as a universal natural phenomenon that is only expressed and developed in various socially constructed categories.[24] The Kantian Captivity of the religious imagination thankfully is now in the past, save in fundamentalistic postmodernism, and theological inquiry is free to look to evolutionary biology and cognitive science as well as to the other sciences, natural and social, to religiously relevant literature and arts, and to experience and public communal dialectic.

The field of religious studies has been exercised for decades by the question of the definition of religion (*III, pt 1*). Historicists and some postmodernists have pointed out correctly that early studies of world religions in the modern period usually employed models of religion taken from Christianity.[25] They countered that religions really should be studied on their own terms, by which they meant that religions are social constructions, each with its own system of Kantian-like transcendentally constituting categories. Perhaps in fact there is no such thing as religion, only religions with at best family resemblances among them (a point from Wittgenstein). In fact, argue these historicists and their postmodern allies, the very attempt to define religion is imperialistically to impose some alien ordering principle on data that should be studied on their own. *Philosophical Theology* rejects this historicist move, however. The models for understanding religion come in significant part from natural history, including evolutionary biology and cognitive science, and from metaphysics, as well as history of religions. The religions are various cultural ways of manifesting and developing religion in the universal sense of engaging ultimacy, which always needs cultural embodiments. Yet many aspects of reality are relevant for religion and all religions have to address these, one way or another. The alternative ways of addressing these realities are to be found as much within religious traditions as between religions. Therefore, the boundaries of religions as cultural traditions do not have to be taken too seriously, although the linguistic difficulties they pose for their careful study likely will reinforce the cultural boundaries approach. *Philosophical Theology* examines how different cultural religious traditions often provide parallel disputed solutions to how to address one or another universal problem. This allows for a much more careful tracking of the interactions of cultural traditions than is possible if religions are defined by separate cultures.

The basic point, however, is that religion can be given what John E. Smith calls a generic philosophic definition, in this case in terms of the symbolic engagement of ultimacy, that is embodied or instantiated in diverse cultural and historical ways, even in diverse individual ways. He writes, in a balanced statement worth quoting at length:

> No serious discussion of religion, East or West, in relation to society and the contemporary world is possible without taking into account a distinction between *religion* understood as a pervasive dimension in human life and the world historical *religions*—such as Judaism, Islam, Christianity, Buddhism and Hinduism. These religions have defined themselves through their respective objects of worship, their religious communities, their sacred literatures, sacred persons, and their systems of morality.... With respect to religion itself as a pervasive fact in human

history, we must resist the nominalist tendency to say that "religion" is merely a collective noun or name for these historical religions because that obscures the fact that religion is a distinctive dimension of human life and experience and that, as such, it is not exhausted in the particular religions that have appeared nor is it confined to the lives of those who adhere to these religions.[26]

Smith goes on to warn that the generic character of religion in human experience is not itself a religion—there is no super or integrated religion: People need to be religious in particular ways, to be analyzed in *Philosophical Theology* in terms of needs for different worldviews.

The most important consequence of the relevance specifically of natural science to theology is that the framing metaphysical symbols of theology are as *extensive* as the cosmos imagined by astrophysics and as *intensive* in feeling the embeddedness of human life in nature as imagined by the physics of biochemistry and ecology. The great religious traditions are replete with symbols for this cosmic extensiveness and natural intensiveness—symbols of creation, the Dao, Brahman, Hiranyagarbha, Buddha-mind, and worlds within worlds (I, 6–7). Nevertheless, theologies of traditions for which historical narratives are central, such as the Mahabharata and Ramayana in Hinduisms, the Exodus in Judaism, the Christ event in Christianity, and the angelic revelations of the Qur'an to the Prophet in Islam, need to recontextualize those narratives in the larger natural context. Human affairs understood narratively are miniscule in the extension of the cosmos and astonishingly superficial in floating across the intensiveness of nature. Because religion is indeed a human affair, such narratives can play important roles in existential responses to what is ultimate. But ultimacy framed with cosmic extension and natural intension cannot be conceived to play roles in human narratives without a complicated set of symbolic transformations, a metaphysics and symbology of incarnations and avatars. Narrative itself bears less ontological weight than some other forms of symbolizing the relation of human beings to ultimacy (I, 8; III, 13).

BROKEN SYMBOLS IN THE SACRED CANOPIES

The fourth distinctive trait of *Philosophical Theology* is the centrality of its thesis that the sacred canopies by which religions identify, orient, and order themselves on occasion, and because of the nature of ultimate reality, break down. A deeper theological truth than is claimed on the surfaces of sacred canopies is what arises in coping with this implosion, perhaps a more nearly ultimate sacred canopy, or the discipline of living alongside imploded sacred canopies.[27] Most theologies are explorations, developments, justifications, and repairs of sacred canopies associated with religious traditions and communities. This is kataphatic theology, and is essential both to the vitality and ordering of religious communities and to the continuity of traditions in changing circumstances. An individual cannot be serious about religious practice without participation in a sacred canopy. Most theologies also, however, have apophatic moments when they recognize the limitations, falsehoods, failures to address realities, and the spiritual bondage of manifest sacred canopies.[28] In this recognition they attempt to articulate more nearly ultimate sacred canopies that address the implosion of the manifest canopies, although these too are limited by the powers of symbolization. The experiential achievement of the apophatic moments is not wholly negative, although the recognition of the implosion of sacred canopies might be. Rather it is something like the peace that passes understanding, mystical joy in the awesome abyss, glorious annihilation in nirvana, the total eradication of self–other boundaries, or the paradoxical sense of being at home in a universe that bears no human meaning (III, 16).

※ ※ ※

Philosophical Theology is divided into three volumes. The first, *Ultimates*, is about the nature of ultimate reality, the second, *Existence*, is about human predicaments and ecstatic fulfillments relative to ultimate reality, and the third, *Religion*, is about how to live in relation to ultimate reality. This division vaguely echoes the traditional Christian division of systematic theology into studies of God the Father, Jesus Christ the Savior, and the Holy Spirit as Guide to sanctification and religious life. The echo is vague, however, because many other motives exist for dividing the subject this way that come from philosophy, the state of religious studies, and religions other than Christianity.

The chief motive for the present division is that most current approaches to theological topics in religious studies bracket out the question of whether the theological claims are true and whether the ways of life they interpret and guide are valid or authentic. Another way of putting this is that they treat religious references to ultimate realities and concerns as if they do not really refer. Volume One, Chapter 2, treats this issue in detail. Nothing is more important to theologically robust people than the truth of what they say and believe about whatever they deem ultimate. Indeed theological life for religious people is a vital symbolic engagement, theoretically and practically, of religious realities. When the various disciplines of religious studies then bracket out the assessment of those references, they give rise to strangely unstraightforward definitions of religion, such as a source of order in society, or a psychological process, or a trait of culture, or a tool in the biological and social evolution of humankind. Religion is all of those things, of course, and many others. But it is prima facie the direct and indirect engagement of what is ultimately real and valuable, and the cultivation of life so as to engage ultimate matters better. Therefore, it is important to address the question of ultimacy from the beginning, so as to justify taking references to ultimate reality seriously.

Ultimates: Philosophical Theology One develops a theology of ultimacy in considerable detail. Part I explores ways by which ultimacy is to be conceived as bearing on human life, focusing on epistemological and methodological issues. This part provides much of the conceptual apparatus for both the ontology of ultimacy and the theory of religion to come. Its tentative conclusion is that ultimacy and human life have real characters that all religions need to engage in one way or another. Part II then explores some of the pressures those realities put on candidate conceptions of ultimacy. This lays groundwork in comparative theology for making good on the general claim that all the major religions with a long civilized literature have addressed the same basic issues of ultimate reality, each in its own ways. Thus, the burden of comparison is not so much among different religious traditions, which are extremely problematic to define as bounded comparable entities, as within religious traditions as each responds to competing elements of ultimacy.

Part III presents a dialectical argument for a metaphysics of ultimacy. It examines the concept of being, and shows it to attain definition in connection with the problem of the one and the many. A theory of determinateness is presented in terms of harmony, which allows for the metaphysical definition of many and one. The part then argues that only an ontological act of creation can function as being, the one for the determinate many of the world. Ultimacy is thus defined in terms of the relations of the ontological act of creation and the determinate things created. Ultimacy cannot have a determinate character apart from creation, for this would require some deeper "one" to relate determinate ultimacy to other determinate things. This is laid out at length in a theory of eternity and time.

Part IV generalizes from the metaphysics of Part III to explore what is ultimate in human beings' orientation to the ontological act of creation and to one another as determinate beings in relation. It lays out in systematic fashion what can be known about ultimacy on this theory of ontological creation, and what cannot be known that some thinkers would like to know. Then it studies how the metaphysical theory of Part III can be used by theologians themselves to engage ultimate reality. It concludes with a discussion of four spiritual paths of symbolic engagement of the ultimate whose structures are revealed by the metaphysical theory. All of this sets up the discussion of human predicaments and ecstatic fulfillments in *Existence: Philosophical Theology Two*.

Part I

Ultimates Defined

Part I

Preliminary Remarks

How does one begin a discussion of ultimate reality? The first quandary is that we are already in the middle of very many discussions of ultimate reality. Some of these discussions are the historical traditions of religions with their manifold genres of scripture, commentary, and evolving cultures of rituals, practices, and historical institutionalizations. Others are more philosophical discussions of ultimacy that in some ways are critical of religious traditions, especially in the West since the Enlightenment. Yet others are discussions of the methodology and content of anthropology, psychology, sociology, economics, and history, as well as philosophical, literary, and artistic endeavors, all having to do with how human beings approach ultimacy. These discussions are diverse and complex. To be involved to a professional degree in any one tempts an attitude of alienation from the others. Yet all have some bearing on ultimacy.

The second quandary with beginning to discuss ultimate reality is to identify the subject matter, "ultimate reality," which has been done implicitly already in saying that it is the topic of many discussions. At this stage of the argument, "ultimate reality," "ultimates," "ultimacy," "ultimate matters," "ultimate dimensions," and similar cognates are mere token concepts pointing toward and awaiting detailed analysis, most systematically in Part III.

The function of ultimate reality as a token concept can be understood somewhat from its history. Until approximately two centuries ago, Western scholars tended to identify religion with the worship and service of gods. This approach dated back to the comparison of the pantheons of different civilizations in the ancient Mediterranean and South Asian worlds, and worked well enough when there was general agreement that gods are supernatural beings with super-human properties. But not all religions have taken their basic principles to be personified beings, certainly not the East Asian religions that look to Heaven-and-Earth, the Dao, the Ultimate of Non-Being, and the Great Ultimate. Nor is this the case with the South Asian traditions that take the gods to be themselves subject to karma. Moreover, sophisticated thinkers for millennia in all the major religions have challenged the personified supernatural-being imagery in their own traditions. Brahman is very little like a person, especially Nirguna Brahman. Rather, the metaphoric base from which concepts of Brahman have been developed is more that of consciousness than of personhood, although Brahman also is identified with person-like Gods such as Vishnu and Shiva. The One of Neo-Platonism is not a person. Rather it is an effulgent reality beyond all determinateness from which everything else emerges, beginning with the emergence of difference per se, then relational soul that emerges from difference, and so on. Neither is the pure Act of To Be in Thomas Aquinas' conception of God much like a person: It is simple and fully actual with no potentialities, and has no capacity to relate to something different from itself. Yet all of these conceptions, derived from persons, consciousness, and emergence models, often seem to be competitors with one another in some sense. And when they are not, as in the case of Hindu traditions in which the world is populated with many gods of the personified sort that are not as important as more transcendent principles, this very difference is important. And so scholars thinking about comparative theologies have sought a term that is vague enough to embrace all these competitive and sometimes contradictory notions.

Vagueness is a technical term in pragmatic semiotics that means a category that is capable of being instantiated or specified by instances that are mutually contradictory.[1] Vagueness is requisite for any comparative category because comparison is always "in some respect," and the respect in which things are compared is the comparative category of which they are instances. Things compared might be similar or different, overlapping or barely commensurable, contradictory or confused. Only the results of comparison can sort this out. But the vague category is required to bring the things into comparison in the first place. The tough problem with comparative categories is that they often are not vague enough to be fair to the things to be compared. It was a Christian or Western Enlightenment bias that suggested that religions are to be compared according to the conceptions of the gods they worship and serve. The conception of God had to be made more vague so as to allow the comparison of personified beings with more transcendent principles such as the Neo-Platonic One or the Thomistic Act of To Be. But then that vague conception of God had to be made even more vague so as to bring Heaven, the Dao, and Nirguna Brahman into comparison. This is the point at which scholars appreciate Paul Tillich's suggestion of *ultimate reality* as a properly vague term. Ultimate reality itself suggests that which is most real, most basic, that which explains without needing explanation, the uncaused cause of everything else, and things like this. Of course, all these notions need to be analyzed in detail as they are instanced in candidate conceptions of ultimacy.

Yet perhaps these connotations of ultimate reality are not yet vague enough. Some Buddhists, especially the Madhyamaka, argue that any worry or even curiosity about ontological realities, ultimate or otherwise, is part of the religious problem.[2] What is ultimate for this kind of Buddhism is not an ontological reality but rather the task or project of obtaining release from suffering. This is an anthropomorphic rather than an ontological ultimate reality. So ultimate reality, ultimates, ultimacy, ultimate matters, ultimate dimensions, and their cognates embrace anthropological as well as ontological instances.

Tillich himself approached ultimate reality through the anthropological route with his analysis of ultimate concern.[3] He held that every person has an ultimate concern with something. An ultimate concern is exclusive, setting all other concerns aside as proximate or preliminary in some sense. In actual fact, we might be self-deceived about our ultimate concern, thinking it is something properly pious or moral but discovering when push comes to shove that something else more egocentric or bizarre functions to make all other concerns preliminary. Whatever we think about our ultimate concern, the functional definition of ultimate concern is that it is the concern we would give up last. Whether every person has an ultimate concern, as Tillich thought, is an empirical question; perhaps not everyone has a functionally consistent set of concerns (I, 5). But for any person who does have an ultimate concern, ultimate reality is the putative object of that concern, said Tillich. Theology, for Tillich, has as its object whatever is worth being an object of ultimate concern. That is Tillich's first formal criterion of ultimacy. His second formal criterion is that whatever is the object of ultimate concern has to determine the being or non-being, in an existential sense, of the person with the concern. Tillich believed that the historical religions provide material criteria for ultimate reality.[4]

Thus, we have two tracks by which to explore ultimate reality. One is the ontological track of inquiry into what is most real, that which conditions but is itself unconditioned, whatever that might turn out to mean. The other is the anthropological track according to which ultimate reality is what is most important to people when it comes to defining their identity and existence. The present volume explores the first track, although with significant discussion of ultimate concern. *Philosophical Theology Two* and *Three* will explore the second in several ways.

The purpose of *Philosophical Theology One*, Part I, is to collect some of the more important tools necessary for a responsible analysis of ultimate reality. Accordingly, its chapters address the following four general questions.

First, what is the primary location in human experience of the symbols that define ultimacy? Chapter 1 will put forward the hypothesis that those symbols are located in sacred canopies that are accepted, more or less, by individuals and groups. An analysis of sacred canopies requires the development of some technical philosophical categories.

Second, do the symbols in sacred canopies that seem to refer to ultimate realities and ultimate dimensions of experience really do so? And if they do so, can they do so truly? Chapter 2 will explore the problems associated with scientific approaches to the study of religion that analyze religious symbols but prescind from asking whether these symbols refer to realities and do so truly. For religious people, whether their theological commitments are true or false is a point of utmost importance about their religion.

Third, by what theory of interpretation or reference can we understand the ways in which symbols of ultimacy in sacred canopies engage their objects? A theory of symbolic engagement will be developed in chapter 3 according to which three kinds of reference are required, iconic, indexical, and conventional.

Fourth, how do sacred canopies, with their symbols for engaging ultimacy, connect with the rest of life, with the "mundane" parts in contrast to the sacred elements? Chapter 4 will develop a theory of worldviews that connect the sacred canopies with other dimensions of experience along three "formal" continua. One is the continuum from the sacred to the mundane. A second is the continuum from intimate (often anthropomorphic) to transcendent symbols of ultimacy. The third is the continuum from sophisticated thinking to folk thinking along all points of the sacred/mundane continuum. Three "existential" continua will be developed in addition to the formal ones, concerning how different individuals share a larger cultural worldview, concerning how comprehensive a worldview is in providing articulation to the multitude of affairs of life for individuals and groups, and concerning how intense the commitment to a worldview is on the part of individuals. The existential continua of worldviews are more important for *Philosophical Theology Two and Three* than for the present volume.

Chapter One

Sacred Canopies

I. A THEORY OF SACRED CANOPIES

The phrase, *sacred canopy*, derives from Peter L. Berger's book, *The Sacred Canopy*. The purpose of that book is to develop a theory of religion with the tools of sociology of knowledge; its argument is closely connected with the book Berger wrote with Thomas Luckman at about the same time, *The Social Construction of Reality*. Berger's general thesis is that human beings need to order their experience, and do so by imposing subjectively constructed ordering ideas on reality. "A meaningful order, or nomos, is imposed upon the discrete experiences and meanings of individuals. To say that society is a world-building enterprise is to say that it is ordering, or nomizing, activity."[1] Although constructed by the human imagination, and thus subjective in this sense, the nomos imposed on the world is taken to be objective and people live according to it. The world, of course, has its own structure, which Berger calls "cosmos" in contrast to "nomos." The human need for ordering experience in ways that relate to purposes of survival and flourishing is extremely practical. The human ordering of experience gives structure to everyday life and also copes with the terror so natural when people face a vast and violent cosmos unscaled to human interests. As people objectify the meanings they project on the world, they construe their nomos to be cosmos. They thus internalize the objective meanings they had subjectively invented and projected. A cyclical relation exists, Berger points out, between inventive subjective projections, objective construals of the world in terms of those projections, and the internalization of that objectified world so that people "know" the world in the terms they have invented for it. This is "the social construction of reality."

But reality has tough feedback and not every human imaginative construction can be lived with as objective meaningful fact. A rough fit is required between actual "cosmic" structures and the "nomic" meanings by which people navigate the real world. So the objectified nomos is constantly being amended, which requires a new internalization, in turn stimulating new inventive subjective projections in an unsteady round of learning and inventing. Although Berger does not in this book relate explicitly to the pragmatic movement in philosophy, he is solidly within the pragmatic frame which says that people interpret reality by means of signs that frequently are amended so as to interpret better or that are abandoned because they miss what is important. The "social construction of reality" is not an idealist philosophy that represents human meanings as mere fictions with no relation to reality or that represents reality as a mere fiction. Rather, it is a realistic philosophy that provides an account for how reality corrects our interpretive, meaning-giving ideas.

"Corrects" is not always the right word, however. Whatever the cosmic structure of reality, from the standpoint of human experience it is terrifying and "anomic" except insofar as the nomos shelters experience with its imposed meaning. "The sheltering quality of social order becomes especially evident if one looks at the marginal situations in the life of the individual, that is, at situations in which he is driven close to or beyond the boundaries of the order that determines his routine, everyday existence."[2] The perceived objective validity of the nomos is precarious in these marginal situations.

Although the social world is supposed to be taken for granted, in marginal situations certain of its elements "stand out" as providing the world-making meaning on which the rest of social world's nomos depends. These constitute what Berger calls the "sacred."

> Religion is the human enterprise by which a sacred cosmos is established. Put differently, religion is cosmization in a sacred mode. By sacred is meant here a quality of mysterious and awesome power, other than man and yet related to him, which is believed to reside in certain objects of experience. This quality may be attributed to natural or artificial objects, to animals, or to men, or to the objectivations of human culture. There are sacred rocks, sacred tools, sacred cows. The chieftain may be sacred, as may be a particular custom or institution. Space and time may be assigned the same quality, as in sacred localities and sacred seasons. The quality may finally be embodied in sacred beings, from highly localized spirits to the great cosmic divinities. The latter, in turn, may be transformed into ultimate forces or principles ruling the cosmos, no longer conceived of in personal terms but still endowed with the status of sacredness. . . . The sacred is apprehended as "sticking out" from the normal routines of everyday life, as something extraordinary and potentially dangerous, though its dangers can be domesticated and its potency harnessed to the needs of everyday life. Although the sacred is apprehended as other than man, yet it refers to man, relating to him in a way in which other non-human phenomena (specifically, the phenomena of non-sacred

nature) do not. The cosmos posited by religion thus both transcends and includes man. The sacred cosmos is confronted by man as an immensely powerful reality other than himself. Yet this reality addresses itself to him and locates his life in an ultimately meaningful order.[3]

The function of the sacred cosmos, according to Berger, is not only to provide meaning at the boundaries of the social world, but also to provide legitimation for the institutions and authority structures of the social world. Because the marginalized situations threaten the sacred cosmos, the sacred cosmos is precarious, and so is the whole nomic world including the society's institutions and authority structures. Berger is concerned with tracing basic philosophical problems, such as theodicy, which threaten just about any given social cosmos. He is also concerned with understanding how modern science threatens the sacred cosmos of Western religion, especially Christianity. The sacred cosmos of our time is disjointed, inconsistent, often inapplicable or inadequate, and much broken.

Although appreciating and building enthusiastically upon Berger's work, the conception of sacred canopies developed in *Philosophical Theology* pushes the notion in directions that Berger himself did not do. Berger himself uses the phrase *sacred canopy* only in the title of his book. In the body of the work he uses *sacred cosmos* instead. But sacred cosmos suggests a contrast with mundane cosmos, or with chaos.[4] However incoherent or fragmented, a sacred *cosmos* does not admit of alternatives, only of amendments or collapse. *Sacred canopy* is a better term because it suggests a great tent over a larger cosmos, a tent that depicts the boundary conditions for the world in which the socially constructed nomos also provides the meaningful details of everyday life. The metaphor of "canopy" is apt because is suggests an artifact shielding the human world from the transcendent void above and also because, when it breaks down, it can be said to be "rent" like torn canvass. In what follows, "worldview" is used, as is explained in chapter 4, to mean something like what Berger means by nomos. A sacred canopy is only the part of a worldview that symbolizes the worldview's boundary conditions.

The study of ultimacy can begin by locating the ultimate in human experience as that to which reference is made in sacred canopies. The symbols in sacred canopies refer to what is ultimate in the sense that they articulate the boundary conditions that define the world. The boundary conditions are the "last" in the various series of conditions that make up the interpretive structures of everyday life. This notion of ultimate boundary conditions is developed in many layers throughout *Philosophical Theology*.

The symbols in a sacred canopy have some degree of coherence, hence the unifying connotations of a "canopy" thrown over the affairs of experience. But the coherence does not have to be great, nor does it have to be formal. The symbols do not have to be consistent with one another as they would be in a theological system of doctrines. When a sacred canopy is functioning well, its symbols work together even though they are not consistent. When the sacred canopy is rent, the symbols do not work together, nor do they collectively address the issues of boundary conditions that arise in marginal situations. Robert Bellah, in *Religion in Human Evolution*, develops an anthropological tradition that makes a strong distinction between the symbols making up the world of ordinary life and those making up sacred or religious life, noting that many things can be approached in both ways and suggesting that the same individuals can step from one to another.[5] That might be the way some religious cultures work. But there is no necessity that symbols of the ultimate constitute a different way of relating to the world than do symbols of proximate things that are part of mundane life.

Many different things can be found in a sacred canopy, from sacred rocks to transcendent, nonpersonified principles, as Berger listed in the long paragraph quoted above. Perhaps Berger did not give enough importance to the roles of narratives, histories, myths, and legends in defining boundary conditions for meaningful life. One of the great contrasts between the Christian theologies of Karl Barth and Paul Tillich is that the former represents the overall frame for Christianity as a *narrative* of creation and redemption whereas the latter represents the overall frame as a *metaphysical structure* relating people as alienated or reconciled to God as the Ground of Being (I, 8, i).[6]

Although Berger recognizes the issues of individuals relating to sacred canopies or a sacred cosmos, he orients the discussion to the externalizations, objectivations, and internalizations of societies. Modern societies contain many religious cultures, and hence the plurality of sacred canopies represented by those religious cultures. Moreover, the major religions each have many overlapping but often contradictory sacred canopies. Each individual within a religious community relates to sacred canopies in individual ways, affirming or supposing some elements, and rejecting others. Individuals in this pluralistic age can relate to several quite different sacred canopies at once, or serially, or according to different situations. So it is important at this early stage of the argument to be somewhat loose, or at least vague, about how individuals and groups relate to sacred canopies as defining *their* world. Chapter 4 introduces more variables to discuss this.

The "sacred" in sacred canopies requires much analysis. Berger's discussion resonates to the traditions of phenomenology of religion that emphasize the quality of uncanniness, as in the work of Edward Burnett Tylor, Gerardus van der Leeuw, Mircea Eliade, and Rudolf Otto. Yet the connection of uncanniness, or *mysterium tremendum et fascinans*, or the *numinous* with ultimate boundary conditions is not obvious. At this stage in the argument it is important to stress first that "sacred" in sacred canopies means the references to the boundary conditions, the world-making things that are ultimate (I, 7).

Living within a sacred canopy, the boundary conditions expressing ultimacy can be taken at face value. Yet most religious traditions, surely those of the Axial Age religions, are aware of the fact that the symbols in their sacred canopy are just symbols, that they are imperfect expressions, that in some sense they are false as well as true.[7] Although no sacred canopy operates within anything other than symbols, their symbols can explicitly point beyond themselves with an apophatic quality. The concept of sacred canopies is an important analytical tool in the discussion both of ultimacy and of religion in this and the volumes to follow. The next step is to define it more precisely.

II. FINITE/INFINITE CONTRASTS

Ultimacy or ultimate realities symbolized in a sacred canopy can be understood as finite/infinite contrasts. *Finite/infinite contrast* is a technical term that will aid in defining ultimacy.[8] *Contrast* is a term taken from Alfred North Whitehead's cosmology that means the juxtaposition in a coherent harmony of two or more different things.[9] For Whitehead, a contrast bears different degrees of intensity, depending on how different the things are that are contrasted together, and how simply they fit together. Kant had defined a concept as a rule uniting a manifold of representations.[10] This is a good definition for some concepts. A contrast, however, does not have a rule over and above the manifold simply being together. A contrast has a pattern expressing just how the contrasted elements are together; but the pattern is not some "third thing" over and above the elements as fitted together. A contrast is a harmony of diverse things that can be grasped in an interpretive judgment.[11]

The finite side of a finite/infinite contrast is whatever finite or determinate thing is taken to be ultimate in a sacred canopy. This could be anything from a sacred rock to a sacred time, a sacred myth of origins, a deity or set of deities, a creator God, the Dao, a divine narrative, or any of a host of things that have been called ultimate. Most Axial Age religions take the radically contingent existence of the world to be a finite ultimate, and have something ultimate as the ground of value or obligation, something that articulates human or cosmic destiny, and so forth. The important point here is that the finite side of a finite/infinite contrast is something determinate, something that can be expressed as being what it is and not something else.

The infinite side of a finite/infinite contrast is the recognition that, without the finite side, some basic world-defining trait would be missing, or would be indeterminate, infinite. The infinite side defines the finite side as being a boundary condition, a world-making condition. Numinous rocks and personal deities might simply be strange components of the world, with nothing ultimate about them; South Asian religions claim an abundance of deities that are not ultimate. What would make them ultimate is that, without them, some crucial world-defining trait would be missing. It is apparent why the creation of the contingent world is such a ubiquitous symbol of ultimacy in the Axial Age religions that symbolize "the world as such": Without the ultimacy of ontological creation of the world, none of the other ultimate traits would have a context.

The infinite side of a finite/infinite contrast need not be thought of as a positive infinite, as in the pure actuality of Aristotle or Thomas Aquinas, or the One of Neo-Platonism. In fact, to the extent that it is conceived in that positive way, the "full" infinite of those creation traditions would fall on the finite side of the finite/infinite contrast, although paradoxically because both are thought to be infinite in a sense. The logical function of the infinite side of a finite/infinite contrast is to be the counter-factual of determinateness: There would be nothing world-making, no world at all in respect of the finite trait, if the finite side were not real. The nothingness or indeterminateness of the infinite side is the only thing that would be real if the finite condition did not obtain.

So a finite/infinite contrast is an ultimate reality, or part of a larger ultimate reality, or has ultimacy, because the infinite side shows the finite side to be an ultimate condition for some dimension of reality. That condition might be the very existence of the contingent world, determinate reality as such. Or it might be the existence of some other ultimate trait defining the world. The next section elaborates a typology of kinds of ultimate conditions that was introduced in the Introduction, Section I. The location of ultimacy within human experience, we can say now, is to be a finite/infinite contrast symbolized within a sacred canopy. Sacred canopies vary enormously in the kinds of things they symbolize as finite/infinite contrasts. This variety is examined in more detail in chapter 4, on worldviews. Sacred canopies also vary in how they put together their congeries of finite/infinite contrasts, with, say, narrative structures, geometric structures, ritual structures, or all of the above, and many more besides.

A theological analysis of ultimate realities involves the articulation of that particular boundary condition or dimension of the world that is ultimate for the finite/infinite contrast in question. A personal deity, for instance, might be a boundary condition for establishing a people as historically powerful over against their enemies. Or the deity might be the condition for natural phenomena such as storms or the chaos of the sea, or for the creation of the world as a whole. Each of these is a different respect in which ultimacy is claimed. Theological analysis is needed to sort these different dimensions of ultimacy or different ultimate realities.

What is claimed to be ultimate in various sacred canopies is a matter for empirical analysis. Nevertheless, some broad categories can be articulated for a rough sorting of kinds of ultimate realities as finite/infinite contrasts. These categories do not capture all the alleged ultimates. But perhaps they articulate enough so that some of the dimensions of ultimacy will be apparent that any good sacred canopy ought to be able to symbolize.

III. WORLD-DEFINING HUMAN PROBLEMS

In a general sense, we can suppose that the basic categories of ultimacy in a sacred canopy are those that make the human world potentially problematic.

These are world-defining human problems and they articulate ultimate dimensions of reality relative to the human sphere. The finite/infinite contrasts are addressed by those symbols that link to these potential problems and, at least temporarily, signify that the world is real and meaningful in that "category." The diverse sacred canopies of the multitude of world religious cultures, of course, vary among themselves, as well as within themselves, because of their different histories. All their symbols are historically situated. Moreover, it might well be that some religions emphasize some sorts of world-defining human problems and other religions emphasize others. Nevertheless, a general thesis of *Philosophical Theology* is that reality is what it is, and that all religious cultures have to address its ultimate dimensions one way or another.

To provide a rough catalogue of dimensions of ultimacy to be symbolized in the finite/infinite contrasts of a sacred canopy, it is possible at this stage of the argument to appeal to some metaphysical considerations about reality that will not be explained in detail or justified until Part III, especially in chapter 10. The argument of this section thus is seriously incomplete without that subsequent discussion. The metaphysical considerations articulate a theory of the conditions for the existence of a determinate world. Of course, few if any sacred canopies contain these or cognate metaphysical ideas per se, although it will be argued in chapter 15 that in some sense this metaphysics constitutes a kind of language for prayer or meditation appropriate for those with a metaphysical bent. Rather, the metaphysical categories name world-making structures of reality for which some religious symbolization in a sacred canopy is appropriate.

Any world, real and as symbolized, is made up of things that are determinate. That is, each thing is what it is and as such is different from other things. "Determinate thing" here can mean objects, substances, events, processes, ideas, classes, changes, or whatever: a thing is determinate if it is what it is and is not something else: so long as it is a what, anything whatever is determinate. A thing need be determinate only in certain respects, perhaps not in all respects; today is quite determinate with regard to the weather, for instance, but it is not entirely determinate today what the weather will be tomorrow—determinateness does not imply determinism. The following is a sketch of a metaphysical hypothesis about determinateness that is defended at length in chapters 9, 10, and 11.

To be determinate is to be together with at least some other things. For, determinateness means that a thing is itself and thus is different from other things, which in turn are determinate in their own ways. Consider a determinate thing, therefore, to be a harmony of two kinds of components ("harmony" is analyzed on many levels in following discussions).[12] One kind of component can be called "essential" in that it contributes to or determines the thing's own being. The other kind of component can be called "conditional" because it derives from some other thing or things that condition the harmony in question. Without conditional components, a thing would not be related to other things and therefore could not be different from them.

Without essential components, the conditional components would not be integrated so as to constitute a thing that is itself and not reducible to the other things. Both essential and conditional components are necessary for a thing to be determinate. It can only be determinate in a world with other things with respect to which it is determinate. And the thing is a harmony of essential and conditional components.

Now there are four transcendental elements of all harmonies: form, components formed, existential location, and value identity. Form is the pattern in which the components are harmonized. Possibilities are forms in which actual components might be harmonized. Some forms are static but many interesting forms are dynamic, unfolding as in a musical piece. The components are all the things that are harmonized within the harmony, and they can be classified in one way as essential or conditional components. But there are many other ways to classify the components of a harmony. In a dynamic thing such as a living organism, many organic processes are formed together to make up the living harmony. All the components of a harmony are themselves harmonies, each with their forms, components, existential location, and value. It is harmonies (not turtles!) all the way down. No basic atomic simples can exist because atomic simples would have no conditional components and thus would not be determinate, which would mean that they would contribute nothing as components of a harmony. The existential location of a harmony is the set of connections by which the harmony relates to other harmonies. Some other harmonies might be wholly internal to the given harmony as components. Others might be wholly external and connected only indirectly by a chain of harmonies. Still others might be partially internal and partially external, or begin as external and become internal, and perhaps become externalized again. Some harmonies are very distant and connected only through extensive mediation. An existential field is itself a kind of harmony and thus has a form. But it is not only a form or pattern of harmonization: It is the real causal network by which things condition one another and take on their own places or existential locations vis-á-vis the others. The value identity of a harmony is the value of having its specific components together in the form it has at the existential location it has (*II, 3; III, 9*). Each component harmony has its value (or disvalue) that is integrated in the existential location with the harmony's form. Sometimes integrating the components in a harmony creates a significantly different value from the sum of the components apart from the harmony; the harmony might be far better than the sum of its separate parts, as a great painting is better than the colors and lines that go into it; or it might be far worse as when the party of the hostess's friends, each of whom is dear, turns out to be a disaster when they are mixed together.

These traits of determinateness and harmony provide a set of categories for articulating dimensions of ultimacy that somehow or other are addressed in most civilized sacred canopies. This set has two fundamentally different kinds of categories. The first category has to do with the very being of determinate things; the others have to do with the nature of determinate things. In list form these categories are:

1. The Being of Determinateness (as harmony of essential and conditional components).
2. The nature of Form in harmony.
3. The nature of Components in harmony.
4. The nature of Existential Location in harmony.
5. The nature of Value Identity in harmony.

Each of these dictates a set of ultimate problems that are ontological in the sense of being the conditions for determinate reality; each also dictates a set of ultimate problems that are anthropological in the sense that human beings are framed with tasks or projects in order to be responsive to the objective conditions. So then there are ten general areas of ultimacy in five ontological/anthropological pairs.

PAIR 1, IN RELATION TO ONTOLOGICAL DETERMINATENESS

The ontological ultimate condition is the radical contingency of the entire collection of determinate things (I, pt 3)

Although determinate things condition one another through their conditional components, they cannot create the essential components of one another but are simply together with those other things with their external essential components.[13] Any kind of causation articulated by science or other forms of inquiry consists in the conditioning of things by one another. The existence of mutually conditioning things presupposes a context other than the mutual conditioning in which the separate essential components of the different things are together. That context of mutual relevance is radically contingent and not explained by any determinate thing or combination of determinate things.

This radical contingency is articulated in many different kinds of finite/infinite contrasts. Some suppose a question of how the radically contingent world of determinate things comes to be, and one position posits an external creator, a God, and another the cooperation of independent principles such as Heaven and Earth in East Asian thought. Some sacred canopies, such as the Neo-Platonic or the Perennial Philosophy, posit an indeterminate fullness of reality that produces determinate realities by a contraction or diremption of itself. Other sacred canopies, such as in the Daoist and Neo-Confucian symbolism of Zhou Dunyi, say that absolute nothingness gives rise to Taiji, the great fruitfulness, which gives rise to extension, which reaches its limits and returns, distinguishing yang and yin which thus makes determinate things (quoted in *I, 12, i.*). Many kinds of creation myths exist in addition to these more philosophical considerations. Some sacred canopies, for instance many but not all Buddhist ones, do not focus on a cause for the existence of a determinate world, but rather on the surprise at its suchness, amazement at its contingent determinateness. The large religious traditions often try several or all of these symbolic finite/infinite contrasts to respond to the world-making trait of radical contingency. The problem of radical contingency is the center of the philosophical theology developed in these volumes, and on it depend all the other senses of ultimacy. Depending on the symbolic structure involved, the other senses might be combined with the finite/infinite contrasts regarding radical contingence. For instance, if the assertion is that the world is created by a personal God, then that symbol might combine with the world-making dimension of value, saying that God creates the world for a purpose.

The anthropological response to radical contingency can be ontological gratitude or rage/denial

As is argued in layers of development in the following chapters and volumes, the radical contingency of the cosmos is gratuitous, arbitrary, undeserved, and surprising. The shock of apprehending this can be ontological gratitude, which has four main forms. One, in response to the gratuitousness of the existence of this or any cosmos, is gratitude as "consent to being in general," as Jonathan Edwards called it (*II, 12*). A second is acceptance of the singularity of existence, of one's particular place and character, in response to the arbitrariness of the cosmos, a point developed in Part III. A third kind of gratitude is humility in the face of the undeservedness of the cosmos from any human point of view. A fourth is awe and astonishment at the surprisingness of the cosmos. All four forms of gratitude in combination or singly constitute ontological gratitude for the existence of the radically contingent cosmos. The other side of the coin of gratitude is resentment, anger, and denial directed at the cosmos, which for many people is nothing but a source of pain and universal death. Because the cosmos has value, as is argued in detail, the gratitude response is appropriate and the other not, even under the circumstance that a person's own situation has more disvalue than positive value.

Pair 2, in reference to form

The ontological finite/infinite contrasts have to do with possibility (II, 1)

The form of a present set of determinate things is possibility actualized. But what about the future? Sacred canopies address the world-making quality of possibility in a number of ways. Some regard possibility as the future in some narrative, perhaps with a destining divinity controlling things, perhaps with decisive events such as battles or the return of gods. Others regard possibility in terms of the order and chaos of nature. Yet others supply finite/infinite contrasts in the forms of rituals for ordering possibilities.

In the human sphere, possibility poses a world-making problem for human freedom. Some sacred canopies deny any meaningful sense in which human beings can make a difference to which possibilities are actualized. Others take serious note of the fact that people do control what happens to some degree. Because which possibilities among options are actualized determines what values come to be actualized, it makes a difference what people choose. This is to say, because of possibility, human beings lie under obligation to do the better and avoid the worse because that makes an ontological difference to the value in the world. Many different symbols have been devised to spell out the nature of the kinds of possibilities facing communities and individuals, and articulating modes of obligation. These in various ways determine ultimacy in possibility.

The anthropological side of the ultimate conditions of possibility is the task of becoming righteous in the sense of living up to obligations (II, 1)

Some sacred canopies articulate this in symbols of obedience to divine law; others in symbols of the cultivation of basic virtues of righteousness. Some finite/infinite contrasts spell out historically decisive acts of righteousness. Others focus on everyday behavior. Rituals are prominent in many sacred canopies for the performance of righteousness. Ultimate reality in sacred canopies sometimes constitutes a sense of justice that combines the project of performing righteousness with recognition of Otherness in those to whom justice is owed. Righteousness is a matter of ultimacy because of the world-making function of form as possibility.

PAIR 3, IN REFERENCE TO COMPONENTS

The ontological side of components is that the world is grounded in what makes it up, and we human beings are grounded in what composes us (II, 2)

We harmonize our components, but the components are the given things in the actual world plus our own subjective contributions. If we did not have actual things to integrate into our lives, we would be but patterns. The givenness of our component processes and ancestors is what constitutes our sense of reality. Most sacred canopies have elements that address the problematic sense of *un*reality. Some have to do with being seen by God. Some have to do with cultivating a sense of embodiedness; others have to do with escaping a sense of embodiedness so as to relate to the "real" components, for instance the Atman that is Brahman. Some finite/infinite contrasts have to do with finding a part in a mythic narrative, or with addressing a component social role as a special responsibility—Jonah became real when he accepted the call to Nineveh.

The anthropological side of the ultimacy of components has many expressions in sacred canopies

Some have to do with the task of developing special kinds of piety toward certain of the components of life, recognizing that they have integrities of their own despite the fact we reduce them to the roles they play in our life's harmonies. This piety involves a kind of deference to the components, not just recognition of Otherness, but deference to the quasi-independent careers of the components. Human beings need food in order to maintain themselves. But eating something destroys what would be the otherwise independent career of the plant or animal. Ritualized sacrifice of animals and vegetables for food is recognition of the ultimacy of components in some religions. Some religions are vegetarian in their piety toward animals. Sacred canopies contain finite/infinite contrasts for honoring the human body as a component in a larger human life, for honoring individuals who are components of families, for honoring families that are components of larger communities. Honoring components and righteously pursuing justice are not always compatible, because sometimes justice requires the diminishment of the component. Sacred canopies have finite/infinite contrasts for recognizing this dimension of ultimacy.

PAIR 4, IN REFERENCE TO EXISTENTIAL LOCATION

The ontological side of existential location is the finite/infinite contrasts defining place in the universe (II, 3)

Some sacred canopies are concerned with the place of individuals, others with particular groups or nations, and yet others with humanity as a whole. Place can be defined in terms of mythic space/time, as in Eliade's studies, or in terms of a national narrative, as in Judaism, or in terms of cosmic narrative as in many forms of Buddhism, Hinduism, and Christianity. Place may be understood primarily in relation to nature, as in Daoism, or in terms of history, as in many strains of the Abrahamic religions. Place also may be understood in terms of contemporary science. Whether there is an especially meaningful place differs from one sacred canopy to another: According to many modern scientists, the human place in the cosmos is meaningless save for what we do in it, and according to some religious groups they have no meaningful place unless they control Jerusalem.

The anthropological side of existential location is the conception of the ultimate project of engaging the things with us in the existential field in the form of the Other, with the task of relating to other things as Others

A person is a harmony that relates to other things as different because of sets of conditional components. But difference is not Otherness. Otherness is the fact that other different things have essential components of their own that are not encompassed within the person conditionally related to them. The existential field connects human beings conditionally to things that are genuine Others. Some sacred canopies register this dimension of ultimacy with symbols of the deep mystery in the beings of things, or of the whole of nature, a mystery that goes beyond lack of understanding of the conditioning causal connections. Often sacred canopies have finite/infinite contrasts concerning the Otherness of other human beings. In pre-Axial Age religions, according to evolutionary biologists, the distinction between people in one's in-group and those outside was of paramount importance: the others in the in-group can be treated as Others, whereas the outsiders can be reduced to their conditional components. A decisive characteristic of the Axial Age religions (*III, 2*) is that they insist that every person, regardless of in-group membership, should be treated as an Other. This takes the form of ultimate obligations for universal justice, based on the dignity of each person having his or her own essential as well as conditional components, and universal love. The subjective side of radical contingency is that we are with Others.

PAIR 5, IN REFERENCE TO VALUE AND VALUE IDENTITY

The ontological side of value is the set of finite/infinite contrasts that articulate the source or ground of value in the world (II, 4)

Value manifests itself in the possibilities of form, in the particular choices for harmonizing components, and in the disposition of actualized things with value in themselves and relative to each other. Some sacred canopies characterize that ground as the expression of some divine purpose. Others characterize divine purpose as determined by value that is otherwise legitimate as independent. Many sacred canopies define value as grounded in the fulfillment of missions or teleological natures of things, individuals, or communities. Some sacred canopies represent the ultimacy of value as residing in a kind of aesthetic beauty or glory. If there were no value, then there would be no sense of accomplishment or failure in life.

The anthropological side of value lies precisely in the ultimacy of accomplishment and failure

Individual identity is made of up what persons do with the conditions of their lives, for better or worse. All the themes of sin and guilt, salvation and redemption, center around the anthropological side of the facts that the universe contains differential values, that the values actualized depend in part on human doing, and that human beings have the value of what they do. The ultimacy of this value identity can be symbolized, among other ways, as a matter of standing under judgment before God, of contributing to the ongoing value of nature, or of abandoning personal value-identity completely in some ultimate sense, as in the Nirvana traditions.

The categories of ultimate dimensions of life, or ultimate realities in sacred canopies, are by no means exhaustive. But they function to indicate just how complex and interactive the finite/infinite complexes are in sacred canopies. All ten categories discussed in this section are, of course, vague in the sense defined in the preliminary remarks to this part. The variety of symbolic finite/infinite contrasts that can specify them is far greater than the examples given here. Moreover, they combine in many different ways in sacred canopies, producing even more complicated finite/infinite complexes. Some of these are explored more systematically in the following.

IV. TRUTH IN SACRED CANOPIES

People bet their lives on the sacred canopies to which they are committed.[14] They take them to be the most fundamental truths about the world, the truths that make more mundane truths possible and orient them to larger meaning. Yet the claims implied in sacred canopies about ultimacy so often are contradictory, even within what is supposed to be a single unified canopy. Huge differences exist among different world religions. Given the historical differences in language and rhetorical tropes, differences in scripture and modes of commentary, to discern just where claims about ultimacy agree and disagree, are similar or different, or are about the same thing or different things, is extremely difficult. Those questions and their cognates are all empirical: Comparative theology needs to do far more work than the relatively new discipline yet has done in order to answer them. Is the question of truth in the claims or assumptions about ultimacy in sacred canopies a matter of distinguishing exactly what is implicitly or explicitly asserted and then determining which claims are true?

To complicate matters, the existential urgency of truth in matters of sacred canopies arises most especially when something causes a sacred canopy or some crucial part of it to become implausible. Peter Berger analyzes in detail the pressure that the existence of evil and gratuitous suffering puts on symbols of a divine creator who is alleged to be personally intentional, all-powerful, perfectly knowledgeable and benevolent, one of the dominant finite/infinite contrasts in monotheistic religions. Events such as the Lisbon earthquake and the Nazi Holocaust raise the question of truth in a powerful way concerning claims about a personal, omnipotent, omniscient, benevolent, creator. Modern science directly challenges many of the symbols of ultimate world structure in ancient religious sacred canopies. Nature is not always as harmonious deep down as some symbols of the Dao would suggest. How can a practical commitment to an Advaita Vedantin non-dualist sacred canopy survive the adolescence of one's children? If the old sacred canopy is rent, by what truth can a new one be woven?

Berger develops the notion of the sacred canopy or sacred cosmos from the methodological perspective of sociology of knowledge. This perspective treats religious symbols as human constructions only and deliberately prescinds from the question of whether they actually refer to what they seem to refer to.[15] In this perspective, the social functional utility of a sacred canopy is the closest thing to the question of truth. An implausible element in a sacred canopy is not so much false as useless or counterproductive in the human project of ordering the world meaningfully. Few religious people view the commitments concerning ultimacy in their sacred canopies to be mere instruments for imagining the world to have an order, or for creating a fictional order in a reality of dangerous chaos.

This chapter has taken the small but decisive step of subverting the social construction view of order making into the pragmatic semiotics of interpretation. The following chapter spells this out in detail.[16] According to pragmatic semiotics, all conventional signs or symbols are human constructions that are used in interpretive acts to refer to their objects. Their reference to their objects is in only certain respects, as determined by the character of the symbols and the purposes or intentions guiding the interpretation. The interpretation can be true or false. In this pragmatic sense, a sacred canopy is a complex, not necessarily coherent, hypothesis about the ultimate boundary conditions of the world. Its objects are ultimate realities, dimensions of ultimacy, and so forth, in the sense defined as finite/infinite contrasts and as illustrated in the previous section.

Treated as an hypothesis to which a deep meaning-founding religious commitment can be made, a sacred canopy can, in principle, be subjected to inquiry about its truth, in part and whole. "In principle" is an enormous qualification. Such an inquiry would have to sort through all the wild systems of symbols used in interpreting ultimacy in sacred canopies. It would have to understand the modes of reference involved in living and thinking according to the sacred canopy. The intentional and purposeful contexts for interpreting ultimacy in life and thought with the symbols of a sacred canopy would have to be identified. A sacred canopy is neither true nor false unless it is used in interpretation, lived-by in some sense, or assumed as the world building background to other interpretations; these are all dimensions of interpretation and interpretation is always contextual. An interpretation that is true in one context might be false in another. Given the enormous complexity of sacred canopies, the question of truth is astonishingly difficult to address.

The complexity having been admitted, the meaning of the truth of a sacred canopy is whether it carries over from the ultimate realities into the interpreter what is important or valuable in those realities, in the respects in which the symbols of the canopy interpret them. This is a formula that will be explained in greater detail in the next chapter.[17] Its point is a fundamental pragmatic one: Does a sacred canopy attune us to ultimate realities so that we can discriminate how we should comport ourselves toward them? If it does attune us so, all things considered (about symbol systems, reference, contexts, etc.), it is true.

Given the unsteadiness of sacred canopies, and the fact that they seem always to be torn and under repair, it is important to distinguish the manifest sacred canopy from the ultimate realities to which it is supposed to refer. Of course, we cannot *say* what the ultimate realities are except by manifesting them in some (hopefully) improved symbols. The tendency in most civilized religious traditions to move from sacred canopies framed in folk symbols toward sacred canopies expressed in metaphysical language reflects this tension. Folk symbols are highly variable in meaning and truth as to context, whereas metaphysical language aims to apply across most if not all contexts.

Nevertheless, the question of the truth of sacred canopies is even more complicated than all this, for two reasons. First, even the most expansive, metaphysically general, logically coherent, consistent, applicable, and adequate sacred canopy, in the form of a sophisticated theology, will interpret ultimate realities in only some respects, not in all respects.[18] Part of the necessity of system in theology is to provide a discipline for attempting to interpret ultimacy in the *important* respects. But that sense of system can never be completed. The potential always exists that some important aspect of ultimate reality has been missed. The vast plurality of sacred canopies is itself a blessing in this sense because it goes some way to get around the blinders that the rhetoric of any given sacred canopy would have that prevent it from addressing other respects in which ultimacy might be interpreted. Even all the sacred canopies together, however, are only a few select guesses at the riddle.

The second complication to the truth question regarding sacred canopies is built into the nature of finite/infinite contrasts. The symbols in the sacred canopy describe only the finite side of the contrasts, along with registering their world-founding functions that derive from the infinite side. But the symbols cannot mediate the finite/infinite distinction. The contrasts remain contrasts. This means that between the infinity of what would be the case if the finite side were not real, and the finite side itself, is an ultimate arbitrariness. Precisely because it is infinite, wholly indeterminate, the infinite side cannot supply a reason for the finite side. Thus even the best sacred canopy, with all possible theological virtues, ends in mystery and surprise, knowing that it cannot be wholly right.

CHAPTER TWO

Reference, Reduction, Philosophy, and Metaphysics

The previous chapter made the point that religious people bet their lives that their religious beliefs are true, especially those embodied in their sacred canopies. Roughly put, their bet on the truth of religious beliefs includes an assumption that they refer to what they seem to refer to and that what they say about the objects of reference is right in some important sense. Further analysis of the point is necessary in order to orient our inquiry into ultimate reality. This chapter explores some ways of looking at the question of reference. Chapter 3 presents a theory of reference that applies to ultimate realities defined in terms of finite/infinite contrasts. The nature of reference is a crucial aspect, but only one aspect, of the nature of truth in interpretation.

I. THE PRESUPPOSITION OF REAL REFERENCE

One of the complications of religious belief is the variety in the modes in which belief is held. Obviously, beliefs can be held as conscious affirmations, which can be expressed in answer to the question, "What do you believe about . . . ?" Consciousness is often deceptive, however. As William James and other pragmatists insisted, what you really believe is what you are prepared to act on. Sometimes you think you believe something but are not prepared to act on the belief; the alternative action you do perform instead reveals that you really believe something else. Two dimensions of this double consciousness should be mentioned.

First, the socialization process within which people mature supplies nests of beliefs including those in sacred canopies, for which there are sanctions. Not only are these beliefs the way the group articulates its world, but people are pressured to accept them and the degree to which they accept the beliefs is correlated positively with the degree to which the people are accepted into the group (*11, 13, 14*). When you think you believe something in the sacred canopy, it might be because this has been socialized into you; when push comes to shove, however, it turns out you do not really accept that belief, contrary to what you had thought, and instead live according to an alternative belief.

Second, many religious beliefs are costly. The cost might be in peer pressure, as in the previous point, or in faithfulness to standards of plausibility, or in the integrity of moral responsibility, or in persecutions by a world hostile to the religious beliefs. What you think you believe perhaps has little cost. But you realize that you are willing to pay some cost, say, standing up to peer pressure, and then you let yourself believe something that is far more plausible. Then you realize that what you thought was plausible is not really, so you let yourself believe something else at the cost of giving up easy plausibility. Then you see that this new belief stands in the way of fulfilling responsibilities, say, to your family, and so you let yourself believe something even more costly. And then you are struck with yet another alternative belief that is so compelling that you are willing to go against peer pressure, your standards of plausibility, and your moral expectations so as to witness to this new belief in a world that is socially, cognitively, and morally hostile (III, 13–14).

Beliefs are held not only consciously but also as unconscious assumptions that serve as background for other actions and beliefs. Behavior is shaped by background assumptions perhaps even more than by foreground actions and assertions. For some people in any religious culture, the beliefs in their sacred canopies are implicit and not acknowledged consciously except insofar as they are expressed in rituals whose symbols might come to consciousness as referring to something. Even then, for many people the explicit religious symbols of belief are performed ritually rather than thought about reflectively. When questioned about their background religious assumptions, many people cannot go beyond one or two exchanges to explain the meaning of the symbols they ritually perform. This does not entail that they do not really believe those assumptions. It suggests only that the mode in which those beliefs are held is that of assumption, perhaps unexamined assumption.

Within some sacred canopies, it is thought that salvation itself depends on believing certain things. Some forms of evangelical Christianity, for instance, hold that if you believe that Jesus Christ is the Messiah and accept him as your personal Lord and Savior, you will be saved, where salvation means going to Heaven after you die. For this kind of Christianity, the content of beliefs and commitment to their truth become extraordinarily important. Much focus is placed on grounds for certainty for beliefs, such as the Bible interpreted literally or the magisterium of the Church with infallible doctrine.

More mainstream forms of Christianity construe the theology of salvation by belief to be a kind of heretical "works righteousness" in which individuals erroneously think to earn their salvation by their work of believing. The mainstream forms would say rather that salvation involves accepting a way of life that involves beliefs but also much more—community participation, ritual organization, cultivation of spiritual practices, and the integration of many dimensions of religious life so as to respond appropriately to ultimate matters; salvation is viewed not as a reward for such participation but as a perfection of that participation. St. Augustine's conversion, for instance, was not a matter of him coming to believe something he had not believed before. It was a matter of his will to put on the vestments of the Christian life, which included theological beliefs that he adopted as his own. Yet he was not bound by those beliefs in any rigid way. More than just about any Christian theologian before or since his time, Augustine transformed the theological belief structure of the Christian tradition that he inherited to "put on." His way of holding the beliefs in his sacred canopy was to accept the sacred canopy as a part of "putting on Christianity" and then improve the canopy to make it more nearly true.[1]

Madhyamaka Buddhism might be seen as a conspicuous exception to the claims that people believe their religious beliefs to be true and that belief is extremely important. In a marvelously complex article summarizing an ironic history of Western interpretations of Madhyamaka, Malcolm David Eckel (with John J. Thatamanil) argues that the Madhyamaka tradition treats "reference" as a "myth" in an important sense.[2] Our words and beliefs do not refer to transcendent objects. In fact, there are no transcendent objects to which reference might be made, nothing with a being of its own as an object of belief or knowledge, only momentary congeries of intersecting conditions. Indeed, part of the religious problem that causes suffering, according to Madhyamaka, is precisely the common belief that there exist transcendent realities, especially ultimate ones that a person might hope to possess or avoid. Attachment to the truth of references is a poison that causes suffering. The Madhyamaka point, according to Eckel, is to transfer attention from concern for ultimate objects or ultimate truths to concern for the project of obtaining release from suffering. To the extent that transfer is made, it is fine to accept the conventional beliefs that our beliefs do have objects because the objects no longer solicit attachment. Yet, according to Madhyamaka, "betting your life" on the truth of religious beliefs is precisely what must be given up if commitment is to be made to the journey toward release from suffering.

This important point qualifies the claim that religious people are deeply concerned about whether their beliefs refer to ultimate realities and do so truly. Nevertheless, the Madhyamaka point is based on the ontological truth-claim that in fact there are no ultimate ontological realities, no own-being in things that endures through time. If that philosophical point were false, then the "medicine" Buddhism prescribes for breaking attachments to objects and thus obtaining release from suffering would not work. Although Madhyamaka does not think its cure for suffering depends on holding particular beliefs in a sacred canopy of symbols about ultimate realities, it is firmly committed to the referential truth of its analysis of the flow of things and the attachments of the mind, and *those ideas* are what are ultimate in its sacred canopy.

Another potential exception to the claim that referential truth in sacred canopies is important to religious people is the analysis of theology by thinkers in the so-called "Yale School," particularly Hans Frei and George Lindbeck.[3] For them, as for Peter Berger, religion is located in religious communities that are to be understood as "cultural/linguistic" systems. The lives of individuals in a community, and the career of the community itself, are guided by religious beliefs, as in sacred canopies. In fact, the real sacred canopies or theologies are the deep structure or the underlying grammar of the community. The function of theology is to ascertain whether actions, practices, and other beliefs are in harmony with or expressive of the deep grammar of the community. The reality of the deep grammar is solely in its function of guiding the life of the community. Although it might contain ideas about God or Buddhist emptiness, these ideas do not refer to anything outside of the community with its deep structure. Rather they refer to one another in ways of systematic meanings that guide religious life. In Lindbeck's case, the conception of cultural/linguistic communities came out of his experience in interreligious dialogue, Buddhist-Christian and Protestant-Roman Catholic. The upshot of his theory is that the different religious communities do not disagree about anything, because there is nothing to which they refer about which there can be disagreement. Rather, they organize their communities and practices differently because their communities have different deep structures. Interfaith dialogue explains these differences to one another.

Although much is to be learned about the contextuality of religious belief from the Yale School, it exhibits two important drawbacks. First, the conception of religious communities as having steady boundaries determined by the specifics of grammatical deep structures is flawed. Communities adventitiously intersect and borrow from one another and the borrowing shifts the deep structures. Especially in pluralistic situations, individuals are tempted by multiple religious community memberships, and can move from one to the other (III, 2–5). Among the reasons people shift religious allegiances is that they find some faults with the community of origin and some greater truths in the communities to which they move. Second, the nonreferential cultural/linguistic model is not persuasive to many of the very people it is supposed to explain. Of course, people can understand their communities to exhibit cultural and linguistic systems. But they do not easily accept that what those systems say about the world in ultimate matters is nothing more than a function of what the systems say rather than claims about what the ultimate matters really are.

So, acknowledging the complexities of the modes by which beliefs are held, noting the variations in the roles religious beliefs are thought to play in religious life, from being essential to salvation for conservative Christian evangelicals and being detrimental to "salvation" for Madhyamaka Buddhists, and accepting the fact that religious beliefs can constitute deep assumptions according to which religious life is lived, we still note the importance of the truth of claims about ultimacy in sacred canopies.

II. THE SCIENTIFIC BRACKETING OF REAL REFERENCE

However much people who take their orientation from sacred canopies are concerned about the truth of those canopies' claims about ultimacy, the various forms of the scientific study of religion scrupulously have attempted to bracket out any consideration of whether those claims have real references and whether what they claim is true. This is done in the name of objectivity (III, 1).

Objectivity does not lie in any simple contrast with subjectivity, although many people do believe, with Feuerbach, that religious beliefs are subjective projections with no real referents. The more scientific meaning of objectivity derives philosophically from Kant. Kant argued that our knowledge can be objective only when we cause things to answer questions that we put to them.[4] The answers then conform to the structures of our questions. Or to put the matter another way, what we know of things is "reduced" to what is revealed of the things when investigated according to the assumptions, structures, theories, and instruments of the investigation. The things might be much more than what shows up in the reductionist inquiry. But what that "more" might be cannot be known objectively unless perhaps it shows up in some other reductionist inquiry.

Kant put his point in a more radical way than many scientists would. He said that all we have in experience is a subjective order of representations that runs through our mind.[5] Some of that subjective order also might have objective validity, but the only way to tell is by seeing which ordered elements conform to regular causal connections in a deterministic sense. Kant said that, objectively, every alteration has a sufficient cause and that the only way to distinguish objective from merely subjective alterations is by finding the ones that have sufficient causes. Only reduction to what fits within a causal scheme distinguishes objective experiences from sheer fantasy.

Most scientists do not tie their methodological reductionism to the whole of Kant's transcendental philosophy. Yet the force of the term *objectivity* comes from that philosophy. For most Westerners after Kant, objectivity connotes knowledge of what is really real, as opposed to subjectivity, which might be sheer fantasy or willful projection. One cultural outcome of this point has been the recent assumption that those things that cannot keep their face-value intentionality when analyzed reductively by some scientific paradigm, things such as the validity of emotions, the real values experienced, and religious beliefs about ultimate matters, are themselves subjective. That they are subjective means that they have no real referents about which the knowledge or experience of them might be right or wrong. The great irony here is that this cultural consequence is the exact opposite of Kant's point. For Kant, empirical knowledge is objective because it is reduced to what can be expressed in the transcendental structures of subjectivity: it is not at all knowledge of the really real, which he called "things in themselves." The things that are really real in the sense of transcending our reductive experience of them, Kant said, are "transcendentally ideal," which is to say we can *think* about them but cannot *know* them empirically or any other way. For Kant, objectively known empirical realities might indeed have transcendent referents but they cannot be known.

The assumptions, structures, theories, and investigating instruments of scientific reductionism have complex histories, especially with regard to religion. Long before Kant, modern scientific philosophers had urged at least the ideal of reducing scientific knowledge to what can be expressed mathematically. Given the mathematics of the day and its modes of deployment, this had the immediate consequence that values in nature and society could not be registered in a reductive scientific account. The cultural outcome of this point was to assume that values are subjective and as such matters of human projection. Another consequence of the mathematical ideal has been that purposes or "final causes" can be given no explanatory power in a reductionist scientific investigation. Only antecedent conditions, or "efficient causes" have explanatory power. By Kant's time, he could define causation in terms of regularity of antecedent-consequent relations.

This mathematical reductionism posed enormous problems for understanding human experience and behavior. Beginning with Thomas Hobbes and John Locke, and culminating in the work of Max Weber, Western scientific philosophy devised an ingenious scheme for addressing these problems. In Weber's terms, human behavior can be studied according to "ideal types." An ideal type is a conception of a general person as defined by certain circumstances and determined mechanistically to behave in whatever ways seem to the individual to be his or her "best interest." For Hobbes and Locke, people in a state of nature find it in their best interest to enter into a social contract, which then opened the way for a rational scientific account of government (and jurisprudence). For more recent thinkers, the ideal type has been an economic optimizer: by figuring out the attendant circumstances and calculated "best interest," economists think to predict economic behavior. This seems not to work well, even when predicting the behavior of large aggregates of people. And it does not even apply to the understanding of individuals who are specific in their own purposes and choices. To accept that the prediction of the statistical behavior of a volume of gas says nothing about any one of the molecules in the volume is one thing, and it is quite another to accept that the prediction of aggregate human behavior says nothing about any individuals. Particularly is this true concerning religious behavior that, in so many respects, is inward and individualistic (*II, introduction, i*).

Alternative to the models deriving by analogy from mathematical physics is a complicated history in the West of observational or descriptive social sciences (*III, 1, i, ii*). Early anthropology, often conducted by or based on data from Christian missionaries in non-Western colonial lands, found it relatively easy to take an "objective" approach to the cultures it studied. The "true" culture with real references to ultimate realities was the Christian, or at least the sophisticated modern Western, and the "other" cultures must be quaint anticipations, deviations, or primitive variants of that. The variations could be marked off objectively as themselves in their sacred canopy having no real referent, or none but what was better expressed in Western terms. As is well known, the reductionist framework of the early anthropologists and religious comparativists consisted of categories derived from Western monotheisms. Much more than anthropology, early sociology began with theories of society, such as Marx's, which served as the reductionist framework for empirical study. Psychology arose with three often-conflicting reductive paradigms, all illustrated in the work of William James. One was the physiological approach that sought to understand psychological behavior, emotions and behaviors in terms of neurology and body chemistry. Another was the hermeneutical approach that sought to understand them in terms of the psychodynamics of consciousness, and the unconscious, a line of development encouraged by Freud. A third was what we now call "empirical psychology" that sought to develop categories and draw psychological generalizations through interviews and questionnaires, an approach in psychology of religion pioneered by James H. Leuba and Edwin Diller Starbuck.[6] All of these were objective because they "reduced" their subject matter to what could be represented according to their assumptions, structures, theories, and observational tools and categories. At the present time, these disciplines are much changed through the correction of the reductive limitations of their assumptions, structures, theories, and observational practices, with much crossover. Yet all would claim to be objective because much clearer and more self-conscious about the reductive characteristics of their approaches.

The postmodern critique of all these classical social science approaches was based on their common privileging of attention to their theories, as well as the unconscious bias that lay in the history of their theoretical developments. According to the postmodern critique, the problem lies in the reliance on theory itself. Any theory with its categories is logo-centric, recognizing those phenomena that its categories register and marginalizing or obscuring altogether those that it cannot register. Theory itself should be held under deepest suspicion, even if one cannot conduct inquiry without it. Moreover, theory never throws off completely the cultural biases of its origins, argues postmodernism. Western orientalism, Christian structuralism, male chauvinism, or the lingering authority of the geniuses of the discipline, all serve to bring a subjective element back into social science inquiries. Postmodernism is acutely aware of the power dynamics in controlling the discourses of inquiry. The way around this, according to postmodernism, is with micro-studies that let local communities, societies, psychological issues, and historical contexts speak for themselves as much as possible, with the assumptions, structures, theories, and investigative tools arising from participant-observation within the local setting.

The postmodern approach makes a decisive advance on Kant's insistence that nature answer our questions. It attempts to derive our questions from nature. The issue then is whether postmodern micro-studies are objective. They do not derive objectivity from reducing their subject matter to their own transcendental grid so as to claim nothing more than what shows up on that grid. Instead, they aim to give a picture of a religious cultural world, say, from the insider's point of view. But they also do not say whether that insider's point of view is valid or true, only that it seems true to the insiders. Because it claims no truth in the insider's view, it is not subjective projection on alleged real referents of that view. It is objective in the old-fashioned sense that it does not comment on the truth of real reference. Its validity has nothing to do with assessing the competing claims in insider views, for instance. Its validity rather lies simply in whether it has uncovered and expressed accurately the insiders' views on the world, including their sacred canopies.

Recently, the biological sciences and cognitive psychology have taken an interest in religion (*III, 1, i*). Evolutionary biology has made enormous contributions to the study of religion in its origins, and it is objectively reductionistic in its strict appeals to evolutionary theory. Neuroscientific studies are objective as well in the old-fashioned sense of reducing their claims to what can be made through the reduction of the subject matter to neurological findings. These studies will be important for the theory of religion to be developed in *Philosophical Theology Three*. Nevertheless, precisely because of their reductionistic objectivity, they do not speak to issues of truth in the real references of religious beliefs resident in sacred canopies.[7]

III. PHILOSOPHY'S CONTROL FOR REDUCTIONISM

In a strict sense, reductionism is good science. It reduces its subject matter to what can be defined in terms of its assumptions, structures, theories, and investigative instruments, analyzes its reduced subject matter in those terms, and then gives its results as strictly limited to what the analysis shows of the subject matter as so reduced to the scientific terms. In the strict sense, it does not say anything about the subject matter as such, only about the subject matter as filtered through the mesh of the inquiries assumptions, structures, theories, and instruments. Scientific theories refer iconically, as Chapter 3, Section III will explain, which means they say their subject matter is "like" what the theory says, as a map implies that the territory is like what the map depicts. But maps refer to territories only in certain respects, for instance with respect to road, property boundaries, population centers, geographic features, or weather. Scientific reductionism is bad when it suggests that the respect in which it is iconic for reality is the only or the most important respect. A higher-order inquiry, such as philosophy, is necessary to note what is filtered out in the subject matter and assess the distortion involved in getting the scientific outcomes about the subject matter as reduced.

In some kinds of scientific inquiry, for example, particle physics, the discrepancy between the real subject matter and the reduced subject matter is minimal, because the subject matter itself is so much a conceptualized product of the theories and instruments for making empirical distinctions. No way exists for identifying the real subject matter known as "quarks" independently of the particle theory and instrumentation that studies them. This is not to say that quarks are not real: Particular hypotheses might be wrong about them as demonstrated in an experiment, and anything that an hypothesis might be wrong about is real in some sense of resisting the hypothesis. Quarks do not have much connection with wider realities, however, that are not themselves already reduced to the terms of particle theory. Quite the opposite is the case with regard to Newtonian or Einsteinean mechanics. Those theories purport to be about the basic laws of physical reality and yet their assumptions, structures, theories, and instrumentations systematically screen out all considerations of the values of things in physical reality. They are not in fact about physical reality but about physical reality as reduced to what can be expressed mathematically.

Given the enormous damage to human civilization in the loss of value-reference and realistic valuation in modern Western science, the price of failure to recognize the difference between knowledge of the physical world as such and knowledge of the physical world as reduced to the terms of non-valuational mathematics has been extraordinarily high. One would have thought that the early modern philosophers, brilliant as they were, would have recognized this difference. But in fact they did not. They were all enchanted by the explanatory power of mathematical science, and often were major contributors to that science. Descartes produced a philosophy that defined physical reality as that which can be known by mathematical science—corporeality in motion, and placed all the rest of rich nature, including value, in what he called mind. Instead of saying that mathematic physics articulates an aspect of physical reality, however, modern philosophers for the most part said that what mathematic physics articulates is the real nature of physical reality. "Objectivity," as noted previously, has come to mean reality itself rather than reality as reduced to the assumptions, structures, theories, and instrumentations of inquiring subjects.

Here, then, is one of philosophy's major difficulties: to maintain sufficient connection with reductive inquiries so as to understand them without being seduced into forgetting that they exclude all aspects of their real subject matters that do not fit their reductive analyses. To be sure, philosophies themselves are reductive in the sense that they interpret their subject matter in and only in the respects in which their ideas can represent that subject matter. This is why philosophy needs to be systematic: to build in a vulnerable vision of the scope and limits of its own categories.

The case with scientific inquiries into religion is vastly more complicated than inquiries in physics or biochemistry. No learned person doubts that religion is deeply involved in culture, especially through social rituals. But, after declaring that his landmark book, *Ritual and Religion in the Making of Humanity*, is anthropological, "exclusively naturalistic" in assumptions, Roy A. Rappaport writes:

> One of its main theses is that religion's major conceptual and experiential constituents, the sacred, the numinous, the occult and the divine, and their integration into the Holy, are creations of ritual. To put the matter into logical rather than causal terms, these constituents are *entailments* of the *form* which constitutes ritual.[8]

Rappaport's theory of ritual will be important for the theology of ritual in *Philosophical Theology Two*. Nevertheless, he does not suggest that religion is more than is known through his naturalistic anthropology, and lists major items common to sacred canopies as entailed by ritual itself. Kathryn Tanner, explicitly a theologian with a philosophical bent, rightly points out that the classical anthropological approach to culture needs to be supplemented with studies of how individuals resist culture and its rituals in the name of religion, which is something more.[9] Similarly in sociology, learned people recognize with Marx and Durkheim that religion functions to stabilize, and sometimes to destabilize, social structures. But does the analysis of religion through the interpretive grid of social analysis really deliver "the elementary forms of the religious life?"[10] Of course religion is psychological, but only that? Of course it played a role in the evolution of humanity, and itself has evolved, but is it only that? Of course like any aspect of experience it has to involve neural cognitive and emotional abilities, but is it only that?[11] All of these studies will be crucial for the theory of religion developed in the second and third volumes of these studies. But all are reductionistic and the abstractions from concrete religion involved in their investigations need to be spelled out.

Happily, the multiplicity of disciplines studying religion and its appeals to and beliefs about ultimacy serve as counterweights to one another. Learned people know that all of them are helpful in some ways, and that they all are "right" concerning something about religion. But they also all reduce away all questions about the reference and truth of beliefs about ultimacy, and the authenticity of life as guided by those beliefs. Only philosophy can say what the price of reduction is when it leaves out the questions of reference and truth as found in the sacred canopies that express finite/infinite contrasts.

Philosophy has two principal tasks in this regard. First, it needs to supply an epistemology that can show how reference to ultimate matters is possible. This task is addressed in the following chapter and then throughout this volume. Second, philosophy needs to develop a plausible metaphysics that identifies ultimate realities in their independence. Only this can show what is left out when scientific and other approaches to religion reduce reference to ultimacy to what people say in reference to ultimacy. The following section describes what is meant by metaphysics in this sense, and Part III of this volume will develop the metaphysics of ultimacy itself.

IV. METAPHYSICS EXPLAINED AND DEFENDED

Critical reflection on the most basic categories and principles of reality, with debates among alternative theories, has been common in the history of the Axial Age cultures. This embraces the great civilized religions of East Asia, South Asia, Europe, and more recently the Americas, and global Islam (*III,2; III, pt 2*). Indeed, the rise of ways of conceiving of the world as a whole, of underlying universal principles, and of the identification of individuals in terms of relations with those principles instead of only in terms of kinship groups, are among the defining characteristics of Axial Age religions. For our purposes, this kind of dialectical critical reflection on basic categories and principles of reality can be called "metaphysics," although that word is of Western, Aristotelian origin.

Of course different styles of thinking about these issues exist in different traditions and the long histories of the traditions exhibit different styles within each one. Nevertheless the mutual interactions and influences of the different traditions should not be neglected. South Asian thinking is an amalgam of Aryan and Dravidian traditions. The Aryan side is cognate with Aryan influences in Persia and Greece and then Rome. Through Buddhism, South Asian thought dominated China for almost a millennium. Buddhism itself was heavily influenced by the Greek philosophy in the Asian kingdoms set up by the royal successors of Alexander the Great, and the Silk Road carried ideas from Europe to East Asia and back. Islam was powerfully influenced by Platonic, Aristotelian, and Neo-Platonic philosophy, and in turn influenced medieval European Jewish and Christian philosophy. Randall Collins' monumental *The Sociology of Philosophies: A Global Theory of Intellectual Change* details many of the important threads of intellectual interactions among traditions, giving the lie to absurd claims about the traditions being mainly linear and relatively isolated. Those claims perhaps are fostered by an intellectual laziness that wants to avoid responsibility for erudition in all the world's philosophic traditions as the background public for philosophic work today. They are also fostered by the practical problem that most people do not want to learn the languages necessary to track global philosophies. Nevertheless, through good translations philosophers can access all the traditions. Philosophic erudition, especially that involved in systematic theology, does need to be global and shaped by comparative considerations. A metaphysical theory appropriate for our time is heir to the tangled roots of global intellectual life.

A metaphysics appropriate to our time also needs to justify itself against the widespread claims in Western philosophy and theology that metaphysics is impossible or inappropriate. The critique of the possibility of metaphysics comes from Kant and will be addressed first. Kant argued that metaphysics claims to determine reality by thought alone, and with apodictic or necessary certainty.[12] He had in mind Descartes' idea that the light of reason allows for the direct inspection and understanding of simple realities, and that the world is a complex built out of simple realities.[13] Spinoza and Leibniz made similar claims for the power of reason to understand necessary traits of reality.[14] Against this, Kant argued that the only way the mind can determine reality is if reality is made to fit the transcendental structures of the mind. Then, we can know a priori whatever the transcendental structures of mind build in to what is experienced through sensation. But we cannot know anything about what reality is apart from its being experienced and thus being conformed to the transcendental conditions of the mind.[15] Metaphysics, he argued, is impossible because it attempts to know things beyond experience and beyond the transcendental structure of the mind. He called metaphysics a "dialectical illusion" because, in effect, all it does is to extrapolate certain ideals of reason, such as wholeness, completeness of a line of causation, and the like, and claim that the extrapolations are real transcendent-of-experience things.[16]

The answer to Kant is to point out that metaphysics does not have to mean the determination of reality by thought alone with apodictic certainty. Rather, as Charles Peirce argued, metaphysics is the development of hypotheses or a grand hypothesis about the most fundamental structures of reality.[17] This is the position on metaphysics of *Philosophical Theology*. For all their claims about certainty arising from the light of reason, the theories of Descartes, Spinoza, and Leibniz are more fruitfully regarded as large-scale hypotheses, and considered in that light. All the great theories of the global traditions of philosophy can be regarded as hypotheses, regardless of the authority their traditions claimed for them from a priori reason or revelation. Metaphysical hypotheses are developed to be consistent and coherent, applicable to experience and adequate to explaining everything. They are argued for in many ways, including the critique of alternative hypotheses and the demonstration that they can represent the truth in the alternatives without the drawbacks. In the long run, a metaphysical hypothesis is defended as being able to make better sense of everything we experience than its alternatives. For all its internal dialectic, a metaphysical hypothesis is an empirical claim.

The hypothetical character of metaphysics in the sense used here needs to be stressed in order to distinguish it from the sense of metaphysics commonly under attack at the present time. Charles Peirce characterized the nature of hypothetical inquiry in the following way.[18] Although thinking (or "inquiry" as he preferred to say) never starts at a fresh beginning, let us suppose as a construct for inquiry that thought begins with an intellectual problem, a perplexity or unanswered question such as the problem of the one and the many. "Musing" about the question, inquiry makes a guess or brings to mind some images that might solve the problem. Peirce called this "retroduction" or "abduction" because it moves from what is to be explained to what might explain it, and said it is an "argument" because it draws a conclusion. Although an argument, abduction is not an "argumentation," which Peirce characterized as an argument that proceeds according to rules, as in logic. Abduction might have *plausibility* because it would, if true, explain what is to be explained; but it is untested. The next step in inquiry Peirce called "deduction" and it has two parts. The first, which he called "explication of the hypothesis," is to work the guess or vague image into a properly logical hypothesis from which logically ordered argumentational deductions might be made. The framing of the hypothesis in formally precise terms is also an argument, not an argumentation. Properly formed, an hypothesis can be explored in terms of its own logic to determine what might be expected in experience if the hypothesis is true, or what in experience might contradict the hypothesis. This is "demonstration," properly speaking, according to Peirce, and is illustrated best for him by a scientist setting up a controlled experiment. Running the experiment is what Peirce called "induction" and for him, unlike for most scientists, induction has three parts. The first and usually neglected part is inquiry into whether the terms deduced from the formal hypothesis accord with actual phenomena in experience, which Peirce called "classification," a "non-argumentational kind of argument." He is very clear to avoid the fallacy of letting a theory (or its instruments, research-program suppositions, etc.) determine what is found in the phenomena it is supposed to explain. The second and third parts of induction Peirce called "probation," distinguishing according to his own logic between negative ("there are no instances of *x*") and positive probation ("the discovered proportion of *x*'s supports or does not support the hypothesis"). These probations constitute the actual assessment of whether the evidence supports the hypotheses' predictions, supposing that there is accord between the theoretical terms and the phenomena.[19] Peirce intended this kind of hypothetical inquiry to be general with respect to all kinds of inquiry.

The sense in which the metaphysics of *Philosophical Theology* is hypothetical can be illustrated in Peirce's terms. Vaguely formulated ontological and cosmological metaphysical questions constitute a field of metaphysical issues out of which many abductive answers have been given over the past two and a half millennia. The first step in addressing these is the abductive speculation of an hypothesis. Peirce himself claimed that in all cultures the abductive inference has been made that any determinate plurality must be created by an act of creation (an empirical generalization on his part about "all cultures" that might not be supportable). The explication of the speculative hypothesis, in the case of metaphysics, is through complicated dialectic that shows how alternative hypotheses are impossible in various senses or can be contained within one's own hypothesis under some interpretation or other. The formal shape of one's own hypothesis, its "explication," comes from the cumulative dialectical arguments relating it to potential competitors. The result, in the case of the metaphysics of *Philosophical Theology*, is an extraordinarily abstract hypothesis about the nature of being, why there are beings, and what it is to be a determinate being (I, 9).

Another layer of metaphysical argument, corresponding to Peirce's deduction, is to show that this complex metaphysical hypothesis is presupposed by all other theories of nature and human life that claim to assert anything determinate. This is to say, regardless of what other theories say, if they claim something determinate, they presuppose some account of determinateness, which in turn presupposes an ontology of how and why there are determinate things. The already explicated complex metaphysical hypothesis shows how it is superior to alternative hypotheses about determinateness and being. Therefore those other less abstract theories are subject to the formal strictures of the metaphysical hypothesis. This necessary presupposition holds because the other theories assert something determinate, regardless of whether what they assert is true, plausible, or even very intelligible.

Corresponding to Peirce's inductive level of inquiry is the use of the complex metaphysical hypothesis to interpret experience in its multifarious avenues. In *Philosophical Theology* the probative fields have to do with ultimacy, human predicament, ecstatic fulfillment, and religion, although a metaphysical hypothesis should also be tested in politics, ethics, science, the arts, and a host of other dimensions of experience. A large part of the probation of the metaphysical hypothesis comes in its interpretive power for making sense of the intellectual traditions of religious cultures and for answering the first-order questions for contemporary religious life. All three volumes of *Philosophical Theology* are needed both for the deductive and inductive testing of the metaphysical hypotheses. As Peirce said, the complex process of abduction, deductive explication and demonstration, and induction, is more like weaving together many strands of a rope than like constructing a chain of arguments that is as strong as its weakest link.

Metaphysical inquiry and its hypotheses are fallible, and it is clear that they are fallible at different levels or stages and in different ways. The abductive guesses are fallible, which can be shown by indicating how they might not be explicable. The explications of the hypotheses are fallible as can be shown in the dialectical debates among competing hypotheses and their explications. The hypotheses are fallible with regard to whether they are illustrated by any theory or claim that affirms something determinate. And they are fallible in countless ways with regard to whether they interpret and guide experience well, in this instance the experiences involved with engaging ultimacy, enjoying ecstatic fulfillments, facing ultimate predicaments, and being religious.

Because they are fallible, metaphysical hypotheses are vulnerable to correction. Therefore, when a valid objection is made, the hypotheses need to be amended to overcome it. If the hypotheses cannot be so amended, they need to be discarded for alternatives. There need be no objection to metaphysics as such, only to particular hypotheses.

The fallibility of metaphysics as hypothetical is crucial to acknowledge in order to see why the many detractors of metaphysics miss the point. Those detractors say that metaphysics is supposed to be apodictically certain and foundational for all other kinds of knowledge, as Kant took the term. But if metaphysics is hypothetical, any objection is only an occasion to amend the hypothesis, not to reject metaphysics as impossible per se. For instance, Kant thought that his antinomies showed metaphysics to be inherently self-contradictory when it attempts to determine real objects, and Hegel followed by a host of others showed why this simply was not so. Kant himself had objections to what he called the "method of hypothesis" because he believed that one needs a transcendental definition of what it means to have a world that constitutes evidence for or against an hypothesis.[20] But this is not necessary. All one needs is an hypothesis about the foundational characters of a world that can constitute evidence, not a transcendental set of conditions.[21] Or, one can treat Kant's transcendental conditions themselves as mere hypotheses. He failed to establish that there are synthetic a priori claims in science and mathematics that justify the transcendental conditions as necessarily transcendental.[22] Many thinkers since Kant have believed that metaphysics as he understood it is impossible; but this does not apply to metaphysics as hypothetical, as has been seen by Peirce, Whitehead, and others.

Another argument against metaphysics, however, is lodged by some postmodern thinkers who believe that the allegedly universal scope of metaphysics is problematic. They cite the evils of logo-centrism that consist in employing universal categories that marginalize or exclude important aspects of reality, especially the experiences of people who are not acculturated by the categories. But this marginalization or exclusion is a fault of the categories at hand that need to be amended in order to take those otherwise marginalized or excluded things into account (*III, introduction, iv*). This is not an objection to metaphysics, only to the particular metaphysics at hand. The metaphysics of *Philosophical Theology* is so abstract that it is difficult to imagine how some possibly excluded or marginalized things or people might be not determinate at all.

A deeper issue lies behind some postmodern objections to metaphysics, namely the supposition that all thinking takes place within experience or consciousness alone and that the realities to which metaphysics refers must somehow be phenomena within experience. This is a legacy of Descartes. It results in the stricture that experience itself is particular, partial, and not given to universal elements, as illustrated in Western phenomenology. Therefore, metaphysics seems to be a non-experiential determination of what should instead show itself in experience, "being coming across the open to us," as Heidegger would put it.[23] The epistemology of symbolic engagement, following the pragmatic theory of interpretation, rejects this experiential consciousness model. Rather, interpreters engage reality in its multifariousness with their signs, and do so more or less well, being vulnerable to correction by the realities they engage. Among the realities engaged are the metaphysically interesting things such as what it is to be determinate at all, and how and why there are determinate beings. How well those metaphysically interesting realities are engaged depends on the merit of the metaphysical hypotheses devised to interpret them. The rejection of a foundational phenomenological frame is a persistent theme of *Philosophical Theology* (III, 1, ii).

Sometimes it is said in defense of metaphysics that everyone necessarily presupposes a metaphysics and that it behooves everyone to develop a good one. The claim is perhaps too strong. What everyone presupposes is that experience engages things that are determinate in part. (Things might be indeterminate in part also, but only in the sense that they are determinately indeterminate, as in it not being decided yet what to have for dinner tomorrow.) Given the determinateness of things, philosophical curiosity needs to give them an account, not only of what determinateness consists in but of how and why there are determinate things. No particular account needs to be presupposed by everyone. But if an account is put forward, as it is here, then everyone who is interested in accounting for determinateness needs to consider it and, if they cannot find objection, include it among their philosophical habits. Although it cannot be claimed that the ontological and cosmological metaphysics proposed here (*I, pt 3, pr*) is in fact presupposed by everyone, it can be claimed, within the strictures of vulnerable, fallible hypothetical inquiry, that it should be accepted by anyone seeking an account.

The great Western metaphysician of the twentieth century was Alfred North Whitehead. In *Science and the Modern World*, Whitehead had argued that modern mathematical science supposes that the relations among things are of a character that would be impossible if the world consists of substances. Given that mathematical science is true, at least in part, a new metaphysics is needed that exhibits how the mathematical theories might apply. This metaphysics he supplied in exquisite detail in *Process and Reality*. That book is the careful elaboration of a grand hypothesis about the nature of ultimate realities, the *res verae*, as he called them.[24] Now, Whitehead's metaphysics might not be the finally adequate philosophy for our time. Nevertheless, it is a comprehensive hypothesis, and it demonstrates the possibility of metaphysics over against Kant. The critiques of it aim only to improve on it.[25]

The charge that metaphysics is not appropriate is different from the charge that it is impossible. Postmodernism sometimes claims that any metaphysical hypothesis would be logo-centric. That is, because it consists of logical categories, it marginalizes or ignores whatever is not registered in those categories, a criticism mentioned previously. The answer to this charge is always to admit it in concrete cases. If someone can show that a person, group, or set of cultural ideas, or philosophical ideas, or kinds of experience, or realities, is not fairly addressed within a metaphysical hypothesis, the hypothesis needs to be amended to accommodate them. This kind of concrete criticism is always valid in that it calls for a reconsideration of the metaphysical hypothesis. Metaphysical categories need to be vague, in the sense defined above in the Introduction and the Preliminary Remarks to this part, and to the extent they are biased they need to be changed to become more neutrally vague.

On the other hand, when the postmodern charge of biased logo-centrism is made generally, not concretely, it can be dismissed at once. Unless a concrete case calling for amendment of the hypothesis is presented, it can be assumed that the metaphysical hypothesis is valid as it stands, other things being equal. A metaphysical hypothesis is always vulnerable to correction, but only when a real correction is called for.

The subtitle of Whitehead's *Process and Reality* is *An Essay in Cosmology*. The force of the reference to cosmology is that Whitehead attempted to give an account of the elementary realities of our cosmic epoch, directly relatable to physical cosmology. A more abstract set of problems calls for a somewhat different metaphysics from what Whitehead supplied. These include the problems of determinateness and being. Heidegger rightly pointed out that the question of what it means to be a thing, to be determinate, is not the same as, although obviously related to, the question of being-itself. The question of being-itself is often called ontology, the study of the nature of reality. Metaphysics as a whole embraces a spectrum of questions from the ontology of being to the philosophical cosmology of how nature is conceived to be. Thus, metaphysics aims to be a system of well-justified hypotheses running that gamut.

One of the functions of metaphysics in theology is to provide a properly abstract theory of ultimate realities so that it would be possible to understand how religious symbols refer to them. The religious symbols in a sacred canopy are far richer and more concrete, and related to the lives and histories of the people within the sacred canopy. Nevertheless, metaphysics is needed to supply some control over those references. When the psalms of the Hebrew Bible say that God is the rock of salvation, the metaphoric point of that can be taken without the assumption that the proper study of God then is geology. As shown in subsequent chapters of this volume, metaphysics is the court of appeal when asking about the limits of our metaphorical symbols of ultimacy.

CHAPTER THREE

Symbolic Engagement

I. INTERPRETATION AS ENGAGEMENT

The epistemology of *Philosophical Theology* derives from American pragmatism with a heavy influence from Confucianism. Knowing, according to this epistemology, is a natural interaction of an interpretive organism with an environment. The interpretation allows the interpreter to discriminate what is valuable (or disvaluable) in the environment so as to engage it better. Knowledge consists of the habits of interpretation an interpreter has ready at hand to engage the environment. Such habits are constantly amended by feedback when they come into play, and so "knowledge" is constantly being shifted. No starting point or foundation for knowledge exists: We always are working with the habits we have. Epistemology therefore is better understood as the study of "learning" rather than "knowledge" in any fixed sense. Some habits are so ingrained, so reinforced by experience, and so steadied by long use, that we do not doubt them and take them to be just plainly true and certain.[1]

Only occasionally are deeply ingrained habits of interpretation overthrown. The slow realization in early modern Western culture (and most other cultures) that Earth is not the center of the universe is an example of the overthrow of an idea that had been taken for granted for millennia and had seemed obvious and certain. So is the realization during the past two centuries in Western cultures that women are not inferior to men or in need of male domination.

This pragmatic epistemology stands in sharp contrast with the representationalist epistemologies of much late modern and postmodern Western philosophy. Descartes proposed that mentality is a substance that is complete in itself, with infinite closure. He also proposed that physical reality is corporeal in the sense that it has geometric extension and patterns of movement and force that can be represented mathematically. For Descartes and the glorious tradition that was persuaded by him, the problem of knowledge is to understand how the mind can represent the physical world. For, there would seem to be no place outside of but connected to both mentality and extension from which the representations in mind could be compared with the extensive properties they purported to represent. Some Cartesian descendants fixed on consciousness and attempted to understand the extended world through that; his present heirs in this line are to be found in Continental philosophy.[2] Other Cartesian descendants focused on the material side, as conceptions of matter have evolved, and would be the scientific materialists of today. Neither line of development has given a satisfactory answer to the dilemma posed by Descartes, namely, to think together the physical universe that we are coming to understand through science and the mind which has such subtlety and complexity.[3]

Our pragmatic epistemology circumvents the dilemma of representationalist thinking. It construes knowing as a part of nature, evolved in animals, and evolved to a high state in animals with semiotic systems. By the same token, nature is taken to be that which is found, interpreted, and engaged by natural interpreters. The understanding of knowing is about how our natural cognitive faculties engage the environment. The understanding of nature is about what our cognitive faculties allow us to discriminate and appreciate concerning things in the environment, assuming that our cognitive and emotional apparatus is part of the natural environmental systems.

Interpretation is by means of signs and what we can appreciate in the environment depends on the signs we have. Animals, including human beings, would not have evolved without the development of signs that distinguish predators from neighbors, food from toxins, and safe environments from the perilous. Signs are intimately tied to neural structures. Reptiles and amphibians lack the neural capacities to rotate images of objects in their imagination so as to plan to go around and sneak up on them from behind: a frog just sits on a lily pad and darts its tongue to catch the prey that comes within its vision. Mammals can plan sneak attacks; the attempt to envision frogs sneaking must be a primordial instance of mammalian humor. Human beings have signs that are arranged in semiotic systems so that one imaginative sign can mean another imaginative sign and that language is possible within which we can talk and think about things without directly engaging them. Far beyond sneak attacks, we can cooperate in complicated social living.

Human cultures have semiotic systems that consist of networks of signs that are related in many ways. Many thinkers have taken language as the paradigm of a semiotic system, with the syntactical and semantic structures associated with language. Although languages are indeed very sophisticated semiotic systems, they themselves are set in with other kinds of signs, "body language," unconscious kinetics, and natural signs, among others. The relations among signs in their networks and the relations among the networks are complicated and shifting. Religious signs, or "symbols" as they usually are called in this work, are often overlapping, contradicting, and nonetheless mutually reinforcing. Within liturgical Christianity, Jesus is called the paschal lamb who takes away the sins of the world. The symbol of the paschal lamb is defined by the network of symbols having to do with the Passover, when the lamb's or goat's blood was smeared over the doors of the Israelites in Egypt so that the divinity who was taking the lives of all the firstborn children and animals would pass over the Israelites and kill only Egyptians.[4] The meaning of the paschal lamb has to do with saving from divinely caused death. The symbol of the lamb that takes away the sins of the world comes from the symbol network of the atonement ritual in which the sins of the people and the priest are put on the head of a lamb or goat (the scapegoat) that is then sent out into the wilderness. The atonement symbol has to do with sins, which are not connected with the paschal lamb symbol, and it has nothing to do with escaping from death.[5] Despite the lack of logical connection, the two symbol systems regarding Jesus as sacrifice resonate together in Christian thinking. Some remote connection can be made so as to say that those whose sins are not taken away will die; but the more prominent parallel in early Christianity to Heaven is not death but Hell.[6]

Without signs of the right sorts, realities cannot be discriminately interpreted in experience. Things can bump us, but they cannot be discriminated in response unless we have appropriate signs. Without signs for micro-organisms, people still got sick and interpreted illness medically, but not as something caused by germs that might be seen only through a microscope. The invention of the microscope allowed for the discriminate experience of realities that had always been with us, with effects, but not noticed. Similarly, ultimate dimensions of reality cannot be discriminately interpreted without signs that do so. The great symbols of ultimacy are signs that allow for the discrimination of ultimate realities that otherwise might be present and operative without notice. Given the complex, multifaceted character of experience, we often know that the signs we have are onto something but are inadequate to the interpretive task. Frustrated physicians before the invention of the microscope knew there were mysteries of health for which they had inadequate signs. Religious people also know that their signs are onto something but are inadequate.

Signs have their network meanings, expressed in terms of the syntax and semantics of semiotic systems.[7] But in order to be involved in actual interpretations, signs also have to have some material quality, some actual embodiment. Engagement is an activity and the activity is based in real processes. For some kinds of analysis, the network meaning of the signs is all that is important and the material quality is mainly irrelevant. For instance, in certain kinds of mathematical calculations the logic of the inferences is indifferent to whether the calculations are carried out by computers with silicone chips or mathematicians with meat brains. The network meaning is the "type" while the material quality of the set of calculative signs might be any number of different kinds of tokens. All verbal network meanings require some material quality in a language. But it does not matter which language is used so long as there is adequate translatability. Where languages are significantly different in structure, and adequacy of translation is elusive, a material difference exists between the languages that also makes a difference to the network meaning. Like languages, religious signs need to be learned, and the learning might be more appropriate at a later stage in life than an earlier; it also might be more complicated later on.[8] Religious signs also need some material quality, and this often means becoming religiously adept to a degree. Religious signs might be possessed in verbal form without being possessed in the ways that genuinely lead to engagement. The material causal quality of interpretation involves indexical reference (discussed in the next section).

The discussion in chapter 2 of scientific reductionism illustrates another aspect of the semiotic dimension of human experience. In a reductive scientific inquiry, only those signs that articulate the assumptions, structures, theories, and instrumentation of the inquiry are allowed for the expression of the phenomenon. All others are screened out. Thus, a kind of controlled objectivity comes with the reduction but it also might foster the systematic exclusion of the need to see what is lost in the reduction and of the need to improve the scientific terms.

In a logical sense, an interpretation takes a sign to stand for its object in a certain respect.[9] This is an indissolvable triadic relation, unlike the signifier–signified dyad of most nonpragmatic semiotics. There is an object, a sign, and an interpreter who takes the sign to stand for the object in a certain respect. Signs, as mentioned, come in networks within semiotic systems or codes. Much of the study of interpretation is the study of the sign systems. The relation between the sign and its object is a matter of reference (the topic of the next section). The taking of the sign to stand for the object in some respect is the act of interpretation itself. As an act, it takes place within a larger context, most likely many contexts.

No sign is true or false in itself. It has to be referred to something in order to be true or false about it. Thus, only interpretations can be true or false. An interpretation is always guided by some purpose or value, because it must select the respect in which the object is to be interpreted, and it does so by selecting among the signs at hand that might stand for the object in that respect. A house, for instance, might be interpreted in terms of its location, architectural style, layout, price, ownership, and so forth, and different kinds of signs are appropriate for different respects in which to interpret. The purpose that selects the respect of interpretation might be conscious and deliberate, as in inquiry. Most interpretations, however, are guided by purposes built into cultures that say that these and those respects are the ones important to keep under interpretation.

Human beings are organisms in environments within which they make many hundreds of thousands of interpretations all at once, interpreting gravity with muscular signs so as to stay balanced, interpreting the social environment with body language, engaging in complex activities such as driving an automobile, which requires visual, auditory, and kinesthetic interpretations of countless conditions, thinking (about theology, surely!) while driving, with the purpose of getting to work so as to support a family. As the Confucians have long known in their understanding of ritual, the learning of habits of interpreting with signs begins at birth as the conventional signs are taught in ritualized behavior.[10]

The general term in *Philosophical Theology* for the interpretive activity of human beings in their environing reality is *engagement*. Engagement connotes that our activity in the world is purposive, with most purposes being given in our habits, many of which derive from culture. Engagement also connotes that interpretation is always contextual. Finally, engagement connotes that there is a back-and-forth feedback relation between the interpreter and the environment, correcting as well as eliciting interpretations. All of this illustrates the claim that the pragmatic epistemology understands knowing to be within nature.

Although acknowledging that engaging the mysteries of ultimacy is a sophisticated step beyond, but in continuity with, interpreting the forest as full of predators, the situation with regard to religious symbols is often that of being stuck with symbols that fail to engage ultimacy, or even impede it. Because the symbols come prepackaged in traditional sacred canopies, they might be inappropriate for the context or purposes involved. As Peter Berger stresses, sacred canopies are often behind the times and in need of repair.[11] So the first question to ask of an interpretation of ultimacy is whether it is a genuine symbolic engagement. It might simply be an interpretive pattern that might engage in some context but cannot in the one at hand.

Only after it has been determined that a sign enables a genuine engagement is it possible to ask whether it is a true engagement. If there is no engagement, there is no intentional relation between the sign and the real object, and the sign is neither true nor false. If there is genuine engagement, it still needs to be determined whether the sign is right about the object in the respect in which it engages it. The asking price of a house is to be given in amounts of money, but not every amount of money is the asking price. So with signs of ultimacy: They might be appropriate to interpret the ultimate reality in a certain respect, but do so wrongly. Truth, as has been argued, consists in whether what is important in the object in the respect in which the sign stands for the object is carried over into the interpreter, a point to be developed throughout *Philosophical Theology*.[12] This is always an empirical question in the long run.

The distinction between engagement and the truth of the interpretation in engagement is more important than might appear on the surface. Religion is the symbolic engagement of ultimacy, according to *Philosophical Theology*, not just the interpretation of ultimacy. The interpretive element is where the interests of theology lie in finding out the truth in the engagement. But the engagement itself, whether true or false, or with some complex muddle of truth and falsity, is the heart of religion because what is engaged is the value in ultimacy, and the value in engaging. People rush to the ultimate because of its overwhelming attractiveness, or terror, or numinousness, or mysterium tremendum, or obligatoriness, or call to wholeness, or self-emptying appeal of the Other, or the promise of meaning or damnation, and these all are ascribed through proximate symbols of the ultimate. As Nathaniel Barrett has pointed out, religion engages people with the value dimensions of humanly affordable reality and this is more important than whether it gets those values right in many senses.[13]

II. THE PRAGMATIC HERITAGE

The pragmatic epistemology outlined in the previous section needs at least briefly to be situated in the recent history of pragmatism. The classical pragmatists, Charles S. Peirce, William James, John Dewey, Josiah Royce (the "absolute pragmatist"), George Herbert Mead, and their immediate students such as William Ernest Hocking and C.I. Lewis, were "systematic philosophers in the grand tradition" in that they, each in his own way, treated a broad array of issues in metaphysics, logic, epistemology, ethics, religion, esthetics, and most especially philosophy of nature. For a variety of reasons, many of which have been analyzed acutely by John E. Smith and his student, Richard Bernstein, classical pragmatism was swamped in the middle of the twentieth century by waves of European interest in consciousness on the part of Continental philosophy, and in language, logical or informal, on the part of analytic philosophy[14] In the late twentieth century, however, there was a strong revival of pragmatism that focused on pragmatic interpretations of social practices, sometimes toward ethics, as in the work of Cornell West, Victor Anderson, and Jeffrey Stout, and sometimes toward epistemology and methodological issues about the nature of philosophy, as in the work of Richard Rorty and Robert Brandom, with much connection between the two. In this revival, sometimes called "Neo-pragmatism" when associated with Rorty, the classical interests in philosophy of nature and metaphysics were simply omitted, mainly because those interests suppose that philosophy can deal with real things and not only with the linguistic means of reference to those things.[15]

Meanwhile, during the middle of the twentieth century, pragmatism was reformed in intimate alliance with process philosophy; Alfred North Whitehead called his theory of truth "pragmatic."[16] Whitehead's student, Paul Weiss, one of the editors of the Peirce papers along with Charles Hartshorne, developed a series of philosophical views that owe much to pragmatism.[17] A number of philosophers, taking Weiss, classical pragmatism, and process philosophy seriously, developed consciously detailed and systematic philosophical theories in "the grand tradition." These include George Allan, Fredrick Ferre, David Weissman, Joseph Grange, Sandra Rosenthal, Justus Buchler, Judith Jones,

David Hall (to some extent), and me, among many others.[18] The philosophy in *Philosophical Theology* is pragmatism in this metaphysical and cosmological orientation. It includes the interests of the pragmatic social constructionists but also sustains extensive development of metaphysical themes. Standard accounts of the revival of pragmatism in the Neo-pragmatism of the social constructionists usually neglect the parallel rich strain of metaphysical pragmatic developments.[19]

The revival of pragmatic epistemology within the philosophical world of analytic philosophy needs comment relative to the theory of engagement developed here. Robert Brandom is the self-avowed "systematic philosopher" of analytical pragmatism.[20] Building especially on the work of Wilfrid Sellars and Richard Rorty, he has elaborated a comprehensive pragmatic epistemological theory that emphasizes the normative rules for inference within thinking and interprets those normative rules as guides for cognitive behavior rather than logical rules of inference; his view is known as "inferentialism." Brandom accepts from Sellars a critique of the "myth of the given."[21] Regarding the orientation of metaphysical pragmatism, Charles Peirce had already critiqued the "myth of the given" in the 1860s with an analysis of intuition; Peirce's naturalism in accounting for the arising of cognitions from the encounter with nature is more robust than Sellars' tendency to nod to science, and hence provides the orientation for *Philosophical Theology*.[22] Brandom, in his development of Sellars' theme, shows in detail how the pragmatic sense of meaning, involving the differential habits of cognitive behavior, leads to fulsome inferential patterns that are developed with and then presupposed within communicative behavior. This effectively subverts the distinction between internalist (perspicacity to consciousness) and externalist (judging thought by its results) approaches to epistemology. Yet from the standpoint of the pragmatic philosophy of engagement elaborated in *Philosophical Theology*, Brandom's approach remains limited to the analysis of discursive behavior, as he puts it, prescinding from the natural objects with which interpreters engage and from which they learn. It is close to an idealism of a very Hegelian sort, in contrast to a naturalism that construes thinking to be a transaction between an interpretive organism and a natural environment, as Dewey would put it. Brandom's idealism suggests a far greater order to the world, because thought is ordered, than metaphysical pragmatism that can find only pockets of order. Richard Bernstein has pointed out correctly, commenting on Brandom (and Rorty and others), that the new pragmatism abandons the category of "experience" that was so important for the classical pragmatists. Imbedded in the notion of experience is what Peirce called "Secondness," the brute resistance of real things to interpretations of them such that the interpretations can be corrected (to be discussed shortly).[23] The importance of Secondness is that the epistemological situation is not only internal to cognitive behavior and the norms for communicative inferences but includes also the real things that such behavior engages. A pragmatic philosophy of engagement, rather than inference, requires a philosophical cosmology of nature to flesh out the epistemological situation.[24] The alliance of pragmatism with process philosophy is important because of the advanced detail of philosophical cosmology (although not metaphysics in the sense of the study of being; *I, 9, i*) in the latter. The resurgence of pragmatism within analytic philosophy, by contrast, is limited by the insistence in analytic philosophies of nearly every sort that the proper subject matter of philosophy is language (Brandom speaks of "vocabularies") and other media by which things are known rather than the things becoming known by improvements in the employment of cognitive media. This channeling of analytic philosophy to cognitive media is a legacy of Kant, and is well summed up in Rorty's phrase, "the linguistic turn."[25]

This caution about the limitations of the pragmatic analytic philosophy applies as well to the discussion of religious belief organized by Frankenberry involving Donald Davidson, Richard Rorty, and Robert Brandom.[26] The focus of that discussion is to insist on the importance of belief, whereupon the roles of normative meaning and legitimate inference are highly significant. If, however, the focus were shifted, as it is in *Philosophical Theology*, to symbolically shaped engagement of ultimate matters, then belief would be set in a larger context of natural engagement, feedback, and the amendment of meaning and inferential practices by really ultimate things as well as by the lessons of communicative engagements. This shift in focus, of course, involves a commitment to the metaphysics and cosmology of ultimacy as evidenced in *Philosophical Theology*. These topics can be excluded explicitly from the analytic pragmatic discussion because they involve things that fall outside of the domain of cognitive behavior interpreted in terms of its discourses and inferences.[27] The naturalism of the metaphysical strains of pragmatism that have developed since the classical pragmatic era does not shy away from approaching ultimacy through metaphysics and cosmology.

III. ICONIC, INDEXICAL, AND CONVENTIONAL REFERENCE IN EXTENSION AND INTENTION

At the heart of the question of whether the symbols in a sacred canopy refer to real ultimate realities is the technical question of the nature of reference itself. Charles Peirce distinguished three kinds of reference, based on his metaphysical theory of Firstness, Secondness, and Thirdness.[28] These are iconic, indexical, and conventional reference (Peirce called conventional reference "symbolic reference").

Conventional reference is of a sign to other signs within its semiotic system, structured by the syntax and semantics of the system. Any linguistic sign refers directly or indirectly to the other signs within the language that give it meaning. For instance, the sign of the sacrifice of the paschal lamb refers indirectly to the network of signs in the Passover story, and the sign of the scapegoat sacrifice refers indirectly to the network of signs in the Atonement ritual. When both signs are referred to Jesus, the reference to Jesus' identity, and the complex of stories about him, is direct. It can be stated in "propositions" such as "Jesus is the paschal lamb" or Jesus is the "lamb of God who takes away the sins of the world."

The indirect references through a semiotic system involve interdefined meanings, analogies, metaphors, and various other kinds of resonances. A storyteller, for instance, calls on many layers of associations within the language, the culture, and the history of the culture, not just the direct references asserted in sentences. The direct references have the form of interpretations, namely, the taking of a sign to stand for another sign as its object in a certain respect. The direct references can be assertive, saying, for instance, that this sign and no other stands for the object sign in this respect.

Within conventional reference, the direct and indirect objects of any interpreting reference are signs within the semiotic system. This is the "extension" of the interpretation, its extensive structure within the semiotic system. Any interpretation that can be expressed in language has an extensive structure that is simply a set of signs within the semiotic system. Except insofar as the interpretation is making analytical claims about the implications of ideas in the semiotic system, the interpretation does not make truth-claims with reference to any realities outside the semiotic system. It does express what *would be* a truth claim *if* the interpretation itself is affirmed in reference to the realities to which the semiotic signs refer. This affirmation is the "intention" of the interpretation. The intention of the interpretation takes the extensive interpretation itself, along with the entire semiotic system that gives its signs conventional reference, to be a complex sign referring to the realities "referred to." In linguistic terms, a proposition, plus the language and (syntactical and semantic) assumptions that give it meaning, is a sign for what the proposition is about when (and only when) an interpreter refers it intentionally. Neglecting the distinction between the extension and intention of an interpretation, philosophers have sometimes concluded that interpretation never refers to real things, because the reference is only to "mental" signs of the real things. Here lies the straight path to metaphysical idealism or the consciousness-only dyadic byplay of signifier and signified. Engagement with real objects involves the intentional interpretation of real objects by means of the extensional interpretation expressed in the conventions of the semiotic system.

The intention of an interpretation requires reference in a different sense from conventional reference, which has to do only with the extension of interpretation. In fact, there are two senses of reference by means of which an interpreter takes an extensive interpretation to be a sign of a real object in some respect, which Peirce called "indexical" and "iconic" reference.

Indexical reference involves a causal connection between the interpreter and the object interpreted, as mediated by the signs involved. An index, like pointing a finger to get the viewer to turn to look at the object, establishes a causal relation between the object and the interpreter. That causal relation allows the interpreter to pick up on what is important in the object in the respect in which the sign refers to the object. The causal relation causes some transformation in the interpreter to orient the interpreter to the object, like a turned head, or a jogged memory, or a feeling of being moved. The causality in indexical reference need not be as direct and immediate as a pointing index finger. A piece of literature, using only signs the interpreter had before, and depicting scenes all of which are familiar, nevertheless can move a person to appreciate something never before appreciated, such as the way Dickens' novels can move people to appreciate the plight of the poor. The novel refers conventionally to the characters in the novel but it also refers indexically to the plight of the poor.

In addition to indexical reference, intentional interpretation can use iconic reference, which says that the object is "like" the sign. Peirce's example was the way a cross in a Christian church is an icon of the cross on which Jesus died. A map is an icon of a territory. Different maps are icons in different respects, such as a street map, a political map, a survey map, or a geo-physical map. Iconicity need not be only likeness of shape, like the cross or a map of a drawing. Mathematical science refers iconically to its objects, with the reference saying that the objects have the mathematic structure expressed in the theory. Descriptive writing says that the object is like what the description says. Metaphors and analogies can refer iconically in saying that the object is like them in some ways but not in others. In the analysis of an engagement with iconic reference the kind of likeness involved needs to be identified.

In many if not most intentional interpretations that constitute symbolic engagement, both indexical and iconic reference are involved, as well as the conventional reference in the signs that have extension. An obvious way of pointing is to say, "look for something that looks like this." But they do not always go together. A person's fantasy world is intentional reference with iconicity but no direct indexicality (the indirect index might be to the person's unconscious processes). The fantasy imagines a real world that at the same time it knows has no connection with the person's real world as expressed in the fantasy. Creative people work to give their dreams indexical reference.

More interesting for religion is the fact that religious symbols can foster interpretations that refer indexically without referring iconically. Meditating on the demon goddess with swords in hand and skulls girdling her waist is never meant to suggest that such a goddess really exists. Rather, the point of the reference is to frighten the meditator into giving up some cherished attachment that inhibits spiritual growth. Sometimes religious symbols are fantastical and absurd if thought to refer iconically, although some believers naively might take them to be iconic. The religiously interesting reference, however, is the indexical one: How is the interpreter transformed when engaging reality with the symbols referred indexically? If something important or valuable in the ultimate reality is carried over into the interpreter by the symbol (a network of symbols with extensive conventional reference) in the respect in which the symbol engages the object-reality, then it is true. This is particularly important in the case of many religious symbols associated with liturgies. Sometimes, employing the symbols in liturgies takes years to transform the interpreters so that they pick up on the real object to which indexical reference is made. Years of sitting in zazen are required for the indexical reference in the symbolic engagement of sitting to transform the sitter.

Much confusion in understanding religion comes at the point where the apparent iconic reference of a symbolic engagement has a different object from the real indexical reference. This is particularly true in popular religion where the apparent iconic reference of much of the religious life is superstitious and patently false to modern reflective thinkers. Yet living a religious life guided by those symbols might very well have powerful and true effects through indexical reference. Praying to the gods of the garden and kitchen might be iconically false but still powerfully true in attuning the cook indexically to properly revere and appreciate the economy of food. Believing that the creator of the universe is a person might be iconically false, because persons exist only within the universe with other things to relate to; but it might be indexically true in causing the interpreter to be in an attitude of profound gratitude for the "gift" of existence.

Animals other than human beings (and perhaps some of the higher primates) symbolically engage the world with iconic and indexical reference, responding causally to predators and prey, conditions of safety and danger, arousal and disgust. Human beings also have conventional reference, and therefore can develop enormously more complex signs with extensional reference, that allows them to be far more sophisticated in what they can pick out as important in the world. Once human beings have the conventional reach of language, the signs for intentionally engaging the world allow for the appreciation of possibilities of elaborate cooperation, for understanding political situations, and for comporting individuals and communities to what is ultimately important.[29]

With this theory of reference sketched, we can now return to the question of how reference can be made to ultimacy in its various modes.

IV. ENGAGING FINITE/INFINITE CONTRASTS

Given ready interpreters in the right contexts, the finite/infinite contrasts in a sacred canopy are signs that can stand for ultimate realities in certain respects. Their real objects, according to the analysis here, are themselves finite/infinite contrasts of the ontological or anthropological sorts. These points can be illustrated with certain of the elements of sacred canopies identified in Chapter 1, Section III.

A finite/infinite contrast in a sacred canopy is first of all defined with the conventional reference of a set of signs, or perhaps several networks of signs. The sacred canopy itself might be a tightly integrated, consistent network of religious symbols, although that is highly unlikely. The sacred canopies of the great world religions are rather loose assemblages of symbols that theologians can tighten up into a consistent systematic canopy only by edging out the symbols that do not fit the theological system. Moreover, the great religious sacred canopies contain many layers of historical development, laid down on one another like palimpsests. The sacred canopy expressed in India's great *Mahabharata*, for instance, has some passages depicting the aim of life at the point of death to be to get to Heaven, other passages assuming a samsaric wheel of lives through re-incarnation, and yet others passages that assume a karmic moral guidance of re-incarnation that is missing in other assumptions about samsara.[30] To understand the network of defining symbols according to which a given symbolic finite/infinite contrast within a sacred canopy works requires sorting through many connections and layers, taking care not to be misled by similarities of symbolic expressions that in fact are defined differently.

According to the argument advanced in *Philosophical Theology*, chapter 1, among the networks of signs involved in the conventional references of an interpretation of an ultimate finite/infinite contrast would have to be those articulating its world-making character. The symbol for the ultimate reality would have to define what basic dimension of the world stands or falls with the finite/infinite contrast. Of course this depends on the conceptions of the world involved. Consider the first problem of world-making discussed earlier, the radical contingency of the world itself. The sacred canopies of all the Axial Age religions include conceptions of the world or cosmos as a whole, although they differ greatly as to its size, age, geography, and composition. The world-contingency in pre-Axial Age religions can be much more localized—the existence of our mountain, our island. The contingency itself needs some network expression: contingency of form in a preexisting chaos, contingency of a particular organization of things, contingency of all determinate reality whatsoever; this is not an exhaustive list of possible contingencies. Contingency might be grasped as simply a vast surprise, or as contingency on a human-like creator-god or gods, or as contingency on some fullness of being beyond determinateness as in Neo-Platonism and the Perennial Philosophy, or as contingency on a creative act or acts, or as contingency of thoughts on consciousness, contingency on a process of emergence—the list has hundreds of variations. The point is, the network of symbols in terms of which a given symbol of ultimacy is defined in a finite/infinite contrast has to be able to articulate these things as matters of conventional reference or meaning. These networks are implicit or explicit parts of sacred canopies. Sometimes, theologians believe their work is finished when they articulate the symbols in terms of their network meanings. But this is only the extensional side of interpretation.

The intentional side of interpretation, by means of which individuals and communities actually engage ultimate realities through the symbols of interpretation, involve iconic and indexical reference. The indexical reference in engagements with ultimacy is far more complicated than engagements with physical objects within the world. You can point to a bird to focus attention, but you cannot point to a creator of the cosmos, at least not except in metaphor or philosophical dialectic of the sort exhibited in Part III. George Lakoff and Mark Johnson have argued that basic metaphors of life come from bodily orientations. Although they have not analyzed religious metaphors of ultimacy to any great degree, it is not hard to see their point in gesturing to the Heavens to indicate a High God, or Heaven itself as an ultimate principle in Confucianism.[31] Gesturing to the expanse of Earth or lying still on the ground staring at the Milky Way at night are metaphoric indications of the cosmos and its radical contingency, perhaps on a creative being or principle.

Nevertheless, even those metaphors work only within an extremely rich context of other mediations. At any given time, our causal connections with ultimate matters—radical contingency, possibility, groundedness, place in the cosmos, the source of values, to name the ontological sides of ultimate realities sketched in chapter 1—are mediated through the thousands of more proximate ways by which we comport ourselves to ultimacy. We causally engage radical contingency mostly through gratitude or surprise concerning this or that thing, bracketed out as world-forming. We engage the ultimate nature of possibility in the ways we come to terms with this or that demand for freedom. We relate to groundedness by relating to our family, or nationality, or physical capacity or incapacity. We relate to the ultimate conditions of our place in the universe through the countless ways we take up and exercise an orientation to Others, nature and history. We relate causally to the source of value in all the considerations about the worth of our own identity. The anthropological side of ultimacy, in which human beings are given world-building tasks by ultimate realities, exhibits the causal connections of small ordinary tasks with the ontological tasks even more obviously. The structures of sacred canopies allow for the finite/infinite contrasts in symbols of ultimacy to be applied to intra-worldly, otherwise mundane, causal engagements and to endow them with ultimacy. We wake up to a beautiful morning with gratitude for the sun and rest and say "Thanks be to God," or "Let me forget myself in the spontaneous flow of the Dao." The connection between the symbols of ultimacy in a sacred canopy and the rest of mundane life is a function of a worldview (the topic of the next chapter).

In the long run, our general causal orientation to ultimacy is the obverse side of the ways by which a sacred canopy can shape daily life and the life of maturation and spiritual growth. The slow feedback tests of a theology expressed in a sacred canopy have to do with whether it guides life well, a point that goes back to Plato's Republic where he argued that the purpose of education, particularly theory, is to guide practice. The mundane matters of life are causally connected to the symbolized ultimate matters because the ultimate symbols make a difference to the mundane matters. The general orientation to ultimacy orients how the rest of life is orientated. Theology needs to be able to sort the causal connections involved in indexical references to ultimacy.

Iconic reference in actual engagements with ultimate matters is to be understood in two ways. In one, from the standpoint of the act of interpretation itself, the iconic reference of a symbol takes the object to be "like" the symbol. If meditation on the Goddess Kali is taken to involve iconic reference, it supposes that there is a Goddess girdled in skulls. If God the creator is envisioned as an old man with a beard, whose portrait was painted by Michelangelo on the ceiling of the Sistine Chapel, this supposes that God is like an old but powerful man. Very few people, however, even those whose experience is limited to the icons of popular religion, would say that these images are literally iconic. They simply do not have other images with which to compare these so as to say these are but metaphors. These images are the only ones they have. If they were to assert them to be literally iconic, they would be false images. The images might be false iconically but true indexically if in fact they carry over into the interpreter's experience what is important in the real objects of those images. Most people would say that the icons of popular religion engage at best in metaphoric ways—like in some respect but unlike in others. Here the reference is metaphorically iconic, which leaves great leeway for huge errors when the limitations of the metaphors are ignored.

To engage ultimate matters with literal iconicity is the goal within theology that serves to explain the limitations of the metaphors. In fact, this goal of literal iconic engagement is what drives every rich theological tradition to metaphysics of some sort. Metaphysics is the attempt to develop hypotheses about the most basic, including most ultimate, realities and conditions that are iconically true in as literal a sense as possible. Metaphysics is so abstract because it aims to be true across all contexts, not just those in which by metaphor a true indexical engagement is achieved. Taken by itself a metaphysical hypothesis is so abstract and thin that it has little power to engage someone or a community with an ultimate reality. But metaphysics should not be taken by itself. It has its plausibility only through the complicated steps of its being articulated, dialectically developed in relation to alternatives, and lived with as it is tested for consistency, coherence, adequacy, and applicability. Most importantly, metaphysics takes on its power to engage ultimate matters as it functions as the criterion by which to articulate the limits of metaphoric icons.

The only religious symbols that might be true in engagements with ultimacy are those that are broken.[32] A broken symbol is one whose iconic reference is known to be only metaphorical, with a need for the limits of the metaphor to be spelled out. A broken symbol *might* be true, but not necessarily. Even where the limitations of the metaphoric iconicity are known and controlled for, the sense in which the metaphor engages might be false in that it conveys something other than what is important in the ultimate object.

If the higher level theories, tending toward and including metaphysics, are called on to critique the reach of metaphors in lower-level interpretive engagements, are the symbols of the higher-level theories also broken? Tillich waffled on this point. He said sometimes that all symbols of the ultimate are broken, and other times that only the symbol, "being-itself," is literal. The waffling can be made consistent by the recognition that properly metaphysical symbols such as being-itself can be broken in the sense that they are recognized as metaphors but examined and shown to have no limitations. That is, they can function as referring iconically and literally. Subsequent investigation might point out that their historical locatedness, their peculiar development within a metaphysical system, still has a hitherto unrecognized limitation so that they were metaphorical after all. Metaphysics can never be more than the best hypothesis that can be advanced at present, tested by whatever is suspected to be able to limit or falsify it.

An important conclusion to draw from the above discussion is that theology no longer should be regarded mainly as the development of a set of doctrines about ultimate matters. Only the metaphysical part of theology might be regarded that way, as Thomas Aquinas knew. Rather, theology is the creation and critique of symbolic engagements of ultimacy. This involves articulating the myriads of symbols that occur in sacred canopies, analyzing their conventional meaning networks, ascertaining how they refer and, given that, what they assert about ultimate realities. Theology needs to trace down the mediations of many kinds of causality in indexical reference. And it needs to be able to outline the limitations in the metaphors of interpretations that refer iconically. The richness of a theology is the accumulation of all these things.

To conceive of theology as the creation and critique of symbolic engagements of ultimacy, rather than the development of a set of doctrines, is an important shift (I, introduction). Systematic doctrinal theology has been an important, if somewhat varied, genre of theological reflection in South Asian religious traditions and in Christianity and Islam. It is less prominent in Confucianism, Daoism, and Judaism, of the current living global civilizational religions. Perhaps the reason for this is that the traditions with strong doctrinal theologies construe their authorities to be revelational in some powerful sense. The Vedas, the teachings of the Buddha, the Bible or the events depicted in the Bible, and the Qur'an are all regarded within their traditions as revelations from some non-ordinary source. These revelations have their extraordinary charismatic powers from their intrinsic expressions. But those intrinsic expressions need to be interpreted or explained in order to be understood. Hence, the need arises for theology to say what is revealed, and in all these traditions systematic philosophy is the means by which theology attempts to say what is revealed.

The traditions of Judaism, to be sure, take the Torah to be revealed and yet systematic doctrinal theology has not been prominent in Judaism.

The doctrinal theology of Maimonides was perhaps shaped as much by his Muslim and Christian dialogue partners as by the commentarial rabbinic tradition to which he was heir within Judaism. Although many senses of Torah revelation have been expressed in Jewish traditions, the center of gravity in those senses is more on the performative character of the act of revelation at Sinai than on the communication of some body of truth. The giving and receiving of the Torah, both as understood in the allegedly historical experience of Moses and as understood in the making of the exilic and post-exilic theology that assigned the Torah its authority, was the act of transforming the people of Israel into God's nation of priests, a Chosen People. The giving of the Torah was construed mainly as the making of the covenant. Rather than the interpretation of the truth claims of the Torah, Jewish theology has been the working out of the implications of the covenant for situations far different from those depicted in the covenant stories themselves, for which rabbinic commentary has been the preferred medium. The rabbis attempted to articulate the sometimes conflicting implications of the covenant for Jews in post-Second Temple times.[33] Systematic doctrinal theology has been prominent when the truth-content of the revelation, as opposed to or in addition to its performative content, has been important.

Certain strands of medieval Daoism have strong revelational traditions, as described, for instance, by Livia Kohn in *Taoist Mystical Philosophy: The Scripture of the Western Ascension* and by James E. Miller in *The Way of Highest Clarity: Nature, Vision and Revelation in Medieval China*. The little systematic doctrinal theology they show manifests its roots in Buddhism, although much transformed from the Buddhist doctrinal language of India and Tibet. As with the Torah revelations, the medieval Daoist revelations functioned more performatively than to convey truths. The revelations focused on images to be contemplated for the sake of personal transformation rather than on truths about ultimate matters. Of course, the Daoist revelations were indeed about ultimate matters. But the explication of this is through the analysis of symbolic engagement, as in the work of Kohn and Miller, rather than through restating revealed truth in systematic form.

In recent Protestant theology, it has been customary to begin systematic theology with a discussion of revelation. The supposition in this kind of theology is that its job is to explicate the revelation in relevant ways for the Protestant Christian communities involved. Although great variety exists in these doctrines of revelation, the common assumption is that the purpose of theology is to address the practical intellectual issues that arise from the conjunction of the revealed sources and the contemporary situation. This kind of confessional theology is a form of membership within the particular religious community, and it takes itself to be able to assume the revelatory authority by which the community defines itself.

Philosophical Theology cannot define itself confessionally in a pluralistic situation in which it is vulnerable to correction from any source that might be critical. Otherwise it would give up its commitment to ascertain the truth of first-order questions about ultimacy. The revelatory claims among different traditions, indeed the revelatory claims within traditions that consider themselves a unified community, are often contrary, mutually contradictory, or incommensurable. *Philosophical Theology* needs to be able to sort these by treating them comparatively as symbolic engagements of ultimate matters.

Claims to revelation, therefore, need to be assessed as sources, perhaps compatible, perhaps rival, for religious truth and guides to practice. All religious traditions have claims to authority, if not extra-mundane revealed authority. The teachings of Confucius, Mencius, Xunzi, and other ancient worthies are authoritative in Confucianism, although they are not claimed to be revealed in any special sense. All the Axial Age religions have authorities that are sources for thought and practice that are not claimed to be revelatory.

Whether revealed or not, religious authoritative sources in theological matters are imaginative productions that create new signs or religious symbols that inspire and make possible new religious ways of life and thought. These new signs are genuinely revelatory, in the deepest sense of the term, when they make possible the engagement of something ultimate that had not been accessible before. They allow something new to be encountered. Sometimes if not always these new signs are modifications or re-interpretations of older religious imagery, but are decisive for establishing new religious communities and directions. Some nineteenth-century European romantics construed every significant act of imagination to be a function of divinity. In this sense, all expressions of religious genius are "divinely inspired." Yet much needs to be analyzed about the intentions imputed to any divine inspirer.

The construction of theology as the creation and assessment of symbolic engagements of ultimacy is a significant enlargement of theology beyond the development of systems of doctrine. As illustrated here, it requires a theory of religion, and access to the means of assessing religious claims.

CHAPTER FOUR

Worldviews

The first three chapters of *Philosophical Theology* focused on ultimacy as symbolized in sacred canopies. The first developed the conception of sacred canopies, including the technical concept of finite/infinite contrasts. The second dealt with the importance of reference in the symbols of ultimacy in sacred canopies, both for people whose canopies they are and for scholars who study them, indicating the importance of philosophy and especially metaphysics. The third presented a theory of reference within a larger theory of semiotic interpretation and focused on the dimensions of reference in acts of interpretation for which finite/infinite contrasts within sacred canopies are the main signs. The topics so far have been conceptual tools for the understanding of ultimacy and of religion as it relates to ultimate matters. One more analytical concept needs development in this introductory part to *Philosophical Theology*, that of a worldview.

I. ORIENTATION AND WORLDVIEWS: THE SACRED/MUNDANE CONTINUUM

The concept of a worldview (*Weltanschauung*) has a long history, particularly in German idealism. In *Philosophical Theology*, a worldview is conceived as a set of signs, more or less coherent, by which individuals who hold the worldview are oriented to the things in the various domains with which they directly and indirectly interact.

Orientation is the important notion here. Any interpretation supposes a background in the context of which its object for interpretation is selected. The selection of an object of interpretation foregrounds something against a background. The selection is partly a function of the purposes and values in the interpreter and is quite specific to the actual context of interpretation. Yet even those purposes and values find their meaning in terms of a background of symbolized distinctions and values carried in the interpreter's culture and personal history. To be an interpretive person is to be oriented, by means of a worldview, to the objects of direct symbolic engagement as resting within a background of important distinctions and values, a background that provides some degree of coherence between the objects of the engagement at hand and those of other engagements.

The orientation of a human being is not given by a system of signs within a worldview all on one level, as it were. Rather, we are oriented to very different kinds of things, in different domains. Xunzi, the great ancient Confucian, distinguished three domains of orientation.[1] Human beings are oriented to the Heavens, he noted, about which we can do nothing but stand in awe; sometimes predictions for history can be made (he thought) from the patterns of stars. Human beings are also importantly oriented to the rotation of seasons, particularly in temperate climates. Seasonal orientations are carried in direct-learning folklore and affect the kinds of work to be done, clothing to be worn, shifting authority structures, and the like. Xunzi said human beings also should be oriented to large-scale surprises such as floods, droughts, famines, pestilence, and the incursion of barbarians; for this orientation we need governments to look beyond the immediacies of seasonal change.

The basic orientations of life are far more varied in their domains than Xunzi's list. Our actions and interpretations are oriented in certain ways within the context of our families, in slightly different ways in the contexts of friends and acquaintances, in radically different ways in the contexts of political communities. The workplace requires an orientation different from that of the home. Orientation for global politics differs from that for local politics. Orientation to global history differs from that for local history. Orientation to natural surroundings is affected by whether or not one is oriented to the changing ecosystems affected by one's local surroundings. Orientation to the dimensions of ultimacy in a sacred canopy determines how one is religious.

Nothing but very rough maps of different domains of orientation exist. Orientations differ by ethnic group, nationality, climate, occupation, gender, maturity, and the blessings and vicissitudes of luck that makes for accidental circumstances. Orientations are articulated by the imaginative arts of every kind, by traditional symbols, by inquiries and special agreements, and by events of personal and historical accident. Orientations are constantly changing in small ways and sometimes change radically. Orientations sometimes are matters of fairly explicit awareness, sometimes are never recognized as orientations although they function that way, and most often are mixtures of conscious awareness and tacit supposition. Times of crisis tend to call attention to orientations.

A worldview is the set of all the domains of orientation for an individual, each expressed in signs, and together given more or less coherence. Cultural anthropologists or historians might be tempted to sketch a worldview as a system of signs with more coherence than they have. But chances are these sketches deal with only a few domains of orientation, for example, communal rituals having to do with the sacred canopy, or the historical situation of conflict among groups. Orientations, and hence kinds and connections of signs in worldviews, are far more diverse than this. By and large, the worldview of an individual is learned from and in conjunction with a cultural group. Still, many individuals rebel against aspects of their communal culture. Moreover, individuals' worldviews are much affected by their personal histories. The aspects of inwardness in religion point up idiosyncrasies in worldviews.

A sacred canopy is only part of an individual's or a group's worldview, involving the finite/infinite contrasts that define the outermost elements of the symbolized world. All the other aspects of life, including the multitude of different orientations, are other elements of the worldview. Thus a continuum can be drawn from the sacred canopy, which focuses on the orientations to ultimate matters, however symbolized, through to less and less ultimate matters and toward more and more mundane ones. "Mundane" has no negative connotations; it does not mean vulgar or low class. In *Philosophical Theology*, the *sacred* is defined in terms of ultimacy, the most ultimate boundary conditions defining the world.[2] The *mundane*, then, is defined in terms of proximity.

The sacred/mundane continuum within a worldview therefore is defined in terms of the relative remoteness or ultimacy and relative proximity or idiosyncratic intimacy of the matters at hand, to which orientation is given. Orientation to one's place in the cosmos is more toward the ultimate or sacred end of the spectrum than orientation to one's place in world history, if the worldview distinguishes these; orientation to the historical issues of one's day is closer to the proximate or mundane end, and orientation to one's community life is more mundane yet. Friendships and family dynamics are yet more mundane, and the routines of daily life, such as eating, hygiene, sex, childrearing, and getting about even more so.

The religiously interesting elements of the sacred/mundane worldview have to do with how elements in the sacred canopy bear on the mundane elements so as to affect their orientations. For instance, if one's sacred canopy suggests that the entire cosmos is ordered toward the human story, as in some traditions of West Asian monotheism, conceptions of ultimacy would have little bearing on one's orientation to the cosmos as such, but much bearing on one's orientation to human history as such. The Chinese sacred principles of Heaven, Earth, and Dao, by contrast, make significant differences to how one is oriented to cosmic nature, and little difference to orientations regarding large-scale human history. Most sacred canopies make important differences to community life, especially as based on ritual, which are studied in *Philosophical Theology Two* and *Three*.[3] Most sacred canopies also make important differences to orientations to family dynamics, although that differs according to the sacred canopy. Traditional Christian sacred canopies put great emphasis on friendship, whereas the Confucian and Jewish sacred canopies often put family relations above friendship, although ultimacy is given to both friendship and family in all three. Islam takes same-sex (nonsexual) friendship to be more a holy obligation than husband–wife friendship. Although nearly all religious traditions value teacher–disciple relations as part of education, the traditions arising out of South Asia take the guru–disciple relation to be central to the attainment of religious virtuosity. The symbols of ultimacy in sacred canopies often, although not always, make a difference to when to go to war, when to have children, and when to wash. The specific differences that sacred canopies make to mundane orientations of course depend on both the characters of the sacred canopies and the mundane matters to be oriented.

The influence along the sacred/mundane continuum is reciprocal. A community besieged in longstanding war is likely to symbolize the ultimate powers as on its side rather than as aloof or neutral. The Axial Age traditions that emphasize universal love and justice are put under heavy pressure when groups within those traditions are fighting each other for their lives and identities. Persons whose lives are filled with unjust suffering are likely to be less tolerant of conceptions of the Ultimate as a good God who always governs things for the best. Critical accidents in some of the mundane matters of life can bring sacred canopies into crisis: The political atrocities of the Nazis on Jews challenged the sacred canopies that said the Jews are God's chosen people and that Christians are loving.

We now are in a position to refine the preliminary definition of religion given in the Introduction: *Religion is human engagement of ultimacy expressed in cognitive articulations, existential responses to ultimacy that give ultimate definition to the individual and community, and patterns of life and ritual in the face of ultimacy.* It should not be thought that "human orientation to ultimacy" is limited to interpreting the boundary conditions in terms of a sacred canopy and its finite/infinite contrasts. Rather, there is human orientation to ultimacy at every point in a worldview where the orientation symbols are affected by the symbols of ultimacy in the sacred canopy. Prayers at mealtime make mealtimes just as religious as prolonged meditation on The Holy One of Israel or Mahayana's Emptiness. Ultimate dimensions to family dynamics, community life, one's occupation, the historical meaning of one's situation, and now practices of recycling used goods, are to be expected. Community festivals, athletic contests, pilgrimages, and political activities can, although need not, have a religious dimension. To understand religion, then, is to understand all those activities to which a worldview gives orientation where those orientations are affected by the bearing of the symbols of ultimacy in the worldview's sacred canopy.

II. THE TRANSCENDENCE/INTIMACY CONTINUUM

The previous section leaves unanalyzed the claims that elements in a sacred canopy can "affect" the orientations of many more mundane matters of life. The examples it gives are enough to make the general point, but it is necessary now to say more about what that "affecting" might be. Much depends on the character of the symbols of ultimacy in the sacred canopy, the particular kinds of finite/infinite contrasts. An important distinction has to do with a continuum of symbols within the sacred canopy from highly transcendent ones to very intimate, often anthropomorphic, ones.

Part II in this volume will argue in detail that reality has structures or characters that any deep and long-lasting culture must address somehow, with some symbols or other. This is true for the nature of ultimate boundaries too. All the world's Axial Age religions have symbols for ontological ultimate reality that are extremely transcendent and abstract. They also have symbols for the ultimate within their sacred canopies that are extremely intimate and in some cases anthropomorphic. And they have a continuum of symbols in between that mix elements of transcendence with those of intimacy and personification, either with different symbols that are more or less transcendent or intimate or with different ways of interpreting the same symbols as more or less transcendent or intimate.[4]

Chapter 5 argues in detail that the real demands of the ontological ultimates push toward greater and greater transcendence while the real demands of anthropological ultimates push toward greater intimacy and perhaps anthropomorphism.

The push toward transcendence has to do with finding the ground or context in which things can be genuinely other than one another while also being so connected as to define one another, at least in part. Another way to put this is that what is ontologically ultimate is the One or unity behind the diversity of the way. The most abstract way of putting this is the classical philosophical problem of the one and the many. Coupled with these metaphysical considerations is the ubiquitous dialectic countering what the West Asian traditions call idolatry, that is, taking something that itself would have to be grounded in a "higher power" to be itself the highest power. Chapter 6 explores this in detail.

The push toward intimate symbols of ultimacy comes from the need to make ultimate realities relevant to human affairs, and this in two senses. One sense is the drive to make ultimacy comprehensible in human terms. A wholly transcendent principle, strictly speaking, is meaningless. Nirguna Brahman is a comprehensible pointer because of its relation to Saguna Brahman: "Nirguna" means "without qualities (the gunas)," whereas "saguna" means "with qualities." Brahman with qualities takes some of its comprehensibility from its formulaic connection with Atman, self, which in turn is understood in a context in which it means a kind of purified consciousness. Although the complex traditions of "purifying consciousness" in South Asian religion are deep, controversial, and not to be explained by quick reference to "consciousness" as if that were otherwise understood, the mediated connection between Atman and Nirguna Brahman serves to give some human tether to the latter notion that is explicitly supposed to deny all tethers. A second sense of the intimate ultimate is that some kind of human spiritual path is itself ultimate and that ultimate dimensions of reality need to be correlated with the humanity of that path. If this does not mean that ultimate realities in the ontological sense need some kind of human face, as it does not for Madhyamaka Buddhism that clearly denies ontological realities, then it means at least that the conditions for the spiritual path have an anthropic character: *Pratitya samutpada* is like the rising and ceasing of forms *in the mind*. Chapter 7 explores this point.

The interesting point of the transcendence/intimacy continuum for worldviews is not so much the extremes but the mixtures in the middle along the continuum. Given that the large religions with extensive theological reflection are pulled toward both ends of the continuum, most of the operative symbols are in the middle of that tension. The earliest religious symbols of ultimacy seem to be anthropomorphic exaggerations of human characteristics applied to works of nature, as in storm gods such as Shang Di in China, Indra in India, Yahweh and Marduk in West Asian Semitic lands, and Zeus in Greece.[5] By the time of the Axial Age in all these areas, however, much more transcendent conceptions also had been developed.

But the major traditions each developed rhetorical centers of gravity along the transcendent/intimacy continuum as they came to formulation in the Axial Age and its sequelae. Prophetic Judaism and Christianity, and later Islam, defined themselves through a rather anthropomorphic set of basic terms for God, with strong connections between human history and God's action within it. This was despite the fact that they were thoroughly acquainted with the abstractions of good and evil in Zoroastrianism and Plato's conception of the Form of the Good; they did, in at least some of their traditions, adopt the genre of apocalyptic thinking from the Persians. The East Asians, on the other hand, adopted a rhetorical center of gravity from much farther along the transcendence direction of the continuum, rejecting the anthropomorphic Shang Di in favor of principles such as Heaven, Earth, and the Dao. Much politics in the Han Dynasty court was involved in giving the transcendent-oriented "philosophers" trumping authority over the more intimate "shamanist" party. In India, the rhetorical center of gravity spread far across the middle, acknowledging a cosmos filled with a variety of more or less anthropomorphic beings but also one dependent on transcendent principles. In fact, the intimate ultimates of most kinds of Hinduism and Buddhism focused on the transformation of the human so as to transcend, or at least relativize, the specifically human traits of intentionality and passion.

Nevertheless, whatever the rhetorical center of gravity, the remains of the other ends of the continua are to be found in all these traditions. The Neo-Platonic One, which is beyond all determinate distinction and is highly transcendent, has been extremely influential in Christian and Muslim theology, and perhaps influenced Jewish Cabbala. Thomas Aquinas' conception of God as the pure Act of To Be was developed in connection with rival Aristotelian notions of his Muslim interlocutors. In East Asia, echoes of Shang Di are heard in Confucian and Daoist references to the "mandate of Heaven." The extreme transcendence of Advaita Vedanta and extreme intimate anthropomorphism of Pure Land Buddhism are still parts of the rhetoric of South Asian sacred canopies.

A worldview is complicated not only by the connections among the points along the sacred/mundane continuum but also by the fact that its symbols of the ultimate realities, and therefore of the ultimate dimensions in all the mundane realities, range across a whole spectrum on the transcendence/intimacy continuum. Imagine the sacred/mundane continuum to be a horizontal line. Then imagine the transcendence/intimacy continuum to be a vertical line that moves across the sacred/mundane continuum point by point. The transcendence/intimacy continuum registers especially profoundly within the sacred canopy end of the sacred/mundane continuum. Nevertheless, it also registers in the ultimate dimensions of mundane elements. For instance, families can pray at meals because God tells them to, or because that is the proper attitude of reverence for the transcendent Heaven about which one can do nothing except be in awe. Because the whole of the transcendence/intimacy continuum is likely to be in a given worldview, although with favored spots for the rhetorical center of gravity, a family might pray for both of those reasons. When trying to understand a worldview, and the bearing of its references to ultimacy on its various parts, the complications of both continua and their possible interactions need to be borne in mind. Simplification is dangerous at this point.

III. THE SOPHISTICATION/POPULAR CULTURE CONTINUUM

Imagine now a third line drawn on the diagonal that can be moved left and right to intersect all the points of the horizontal sacred/mundane continuum and also up and down to intersect all points of the transcendence/intimacy continuum. This third line is a sophistication/popular culture continuum.

Toward the sophistication end of the continuum is found the disciplined thought and resulting symbols of intellectuals who devote themselves to critical reflection. Here is sophisticated theology, science, art, and self-conscious literature. Generally speaking, greater sophistication means taking account of more variables, and hence employing the abstractions that can hold many variables together. Toward the popular culture end is folk culture, the ways by which people act and believe who do not engage in critical thinking but accept what is taught by face-to-face communications and popular media. There is university psychology, and folk psychology; university physics and folk knowledge of nature; university biology and folk biology, university sociology and folk sociology; university history and popular legends. And then there is sophisticated philosophy and theology, and popular philosophy and religious beliefs.

Some people have a tendency to confuse the transcendence/intimacy continuum with the sophistication/popular culture continuum. But this is a mistake. Very sophisticated philosophers and theologians hold to quite intimate, indeed anthropomorphic, views of ultimate reality, although usually also acknowledging reasons for qualifying that view. It is also a mistake to say that the sophistication end of the continuum is more intelligent or rational than the popular culture end. Wiley Odysseus was a master of popular culture.[6] Some of the greatest masterpieces of recent art have been in the popular medium of film. Film lends itself to great sophistication, to be sure, with layers upon layers of meaning; but film also can be appreciated in unsophisticated ways reinforcing the thought-forms of folk culture. The symbols themselves, say a film or a religious text, are not necessarily either sophisticated or tending to folk culture except insofar as they are interpreted, and the interpretations are what differ along the sophistication/popular culture continuum.

On the sophistication/popular culture continuum, popular culture is shaped by the orienting symbols that make social interactions possible among people, many of whom lack much sophistication. Among the vast array of signs available, the minimal requirements of social cohesion, or partial cohesion, select those that will tend to be used for common discourse. The sophisticated people within the society might "know better," and speak in a sophisticated fashion among themselves; nevertheless they accept the need to operate within the larger society with the terms of popular culture. Most readers of this *Philosophical Theology* would imagine themselves to be among the sophisticated thinkers of their society; nevertheless they drink water rather than H_2O.

Different cultures have different versions of sophistication and popular culture. Evolutionary biologists tend to think of popular culture as the more ancient or primitive, something to be understood in terms of what it is adaptive to think rather than what is learned through intellectual discipline. There might be something to this. The popular culture of a contemporary society within which very few people are literate, however, such as Darfur, is likely to be very different from, perhaps more primitive than, a society in which nearly everyone has a high school education and a very large portion are college educated.

With respect to religious culture, great sophistication in religion exists alongside folk religion. Or rather, a continuum exists within religious culture between sophisticated theology and philosophy on the one hand and the symbols, music, stories, and practices of folk religion. In a religious community, say, a liturgical or ritually defined community, these are mixed together. In a typical Christian liturgy, for instance, references to the Trinity, one of the most abstract religious doctrines in any religion, are combined with petitions for favors, a trait of shamanistic folk religion (*II, 13*). Few people in the worshipping congregation are likely to have thought that the Trinity means that the Father (the First Person) is the simple, pure, indeterminate principle of being and that the Son (the Second Person) is identical to the Father, that is, without specific character, except that the Son is derivative from the Father, whereas the Father is self-existent. This is the position with regard to the first two Persons of the Trinity worked out by the Cappadocian Fathers and presupposed in the great creeds that defined the doctrine of the Trinity (the Third Person never has been given much definition and was the source of the split between the Orthodox and Roman Churches). But those abstractions are rarely in mind in the liturgical references. On the other side, in most North Atlantic Christian congregations, few people would believe that they could manipulate God, shaman-wise, to get what they want in prayer; rather, prayer is more like exposing the deepest desires of one's heart to God. In some other areas of the world, Christian congregations are much more shaman-like in their folk religion. By and large, most religious communities operate with a not altogether consistent set of symbols ranged along the sophistication/popular culture continuum.

Robert A. Orsi has written magnificent descriptions of actual American religious practices, for instance among Italian-American Roman Catholics of the mid-twentieth century.[7] He points out that in this Catholic piety "transcendent" matters are embodied in very concrete artifacts and incidents—statues, pictures of saints, physical disabilities, funeral practices, and the like. These concrete things are not symbols of more transcendent symbols, but of the ultimate matters themselves. He insists, rightly, that for this kind of religion—and analogies of folk cultures in all religious traditions—these concrete things are the stuff of religion, just as, for sophisticated theological types abstract ideas and "theologies" might be the stuff of religion. To say that the more sophisticated kinds of symbols are "better" than the concrete practices and ideation of folk religion is without warrant, he claims, even though the belief that they are has been instrumental in establishing the discipline of religious studies in America, on his account.[8] Orsi tends to give preferential treatment to the more concrete practices of his favorite kinds of actual folk religion (not his descriptive phrase) than to more sophisticated kinds. In both cases, at opposite ends of the sophistication/folk culture continuum, whether the religious practice is "true" or "valid" depends on assessing whether what is really ultimate is carried across through the practices and beliefs into the practicing religious people. The interpretation of truth in *Philosophical Theology* helps Orsi and other scholars of popular religion make the case for taking such religion with seriousness equal to that with which scholars comfortably take religious forms that are more sophisticated in the senses defined here.

Much to the disappointment of some sophisticated theologians in the Axial Age religions, to drop the popular culture out of the beliefs and practices of the religious community is usually impossible. The reason is that the beliefs and practices of the religious community include all the mundane matters of life whose orientations are connected with the finite/infinite contrasts of the sacred canopy. Even when worship is cordoned off into a sacred space, it is assumed to address the issues of the mundane matters of life. In fact, for many religions, the ritualized forms of worship are, among other things, training grounds for how to behave and what to think about everything else in life. So long as the larger society is articulated in part by folk physics, folk psychology, folk biology, pop music and art, the symbols of the religious community need to connect with those mundane realities. Precisely because the symbols of the ultimate within the sacred canopy are affected by their connections with the mundane matters of life, the sacred canopy will have to have symbols reflecting popular or folk religion. If they did not do so, then they could not affect the orientation in those parts of the worldview that cover the mundane elements of life.

The complexities of identifying religion through the ultimate dimensions of all the matters encompassed within a worldview are enormous. Systematic philosophical theology needs to be alert to the variables of all six continua discussed in this chapter, which can intersect each other at every point along each. This shows something of the enormous wild proliferations of variables that make up religion. The discussion stands as a warning against identifying religion only with the sacred canopy, or only with its popular expressions, or only with its sophisticated expression, or only with its transcendent symbols of ultimacy, or only with anthropomorphic and other intimate ones. Religion is all of these.

Not all religion is true and valid, however, and one of the functions of systematic philosophical theology is to discern and defend the better versions of religion. In terms of the present discussion, theology is about discerning what is true in a worldview with respect to ultimacy in its various dimensions, including thought and practice. This too is complicated. It might seem as if we should simply devise a worldview of the most sophisticated symbols of the ultimate and of all the other dimensions of life—science, history, art, and so forth. Because these are sophisticated, they would tend to refer more nearly literally and could be envisioned as somewhat descriptive of the world. Yet reference is not only iconic. Indexical reference is perhaps more important for religion than iconic reference. Believing and acting on unsophisticated popular culture beliefs might very well carry over what is true and valid in the ultimate dimensions of things for engaging individuals. For most people, somewhat popular notions are the only ones that engage ultimate issues, and so the extremely sophisticated notions could be neither true nor false for them. The engagement of the ultimate with folk religion might be the only possible means of engagement for some people. And that engagement might be true in the sense of carrying over what is valuable in the ultimate object in the respect in which those ultimate popular symbols actually stand for their ultimate object in the actual interpretive engagement. Of course, it might also be false, even demonic. Therefore, sophisticated theology needs to find ways of triangulating in on what is actually carried across to judge whether the engagements by means of this or that orienting symbols in the worldview are true.

IV. THE EXISTENTIAL CONTINUA: SHARING, COMPREHENSIVENESS, INTENSITY

The purpose of *Philosophical Theology One* is to deal with questions of ultimates, and the three continua within worldviews discussed previously all focus on ultimacy. These are not the only continua, however, in terms of which the religious dimensions of worldviews are to be understood. *Philosophical Theology Two* deals directly with the existential definition of individuals by their relations with ultimacy and *Three* deals with the existential definitions of both individuals and groups. Therefore, three more continua within worldviews need mention here, with greater explication to come in subsequent volumes (*III, 2, iii; 12, iii*).

The "sharing continuum" has to do with the extent to which an individual's worldview is shared with others in a larger culture. At one end is an inherited cultural worldview that an individual might buy into wholeheartedly with no demurrers. At the other end is a worldview hammered out by an individual idiosyncratically, doubtless starting with culturally given elements but reflecting the incidents, accidents, and decisions of the individual's life. Perhaps no person's life is so typical of a larger cultural worldview that the worldview can be borrowed effectively without alteration. Nearly every individual's life has unique aspects and these need orientation in a tailored worldview. Therefore the worldview needs to be adapted to orient them. In the discussions of this chapter the worldviews are analyzed most often in terms that apply to the larger culture, with only passing reference to exceptions for individuals. The exception is analyses of great religious founders or leaders whose own experience causes a significant change in worldview that then becomes objectified in some larger or new community.

In our time, however, the need to be sensitive to the idiosyncratic individuation of worldviews is particularly important (*III, 3, 4*). Social change in most parts of the world is so great that a worldview fit for one generation is ill fitting for the next. Forced or sought, economic mobility threatens family structures, which usually leads to a defensiveness regarding the family worldview, thus exacerbating rebellion among those who want out. Ours is a pluralistic time when many worldviews are offered as options for choice, and many people cobble together a worldview for themselves that borrows from several. A worldview that is a tradition within one group is inevitably changed for an individual from another group that adopts it.

The twentieth century was a disaster for traditional religions and their worldviews. The European world wars sealed the coffin on the worldview of European Christendom. The Buddhist-Confucian cultures of China, Japan, and Korea warred destructively. Islam demonstrated that even an external enemy is not enough to prevent violent conflict between Sunnis and Shi'ites. Many people the world over are disillusioned with the worldviews of traditional religions. This by itself has occasioned a reaction of return to an extreme fundamentalism, to the re-creation, allegedly, of old communities that were supposed to work better, to "roots." The attempts to find and inhabit ancient worldviews, however enthusiastic, are in reality constructions of new worldviews. This highly "creative orthodoxy" is especially true of the extraordinary expansion of Christianity in the Southern hemisphere and in East Asia.

In all, our recent history has produced imaginative creations of new worldviews, often idiosyncratic to individuals who do not accept full membership in any community and whose worldviews are unique to themselves, changing as they themselves change. In no other way would people find orientation in such an age of change, mobility, and destruction of tradition. So, part of understanding religiousness is understanding how an individual's worldview relates to other worldviews, perhaps vaguer but perhaps more specific, that are to be found in the environment. This question of the extent to which a worldview is shared is not the same as the distinction between existential inwardness and external belonging, although it might be affected by that distinction. It rather is a distinction between individual and communal imagination in orienting things with a worldview. Thus, it defines a difference between the ways an individual relates to ultimacy and the ways that person's neighbors do.

A second existential continuum is the comprehensiveness of a worldview. Some worldviews provide orientation for just about everything in life. Others provide orientation for only a few things. For the former, the worldview constitutes something like a "total institution" for orientation.[9] For the latter, the worldview leaves many aspects of life without overall coordinating orientation. Not everything people do and believe needs to have an orienting context. Much of what people do is meaningless beyond the acts themselves. Sometimes social critics complain about this: A consumerist society, for instance, is one where the orientation involved in spending money is too narrow, touting satisfaction with goods that do not satisfy. The failure of the consumerist worldview is that the spending of money is not given a wider orientation that relates it to true human satisfaction, good uses of money, critical attitudes toward social manipulation in advertising, and so forth. But no contemporary worldview makes everything meaningful within a wider orientation. Many things are done just by accident, for fun, for no reason at all. The value of this non-orientation of certain things needs to be assessed in the various cases. Worldviews vary in their comprehensiveness.

Some worldviews have a degree of comprehensiveness that does not include orientations to ultimacy. Not all worldviews have sacred canopies, and many that do have sacred canopies that are minimal in scope. Perhaps most modern Western people believe that individuals have some kind of ultimate importance, which they would symbolize in a minimal sacred canopy by celebrating birthdays and perhaps funerals. Many people affected by European modernity rebel against the explicit symbols of religious traditions and think of themselves as secular. In the name of secularity some of these devise or adopt other, nontraditionally religious, symbols that refer to the ultimate glory of radical contingency, to awesome beauty, and to other finite/infinite contrasts also addressed by traditional symbols. But perhaps more often among people who think of themselves as secular, the orientation to ultimate matters is rather thin, just birthdays, not even funerals. This is to say, they have functioning worldviews for other parts of their lives but not for providing much orientation in ultimate matters. To have an ultimate concern in Tillich's sense is difficult without an orientation to define it. So Tillich likely was wrong to believe that everyone has an ultimate concern (I, 5). To understand a person's worldview requires understanding how comprehensive it is, and just what it comprehends as a provision of orientation.

The third existential continuum is the intensity with which a person holds to a worldview. For some people a worldview is extremely important. Functionally, this is to say that much of what they do needs to have orientation in terms of its roles within life. Other people are only mildly oriented in their beliefs and activities, even if the worldview to which they are mildly committed is very comprehensive and might orient the bulk of their activities and beliefs. Most people are in the middle of the continuum between intense devotion to an orienting worldview and mild use that comes into play only occasionally. Persons attracted to different, seriously incompatible worldviews in different portions of their lives might find it prudent to be mild in their devotion to each; on the other hand, they might give great intensity and contrast to their lives by being intensely devoted to each.

The intensity continuum is a function in part of all the issues of membership and alienation discussed above and in *Philosophical Theology Two*, chapters 14 to 16, and *Three*, chapters 2 and 12. But it also has a developmental dimension. Children learn and assume the worldview of their parental culture, only slightly modifying it. Coming to adolescence they find the need to affirm some worldview intensely—existential identity is defined in terms of worldview commitment for adolescents.[10] Sometimes the commitment is merely the existential affirmation of their inherited worldview. Other times adolescents need to work things out for themselves, with idiosyncratic or generation-specific worldviews, in order to have an object of intense devotion. Adults appear to go through stages when their worldviews are more or less intensely held. Many Western college students practice aloofness and think of themselves as liberated from their worldview only to return to intense practice when they become parents and need an orienting context for family life. As family responsibilities lessen, people typically sit more lightly with the worldview, perhaps experimenting with alternatives. Aging people often return to intense devotion as they try to assess the meaning of their lives and face death.

The three existential continua have to do with how worldviews function in the lives of individuals and communities. Because the concept of a worldview, now defined as a term of art for *Philosophical Theology*, is important for understanding religion, and religion is important for understanding ultimacy, all the continua need to be developed together.

Part I

Summary Implications

The purpose of Part I of *Philosophical Theology One* has been to introduce some of the major conceptual tools necessary for an analysis of ultimacy or ultimate reality. These tools have been introduced but not developed much in use. A brief summary allows for some conclusions to be drawn about the shape of the inquiry to come.

The Introduction to this volume includes a stipulative definition of religion in terms of relations to dimensions of ultimacy or ultimate reality in human life. That the definition is stipulative means that its worth in the long run depends on how helpful it turns out to be in the analysis to come. The definition uses *ultimacy* and its cognates as a kind of token without much analysis of what it means, although with the hope that it carries enough commonsense recognition to move the definition forward. Part I has attempted to gain ground in the definition of ultimacy.

Traditional Christian systematic theological expositions often have begun directly (or after an introductory discussion of revelation) with a discussion of God as the Ultimate, and moved to discussions of religion only later, often in connection with the theological topic of the Holy Spirit. *Philosophical Theology* begins, however, by interpreting them together in terms of one another. The principle behind the mutual interpretation is the conviction that theology never really begins but is always in the middle. To attempt to characterize the ultimate without a self-conscious background of the religious and intellectual context for thinking about ultimacy is to fall into an unnecessary bias-pit. On the other hand, to begin with a discussion of religion without an intrinsic connection with ultimacy is to treat religion as a non-religious phenomenon, in the sense discussed in chapter 2. The strategy of discussing several things at once in terms of one another does not allow for a building-block progression in theology, as has been the ideal for many theologians. But it does allow for increased clarification, correction, and nuance, step by step, that promises a new way of understanding a great many things together.

The Preliminary Remarks to Part I introduced the problem of "beginning" a discussion of ultimacy by putting it in the context of how ultimacy has been handled in the multiplicity of world religions. This established early on that the public for *Philosophical Theology* recognizes the pluralism of the present religious situation (and the situations of many other eras) and expects discussions of theological issues to be in a global context.[1] The character of this pluralistic public thus includes a background in comparative theology. Comparative theology still is a nascent discipline, and so the actual preparation of the public, including its genres of speech and writing, remains spotty.

The crucial conceptual tool for comparative theology is the notion of a vague comparative category. Such a category constitutes the respect in which two or more positions might be compared, and is unbiased to the extent it can accommodate the expressions of the various positions without reducing one to another or any position to its own theoretical elements. The category is vague in the logical sense that it can accommodate positions that contradict one another. If positions that contradict one another cannot be compared, then the language of theology cannot fairly acknowledge diverse claimants for truth and genuine guidance.

Setting the terms of the discussion of religion and ultimacy in a comparative context has involved the use of many comparative categories in Part I. At this stage of the discussion, the references specifying the categories in different traditions or positions have been fairly nominal. At some point, those references will have to become much more specific, or the comparisons themselves will be vague and useless. It might be thought that "real" religion or theology uses only completely specific categories, and in contrast to vague generalizations this is true. But even so-called specific categories themselves are often vague with respect to further specification. So, for instance, the vague category of Christian conceptions of God can be specified by determinate-God conceptions as well as ground-of-being conceptions (Tillich). Determinate-God as a category is vague with respect to conceptions of God as finite versus those of God as infinite. The category of finite conceptions is vague with respect to metaphysical finiteness as in Whitehead or narrative finiteness as in Dispensationalist theology. And so on. The discussions of issues of ultimacy in the chapters of Part I have treated the comparative conceptions at various levels of specificity. In the long run, a rich fabric of these conceptions needs to be woven for comparative purposes.

The general rubric for Part I is the study of ultimacy in life, that is, in religion. Chapter 1 introduced the conceptual tool of sacred canopies as networks of symbols representing ultimacy that articulate the ways individuals conceive the boundary conditions, that is, the ultimate limits in this or that dimension, of their world. The notion of sacred canopy serves to articulate subjective ideas, the objectification of those ideas in social life, and the response to those ideas as they are employed to guide life. Chapter 1 then added the metaphysical conception of finite/infinite contrasts to define more precisely what symbols of ultimacy might be and how they mark the boundary conditions of worldliness. The conception of finite/infinite contrasts is developed throughout the volumes of *Philosophical Theology*: any ultimate is a finite/infinite contrast.

Just what things are ultimate in various sacred canopies is a matter of empirical study, and no a priori list can be drawn up. Nevertheless, chapter 1 argued that some metaphysical characteristics of reality constrain every well-developed and thorough sacred canopy to include finite/infinite contrasts that symbolize those characteristics as boundary conditions. This metaphysical hypothesis is empirical in the long run, not a priori. The thesis that religions are constrained to address real conditions of the world is argued in detail in Part II. The hypothesis about the metaphysical characteristics is defended dialectically in Part III. The metaphysical model sketched in chapter 1 hypothesizes that determinate things are harmonies with essential and conditional components and that, in order to be connected with and yet different from one another, each with the others must be recognized as radically contingent of an ontological creative ground. Every full-blown sacred canopy needs symbols for radical contingency. Moreover, every harmony has form, components formed, existential location, and value identity. Thus sacred canopies need symbols that deal with the ultimacy of possibilities, of grounded wholeness in components, of existential location, and value. Moreover, they need two kinds of symbols for each of these: transcendent symbols of their metaphysical structure and intimate symbols for how human life relates to them. Many symbols function both transcendently and intimately in mixed, sometimes confused, ways. Other topics of ultimacy also might be found in sacred canopies, of course, perhaps universally so.

To function with a sacred canopy is to take it to be true in some sense. The nature of truth in reference to ultimacy is a topic developed throughout these volumes. Chapter 2 discussed how people are committed to the beliefs that their symbols of ultimacy refer to something real. It also discussed how the properly reductive sciences of religion prescind from precisely this commitment so as to note that people are indeed committed but not assess the validity of the commitment. Chapter 3 then introduced a theory of interpretation, called symbolic engagement, which provides an epistemology of reference that applies to religious reference through the interpretation of finite/infinite contrasts. In particular, the hypothesis was introduced that symbolic engagements of ultimacy are acts that take elements of the sacred canopy as signs of ultimacy. The question is how those interpretive acts are true or false. The thesis was put forward, to be defended at length in following chapters, that the truth of an interpretation consists in what is valuable or important in the interpreted object being carried over into the interpreter by the sign in the respect in which the sign stands for the object. This general thesis about truth applies to ultimate objects as well as proximate ones.

Finally, the concept of worldviews was introduced in chapter 4, according to which worldviews provide orienting signs for the various direct activities and reflections of life. Sacred canopies are those portions of worldviews that contain finite/infinite contrasts symbolizing various aspects of ultimacy. But worldviews also contain signs that deal with many other aspects of reality, mundane aspects in contrast to ultimate ones. Six continua of signs were distinguished according to which subsequent analyses of the place of ultimacy in life can be analyzed. One is the continuum from ultimate to proximate, or sacred to mundane matters. A second is the continuum from transcendent to intimate conceptions of ultimacy, a continuum that might bear on mundane matters at any point. The third continuum is from sophisticated to popular-culture symbols within a worldview. Any point on the sacred/mundane axis can be articulated on a continuum from sophisticated to popular ways, as can conceptions of ultimacy from the transcendent to the intimate. These three continua characterize the contents of worldviews. Three other continua characterize the relation of individuals to worldviews. The first is the continuum from the worldview that is idiosyncratic to an individual to worldviews that are more or less shared in cultures. The second is a continuum from a very dense determination of many or all aspects of life by a worldview to a loose and general determination of some aspects of life. The third is a continuum from an intense commitment to a worldview to a relaxed, tentative, experimental, or transient commitment to one or several worldviews. These continua articulate schemata according to which the connections of various parts of life with ultimate realities can be understood. The result of this is that the understanding of the place of ultimacy in human life is very complicated indeed.

PART II

Ultimates Symbolized

Part II

Preliminary Remarks

Without significant elaboration Part I of *Philosophical Theology One* put forward the hypothesis that reflective religions evolve theologies in response to structures of reality with which all cultures and individuals need to cope in one way or another. Of course, religions are historically diverse, wildly so, and their categories should be seen in their own integrity even as integrations and classifications are undertaken (*III, pt 2*). But just as certain aspects of religion are adaptive in a biologically evolutionary sense to the evolution of humankind as such, so other aspects, especially those that show up in theological symbolizations of ultimacy, are adaptive to what in fact might be ultimate structures of reality (*III, 2, iii, iv*).

Evolution is a complicated idea, with both technical and popular meanings (*III, 1*). Biological evolution has to do with the passing on of genes for certain traits that are adaptive in the sense that the individuals or groups that have those traits are better able to reproduce than individuals or groups lacking them.[1] Biological evolution aside, at some point human beings evolved semiotic systems sufficiently subtle that people became able to learn from their experience. This is to say, people came to believe things in part because they had evidence for them, or at least counter-evidence for contrary beliefs. Human beings developed beliefs for reasons, however good or bad. They did not hold beliefs for no reason except that believing them had some biological advantage in passing on the genes for believing them. Beliefs had pragmatic advantage for achieving many kinds of specific human purposes and pragmatic considerations directed the modification of beliefs. Of course, our semiotic systems employ the semantics of signs produced through imagination and this imagination has been shaped in some respects by purely biological evolutionary considerations, for instance the over-eager imputation of agency. So when human beings became able, through the complexities of their semiotic systems, to ask basic questions about the contingency of things, the meaning of human life, and the rest of the big religious questions, one available set of signs that could be used to symbolize that question was that involving supernatural agency. Belief in supernatural agents remains a strong strand in many religions today. But non-agential signs were also used to interpret those questions, as in notions of the Dao, Nirguna Brahman, or the Neo-Platonic One; often these signs were elaborations of ideas of consciousness and spontaneous emergence used to symbolize ultimacy.

The point is that the evolution of religion, whatever its roots in biological human evolution, came to be affected, indeed directed, by human learning. Cultural evolution is the development of semiotically structured elements of human life based on what is thought to be learned about reality. Although to discover which human traits have their roots in biological evolution and where their advantage is or was for the passing on of the genes of the population is important, to discover in respect of religion what is learned about reality and how religion responds to that is more important. The line between biological and cultural evolution is by no means sharp and many phenomena overlap. The neurobiology of semiotic thinking is to be described both in terms of the causality of biochemistry and the causality of semiotic connections, and these causalities need to be integrated, although that is not the topic here.[2]

Having established the general point that cultures, particularly religious cultures, can learn from reality and develop improved conceptions and symbols, we can now ask about the structures of reality that demand religious, theological, responses. A first pass at this inquiry was made in chapter 1, in which a series of fundamental world-defining boundary conditions were reviewed as constituting more or less universal human problems that require symbols of ultimacy. Part II returns to the question of responses to reality by asking four basic questions.

The first is the question of the relation between ontologically real ultimate structures and the anthropological issues of human ultimate concern. The former put pressure on symbols to be more transcendent. The latter put pressure on symbols to be more and more intimate and humanly meaningful. This does not mean that human beings, out of their ultimate concern, need necessarily to symbolize ultimate realities in anthropomorphic terms. Indeed, Tillich, who developed the notion of ultimate concern, explicitly rejected all anthropomorphism. But it does mean that circumstances might exist, and indeed do, when it is legitimate for symbols to personify what is not personal. Nevertheless, the prior question is whether all people have ultimate concern. The strategic answer is to analyze a continuum between those who are deeply defined by an ultimate concern and those who take few if any things with ultimate concern. This is the topic of chapter 5.

Second, what is there in reality that applies the pressure for transcendent symbols of ultimacy? First are issues of cosmic scale, which quickly transcends anthropomorphic organization. Second are issues of idolatry in which something that is not ultimate is taken to be ultimate in inappropriate ways. Third are issues of explanation and ultimacy in what explains what.

Fourth are issues, arising in the context of mysticism, that employ the first three kinds of issues to develop apophatic experiences and theologies. This is the topic of chapter 6.

Third is the question of ultimacy in the structures proximate and intimate to human experience. Again, four topics are analyzed. First are issues about human life lying atop a vast depth of nature, which bears directly on the relative importance of human history. Second are issues of the uncanny in daily life, the numinous as it arises in familiar circumstances in nature and domestic affairs. Third are issues that have to do with giving meaning to human life, to the mundane affairs of life embraced within a worldview that includes a sacred canopy of symbols of ultimacy. Fourth are issues concerning the correction of human life, with responses to the human predicament, a topic that is central to *Philosophical Theology Two*. This is the topic of chapter 7.

Beginning with the anthropological issues of ultimacy in chapter 5, moving to ontological ultimacy in chapters 6 and 7, chapter 8 returns to the anthropological question of the rhetoric with which to mediate between the demands of transcendence and those of ultimacy. Its question is whether the ultimate framing rhetoric of theology should be about ontological relations between human beings and ultimate reality or about fundamental narratives with both transcendent and intimate interests. In many, but not all, religions, ultimacy is sometimes but not always symbolized through a divine narrative of creation and redemption, or a cosmic natural history. What are the consequences of making ultimate realities players in a narrative? In some religions, but by no means all, the ultimate existential location of a people is understood in terms of a narrative or series of narratives. Often the narratives of the divine and the narratives of the people are united. Nevertheless, it is argued, narratives of ultimate dimensions of reality are always mistaken, and in certain crucial respects viciously misleading. Rather than a narrative frame for symbolizing the ultimate, a metaphysical or ontological frame is to be preferred. For compelling reasons, however, religions learn to live with broken narratives and anthropomorphic images that are recognized as personifying projections (II, 9).

CHAPTER FIVE

Ultimate Reality and Ultimate Concern

The distinction between ontological and anthropological ultimates has been observed from the beginning of this study (I, *Preface*). Roughly, ontological ultimates are realities on their own, whereas anthropological ultimates are human projects of ultimate importance. Part of the significance of the distinction is that some important religious traditions, particularly those of Madhyamaka Buddhism, deny that any ontological ultimates exist and insist that religion has to do with the human project of overcoming suffering.[1] As observed earlier, this Buddhist argument is itself based on ontological views about what is (or is not) real (I, 1, ii). Nevertheless, the distinction between ontological and anthropological ultimates needs to be explored.[2]

I. ULTIMATE AND PROXIMATE CONCERNS

Paul Tillich claimed that every person has an ultimate concern, which he contrasted with all proximate concerns.[3] In one sense, ultimacy in a concern merely means the concern that will be held onto until the very last when every other concern has been given up. Tillich thought that for some if not many people the ultimate concern is for money or power. They might tell themselves that their ultimate concern is for something nobler, but in practice everything else is made secondary to the concern for money or power. In another sense, for Tillich, a person's ultimate concern is what defines the person's existential being. For Tillich, a person's ultimate identity is defined by that person's ultimate concern. These two considerations are not incompatible: A person ultimately concerned for money or power is in fact defined existentially by that ultimate concern.

Tillich's theory of ultimate concern reflected his more basic commitment to the general conception of the person in German idealism according to which a self has a core unity, however misguided unity might be. So he assumed that every self is "centered" and that the issues of true selfhood have to do with the character and orientation of the center. Most people are not centered enough, or centered properly. Every person has an ultimate concern, although often badly organized and aimed, and the most serious question is with regard to its object, he thought.

Contrary to Tillich's German tradition, the pragmatic tradition suggests that the self is an achievement of integrating diverse processes of thought, emotion, and behavior and that unity is by degrees, and in fact is sometimes absent. This follows from Plato's preoccupation with the diversity of different elements in the person that need to be harmonized and often are not. The neuroscientific understanding of the self supports the pragmatic hypothesis.[4] Consciousness itself waxes and wanes. Attention wanders, and is subject to discipline. The possibility exists for people to be ultimately concerned about one thing today, another tomorrow. Some days, people do not order their concerns enough to have any concern be ultimate. People's existential value-identity (a notion thematized in *Philosophical Theology Two*) is determined by many factors, and self-definition by individual will, so important to existentialist thinkers such as Tillich, might not be universal. Kierkegaard's striking title, *Purity of Heart Is to Will One Thing*, expresses the profound truth that having an ultimate concern is an ideal to be achieved only with purity of heart.[5] Even the forms of Buddhism that eschew any attention to ontological ultimate realities acknowledge that many people are not ultimately committed to overcoming suffering. No one enjoys suffering, of course, and everyone wants to avoid or get rid of it. But only a few take the journey toward enlightenment and release. This often would involve monastic commitment, and one becomes a serious seeker, according to Mahayana Buddhism, by taking the vows of a bodhisattva.[6] Buddhism would not claim that everyone has a commitment to an anthropological ultimate journey or transformation.

Regardless of Tillich's theory of the universality of ultimate concern, we should acknowledge as part of religion a human concern for ultimate matters that is expressed on a concern continuum. At one end of the continuum is the perfected ideal, the purity of heart, which is to be ultimately concerned in such a way as to give ultimately commanding existential definition to the self. Many models of this are to be found, of course. Kierkegaard's ideal of the purified-in-heart selfless lover, integrated beyond the aesthetic and moral selves to the self of the "knight of faith," expresses a long-standing martial tradition within Christianity.[7] The perfected Confucian sage is rather the opposite of the martial model, with the possible exception of Wang Yangming, a general; yet Tu Weiming likens the commitment to become a sage to a Confucian variant on a Kierkegaardian leap of faith.[8] The "renouncer" traditions in Indian religions manifest many variations on the theme.[9] The ancient Brahmanical scheme of student-householder-forest dweller-wandering ascetic culminated in the ascetic renouncer; in practice, those four might not have been stages in life but rather separate ways of life that people were free to choose, the life of the renouncer being one of them. Buddhism and Jainism in the middle of the first millennium BCE were renouncer traditions requiring commitments to rigorous disciplines of perfection. In the Buddhist case, the ideal was the elimination of the illusion of the integrated self. In the Advaita Vedanta of Shankara, the ideal was the elimination of the illusion of a self that could act so that the seeker could realize full identification with Brahman that simply is and does not act. In all these cases, the ideal is a rare and difficult achievement that most people only approach at a distance, even those who bind themselves on the path with a profession of faith or bodhisattva-style vow, going through sometimes arduous rites of initiation.

At the other end of the concern continuum is mere interest in or about ultimate matters. Most likely "ultimate matters" are identified by a sacred canopy within a person's worldview. But as illustrated in the "intensity continuum" regarding commitment to worldviews in chapter 4, some people might not be much concerned about what the worldview symbolizes as ultimate. Moreover, as illustrated in the "comprehensiveness continuum," a person's worldview might not have much to say about orienting many of the diverse domains of daily life to ultimate matters. Not everyone need have even a mild interest in ultimacy. A person might well have grown up within a sacred worldview but rejected much or all of it, dabbled in alternative cultural worldviews, or knocked together an idiosyncratic worldview that expresses some ultimate realities, as in the "sharing continuum," with the result of a mild interest "about" ultimate things. People can live ordinary lives within recognized religious traditions, ostensibly oriented by their sacred worldviews, but without sufficient passion about ultimate things that could be dignified by the term *ultimate concern*. "Ultimate curiosity" might be better, "latent curiosity" even better.

Nevertheless, human life in most times and places has its crises. Some are tragic, such as sickness, suffering, death, displacement, the destruction of a people. Others are ecstatically glorious, such as the birth of a child, coming of age, acquisition of a new start in life or a new place, sudden encounter with great beauty in nature and art. Although not always, these crises frequently prompt people to raise ultimate questions for themselves, questions that are ultimate in the sense defined above as world-making, expressed in finite/infinite contrasts, involving some combination of concern about ultimate obligation, wholeness, engagement, meaning, or comportment toward existence as such. Take-it-or-leave-it attitudes or mild interest in a sacred canopy's expressions of ultimacy can become transformed into questioning, serious questioning, questing. Ranging from mere interest to deep renunciation of all concerns except for a clearly defined ultimate one, the concern continuum has many stages expressed in various ways.

The anthropological ultimate is to be understood in terms of the demands on symbols of ultimacy in sacred canopies made by various stages and affairs along the concern continuum. This is thematized in greater detail in *Philosophical Theology Two* and *Three*. But the rough point is expressed here.

At the mild interest stage of the continuum, the symbols in the sacred canopy at least must make ultimate matters accessible to people. For this reason, the cultural worldviews need sacred canopies with folk-culture expressions of the ultimate and of ultimacy's bearings on daily life. Anthropomorphic symbols are readily accessible ways of expressing ultimacy, although not the only ones. However much theologians might want to purify the symbols of folk religion, the concern continuum shows why there is powerful pressure not to do so in ways that would make the ultimate symbolically inaccessible.

Moving beyond the mild interest end of the concern continuum to the point where ultimate matters become seriously engaging, the finite/infinite contrasts in a sacred canopy need to express how the ultimates orient life's crises. The birth of a child seen as a transformative event, the death of a child as equally transformative, an encounter with transcendent beauty, coping with one's own mortal illness—crises such as these require the symbols of ultimacy to give meaning to life in terms of the crises. As these issues become more serious, the symbols of ultimacy need to be able to give meaning in the sense of prioritizing concerns: which ones are merely proximate—which are more nearly ultimate in importance? Death and serious suffering, in nearly all traditions, are occurrences that require ordering and meaning-giving answers from the symbology in sacred canopies. The predicaments built in to human life, analyzed in *Philosophical Theology Two*, call for prioritizing life according to religious practices related to sacred canopies. When the predicaments become self-negating, however, and the concern reaches for the ultimate with only trivial attention to how the ultimate prioritizes life, religion becomes apophatic and mystical.

Toward the ultimate concern end of the concern continuum, people begin to change their lives to live in accordance with what they take to be ultimate. Not always does this involve the renunciation of a previous way of life. But it does mean that people begin to define themselves in terms of how they relate to what is ultimate. It means they seek an ultimate existential determination of themselves, as Tillich would say. When these stages of serious religious journey or transformation are reached, the pressures on the symbols of ultimacy in sacred canopies shift. No longer is it enough that they be accessible or give guidance with regard to ordering what is important in life. They need now be *true* to what is really ultimate because that is the point of ultimate concern: how to respond to ultimate reality as such. At this point the symbologies are under pressure to attain transcendence of facile accessibility and responsiveness to human need. The real human need is that they speak the truth, which might not be humane, treating people like straw dogs.[10]

In many if not all traditions the transcendent representations of ultimacy take on an apophatic character. The ultimate seems to be retreating from grasp, almost inaccessible, no longer a comforting presence. It ceases to give directions about how to order human life with the right priorities—life's wildness becomes manifest as a little beyond good and evil. The purifying stages of ultimate concern break symbols of the ultimate as they also break organized structures of the self: The lover abandons love in bliss; the enlightened one abandons all self-identity in identity with Brahman; full release means the end of the self. Many conceptualized ideals manifest this merging of the perfection of the spiritual adept with the symbols of ultimacy in their transcendent purity. Truly serious ultimate concern encounters the infinite side of the finite/infinite contrasts defining ultimacy.

II. ULTIMACY AND DIALECTIC

Our argument now is in a position to revisit the conception of ultimacy. Chapter 1 characterized ultimacy in terms of the boundary conditions for a socially constructed sense of the worldliness of the world, a sacred canopy, and defines those boundary conditions generally as finite/infinite contrasts. Chapter 4 characterized sacred canopies, with their assemblages of symbols of ultimacy, as at one end of a continuum within a worldview that embraced also many other ways of orienting the mundane, non-ultimate, domains of life. Now we can be more precise about what boundary conditions are relative to human concerns, a question more detailed than Peter Berger asked.

First, corresponding to stages of mild concern, the boundary conditions are simply those things that give orientation to any, some, or all affairs of life without any further conditions beyond them. The limitations of this should be noted immediately. For some people, many affairs of life have no orientation beyond the affairs themselves, and are "meaningless" in this sense. For some people, many affairs of life are oriented beyond themselves but not in connection with anything ultimate. In this instance, mundane affairs within a worldview can be oriented more or less to one another, so as to achieve some kind of cultural or personal integration, but without any reference to ultimate conditions. Things are understood simply in terms of one another, to the degree that they have much orientation across a worldview. In other worldviews, however, many mundane things are oriented at least in part by connections with finite/infinite contrasts in sacred canopies. For instance, people can pray before meals because of divine command, think of themselves as people of a tradition dating back to the founding of the world (as in Shaivism), defend their community because that is the very meaning of life, have children because that is the very meaning of being natural for a human. People do not have to feel deeply about the ultimate dimensions of these things. Those dimensions might simply be the ways the worldviews are constructed and the ultimate dimensions are taken for granted. The ultimate dimensions shape the ways people do things, but not necessarily with much concern for the ultimate elements.

Perhaps the best way to describe ultimacy from the perspective of the mildly concerned end of the concern continuum is to say that it is what sociologists and anthropologists find when they ask people to describe the boundary conditions of their world (in appropriate "participant-observation" terms, of course). Social scientists can take this description at face value as a "socially constructed" world. Of course, this social construction needs to be realistic enough about the real world to be pragmatically useful—else the people living according to it would not survive. But at the mildly interested end of the spectrum, the symbols of ultimacy are simply what the people whose sacred canopy they constitute take to be the boundary conditions of their world, about which they might be mildly curious and concerned. Moreover, in most instances those ultimate boundary conditions make certain demands on individuals and groups that can be treated as the cultural demands under which they live. Thus in a broad cultural sense, the people of the culture live under obligation to treat aspects of life as of such significance that there is no going beyond them.

In the middle ranges of the concern continuum the ultimacy attached to the mundane aspects of life begins to exact a price. Sometimes the price is coming to terms with unexpected or unwanted disasters, or transcendently attractive visions and opportunities. Other times the price requires ordering life's choices in ways that are pricey or painful. Obviously, degrees of both exist. The point is that the nature of ultimacy is seen to order priorities and make demands on human belief and behavior. More than at the mild end of the concern continuum, in the middle the ultimate takes on normative characters for human life. Middle symbols of the ultimate need to have such form as to order priorities normatively, whereas at the mild end of the continuum one behaves a certain way merely because that is the way the group inherited its identity in a founding sense. Toward the middle of the continuum, the normative question arises as to what should be sacrificed in order to live according to the ultimate priorities. Should you say grace when meals are rushed and busy? Why should you struggle to conform to the Dao when relaxation is so much easier or strenuous struggle seems not to promise success? Should you wear the distinct clothing of your religious group when living as a minority in a larger population hostile to your group and its badges? What should you sacrifice in order to live in harmony with your environment? What images of a God should you give up in the face of unwarranted suffering and other theodicy issues?

The issue here is that symbols of ultimacy need to have such form as to dictate or elicit ordering of priorities. One of the most common devices is to employ anthropomorphic symbols that simply tell you what the priorities are. Revelatory law codes and divine dictates give clear priorities. So do revelatory visions of deities who prescribe priorities of action and belief. Monotheistic sacred canopies are less ambiguous than those where competing gods vie for priorities. All the problems of the interpretation and authentication of revelations arise here. Anthropomorphic "divine word" symbols of priority are not the only kind, however. Some traditions have normative grades of enlightenment, for instance, such as the two-truths doctrine in Buddhism. Others have normative grades of harmony, as in Chinese religions. All these are conceptions of ultimate matters that focus concerns with prioritizing beliefs and actions. Obviously, much of human concern is *projected* onto symbols of ultimacy in this middle phase because urgencies of human decision exist that depend on how the ultimate is conceived. Here the conceptions of ultimacy relative to possibilities for human freedom, the groundedness of human life in ultimate matters, the human place relative to cosmic existential location, and value as defining human identity, are in great demand.

The more demanding the priorities derived from ultimacy, however, the more important it is that ultimacy be seen for what it is. When a price is to be exacted, one wants to know whether the demand is real. As concerns become more and more nearly ultimate, the pressures on symbols of the ultimate have to do with not being mistaken. Skepticism and doubt need to be internalized to the process of defining the ultimate, as Tillich and countless others before him argued.

The projection of human need onto ultimate symbols, in a strange reversal, itself becomes a problem, as does the danger of idolatry. Understanding the distinctions between the infinite and finite sides of the finite/infinite contrasts is problematized and internalized to the process of theologically conceiving the sacred canopy. This constitutes a tremendous pressure toward the transcendent pole of the transcendence/intimacy continuum.

The topic here is the *conception* of symbols of ultimacy within a sacred canopy. An intensification of concern to ultimate levels need not have as much to do with reconceiving the ultimate as it does with being in accord with what deserves to be the object of ultimate concern. Most great religious traditions are hospitable to strains of bhakti devotion, the pursuit of which can involve exhaustingly demanding practices of ultimate concern but often directed at conceptions of the ultimate that are extremely anthropomorphic or given to the intimacies of folk religion. One thinks of Sufis, Pure Land Buddhists, Shaivite renouncers, and evangelical Christians. Extreme ultimate concerns can take as objects symbols of the ultimate that would not stand intellectual scrutiny as having ultimate, world-founding dimensions. The Buddhist Pure Land, like the heavens in so many traditions, is much like this land except without suffering and with infinite joy; what are the founding elements of *that* land, we might ask? Whence its existence, its possibilities, its make-up, its existential locales, its value? The failure to answer those questions does not lessen the existential function of those symbols as objects of extremely passionate, life-defining, ultimate concern.

The issue for systematic philosophical theology, however, is the theological one. What does the continuum of concern, from mild through prioritizing to ultimately demanding of truth about ultimate matters, have to say about how the ultimate is truly to be conceived theologically? The answer is that truly ultimate concern requires conceptions of the ultimate to be the result of dialectic that itself attempts to get beyond all further conditions. To employ Anselm's phrase, the ultimate is "that than which nothing greater can be conceived."

The term *dialectic* has a checkered history in Western philosophy. For Aristotle, it was the name of a bad argument because it lacks true premises but attempts to draw true conclusions. For Hegel, it was the name of the structured unfolding of conceptions of reality from the simplest to the most comprehensive; he correctly understood that the complex cannot be explained in terms of the more complex because the complex is precisely what needs to be explained. For Plato, however, the founder of systematic Western philosophy, dialectic was the intellectual process of examining the presuppositions of theories to find that which conditions all structures of reality and thought without itself being conditioned by something further. Surprisingly, he called this ultimate condition the "Form of the Good," thus making aesthetic judgment basic to rational recognition. Plato's sense of dialectic is the one used here, the inquiry into what conditions or explains without itself being conditioned or in need of explanation.

The shape of the dialectic defining ultimate reality, demanded by the most stringent ultimate concerns, is complicated but not all that obscure. First of all, it needs to find or develop conceptions of the world and examine the presuppositions of those conceptions. In contemporary terms, this is philosophical cosmology, although there have been versions of this in religious traditions since ancient times, indeed, since the Axial Age which is defined in part by its development of such conceptions.

Second, dialectic needs to find, develop, and examine the presuppositions of theories that articulate and explain how the world is known. This has two broad avenues. The first is the examination of how knowing functions in societies, which we now associate with the social sciences; Berger's theory of the social construction of reality is a contemporary example. The second is epistemology in a more philosophical sense that investigates the logical grounds of knowledge. These two avenues are now being connected by cross streets of evolutionary biology and cognitive science. Dialectic is not the pursuit of these approaches per se but rather the examination of their presuppositions, including their historical locatedness and their dependence on higher-order conditions, such as intelligibility and determinateness.

With philosophical cosmology as well as social and philosophical epistemology in hand, dialectic is in a position to articulate conceptions of the ultimate that aim to be true for themselves and not merely true as in answer to the projection of human needs and priorities. These conceptions would be historically conditioned, but the dialectic would know and control for that. The conceptions would be relative to the best knowledge of the day, and would reflect the limitations of the cultures involved, including that of the dialectical theologian, and the dialectic would know and control for that. Most important, the dialectic would understand just how the conceptions of the ultimate are finite/infinite contrasts, articulating the absence or emptiness of what would exist if the finite/infinite contrast did not obtain. In the case of finite/infinite contrasts articulating the radical contingency of the cosmos as such, the dialectical conception would include the abyss of non-being.

Dialectic moves as a heuristic process through the conceptions of world and knowing that are at hand and in their terms. Dialectic as constructive explication of ultimacy, however, also develops metaphysical language to articulate its findings. Metaphysical language attempts to be general with respect to all contexts so that it does not become metaphorical when moved across contextual limits or into new contexts (I, 2, iv). Any given metaphysical system, of course, is contextually limited. But the very meaning of dialectic in metaphysics is that, when the contextual limits are recognized, the metaphysics must be amended to become general with respect to what stands outside the original. As Hegel pointed out, to say a metaphysical system is inadequate is already to be standing outside the context in which it had seemed adequate. The only hope for dialectic in metaphysics is to keep it vulnerable to correction at all points. Thus, no metaphysics can ever be known to be final.

The importance of this metaphysical hope in the efficacy of vulnerability is that it answers to the most ultimate concern to discover what is truly ultimate. All this is to say that systematic philosophical theology finds its justification in the attempt to articulate what the ultimate truly is in response to the ultimate human concern to relate to what is really ultimate.

III. ULTIMATE CONCERN AS A FUNCTION OF TRUE ULTIMACY

Reversing perspectives, we can now ask how ultimate concern itself, the ultimate anthropological quest, is affected by what is really ultimate, to the extent the latter can be known and symbolized. The answer is that the ultimate concern is progressively decentered from the needs of the person, or persons in community, in order to come into conformity with or appropriate responsiveness to the ultimate and its various dimensions in life. Three important variables are at stake here: the understanding of the self or person, the understanding of the ultimate or assorted ultimates and their dimensions in mundane life, and the process of decentering.

Conceptions of self or personhood vary tremendously among religious and cultural traditions. So, the abandonment of self in favor of the quest for conformity to ultimate conditions means many different things. In major traditions with rich enough histories to respond to the rounded demands of reality, however, the abandonment of self follows upon at least two senses of self that underlie and remain within the project of the abandoned self. Perhaps Buddhism has the most direct approach to this. In nearly all of its branches, going back to the original Deer Park sermon of the Buddha, the ordinary character of the self is presumed to be involved with the typical projects of life as defined by the culture's worldview, complete with duties appropriate to one's station. Living well, even as a faithful Buddhist, is a mild and often unnoticed concern in Buddhist cultures. Life is filled with suffering, however, and for some people the surmounting of suffering becomes a life project, re-ordering ordinary priorities. At this point, the teachings of the Buddha concerning the Fourfold Noble Truths become serious orientation points in life and the Eightfold Noble Path sets priorities for restructuring the self and its activities. Now, Buddhism deals directly with the conception of the abandonment of the self and its interests by saying that there is no real underlying substantial self. This is in explicit rejection of the Brahmanical notion that the self is so underlying and substantial that it is identical with Brahman and, as such, each person's self is one with each other's. The ultimate reality recognized in Buddhism, expressed in different ways in its various branches, is that nothing at all, let alone a self, has underlying substantial identity lasting through time. Personal conformation to this ultimate truth, this ultimate ontological reality, requires a discipline of ordered life, and serious meditation, and finally enlightenment, such that the "self," the conscious ego of the person, recognizes its own insubstantiality and simply lets the appearances of consciousness be what they are. Theravada schools emphasize the discipline of observation of the dharmas in consciousness so as to let go attachment to them. Yogacara Mahayana schools, such as Zen, emphasize the point that only transitory bits of consciousness are real. Madhyamaka Mahayana schools argue that even consciousness, in bits, has no substantial reality. When the "self" comes to terms with this, it gives up on itself, gives up on attaining enlightenment, gives up on surmounting suffering, and just admits to the reality of experience. This is perfected conformity to ultimate reality, which is insubstantial in any of a number of possible ways in Buddhist theory.

In Buddhist theory, the ordinary self and the self of the seeker of discipline and enlightenment live according to the first of the "two truths." The self is caught in the wheel of action, Samsara, which applies as much to the devoted seeker after enlightenment as it does to the ordinary person. Attainment of enlightenment and the realization of the insubstantiality of ultimate reality and of the self, and the practical conformity of the self to this, is the "second" or "higher truth." But what is left with the attainment of enlightenment, the higher truth? Nothing but the way of Samsara. So, many Mahayana traditions say that Nirvana (when the flame of the illusion of the self is blown out) is the same as Samsara, and that one has to go on to live ordinary life with all its vicissitudes. No more strenuous efforts at monastic life or meditation, just ordinary life, except that now the person realizes that ordinary life is only an array of mundane concerns with nothing ultimate about them. Nothing is ultimate for life, once the self has conformed to that reality, and one should pass on big deals.

Christian traditions generally do not go so far as to say that there is nothing lasting or substantial in the world or that there is no real individual self. But most Christian traditions do say that everything in the world is created by and thus subordinate to God the creator. To abandon itself, therefore, the self has to be humbled before God, sloughing off pride and anything else that would give self-interest any ultimate place. The power of this abandonment is in the capacity to love others for their own sakes as creatures of God. Many Christian disciplines are aimed at developing the capacity to love. The real tests for this are the capacities to love enemies and God. These are not so different, enemies and God, because, if God is viewed as an agent within the world whom we might love, it is clear that God creates for us a life of suffering as well as joy, and in the end kills us all. Jesus' identification of loving neighbor and loving God means that abandonment of the self to God includes abandoning oneself in the loving of God, who is not easy to love. Of course, what loving God means depends not only on the loving but also on the nature of the God loved.

Other models of the self are to be found in the great religious traditions, many occurring in more than one, and sometimes many competing within a putatively single tradition. As mentioned, Brahmanical Hinduism affirms the identity of the individual self with Atman, which in turn is identical with Brahman. Abandoning the self to the truth of Brahman thus means finding the true self, or the self without delusions of individuality, especially agency or action, although many variations exist within these traditions concerning dualistic and non-dualistic senses of identity. The dualistic strains tend to liken identity to that between lover and beloved, as in the dominant strain of Christianity. Daoist conceptions of the self view abandonment as the coordination of the person's harmonic structures with the overall harmony of the Dao. Confucian conceptions of the self look on its abandonment to the structures of ultimacy as the perfection of the self's sincerity so that its ritual roles are perfectly individuated with both accurate sensitivity to the worth of those affected and competence to accomplish what is appropriate. Confucians are not likely to use metaphors of abandonment for the self's conformity to the ultimate—Heaven, Earth, and the Dao; Confucians would talk only about abandonment of selfishness and egoism.

Ultimate concerns are shaped not only by different conceptions of the self to be concerned but also by different conceptions of the ultimate with which it is concerned. The conceptions of the ultimate that have been manifested in religions are even more varied than conceptions of the self. For purposes of this place in the argument, however, a schema suffices to allow for discussion of how concepts of the ultimate shape transformations of ultimate concerns. The question is how the task of conforming or abandoning the self to what is best understood as truly ultimate is a function of what is understood as truly ultimate.

The schema derives from the structure of finite/infinite contrasts. The first division is between the finite and infinite elements in the contrast. Then each of them is divided into two. The finite side of the finite/infinite contrast is that character or trait of the world that is world defining, without which the world as grasped would be radically different. The basic contrast here concerns the radical contingency of the world: without some finite/infinite contrast regarding the contingency, the world would not exist, would not even be what it is, and this shall be our example (although to be complete we should illustrate contrasts regarding form, groundedness, existential location, and achieved value). Within the finite side exists a structural distinction between (a) conceptions of the ultimate to which the self is ultimately concerned to conform itself *proximate* to the context of the self and (b) those that articulate the *general or universal* finite component of the world. Within the infinite side exists a distinction between the infinite with reference to the finite in the contrast, and the infinite as truly infinite and therefore not determined by the contrast. In many if not most religions these distinctions are blurred and a single symbol, such as God or Emptiness, is used to cover all four positions. Nevertheless, those symbols function differently to determine ultimate concerns according to these distinctions. Hinduism has been friendlier than other religions, especially monotheisms, to allowing the coexistence of many symbols of ultimate ontological reality along the structures of finite/infinite contrasts. Hinduism often hosts the generous view that the ultimate manifests itself in any way that best meets the need for manifestation. In religious practice, the structures of the finite/infinite contrasts blend into a continuum with much overlap and ambiguous semantic slippage.

To illustrate the continuum, consider the dominant Hindu approach to radical contingency. On the finite side, this contingency often is expressed with symbols of a world-creating deity. Many such symbols exist within the varied Hindu traditions, including Isvara, Narayana, Shiva (Shakti), Brahma, and Vishnu. Different authors and sects nuance these in particular ways, and relate them together as objects of one's cult versus objects of others' cults. However these are articulated in a particular religious context, they are intended to be creators of the world as such. In distinction from these are their avatars that represent the ultimate creator in ways appropriate to some human context for the sake of the ultimate concern of abandonment to ultimate reality. For instance, Ganesh, the elephant-head god, is an avatar of Shiva with respect to a number of contexts in which people with ultimate concern concretely need to conform themselves to ultimacy, among which is the work of understanding or intellect; philosophical theologians do well to have a statue of Ganesh on their desk. A better-known (in the West) instance of an avatar is Krishna who is the avatar of Vishnu in the Bhagavad Gita. Krishna came as a charioteer to Arjuna, the greatest warrior of his faction, at a time when Arjuna was psychologically or spiritually undone by the ultimate (tragic) meaning of his fighting. Krishna counseled Arjuna with cognitive and practical practices so as to convince Arjuna of the need to play his role in the battle situation; this included Krishna's claim to be the reality in all the surrounding contextual elements. Then Krishna transfigured himself before Arjuna as Vishnu, the Creator with innumerable heads who is "brighter than a thousand suns." In context, Arjuna could abandon himself to Krishna and simply be the warrior carrying out his ultimate (in that context) identity as warrior. The transfiguration set the identity of Krishna in the larger universal context of Vishnu as creator. Of course, both Krishna and Vishnu could function in people's lives short of defining ultimate concerns, say, as answering particular needs. At the beginning of the Bhagavad Gita, Krishna functioned to prioritize Arjuna's actions, causing him to stand up and fight. But in the drama, that prioritizing function gave way to Arjuna abandoning himself to what is most real; then at the end of the Gita, Arjuna returned to the battle with the right priorities.

On the infinite side of the finite/infinite contrast, the Brahmanical lines of Hinduism (those descending from the religio-philosophic practice of the Brahmin or priestly Aryan caste) characterize the infinite as Brahman. Brahman is a symbol derived according to various routes from the purification of notions of consciousness. As the infinite reality behind the creator-of-the-world gods (Ishvara, Vishnu, etc.), Brahman has the qualities of being just that. As the infinite reality behind the creators, Brahman has the qualities of being nonpersonal, not relative to others or to the world, and so forth. That Brahman is called Saguna—Brahman with qualities (gunas). But the very meaning of being so transcendent is to be without qualities: Nirguna Brahman. Nirguna Brahman is absolutely indeterminate, a point that can be made only negatively by denying determinations. To the extent that the creator-gods are conceived to be persons, themselves with intentions and subject to the law of Karma, this transcending move rejects that consciousness-oriented model to one of absolute indeterminateness. The ultimate concern to abandon the self to Saguna Brahman is to "attain to" the creator without the creation. The ultimate concern to abandon the self to Nirguna Brahman is to attain to the nothingness of that, but as the object of ultimate concern dialectically moved through the finite/infinite contrast.

The symbols in Buddhism, for instance illustrating the continuum across the finite/infinite contrast for radical contingency, are different from the theistic genre of Hinduism, and also from the monotheistic symbols. There is the ultimate truth of the surprising suchness of one's personal experience, recognizing the emptiness or non-enduring reality of the elements of one's life; there is also the ultimate truth of the fact that this is just the way things are, the true cosmological character of the world in which elements (dharmas) just arise and cease. These illustrate the finite side of the contrast. On the infinite side, is the point that the suchness of the world depends on nothing, no ontological reality; it is just there, surprisingly. Beyond that is useless speculation, which is to be avoided by getting back to work in your context such as it is, as Arjuna goes back to battle. Of course there exist many different interpretations within Buddhist traditions of the nature of suchness, emptiness, and how dharmas arise and cease, especially as distinguishing the Theravada, Madhyamaka, and Yogacara traditions.

In most Christian traditions both Jesus Christ as the Second Person of the Trinity and the Holy Spirit as the Third function as contextually relevant avatars of God the Father-Creator. On the infinite side of the Christian ultimacy symbols for radical contingency are the conceptions of the Creator as transcending all distinctions, as in the Neo-Platonic One, Thomas' Pure Act of To Be, or creation-*ex nihilo* theologies. To some of these conceptions are attributed the qualities that receive finite determinate form within creation, so that it is possible to say, with Thomas for instance, that God is infinitely good, wise, and so on, because God is the creator of finite goods and wisdom. These conceptions attribute a nature to God even though it is not determinately finite. Other conceptions recognize that the truly infinite in itself cannot be defined by causal connections with the finite.

According to this schema of the finite/infinite contrasts, the movement from the contextualized ultimate to the infinite-beyond-connection-with-context ultimate is a move toward greater and greater apophatic mysticism (I, 15, 16; III, 15, 16).

The third element in the existential transformation of ultimate concerns by that which is the best understanding of the true ontological ultimate, is the process of transformation itself. This topic is the main subject of volumes two and three of *Philosophical Theology* and so barely is broached here. For the moment, the Bhagavad Gita again can be our guide to an illustrative typology. Transitions of ultimate concern conforming the self to ultimate reality are "yogas," of which there are three principal ones. First is the yoga of practice or action (karma yoga) according to which the self is conformed to ultimate reality. Often in religious traditions this is thematized as the spiritual discipline of the soldier. Second is the yoga of cognition or dialectic (jnana yoga) according to which the mind and spirit are conformed. This is the spiritual discipline of the sage. Third is the yoga of devotion (bhakti yoga) according to which the self, defined by concern itself, is conformed, the spiritual discipline of the saint. These illustrations are sufficient to make the point relevant to the argument here (III, 11).

IV. TENSIONS ALONG THE WORLDVIEW CONTINUA

No matter how complicated our discussion of ontological ultimacy and anthropological ultimate concern, it is still too simple. For instance, the discussions in the previous two sections have assumed that the concern in question is that of an individual. The senses in which individuals are defined by their social and natural relations have been reduced out. Even more, the senses in which communities or a few individuals in interdefining relations, such as nuclear families, have ultimate concerns have been neglected. The following two volumes of *Philosophical Theology* remedy this reductionism to some degree.

At this point, however, it is possible to call attention to another kind of oversimplification in this chapter for which we need to control. The discussion has not made explicit the variations along the continua of the worldviews within which people live with concerns for ultimate matters (I, 4).

Relative to the sacred/mundane continuum, the discussion has spoken as if the concern is oriented primarily to the ultimate as expressed directly within the sacred canopy. This is not problematic when speaking of the ultimate as appearing in meditation or worship as an object of concern. But the ultimate is also present in all sorts of mundane matters in worldviews, and the crises that are likely to move a person from mild to prioritizing, and thence to the most serious ultimate concerns, usually arise in mundane circumstances, such as the death of a loved one or a sudden emergency to go to war. Arjuna's crisis was of the latter sort. Therefore, the symbols of the ultimate, especially in their proximate contexts, are those appropriate for their mundane embodiment: Krishna was the driver of Arjuna's war chariot. To understand the particularities of actual religious contexts or texts dealing with ultimacy in ultimate concerns, it is necessary to see how the ultimate is expressed as ultimate dimensions of mundane things.

Relative to the concern continuum, the temptation arises to correlate this to the transcendence/intimacy continuum within finite/infinite contrasts; to some extent this is valid. Within Buddhism, Confucianism, and Daoism, however, little anthropomorphism arises except in the proximate contexts of ultimacy. The reasons for the spread within the transcendence/intimacy continuum are due to other factors. Yet all the symbols of ultimacy, the self, and the character of transformation need to be understood according to their places on that continuum.

Similarly with respect to the sophistication/popular culture continuum. No matter where one is on the concern continuum, from mild to ultimate, popular culture as well as sophisticated culture and mixtures of the two can express the self, ultimate realities, and the nature of disciplined transitions in order better to conform to, or to abandon oneself to the reality of, ultimacy. This is not to say that all points on this continuum are equally good or helpful. One would hope that the sophisticated forms are better, although their employment in communal practice is always likely to have limitations.

With these qualifications in mind, the argument can now turn directly to the pressures in reality that push toward transcendent symbols of ultimacy, and then to those that push toward more intimate symbols.

CHAPTER SIX

Toward Transcendent Symbols of Ultimacy

The purpose of this chapter is to explore what exists in the nature of things that puts pressure on symbols of ultimacy to take form and interpretation toward the transcendent end of the intimacy/transcendence continuum (I, 4, ii). The range of symbols prevalent in religions is indeed along a continuum. To say what a "totally transcendent" symbol would be is extremely difficult. Brahman without qualities is a good candidate although it is defined through denial of qualities; the symbol of "the Dao that cannot be named" is in a similar situation. If total transcendence means complete indetermination with regard to any connections with other things, that still is a characterization in terms of the denial of whatever is meant by determinateness. The point of the present chapter, however, is not to define total transcendence, which is the point of the entirety of Part III, but to identify factors that put pressure on given symbols within the continuum to be "more transcendent" in some sense.

I. SCALE

The first factor to consider is scale. A symbol of ultimate reality is insufficiently transcendent if the aspect of the world it founds is larger in scale than the symbol is able to found. A major distinction to consider here is between pre-Axial Age and Axial Age religions.[1] In pre-Axial age religions the world is conceived as centered in the tribe or in-group, with its living geography, its ethnic identity, and the natural forces and personal spirits appropriate to its territory and ancestral history. The "world" includes the neighboring territory of aliens, the specific out-groups that bound the in-group, and the gods and spirits of those other peoples and places. The geographical, tribal, and spiritual boundaries beyond those specific "others" are left vague. The issues of transcendence have to do with questions such as whether the gods founding one's own people also founded the others, whether the gods who rule the tribe's hunting grounds also rule those of the other tribes, whether there are intertribal interactions of ancestors. A highly sophisticated form of pre-Axial Age religion is found in parts of the Hebrew Bible where, for instance, God insists that the Israelites take themselves to be his people and forswear the gods of their neighbors. Yahweh is shown to be more powerful than the Egyptian gods in Moses' contests with pharaoh.[2] The problem for the Israelites in Canaan was not just that they did not perform the rituals of Yahweh correctly but that they also worshiped other competing gods.

Axial Age religions arose as conceptions of the world as a whole developed, although there were many such conceptions (*III, 2*). This coincided with the development of large empires in China, India, and the Near East. However the empires differed in culture and organizational form, all of them forced different tribes to live under a roughly common rule. Tribal languages were supplemented with imperial languages. The old virtue of military aggression against one's neighbors became a vice in the view of the imperial government that needed peace and cooperation. Tribal attachment to territory was disrupted as peoples were dislocated, moved, or even dispersed. Imperial armies marched on other empires, vastly enlarging people's sense of world geography.

In Axial Age religions, conceptions arose of the totality of the world. Conceptions of how to understand that total world's radical contingency led to symbols of monotheistic gods, or of hierarchies of principles, or of cooperations of ultimate beings or principles to account for the world. Possibilities were not limited to the habitual expectations of the tribe but were expanded to possibilities for human nature as such, however that was conceived. The conditions out of which human individuals and societies arise and by which they are sustained were conceived to be common and integrative. The existential locations of peoples and places were conceived to be unified, even if the different positions were thought to be oddly distinguished by our standards, for instance in the ancient Hellenistic conception of the cosmos as a stack of heavens and hells above and beneath the plane of the Earth, all of which are part of nature. Conceptions of value, beauty, and truth were thought to be transcendental to all cultures and built into the nature of things.

The scale of the symbols of ultimacy was shaped by the scale conceived of those aspects of the world they were taken to found, including the symbols for the contingency of the entire cosmos. At some periods, the cosmos in China was conceived to be eternal, always in existence however much that existence had to be sustained by grounding forces. At some periods, the cosmos in India was conceived in terms of an expansion from a cosmic golden egg through eons of time toward the end of which it contracted back to the egg, to begin another cycle, on and on. At some periods, in West Asian cultures, the cosmos was thought to be started in time with an anticipated ending point. Versions of the alternatives were to be found in nearly every culture, however.

In our own time, science has altered our sense of the scale of the cosmos drastically. The cosmos is far older and more extensive than anything conceived in the ancient world when the Axial Age religions developed their rhetoric, save in the religions of South Asia. Furthermore, the same basic causal properties that govern the human sphere on Earth apply in the most distant reaches of the cosmos, save perhaps in proximity to the Big Bang; or, more dangerously said, the causal properties of the cosmos of expanding gasses also apply to the human sphere. Given the scale of things, it is implausible to think of the human sphere as the center of the cosmos. The human story cannot be the purpose of the cosmos, as suggested by Genesis 1–2, because most of the cosmos is incommensurable to human narrative (I, 8).

The result of this is that the controlling images for ultimacy with regard to the existence of the world, its possibilities, its components, its existential places, and its values have to be scaled far beyond the limits of the human scale of things. If God as creator, for instance, or the Dao is conceived to be particularly oriented to some human situation or event, that conception will have to be understood to be "merely metaphorical" relative to a more literal symbology. Occasions might indeed arise when anthropomorphic symbols are appropriate, because of human needs for orientation. But these symbols are to be trusted only to the extent they are seen to be metaphorical diminutions of the scale of the more nearly literal symbols that cannot be anthropomorphic. Symbols of a god, for instance, depicted as a warrior fighting for his people, or as a king ruling over a kingdom, simply are too small to apply to the creator of a 13.6 billion-year-old cosmos within which human beings are on the edge of a small galaxy. The Dao of mountains and streams is too small for a world in which galaxies collide. In a fairly strict sense, the use of small metaphors for ultimate conditions that are vast needs to be controlled by the transcendent qualities of the vast scale.

The perennial issue forcing this pressure of transcendence is the theodicy problem within those traditions that have some other motive for thinking of the ultimate as a personal god or gods, a person with intentions for goodness and a capacity to interact with things in the world as a special finite agent. Popular theisms in South Asian religions as well as West Asian religions— Paganism, Zoroastrianism, Judaism, Christianity, and Islam—often take images of personal theism as dominant. In the face of undeserved suffering and evil, these images are challenged. Why would God, construed as an infinitely effective moral agent, allow this? None of the solutions is satisfactory. The karmic religions by contrast might say that people who in fact suffer must somehow deserve to suffer. But great disasters, natural as tsunamis or social as the Nazi holocaust, usually make this implausible: Job argued that case successfully. God might be said to be finite and therefore unable to thwart suffering and evil, as claimed in Christian process theology. But then God is not the boundary condition for the world—something else must be more ultimate. The universal lesson from theodicy is that the symbols of God as a supervenient person can at best be metaphors and we know that they do not apply to God as the ultimate condition of the world.

The more general lesson from considerations of scale in our time is chilling. If the primary data for the character of the ultimate principle, for instance, God, the Dao, Brahman, or Ein Sof, is what comes from being the source of the particular world that we have, this world shows little that would indicate an intentional creator. All determinate reality arises with the Big Bang. Therefore, the creator could not have determinate imagined options prior to creation, nor be capable of thinking about a world as a potential object apart from divine subjectivity. The image of creation as a selection among options cannot be sustained when all options are consequent to creation.

The negative of this point is telling in the context of evolution. Suppose that we say, as many do, that God creates the world through the mechanisms of evolution. In some sense, this must be correct. But if we go on to say, as much popular religion does, that the creator is a personal, intentional agent, intervening to affect outcomes within the world, then the vast waste of species, the costliness of evolution in terms of genetic failure, the nature red in tooth and claw, means that the creator is a moral monster, intending untold suffering, waste, and meaninglessness. If God is intentional, the created world of cosmic collisions and dissolution, of species that arise only to die off when their niche becomes untenable, entails that God is just some hideous strength.

The vastness we now recognize in the cosmos means that we cannot interpret suffering and evil as affairs to be justified according to human deserts. It means that we interpret the ultimate components of existence, possibilities, conditions, existential location, and value to be of a scale for which the human scale of justice and compassion is trivialized. Personalized conceptions of deity and of the forces of natural processes, as in the Dao, are pushed toward more transcendent notions. Of course, religious traditions abound with these more transcendent symbols. The God of the Hebrew Bible is more awesome than nice and, according to Jesus, sends the rain and sun on both the just and unjust indifferently. Shiva is both the creator and destroyer. According to the Daodejing, Heaven is not humane but treats people like straw dogs, sacrificial objects to be discarded in the fire after the ceremony. Part III reviews some arguments that give specificity to this push toward transcendence according to scale.

II. IDOLATRY

The second consideration that presses toward more transcendent concepts is idolatry. Idolatry is the construal of a less-than-ultimate symbol as ultimate. This is not quite the same as metaphorical symbolization of the ultimate when a more nearly literal symbol is available. The Israelite psalmist was not idolatrous when he said, "God is the rock of my salvation." Everyone recognizes this as a metaphor. The psalmist instead might have said that "God is the source of all being and the power of renewal in all that is threatened." But that psalmist would never have found a publisher: The metaphor carries far more important and accurate information.

Throughout the Hebrew Bible and the Christian New Testament, however, God is often referred to as a king and the world is likened to a kingdom. In an obvious sense this is a metaphorical network. But in a not-so-obvious sense it is often taken as nonmetaphorical. For many people it has been and still is a kind of "final" language, which means ultimate language. Associated with it are political symbols of relationships, as when people construe themselves to be vassals of God, and call God "Lord." In this symbolic network, relationships are defined primarily in political terms of obedience, authority, reward and punishment, the administration of justice, and the practice of clemency; human affairs are reduced to interhuman relations, with God the king playing a kind of human social role. Relations with nature, and nature's interrelations among its various parts, are suppressed. God's creation of the cosmos is misconstrued as the giving of order like a king giving laws and its vastness is obscured. The previous section details the difficulties with this misconstruction in light of our contemporary science.

The biblical theme of kingship/kingdom was in tension with more transcendent conceptions, recognized to be truer to nature even in ancient times. This theme is not limited to the Abrahamic traditions that take the Bible as revelatory. It occurs also in Indian thought influenced by the great epics, the Mahabharata and the Ramayana. Strangely enough that image is prominent in medieval Daoist imagery of heaven's bureaucracy as well. In all these cases the king/kingdom symbolic network for articulating the connection between God and the world has at times functioned as if it were ultimate. Although recognizably metaphorical, it did not always or easily point beyond itself or suggest its own limitations.

Idolatry is not merely the cognitive error of mistaking a less-than-ultimate symbol for an ultimate one. Rather, it is the placing of ultimate commitment on the less-than-ultimate symbols. The most flagrant examples of this are when people construe their political agenda as being divinely sanctioned, which has happened so often in nearly all religious cultures (save the Buddhist and Confucian). The phenomenon is easily understandable. If the ultimate symbols within a sacred canopy say that God is king of the universe and those symbols are connected within a worldview to the mundane affairs of the nation's politics, particularly its wars, the step is small to saying that God is on the side of one's nation and against its foes. This was explicit in most of the references to God as king in the Hebrew Bible. God was the special God of the Israelites and fought with and for them against their foes and their foes' gods. As the ideas of monotheism clarified and strengthened, Jesus in the New Testament could speak of God as king of the whole world, contrasting the competing kingdoms of "this world" with the true and universal kingdom of God. As Jesus urged in many parables, appropriate occasions exist for thinking of oneself as being in the kingdom of God, especially those occasions where one needs to wake up from delusions of petty selfish secular involvements. Nevertheless, this line of thinking becomes idolatrous when it evokes ultimate concern and commitment so as to obscure the greater and deeper truth of God as creator of the whole cosmos, including the non-human natural parts.

Recognition of idolatry has been a persistent theme in the religions of West Asia. One can read the historical layering of concepts of God in the Hebrew Bible as a succession of critiques of idolatry. Close to the earliest layer is the borrowing from the earlier Babylonian myth of Marduk (for instance as reported in the Enuma Elish), who was one god among many, most of whom were children or grandchildren of Tiamat the sea-god of the salt-sea and Apsu, god of the freshwaters. The chaos of mingled salt and fresh water gave rise to a disruptive bevy of gods who annoyed Apsu so much he tried to kill them. Ea, however, killed Apsu. Tiamat made war on the party of the regicide gods and was winning until Ea's son, Marduk, defeated her. Marduk's siblings agreed that he could have first place among them if he would kill their mother, Tiamat. He did so by creating a mighty wind that blew open her jaws so that he could slice her in half. The upper part of her body became the heavens, whence fresh water, and the lower half the earth with its salty seas. Chaos, symbolized by the mixing of the waters in flood, a real concern for people of Mesopotamia, always threatens to undo the Marduk-made order and Marduk had a permanent job as the container of chaos. Similarly, Yahweh in the earliest representations is depicted as defeating the sea-monster of chaos, Rahab, although Yahweh is never given a genealogy of descent from other gods—there is no Hebrew theogony.[3] Provoked beyond measure by people in the time of Noah, Yahweh opened the heavens to mix fresh and salt water so that there was a return to almost total chaos with its massive slaughter of nearly all living things.

Yahweh retained the symbolic identity as chief warrior among the gods, especially as He (yes, He) helped His people Israel prevail against its foes. He used the supernatural power of His mighty wind and destructive waters to destroy the Egyptians at the battle of the Sea of Reeds and Sisera's mercenary army of nine hundred chariots of iron at the battle of Keshon Wadi. Although they contain older interpolations, the books of Joshua and Judges witness Yahweh gradually withdrawing from the warrior role, leaving the fighting to the Israelites, and assuming the kingly role, ruling through the judges as surrogates. By the end of the book of Judges, however, that arrangement proved unworkable. The final story there is of the Levite whose concubine was raped to death by the men of a town in the territory of Benjamin. The Levite cut her body into eleven parts and sent one to each of the other tribes of Israel, requesting vengeance on the tribe of Benjamin. With Yahweh's blessing the other tribes assaulted Benjamin, killed all the women and children, and surrounded the last of the Benjaminite warriors on a fortified hill, about to attack and destroy them. Someone suddenly realized that it would be wrong to obliterate one of the twelve tribes of Israel and, against Yahweh's directions, sued for peace. In order to get wives for the remaining Benjaminite soldiers they arranged for two mass rapes. Throughout this sordid story the phrase,

"There was no king in Israel, and every man did what he wanted," occurs twenty one times. By the eighth chapter of 1 Samuel, which immediately follows Judges, a real human kingship is established in Israel, first under Saul and then David.

The line of transcendence thus moved from Yahweh as cosmic battler of chaos, among other gods, to warrior battling Israel's foes and their gods, albeit with wind and water, to king establishing a political economy, to overseer of a human kingdom in which the human king mirrors on Earth the divine kingship in the Heavens. In all this save the first Yahweh was still understood to be one god among many. The divine kingly lawgiver on Sinai (or Horeb) commanded the Israelites to have no other gods before Him, which assumes that there are other gods. The Sinai covenant established a special cult for the chosen people of Yahweh, distinguished from alternative cults for other gods. The push toward monotheism came from the series of disasters that befell Israel from the eighth through the sixth centuries BCE, first from the Assyrians and then from the Neo-Babylonians. Could Yahweh be too weak to defend His people against the invaders? No, Yahweh was reconceived to be the God of all nations, who must be using the others to chastise Israel; Yahweh was the creator of the entire cosmos. The Exile in Babylon and Persia acquainted the Jewish intellectuals with the Axial Age conceptions that were reflected in the late prophetic writings such as 2 Isaiah. The New Testament authors and the Qur'an assumed that Yahweh was the High God who creates and rules the entire cosmos.

Although the progression in Israelite history was not as neat as represented here, and the older symbols were retained alongside the newer ones, the progression of anti-idolatry is illustrated. When faced with a liberation struggle, it is idolatrous to symbolize Yahweh as merely keeping the forces of natural chaos at bay. Yahweh must take sides as the divine warrior. Yet when faced with the issues of establishing a political economy, the warrior is not sufficient. A kingly lawgiver is required. When faced with the real management of a kingdom, however, management by priestly surrogates does not work and the divine sanctioning of an effective human king is required. When political fortunes fail utterly, Yahweh cannot be conceived as a divine Loser, and so is radically reconceived as the Axial Age High God. Giving ultimate loyalty to anything less is idolatrous. The conception of God as creator in Genesis 1–2, which is from the Exilic period, is of a wholly transcendent order of primeval waters.

III. EXPLANATION: METAPHYSICS

By the time of the Axial Age, philosophy was forming in all the Axial Age cultures: Confucianism and Daoism in East Asia; Buddhism, Jainism, and Hinduism in South Asia; and Zoroastrianism, Greek philosophy, and monotheism in West Asia. In all these philosophic movements, older traditions were objectified, interpreted anew, and sometimes rejected. In all the movements arose conflicts of interpretation and theory, with arguments back and forth and the establishment of competing schools. In all the movements, philosophy became an elite activity, requiring special knowledge and a capacity to communicate with peers, whether or not the philosophers were also priests. Although the styles of writing, thinking, and arguing differed among the movements, and within the movements, these general traits obtained.

Among the works of the philosophers was the creation of conceptions of the world as a whole, however different these might be from one another. The pre-Socratics said everything is water, or air, or the indefinite: who thought about "everything" before them? In East Asia "all under heaven" was conceived to be pulsing energy of yin-yang vibrations with a variation from rough (physical) to subtle (mental and spiritual) forms, with microcosmic and macrocosmic mirroring of kinds of changes. In South Asia, consciousness and its potential contents, or emptying of contents, came to define the character of worldliness. Human beings came to be thought of in terms of their humanity, not merely or most comprehensively in terms of their kinship identities. Humanity was variously understood in terms of the relations of people to the universal characters of the cosmos.

Within their developments, the philosophic movements came to ask "why questions," requiring explanations. They variously gave rise to wildly differing answers to the why questions, with different models of causation and conditioning. But in all the philosophic movements existed a drive to order explanations, saying what explained what. Moreover, they all searched for ultimate explanations that explained other things but that themselves did not need explanation. The drive toward the explanations that do not themselves need explanation exerts tremendous pressure on symbols of ultimacy to become more and more transcendent.

Can we ask what form explanations toward the ultimate end of the spectrum might take? In one sense we cannot, given the great diversity of philosophical languages among and within the world's great intellectual cultures. In another sense, we can note that all of them strive for languages that are not relative to specific context. One way of characterizing metaphysics is to say that it is the attempt to understand things in terms that do not have to be changed when moving from one context to the next. Most of the time, our language gains richness, nuance, and resonance precisely because of its contextual embeddedness. To become a competent "speaker" requires intense immersion in a context to learn the idiosyncrasies of its metaphoric plays. But then that contextually embedded language cannot be taken out of its context without losing control of its metaphoric reaches. The Dao that can be named in any context is not the true Dao in which all contexts rest. The language of the aristocracy distorts the reality of the poor. Most religious studies scholars are embarrassed by the history of that discipline that has, in its early forms, imposed the terms for understanding religion that come from

Christianity, with a little awareness of Judaism and Islam, on the rest of the world's cultures. So, from the earliest days of philosophy the great traditions have attempted to develop language they believed was abstract enough to be applicable and true across diverse context. Of course, their languages all had histories and reflected their cultures. In comparative perspective we can see how truly nonabstract they are. East Asians developed naturalistic emergence metaphors such as Heaven, Earth, and Dao into technical, literal terms about which they could argue univocally. South Asians developed metaphors from consciousness into equally technical terms. West Asian thinking most often used the language of causation to indicate the relation of the ultimate to the more proximate conditions, although there have been many senses of ontological causation. Causation in Buddhist thought, by contrast, is exclusively limited to proximate relations and denied ontological standing.

The lesson to be drawn from this is that the comparative perspective is essential for the development of a properly abstract metaphysical language that might be true across all contexts. Although it is impossible for language not to have a history, it can be developed with special pains to control for that history. Metaphysical categories need to be developed as comparative categories, in the senses explained earlier. They need to be fair to register without distortion the issues and phenomena that arise within and among any contexts, and they need to be under constant correction as they are employed across new contexts. Contemporary metaphysics requires a comparative context as its paideia and public, unpopular as that might be within noncomparative academic philosophical conventions.

The metaphysics that will be developed in Part III here uses causal language that arose within Western philosophical and religious thinking. But it does so in ways explicitly enriched by other metaphors for ontological conditioning in ultimate and proximate ways.

With the discussion of the explanations of conditions (ultimate and proximate) seeking abstract universality with regard to context, the pressures for ever more transcendent, now meaning "abstract," conceptions are apparent. The extraordinary successes of modern science have come in part from its ability to universalize across all contexts with the language of mathematics. Yet mathematics is not properly abstract for metaphysics. It is reductionistic and cannot register most kinds of value, only those in the aesthetic components of mathematical expressions themselves. Mathematical science explicitly distorts any context containing valuable things whose value it cannot register. As such, its application across most contexts of human engagement of the world, and most likely across any natural contexts that embody value, is that of a very bad metaphor, bad in the sense that it is out of control. It leads to disastrous practical conclusions, such as treating nature, sometimes including human beings, as value-neutral and therefore ready to be used in any way that those with the power want. The cultural downside of modern mathematical science has been to teach four centuries of Western and now global culture that the only value things have is that which is instrumental to human will.

Metaphysical abstraction, by contrast with reductionistic abstraction, is such that all things whatsoever must be able to be specified within its categories without distortion. So, metaphysical categories must be able to account for the value of the beautiful rose, the civilized arts, and the dignity of the human person, none of which register in mathematical biophysics. Whereas reductionistic abstraction makes progress by leaving out as much as possible, identifying regularities exclusively within the parameters of its theories, procedures, structures, and instruments, metaphysical abstraction is faulty to the extent that it is not adequate to everything.

A final point needs to be made about the power of explanation of ultimate matters to press symbols of ultimacy toward transcendence. For some people, the explanation of a thing must be as complex as the thing explained. Those defending teleological arguments for the reality of God in European philosophy, for instance, have argued that, because the world has a complex organization in which some parts are designed to fit into other parts, therefore there must be a divine designer: If the world is like a watch, there must be a watchmaker. Contemporary defenders of intelligent design make variations on this argument, substituting biological complexities for watches.

But complexity itself, order, is the very thing that needs explanation. Chaos or sheer indeterminate componentlessness does not need an explanation. It has nothing to explain. The complex must be explained by the simple. Conditions with characters need to be explained by conditions that have no character, which if they did in turn would need explanation. The conclusion sought by the teleological argument for an intelligent God multiplies the problems rather than solves them. How does one explain the complex intelligent, intentional, agential God? If it does not need explanation, then why does the complex world need explanation? If the intelligent complex God does need explanation, then it is not really the ultimate condition.

This point has been recognized in the major traditions since ancient times. Earlier in this chapter, the dialectical connections were traced in South Asian religions between very complex and humanly real avatars to Brahman with, and then without, qualities. The metaphors in this metaphysics are not those of ultimate conditions causing more proximate ones. But they do express an order of understanding. That which has qualities is to be understood as a manifestation of that which is more real and does not. Mention has also been made of the Western metaphysical traditions of Neo-Platonism and Thomism according to which the ultimate principle must be simple and beyond any distinctions. For Plato, the Form of the Good is the ultimate cause of everything knowable and all powers of knowing, but itself has no determinate form. In Chinese philosophy the early abstractions of Heaven, Earth, and Dao were further abstracted in Neo-Confucianism in the cosmogony of Zhou Dunyi: non-being gives rise to the Great Ultimate which gives rise to extension

(Yang) which reaches its limit and returns to its matrix (Yin); yang and yin together distinguish differences in vibration that give rise to the five elements, time, space, and change, that in turn give rise to "the ten thousand things." Only non-being does not need explanation. The simpler the symbol of the ultimate condition, the more likely it is to be really ultimate, the condition that is unconditioned.

IV. EXPERIENCE

The final consideration to be noted here, concerning the pressure to make symbols of the ultimate more transcendent, arises from experience. As noted already, symbols of the ultimate are not only for the purpose of conceiving of ultimate reality and its cognates, although that is the purpose when we are concerned with explanation. Most generally, symbols are for the purpose of engagement of what they symbolize. Symbols of the ultimate are set, as we have seen, in the context of sacred canopies. Sacred canopies themselves are dynamic, constantly changing as personal, social, and natural pressures call for their amendment. So, when symbols of ultimacy are employed to engage ultimate realities, the whole dynamic and somewhat inconsistent sacred canopy is part of the sign in the interpretive engagement insofar as the canopy gives meaning to the symbols. This is part of the meaning of interpretive engagement as *intensive* rather than merely *extensive* in its reference, as chapter 3 discussed.

Rarely is engagement with ultimate reality focused exclusively on the symbols as contained in a sacred canopy alone. Perhaps that happens in practiced meditation and certain kinds of worship. Rather, ultimate realities are engaged most often in terms of how they bear on the vast array of issues of life that themselves are mundane, proximate, not ultimate. These bearings are articulated in worldviews. "Ultimate matters," "ultimate issues," "ultimate dimensions" all refer to mundane things on which ultimate elements in the sacred canopy bear in ways expressed in the worldview at hand. So it is both possible and common to engage ultimate realities through their bearing on crucial life decisions, on the significance of the birth of a child, or tragedy, sickness, death. Ultimacy can be engaged in great beauty, natural or cultivated, in overwhelming forces of nature, in knowledge and imagination of the intricacies or vastness of nature. Kant saw ultimacy, which he called the sublime, in the "starry skies above and the moral law within."[4] Not only sacred canopies but also entire worldviews are involved as the semiotic setting of symbols of ultimacy when we engage ultimate matters. Worldviews themselves are not fixed but are under constant shift. The shifts involve additions and subtractions, confusions and separations, melding and resorting of positions on the sacred/mundane, intimacy/transcendence, and sophisticated/folk culture continua of worldviews. They also involve shifts on the sharing, comprehensiveness, and intensity continua for individuals and communities.

So all in all, the understanding of the engagement of ultimate realities with symbols of ultimacy is extremely complicated. A proper analysis of any given experiential interpretive engagement would have to sort out how all these variables apply to the instance.

Nevertheless, a dimension of any symbolic engagement of ultimacy constitutes a possibility that the experience will push for a more transcendent symbol of ultimacy than those directly involved, or a more transcendent interpretation of the symbols. Any symbol of ultimacy, whether regarded in its form within a sacred canopy or in its bearing through a worldview on some otherwise mundane matter, is a finite/infinite contrast. The infinite side of that contrast is a potential reminder that the finite side is "ultimately" arbitrary. The recognition of that arbitrariness itself constitutes a transcendent move beyond the grasp of the contrast in terms of the positive finite side alone. Put in more common language, recognition of the arbitrariness in the contrast between the finite and infinite sides feels like a mystery. Even when the symbol itself points out the mystery in the arbitrariness of the world-founding condition, the recognition of the fact that this itself is also mysterious pressures the imagination for an even more transcendent way of symbolizing what is at hand. Recall the Brahmanical dialectic of moving from the mystery of creation in Ishvara to Saguna Brahman apart from creation, to Nirguna Brahman who does not even have the qualities of being without qualities. Because the advance is made by negation, there never is an end to the transcendence of one negation by the negation of that. Ontological arbitrariness in world-founding finite/infinite contrasts is not the only religiously significant sense of mystery. Chapter 7 deals with another sense, the uncanny. Nevertheless, ontological arbitrariness as mystery is an important pressure placed on symbols of ultimacy to move to greater transcendence that internalizes the mystery.

Of course, the experience of mystery in this sense is only a possibility in symbolic engagements of ultimacy, and perhaps a rare one. Far more common is the simple adjunctive grasp of the ultimate in the form of the finite side of the finite/infinite contrast as it bears on the matter at hand. The joyous birth of a child is celebrated as a blessing of God, or a new mixture of forms within the Dao, or the tragic reincarnation of some trapped soul once again. A death is construed as the vengeance of a God, as the dissolution of an illusion, as the loss of a founding hero, or a home going to the soul's rightful place. Insofar as religious and cultural experiences are ritualized, the mystery in the bearing of the ultimate on life's affairs is suppressed. Even in worship, when at least some people are hoping for experiences of the transcendent, the symbols of the ultimate can be domesticated to their finite, positive, side only. Symbols of ultimacy are domesticated when their feeling tone picks up on the finite side and suppresses the infinite side, or substitutes another finite symbol for the infinite side. For a theist to experience God as an intelligent designer is to be cursed with a domesticated God—some people seek to live under that curse.

These qualifications having been registered, the point remains that in the experiential symbolic engagement of ultimacy, it is possible to feel the balance of the finite and infinite sides in the contrast, and to recognize this as mystery. The recognition at hand is a bid to press on to a more transcendent symbol.

One line of mysticism is quite conscious of this dialectic of experiential transcendence, the line that moves beyond the determinate, however that is articulated, to the indeterminate, however *that* is articulated. This is illustrated in the "Perennial Philosophy" that has found expression in many traditions, through the pervasive influence of Neo-Platonism.[5] But it is not caused by the influence of that tradition, which only supplies a vocabulary. It is caused by the nature of symbolic engagement through symbols that articulate ultimacy in finite/infinite contrasts.

The symbols of ultimates at the transcendence extreme rarely are those that closely address human predicaments. But they are very important for giving articulation to certain kinds of ecstatic fulfillments, those of the adepts who are able to abandon most of the concerns about themselves and turn themselves into signs, almost self-interpreting signs, of the ontological act of creation itself. Chapters 15 and 16 develop this point with regard to religious virtuosi. *Philosophical Theology Two*, Part III, spells out what this means with regard to modes of virtuoso ecstatic fulfillment in time, in eternity, in love, and freedom.

Chapter Seven

Toward Intimate Symbols of Ultimacy

Whereas issues of scale, idolatry, explanation, and experience put pressure on religious thinking to develop increasingly transcendent symbols, something parallel exerts an opposite pressure to develop increasingly intimate symbols, symbols proximate to the exigencies of life. These are the issues that in summary fashion can be called, respectively, the intension of nature within us, the uncanny, meaningfulness, and the correction of meaning.

1. NATURE'S DEPTHS

The "intension" of nature stands in parallel contrast with the "extension" of nature discussed in the previous chapter under the rubric of scale. Nature is vast in its extension beyond anything the ancient traditions imagined. Symbols of ultimacy regarding the radical contingency of the cosmos need to be scaled to that immensity. Similarly, nature here and now consists of a depth of layers of physical organization that is seemingly infinite in its intensity, or intension.

The elementary particles and forces that sorted themselves out in the first minutes after the Big Bang have instances with existential location within the atoms that make up our bodies. Those atoms exist within the molecules of our bodies that transform one another through biochemical processes. These molecules exist within us carrying the history of evolution whereby they are formed into organic environments for themselves. This evolutionary history has resulted in layer upon layer of inorganic and organic organization that constitutes the existential location for us as bodies. Part of our nature is to be on a planet with the approximate gravity of Earth, within certain limits of tolerance of air pressure and atmospheric chemical composition. In order to have any existential location, we need to be a certain distance from a heat source such as the sun, which itself has to be of a certain temperature; that relation to the sun would be intolerable for our existence if there were not atmospheric protections from harmful solar radiation: The ozone layer is bone of my bone.

What is my body? Is it the organization of cells that carry my DNA? Yes, but more. My cells are organic but contain, indeed require, all sorts of inorganic substances, "minerals" of the sort listed under that head on the vitamin bottle. Many of the particular particles of these inorganic substances began eons ago and will continue for eons after my organic body is no more. Even the highly evolved and complicated organs of my body, which interact intensively on so many levels to keep me alive as a whole, are themselves involved in metabolic chains that extend far beyond my body. Within me are the nourishing chemicals from my breakfast banana, flown to me on an airplane made of metals formed in the Earth's core and powered by gasoline that once was dinosaurs, from the tropical rain forest whose ecology is vastly different from my neighborhood ecology that won't grow bananas, which provided it with a banana DNA that gathers light generated by the sun: my body right now is being renewed with banana-reconstituted sunshine. Internal to the existential location of my body, bounded by my skin, are elements whose own existential location consists of systems of systems of causal interactions, each as intensionally deep as what is "within" me.

What is "within" me, however, is not only the material organized according to my DNA. Uncounted numbers of microbes live within me, in my mouth and gut, within my organs, and on my skin.[1] My organs could not function if it were not for some of these microbes, and my body is the living environment for them. These and other microbes provided the environment within which my species evolved, and they are crucial for my continued existence. When I die, much of my body will be returned to its microbial elements.

Of course, I am not only my body, its sustaining causal environment, and the elements to which it is host. My DNA is possible and composes me because of my parents and their lineages, all of which depend on social organization. For the last several scores of million years that social organization has been vertebrate, and then mammal; for the last several scores of thousand years that social organization has been human, structured by communication through semiotic codes. I bear within me now, not only the past history that led up to the present, but the layers of social structure embodied in me. By and large the social organizing principles of high civilization provide top–down oversight of my social behavior. On the occasion of fiercely bad traffic, however, with intense stimuli to road rage, the velociraptor in my "old brain" will govern my social behavior.[2]

Given our evolved minds, we can include within ourselves many things remembered and anticipated. These are objects of symbolic reference and legitimately can be considered part of us, providing conditions for our life and behavior and themselves conditioning what we are and do. But for the moment let us distinguish these things that become part of us through symbolic reference from those things that make up our bodily life and social practice that define our existential location and that can be called our "natural constitution." That natural constitution is infinitely dense, as illustrated here.

Several times in this book reference has been made to the theory of harmony that depicts a harmony's form, components formed, existential location, and value-identity. These have been illustrated in the previous discussion, making the points that our natural bodies are an infinity of components of components, each a harmony, each with its structured existential location that collectively define our natural existential location, achieving the multitudes of kinds and degrees of value that result from getting these components together in these locations in these patterns of structure, of coming to be, and of dissolution. In this example, the focus has been on an individual body. But of course the social nature of human life means that the more interesting units are groups of people, sharing microbes through a friendly touch and passing around the bananas. Whenever we focus on the foreground of our affairs, an intensive depth of nature gives it its existential location and groundedness. Most of the time we pay little attention to that depth, thinking only or mainly of the affairs in terms of their semiotic interactions on the human scale. But 99 percent of the reality is the intension of nature. My garden has a particularly beautiful rose blossom, which I bend to show my wife, pricking my finger on the thorn anciently evolved to keep pluckers away, tearing the skin to open the muscle cells beneath to the microbes—ah! the infecting microbes, toward which blood rushes to flush the wound and carry microbe-killing defensive cells developed by my fishy ancestors who first grew skin. What an event!

Now the symbols of ultimacy regarding the radical contingency of the world, as well as those founding possibilities, groundedness in components, existential location, and value, need intensive symbolic depth to register nature's depth. The most nearly literal symbols of ultimacy need to register at least this much natural depth. Only modern science has revealed the intensity of nature's depth as we know it now. The ancient traditions were somewhat oblivious. Ancient Daoism had some idea and correctly registered that nature's non–human-scaled causal patterns provide the context within which humans need to work out their affairs. The Confucian notion of the intensity of ancestors read natural intension through a human frame. Buddhists, for instance in the Lotus Sutra, have notions of worlds within worlds, which is another metaphor for natural intension. But by and large it is only since the development of cosmic natural history and biological evolution that we have recognized something of the intensity of nature's depths.

Regarding the depth of nature, human affairs with their histories, especially conflicts and searches for heroic meaning, are like tiny spots of oil floating atop a shoreless ocean. The controlling symbols of ultimacy need to register this depth of nature's intension. The symbols that are scaled to human affairs, such as personal gods who intervene to take sides in human battles, are broken metaphors that should be read against the background of nature's scale of ultimacy. Just as ultimate realities founding the vast extension of cosmic existence are far more transcendent of the personal than many traditional symbols of ultimacy, so the ultimate realities founding nature's depths are vastly more intensive through natural layers than many traditional symbols.

But whereas ultimate realities founding cosmic extension are transcendent of most traditional symbols, those founding nature's depths are more immanent or intimate than most. Nature is not just "out there" in symbolic reference, it is "in here" in my body, in my gesture with the rose. The ultimate (regarding at least existence, possibility, components, existential location, and value-identity) is closer to me than I am to myself, defining me symbolically, closer than my jugular. It is in every breath, heartbeat, step, and rose touch.

Therefore, nature's intension provides pressures for finding and symbolizing the ultimate in the close at hand. Theisms might symbolize God in terms of participation in human interactions. But the more nearly literal presence of an ultimate condition is in the natural loci and components of human interactions. Daoism might symbolize the ultimate in terms of the natural forces around which human social and personal intentions need to organize themselves. But the more nearly literal presence of ultimate conditions in the Dao is in the extraordinary depth in any single move. Buddhism has spiritual practices for focusing on the moment, the immediate suchness of what appears in consciousness. But these practiced focusings of conscious attention rarely grasp the depth in the preconscious dharma. The pure surface of the dharma is blind to the intension of the nature within it.

Both the cultivation of more transcendent symbols of ultimacy because of the newfound scale of the cosmos and the cultivation of more intimate symbols because of nature's intension call for a new piety that modifies and extends the traditional pieties had shallower visions.

II. THE UNCANNY FAMILIAR

A second consideration concerning pressure on symbols of ultimacy to take a more intimate or immanent form is that experience, as described in many religious traditions, includes manifestations of the uncanny. The *uncanny* is a term with a complex history in the Western study of religions, and therefore it can be used here only as a technical term of art defined in reference to alternative meanings. From Edward Tyler in the nineteenth century to Gerardus van der Leeuv and Mircea Eliade in the twentieth, the uncanny was considered a trait of the sacred, and was coextensive with it. In the present work, however, the "sacred" has been limited to the ultimate as expressed in sacred canopies, and stands in contrast to mundane areas of life that might or might not have dimensions of ultimacy because of worldview connections to the sacred canopy. The uncanny in the terms of *Philosophical Theology* is not a characteristic of the sacred canopy or its elements, but only of mundane things that are touched by ultimate elements in the sacred canopy so as to be uncanny.

Rudolf Otto brilliantly elaborated the idea of the numinous in religious experience, which he categorized as *mysterium tremendum et fascinans*.[3] In the scheme of the present study, the numinous can apply all across a worldview's embrace of objects, both sacred and mundane. The numinous is shocking and powerful. In mundane things, the numinous is always uncanny, although not all uncanny things have the power and shock value of the numinous. The uncanny in the present study means a quality in something supposedly understood (about which we are "canny," or familiar), but that indicates that our understanding is wrong, inadequate, perhaps even perversely off the mark. Instead, something manifestly *not understood* is going on. As a result, the experience is interpreted with a bizarre, nonordinary, explanatory reference. A series of illustrations can make this clear.

Anthropologists have long noted that in savage or primitive societies the natural and social world is filled with spirits and supernatural forces. In those societies a great many phenomena are not understood in the modern scientific causal sense of understanding.[4] The default position seems to be to attribute the phenomena, or the uncanny aspects of them, to the intentional causal processes of agents because personal causal agency is familiar to human beings in the most elementary of cultures. Savage cultures do attribute many kinds of events to the will of spirits or supernatural agents of some sort or another, not always humanoid in form.

Some evolutionary biologists speculate that a great adaptive advantage lies in the overattribution of agency to natural phenomena. To use Wesley Wildman's example cited previously, a person who hears a rustling in the bushes can attribute it to the wind or a predator. People who react as if to a predator are more likely to live to pass on their predatorial nervousness genes than those with a less agential imagination. Small children in all cultures develop conceptions of agency, including conceptions of supernatural agents who can read their minds, even if parents have been careful to not teach this, or to teach the opposite. Some deep genetic basis for the overattribution of agency must exist.

The attribution of supernatural (from our standpoint) agency in savage societies involves worldviews that integrate the agencies in complex stories, stories of gods and their relations, of epic journeys, divine geographies, and the like. Although it might well be the case that the attribution of intentional agency is mistaken as a causal account of many dimensions of life, worldviews that are attribution rich often give extremely meaningful orientation to life's affairs. Worldviews that are more "realistic" in giving scientific explanations seem impoverished in orientational meaningfulness compared with worldviews that attribute a plot to the spirit world behind just about everything that happens. Meaningfulness is not the only positive contribution of worldviews, to be sure: Truthfulness is also crucial. A worldview that is untrue in the sense of providing causal orientations that are false leads people holding those views to live in a dream world. Dream worlds are meaningful, even when false, and the loss of innocence regarding a dream world can lead to personal and communal alienation and meaninglessness. One of the important contributions of theology is to help build a worldview that is both true to the best we can know and also that provides meaningful orientation. As explored in *Philosophical Theology Two* and *Three*, truth in theology applies not only to theological claims in symbolic engagements, but to truth in sacred canopies as those are involved in symbolic engagements, as well as to truth regarding the religious dimension of otherwise mundane elements of life.

The false attribution of agency to a phenomenon, or to a world of phenomena, illustrates the uncanny in familiar aspects of life. But the uncanny occurs in many circumstances where there is no attribution of agency, as in the overpowering experience of a sunrise, or the numinous feeling of a particular place—a grotto, a tree, or a windswept cliff.[5] What makes such phenomena sometimes uncanny is the contrast between what is expected of them in their ordinariness and what they reveal themselves to be. The quality of the uncanny requires a contrast between the expected understanding of something and the failure of that understanding. Therefore, if a culture so routinizes an attribution of supernatural agency to a certain phenomenon that the supernatural cause is taken for granted, then the phenomenon is not experienced as uncanny, just as "unscientifically" caused. In uncanny phenomenon, the dualism of the canny and uncanny remains as a background feeling. If a person gets sick, and the cause cannot be understood in natural terms, e.g. food poisoning or wound infection, the condition might be experienced as the uncanny operation of a witch. Or if a person unexpectedly gets well, it might be experienced as an uncanny miracle. Or, radically undeserved suffering might be attributed to some out-of-sight moral operation, such as karma. Or to the vengeance or justice of a god, or as the result of wars among gods.

Natural phenomena carried to an extreme are uncanny, a wind of typhoon force, rain that floods, crops that fail, prey in unusual abundance, ground that dances. Even the regularities of nature, when grasped as such, can be uncanny, the rotation of seasons, the seasons for rain and drought, planting and hunting. Moreover, certain places seem filled with spiritual presence more than others, "sacred folds," as Robert S. Corrington calls them. Geomancy and feng shui are common powers of religiously sensitive people.

Modern Western Enlightenment cultures tend to downplay the uncanny in familiar life. The power of mechanical models of causation, indeed the power of all models of causation that are reduced through expression (ideally) into mathematical terms, to debunk the experience of things as uncanny has been devastating to the uncanny in religious sensibility. Modern science is a deeply influential filter for much of experience. Nevertheless, such modern cultures are also friendly to countermovements. Just as Whitehead cited the Romantic Rebellion against eighteenth-century science, so the countercultural movements from the 1960s of New Age spirituality are intrinsic parts of modernity. As a religion taken in its own right, New Age spirituality is thin soup. Taken as a corrective to the scientistic filtering out of the uncanny, however, that spirituality is a vital force. The uncanny is found even within the precincts of science itself. The more science reveals about the workings of things, especially in biology, the more phenomena it exposes that it does not understand, and these (at least temporarily) are appreciated as uncanny. The proper scientific response is to set about understanding them, and in the course of time this might happen, at which point the phenomena will no longer be uncanny. Yet the feeling of the uncanny is an intrinsic goad to inquiry.

With respect to symbols of the ultimate, the uncanny in ordinary life puts pressure on the symbols to attach themselves to mundane things so as to give them an ultimate dimension. Conceptions of divine agency are obviously good for this. Yet there are more and less transcendent images of divine agency. Conceptions of the monotheistic God who intentionally creates an ordered universe, perhaps a universe as understood by modern science, are wholly inadequate to provide orientation for the uncanny experience of the birth of one's child, or of the sacred hollow at the low point in the woods. Extremely anthropomorphic conceptions are far better, the God with whom one is in daily communion, the household gods, the recently dead ancestors. Intimate symbols of the ultimate include the spirit of the place, the sublimity of a climatic phenomenon, the feeling of "rightness" about being in a certain place.

What theology is to make of the pressures toward intimacy exerted by uncanny experiences is complicated, and the topic receives development through all three volumes of *Philosophical Theology*. Given the drive for truth, with its aim for metaphysical literalness, the pressure toward greater intimacy of symbols of ultimacy seems a move in the wrong direction. Surely the intimate symbols are at best only metaphorical! Yet given the drive for the acknowledgment, critical embrace, and understanding of the intimacies of experience, which include the uncanny deep in the heart, it is the metaphorical symbols that carry the truth, and the transcendent ones that lose it. This leads to the importance of meaningfulness.

III. HUMAN MEANING

The argument so far has claimed that at least one dimension of human meaning comes from the ways in which concrete affairs are oriented against the backdrop of a worldview. A worldview, it has been argued, has many elements for the orienting of different kinds of things, such as Xunzi's orientations to the heavens, to the rotation of the seasons, and to unpredictable phenomena that require good government. We have noted orientations to home life that differ from those of the working environment, to global politics that differ from local politics, and so forth. Worldviews differ according to how they put these various domains of life together, some closely, some distantly, some nuanced, some crudely bundled. They differ also in how they connect the various domains with their sacred canopies. The "meaningfulness of life" consists in how the worldview functions so as to orient life's mundane affairs individually and in reference to one another.

Some thinkers take a strong view on the human need for meaning, claiming that people cannot tolerate meaninglessness and therefore fabricate symbols that are pure fictions, false fictions. Some scientists hope to understand religion scientifically by constructing an ideal type for human beings according to which people necessarily are driven to meaning-making and whose religious symbols are seen as rationally instrumental to providing meaning. The assumption in this argument is that there is no real religious meaning and that religious symbols are mere projections; otherwise the scientific study of religion would be the empirical examination of religious meaning and the assessment of how well various religions get it right.

Nevertheless, there is no need to employ the ideal type of human beings as driven to construct meaning even if they have to lie to themselves. The simpler observation is that human beings are curious and naturally try to understand their affairs in larger contexts. We see particular things, events, and actions within domains in which they make sense together. For instance, feeling hungry, the presence of something edible, and the act of eating it, all make sense together in an orientational domain of eating. The activities in the eating domain also make sense in a larger context of nourishing people in family life, sustaining all the adults, finding good food for children, and the like. The act of eating means one, fairly narrow thing in the orientation to the eating domain; it means something larger in the orientation of family nourishment over time. Family nourishment is closely associated with the orientation of a much larger domestic economic domain for a community, which includes not only matters of food but relations to animals, growing things, shelter, and so forth. When the domestic economy is large enough to involve trade, it becomes associated with other aspects of economy and relations with strangers. The simple act of snacking in Boston on a banana that has come from Brazil finds different elements of orientations to simple eating, to personal nutrition, to a city organized with food stores, to the heavy industry of airline manufacture, the business of airline trade, the oil industry with its attendant global politics, and to the distant local economy of Brazilian banana growers. In a given instance, most of those domains of orientation might be ignored, although a reflective person might contemplate them all while enjoying the snack. Whether and, if so, how the different domains are related to one another depends on the worldview at hand. Nearly every Bostonian can relate to each one of those domains, especially if they are pointed out. Most Bostonians can connect the domain of the banana in hand with the domain of the food market, and that with the domain of importing food grown elsewhere. But a much smaller percentage of Bostonians have a worldview in which having a diet of tropical fruit is implicated in the distressing global politics of controlling access to oil.

Some people live with minimalist worldviews that make few connections between domains of orientation, and that fail to provide any domains of orientation at all for many of the activities of life. But even they might be curious sometimes about how to think about what they do in larger contexts. Nearly every one faces disruptions and crises that cause them to ask about the meaning of something whose context they had not questioned before. When the stores suddenly stop carrying bananas, just about any banana eater will ask why, and begin to trace the different domains of life that are involved. Larger crises of the existential sort, such as asking how and where to live one's life, put pressure on the search for meaning in the sense of seeking out a worldview that makes connections among the important domains.

One's culture supplies the terms at hand for understanding particular things, their larger context or domains of orientation if they have them, and their connections with other domains. One's worldview is an important array of terms and interconnected meanings within that culture. But just as language does not tell people what to say, although it is necessary in order to say anything and sets limits to what non-poetic people are able to say, so culture does not necessarily provide the answers to questions of meaning, although it provides the tools for framing both questions and answers. Of course, in one sense a culture, particularly the worldviews in it, does provide answers to the questions of meaning—worldview orientation itself is a meaning structure. But when a *question* of meaning arises because of some crisis, or even just a stimulated curiosity, the answers provided by the culture are obviously not enough. A first response to a question of meaning might be to say that the person's actual inherited culture is a shallow version of a rich culture that is available, and that the person should pursue the richer culture. Turns to religion in times of crisis are often like this. But it might be that a question of meaning arises for which there is no preexisting answer within the culture, and creative inquiry is called for.

The meanings of things are not always good, and sometimes we would prefer to deny them. Favorite foods might mean a threat to health, not just a way of satisfying nutritional needs. The prosperity of Brazilian banana farmers because of the transportation system connected to the Boston market might be a good meaning of the banana snack, but the connection of all that with a world too heavily dependent on oil with its attendant murderous politics is bad, and some people are motivated to deny that meaning connection.

The quest for meaning in religious questions is particularly tricky. Its form is to ask whether something in a mundane domain has a connection with the domain of the sacred canopy such that the mundane domain has a religious or ultimate dimension. A given worldview provides an answer: there is a connection of a certain sort, or there is not. Consider the surely universal example of the meaning of death. A person dies, and people ask whether that is all there is to the person's life. A broad array exists of different worldviews that answer this question. Some say that death marks a transition to another life, reincarnation, possibly with moral or karmic implications; on most of these worldviews, reincarnation is the religious problem to be solved by finding true death from which there is no rebirth. Other worldviews say that death is followed by life not on this earth but on a different plane, a heaven, hell, or purgatory where the soul stays forever, or for a finite period before moving to a different plane. Worldviews of this sort differ according to whether only a soul survives to a new embodiment or whether the dead person, body and soul together, are resurrected in the new plane. Yet other worldviews say that there is no life after death of any sort but that the meaning of the life lived between birth and death has an eternal significance in relation to ultimate things that is more than the temporal life as usually understood. Other worldviews claim that there is no life after death except insofar as one contributes objectively to subsequent generations, "living as an ancestor." Other worldviews say that the significance of the person's life is in a larger story of ultimate significance, fighting for good against evil, perhaps, or playing a role in a history of redemption. Other worldviews say, Yes, this here is all there is with no significance beyond what is apparent.

Death is often an ontological shock, and it occasions the questioning of worldviews and their answers to the meaning of life and death. This is particularly true in a pluralistic society in which different worldviews are in competition and the weight of inherited tradition has lost its force. So the question arises, which worldviews are true in the connections they make between ultimate realities and mundane affairs such as death. Here the complexity of the question of truth in matters such as these needs to be remembered. Truth is the carryover of what is valuable in the object interpreted into the interpreter in the respects in which the interpreting signs and symbols stand for the object. Does the symbolic construction in the worldview carry over into the questioner what is important about the meaning of death? This varies, of course, with the particular context of the questioner and the readiness of the questioner to interpret the object (the meaning of death) with the signs at hand; the symbolic construction might carry over truly for some people but not for others, depending on their contexts and readiness. Perhaps more important is the question of reference in the interpretation. If the symbolic construction referred only iconically, the question of truth would be whether the construction accurately describes the situation (e.g., life or no life after death, of such and such a sort). In the folk-religion end of the sophistication/folk culture continuum within a given worldview, reference is usually construed mainly iconically. This is also the construal of those who are hostile to religion and want to debunk it by taking it literally and showing it to be silly.

But reference in most religious interpretations is also, and sometimes exclusively, indexical. That is, the symbolic construction reorients the interpreter so that what is important in the object gets carried across in the right respects. To discern whether this happens in a particular interpretation requires triangulating both on the nature of the object independently of this interpretation and on the interpreter to see what difference the interpretation makes. It might well be that interpretive belief in an afterlife of reincarnation or heavenly (or hellish) relocation is descriptively (iconically) false but indexically true because it embodies within the interpreter the ultimate meaning of death. The great Axial Age religions have metaphysical conceptions, aiming at literal descriptive truth about ultimate realities, conceived as finite/infinite contrasts, to which they would relate the ultimate meanings of finite human life. In all of them save perhaps Confucianism, the literally inconceivable relation between finite human life and the infinite side of the finite/infinite contrasts is schematized, in Kant's sense of "schematism," with conceptions of an after-death life in a kind of time and geography.[6] Usually, the relation between the ordinary finite life just past and its ultimate fulfillment is expressed as some kind of journey. The relation between the finite and infinite is expressed in (finite) temporal and spatial terms, although with radically different imagery. Daoists imagine infants floating among the clouds, Muslims imagine luxurious gardens, Buddhists and Hindus imagine palaces set in parks, Jews imagine judgment halls, and Christians dining halls in well-ordered cities. Does interpretive belief in these terms carry over whatever the ultimate meaning of human life/death is when that cannot be expressed adequately in finite terms? Perhaps.

Now we are in a position to see something of how issues of human meaning concerning ultimate matters put pressure on symbols of ultimacy to be more intimate. They are metaphorical to be sure, with a need, from a theological perspective, to be understood in terms of their metaphorical limitations. But the people living by the metaphors in dealing with the ultimate religious questions such as the meaning of death do not have to be aware of those limitations for the symbolic constructions in fact to carry across the truth. They can simply live within the world of those symbolic constructions with a kind of innocence and still be living in the truth. Of course, in practice they should be aware of the symbolic limitations so that they do not draw inappropriate conclusions from the symbols, such as ending a good life prematurely so as to get to an imagined better life. Paul Ricoeur has popularized a distinction between first and second naiveté. First naiveté is living according to the symbols with little or no awareness of the fact that they are symbols with limitations. Because of the dangers of inappropriate conclusions, however, especially in the late-modern world people are prone to break that naiveté and declare the symbols to be broken. Second naiveté is when people live with the broken symbols, aware of their limitations and brokenness, and yet allowing the symbols to carry across what they can.

Metaphorical symbols of ultimacy need to be intimate to the affairs of human life that have ultimate dimensions. The ultimate meaning of death (or life that ends) is not the only serious religious question of meaning. The ultimate significance of one's community is sometimes symbolized with a sacred history intimating a special relation to a god or place, even though other communities might have competing symbols. The ultimate meaning of life's developmental transitions—birth, puberty, the responsibilities of adults, old age, death—are often symbolized in terms of special relations with ultimate matters. Household gods, revered saints, and ancestral spirits are common in worldviews even with monotheistic or anti-theistic sacred canopies.

To be sure, these intimate symbols of ultimacy accommodated to questions of the ultimate meaningfulness (or not) of mundane affairs are metaphors. Few if any could stand up to examination regarding their literal truth. But this does not mean that they are not true. Their indexical reference might indeed provide for the carryover of ultimate meaning in a true way.

IV. HUMAN CORRECTION

The question of the intimacy of symbols for ultimacy in human meaning is intensified when the questions of meaning have to do with the human predicament, which is the first main topic of *Philosophical Theology Two*, Parts I and II. Human beings typically, or ordinarily, or perhaps universally, have something wrong with them to which religion aims to supply some remedy. In West Asian religions, the rhetorical center of gravity has been on problems of good and evil, with people being in need of salvation from evil intent and guilt. In South Asian religions, the rhetorical center of gravity has been on problems of suffering and harmful ignorance, with people being in need of enlightenment and liberation from transitoriness and separation. In East Asian religions, the rhetorical center of gravity has been on problems of disharmony, imbalance, and running contrary to nature, with people being in need of harmonization in fulfilling ways with nature, sometimes construed as destiny, and social realities. Yet all the Axial Age religions have thematic considerations of good and evil, with an ultimate return to righteousness, of change and loss, with an ultimate enlightenment, and of disharmony, with the achievement of fulfilling harmony. These themes have many competing variations, even within seemingly coherent religious traditions.

Behind these highly civilized articulations of human predicament and religious soteriology is a more primitive sense of the human predicament that Paul Ricoeur characterized as "stain."[1] In pre-Axial Age religion "impurity" is viewed as a kind of ontological wrongness, which can be set right, or purified, only at a price. Animal, including human, sacrifice is typical of religions dealing directly with impurity or stain. The primitive sense of impurity is overlain by more sophisticated versions of human predicament in Axial Age religions. But they do not replace it. In various ways, many of which are discussed in *Philosophical Theology Two*, the sense of stain and versions of sacrifice are incorporated, often with little change, in the problematics of righteousness, enlightenment, and harmony. The Christian Eucharist, for instance, is a symbolic cannibal rite that Roman Catholics call the "sacrifice of the mass." The ancient Confucian emperors conducted bloody sacrifices to mark or effect the change of the seasons.

Underlying both Axial Age and pre-Axial Age interpretations of human predicament is the special predicament that comes on occasion when one's sacred canopy implodes, taking the worldview with it. Sometimes this is a community event, as when the Holocaust caused a radical rethinking of the Jewish conviction that they were God's chosen people. Sometimes it is an individual event, as when some great ontological shock undermines the plausibility of one's sacred canopy. Sometimes it is a cultural event, as when the sacred canopies of traditional religions are undermined by elements of a new culture of modernity. Torn sacred canopies might be repaired with amended symbols, reaffirmed without repair in a kind of fundamentalistic intensity, replaced with other sacred canopies, discarded without replacement or lived with in broken fashion, in a kind of despair about ultimate things.

The *brokenness* (to use a vague term for human predicament) of human life is felt existentially in first-person token-reflexive ways: It is *my* sin, *my* ignorance, *my* imbalance that needs correction; it is *our* deviance, *our* blindness, *our* cultural chaos, which needs correction. *Our* stains must be removed as a people as well as those of each of us. *My* sudden loss of meaning regarding ultimate things is *our* culture's problem. Sometimes the collapse of a worldview is so great that individuals lose the plural sense of identity and have difficulty identifying with any ultimately significant "us." Religious corrective to the first-person predicament needs to be symbolized in terms that can address the first-person perspective. Perhaps the most common way to do this is to symbolize the ultimate in anthropomorphic terms, on the model of person-to-person address. Many monotheists view God as personal in some sense, with whom they can have a personal relation. A similar situation holds with regard to Hindu representations of creator deities such as Ishvara, Vishnu, Shiva/Shakti, Brahma, or Narayana. Even anti-anthropomorphic Confucians look for the "mandate of Heaven" for them personally. The first-person need for personal salvation, enlightenment, re-harmonization, purification, or courage in despair elicits symbols of the ultimate in avatars such as Jesus, Krishna, and assorted Daoist visitors from Heaven. The personalities of founders of faiths, such as Abraham/Moses/David, or the Buddha, or the sage reciters of the Vedas, or Confucius or Laozi, are important ways of making ultimate correction first-person directed.

Anthropomorphic representations of ultimacy are not the only ways to symbolize ultimate reality's corrective force for first-person predicaments. Symbol systems have been developed from the personal experience of consciousness, and the experience of new emergence. All people need to cope with the possibilities of their time, but those possibilities address the person in first-person fashion when they become the individual's trial of destiny and freedom. All people are composed of multiple processes of nature and society, but these address the first-person predicament when symbolized as the way by which the ultimate constitutes the individual or group particularly and specially. All people have existential location, but that becomes ultimately relevant to the first-person predicament in the symbolic guise of home. All people have value, but this addresses the first-person predicament when symbolized as ultimate identity, perhaps recognized in ultimate judgment. All people relate to other people, to social structures, and to various levels of nature in subject–object fashion. This is expressed also in the first-person token-reflexive sensibility regarding human predicament. Experiences of the transcendence or obliteration of the subject–object distinction in meditation or other ecstatic activities are a kind of ultimate first-person symbolization of existence as such, finding correction in some symbolic appropriation of the radical contingency of the world.

Insofar as ultimacy is to be symbolized as relevant or responsive to individuals and groups in an ultimate human predicament, that symbolization needs to be intimate enough to be conjoined with first-person token-reflexive symbolizations of the self or community. This constitutes a powerful pressure to develop symbols of intimacy in contradistinction to transcendence. If we were interested only in developing symbols that accurately describe human connections with nature internal to the individuals themselves and their affairs, that articulate experiences of the uncanny–familiar, or that relate human affairs meaningfully to ultimate things, the greatest theological problem would be controlling for the limitations of metaphors. The deepest question would be whether and under what conditions the metaphorical symbols are true.

Human predicaments requiring correction are not the only ultimate dimensions that define people in religiously existential ways. People also engage the ultimates in ecstatic fulfillments. Some of these ecstatically fulfilling experience take place at the extreme transcendence end of adept development (*I, 15, 16*). But others engage the ultimate through affairs that might seem very mundane. A person faced with an extremely powerful moral dilemma who knows the better but very much wants the worse and yet who prevails with the moral path can find that ecstatically fulfilling relative to the ultimate of obligation. A person whose world is in pall-mall turmoil and yet is able to find a still point within it can find that ecstatically fulfilling. A person hard-pressed not to forgive an oppressor but does so can find that ecstatically fulfilling. A person whose value-identity is a profound disappointment but who accepts that for who he or she is can find that ecstatically fulfilling. A person profoundly shamed but who still can affirm going on with hope can find that ecstatically fulfilling.

But, insofar as the theological question is from the side of persons caught either in some human predicament or on a path of ecstatic fulfillment, symbolizations of ultimate realities that can relate to the first-person token-reflexive character requiring naiveté, either first or second, is absolutely demanded. A mere metaphor, however true, will not suffice unless it addresses *my* predicament, *our* predicament, my point of ecstatic fulfillment or ours. Because modernity breaks traditional religious symbols in so many ways, it not only makes religion seem implausible to many. It also makes religion ineffective as ultimately corrective to the human predicament or as venues of ecstatic fulfillment unless people can achieve second naiveté with broken symbols that address them in the first person (*III, 13, iii*).

CHAPTER EIGHT

Ultimacy in Theological Framing
Ontology and Narrative

I. NARRATIVE OF THE DIVINE

One of the most important distinctions within theology is between two structures of the broadest frame for theological discussion. One structure is a kind of cosmic or ultimate narrative. The other is an ontological structure articulating relations among finite affairs, natural and human, and ultimates that are infinite in crucial aspects as finite/infinite contrasts. *Ontology* in this anthropological context is used in the sense popularized by Heidegger and Tillich as "fundamental ontology:" how the human is structured by its relations with ultimate reality. The distinction here is in reference to the broadest or "ultimate" frame for theology. The ultimate frame surely affects and reflects the rhetoric of theology, and so it might be called the "ultimate rhetorical frame." More than rhetoric is involved, however. In some sense, the ultimate frame is how religion or theology is "given," and so it might be called the "ultimate revelatory frame," although revelation is an extremely complicated notion (*I*, Introduction). For the purpose of this discussion, the ultimate frame can be called the "ultimate cognitive frame." The great narratives themselves presuppose and articulate ontological or metaphysical relations between the ultimate and non-ultimate. The great ontological structures in turn contain narratives on many levels. What is at stake in the distinction is the outermost frame because it conditions everything within it.

Most religions have theological traditions representing each side of the distinction respectively, although the discussion here focuses on the Christian. Karl Barth, the great twentieth-century Protestant Christian theologian, framed his theology as a grand narrative of creation, fall, and redemption. He construed the Bible to be a grand telling of that story, something like a loosely integrated nonfiction novel.[1] Much of the Christian Bible can be read as contributing to that cosmic story, including the Torah, minus the legal passages, the books of history, Daniel, the authentic letters of Paul (i.e., excluding Ephesians, Colossians, and the Pastoral Epistles), the letters of Peter, and Revelation; the four Gospels in their own frames as "biographies" of Jesus, plus Luke's Acts, are narrative.

Tillich, an equally great twentieth-century Protestant theologian, framed his theology in the ontology of depth, relating human concerns and history to God as Ground of Being. Although people's lives have narrative form, and people live in history, for Tillich theology did not try to articulate how those personal and historical narratives relate to a larger cosmic narrative. Rather, theology for Tillich articulated how those narrative-shaped aspects of human existence relate to the Ground of Being. Much of the Bible supports that relational view rather than a narrative of creation, fall, and redemption. Consider, for instance, the covenantal or legal aspects of the Torah, the wisdom literature including most of the Psalms, Proverbs, Ecclesiastes, Job, much of the major prophets, the teachings of Jesus, including the parables and the Sermon on the Mount, Ephesians, Colossians, the letters of John, James, and Hebrews, and the Pastoral Epistles.

Much is at stake in the ways these ultimate cognitive frames situate a theology. A narrative, however cosmic its extent, is particular, one story among other possible stories. Thus, it excludes those other stories, and excludes the nature, societies, peoples, and persons that are not part of it, though they might be parts of other stories. Karl Barth's story of creation and redemption in Christ has no roles for Buddhists or Confucians, and the Jews and Muslims show up in the story only because of their connections with Christianity.

Barth's narrative thus has great power in giving identity to Christians who want to be distinguished from people of other or no religions. Indeed, Barth represents in this respect a fairly large delta of Christian traditions that believe that becoming a Christian means adopting as one's own story the ultimate Christian narrative of creation and redemption. Surely there is a large Christian truth in this. Consider the Gentile Christians to whom Paul wrote in the first century. Although they came from a variety of Gentile cultures, each with its own narrative, to become Christians they had to adopt the narrative of Israel and its historical relation to Yahweh as told to them in the Septuagint as their own, most true, story. From Barth's perspective, for practical purposes the alternative stories could be forgotten, as well as the people in them who were and are not related to the Christian narrative.

Wide variation is to be found in ultimate narratives, and even within different views as to what that might mean. Nearly all religions, Axial and pre-Axial, have creation stories. Mircea Eliade argued that the latter do not tell a story in any modern sense of historical time, but a story within repeatable time in which the founding event can be made contemporary to any worshipper through liturgies. For Eliade, Judaism and Christianity had conceptions of historical time, with a beginning for the world and also an end. But for both, the founding events were sacred, in his sense of the term, *illud tempus*.² Eliade himself held strongly to the view that the ultimate cognitive frame for theology, at least for the kind of "normative phenomenology" that he did, is the metaphysical sort, not the narrative sort, and for this he has come under much criticism.³

The ontological ultimate cognitive frame is not necessarily "metaphysical" in dialectical argumentative senses discussed previously (*I, 6, iii*), although dialectical metaphysics is required to flesh out such a theology. Rather, the ontological ultimate cognitive frame is "ontological" in that it is concerned with the relation of human beings, in their natural settings, communities, and historical circumstances, to ultimate realities as these are articulated in a related sacred canopy.

The dominant ultimate cognitive frame in most forms of Buddhism is ontological in that human suffering is understood and treated in relation to the ultimate reality of no underlying own-being for things. The Four Noble Truths articulate this relation in a practical way. Buddhist metaphysics, say in Nagarjuna or Vasubandhu, articulates versions of the ultimate reality of transience, always with an eye to how the ultimate reality of transience (of dharmas in some sense or other) determines or guides the anthropological ultimate reality of discovering release from suffering. Of course, Buddhists understand this ontological frame to have a history, from Gautama Buddha and his disciples. Within Buddhism there is a meta-narrative of Buddhas coming in different epochs with the true teaching of enlightenment, with Maitreya being the next appointed. Moreover, within certain kinds of Buddhism, for instance Hwa Yen, is an elaborate cosmology of entire universes being contained within each speck of dust on the floor, and a story can be told of the evolution of each universe.⁴ But these narrative elements by and large are treated within the larger, more ultimate, ontological frame of suffering relative to the character of ultimate reality.

Confucianism too is most usually understood within an ontological ultimate cognitive frame. As the Doctrine of the Mean argues, Heaven provides the inmost heart of human nature and the ultimate anthropological concern of human beings is to find the way or Dao that allows for Heaven's mandate to find expression in one's personal and historical situation. Like Buddhism, Confucianism is defined by the ultimate anthropological concern of attaining sagehood (not the same as enlightenment, but close), and that in turn is defined by the ultimate ontological reality of Heaven and its Principle that defines harmony for each circumstance.⁵ Within this ultimate ontological frame exists a history, going back to the ancient sage kings, and several versions of models for the rise and fall of dynasties. With help from Daoism and Buddhism, Neo-Confucianism developed an elaborate metaphysics of the origin of the cosmos from non-being (wuji) to taiji to yang to yin to the basic elements to the ten thousand things. This ontological uprising of the world as we live in it is not historical in the sense that it had an original moment, but is a kind of continual emergence that hides the subtlety of the originating phases in the passage of ordinary time. The emergence theme in Confucianism is a parallel alternative to the metaphors of divine creation in Christianity.

Within Christianity the ontological and narrative ultimate cognitive frames compete, as in the cases of Tillich and Barth. The former takes as its ultimate cognitive frame the problem of establishing the right relation between human beings and God, the ultimate ontological reality. In the Hebrew Bible this is expressed as the covenant relation and the vicissitudes of Israel being in (or out of) the covenant. The revelation at Sinai is taken to be an historical event that is sacred because of its establishing of this covenant. In the New Testament, Jesus and Paul taught somewhat different versions of the covenant, at least with regard to who could enter into it and how covenant-breakers might be reconciled to God. Jesus and his disciples are sacred, in the many sense of their being sacred, because of their revelation and establishment of this new covenant. In both instances, on this theological view, it is the ontological covenant relation that makes historical events and people sacred because of their roles in revealing and establishing the covenant. In the narrative Christian ultimate cognitive frame, God appears as the aboriginal historical agent creating the world, which struggles with evil causing the fall of human beings from covenant, with the result that God sends Jesus his divine son to redeem the world, a redemption that can be felt in present time but that will be complete only with an ending of the narrated history of creation and redemption. The real agents in this narrative, according to Barth and several other narrative traditions, are God, Jesus Christ, and the forces of evil. Human beings are what they fight about, but human beings are not real players in the drama—salvation comes from God in Christ triumphing over the forces of evil. The human part of the drama is to be on the right, that is, divine, side of the contention between God and evil, which is accomplished by faith, not works such as personal struggle against evil. To be a Christian is to buy into this story and see one's own ultimate identity as the place one has in that history of creation and redemption. Of course, living out this historical place means that human beings do struggle against evil, practice at being imitators of Christ, and imbed themselves in one or another of the rich traditions of piety. It means aiming to perfect one's relations with God and Christ (and the Holy Spirit), and those relations can be "ontological" in the sense meant here; but those relations are set within the larger more ultimate narrative cognitive frame.

Philosophical Theology opts very clearly for the ontological ultimate cognitive frame in several ways. First, it insists on a comparative base for theological reflections, taking seriously the experiences and interpretive frameworks of as many religious traditions as possible. This undercuts any grand narrative from the very beginning. Second, it insists that theological claims, about narratives, doctrines, special revelatory events, or anything else, be interpreted and adjudicated from as many perspectives as possible, not only from alternative religious traditions but also from as many intellectual and practical disciplines as are relevant. Third, it aims to be systematic in the several senses discussed in the Preface and Introduction, and therefore it must look at any narrative from the standpoint of those events and at figures excluded from the narrative, necessarily treating the narrative as one among many. Fourth, it argues in *Philosophical Theology Three* that a crucial part of the human predicament is that sacred canopies that serve to provide religious identity are fragile and collapse, and that a more important element of religious identity is how one copes with that implosion. This holds for any ultimate narrative that might be employed to give identity.

Furthermore, any conception of the ontological ultimate as being within a containing narrative makes the ultimate finite in an unsustainable way. Perhaps the ultimate does not have to be viewed literally as a personal God, which surely is a finitized conception: Persons are necessarily related to others. But a narrative ultimate cognitive frame makes all ultimate realities actors in the narrative drama. This is to say, they play some roles but only relative to other roles, as in God dealing with recalcitrant human beings. As argued in Part III, all roles and role players are ultimately derivative from an ontological creative act.

To be sure, *Philosophical Theology* is committed to understanding the created cosmos as science best depicts it. The reigning astrophysical paradigm is the Big Bang, which is usually interpreted to be a "first moment." Science is thus the "natural history" of the Big Bang and its sequelae. Moreover, with regard to organic life the theory of evolution has proved to be extremely powerful. Therefore, we understand the situation of our natural and social environment as historically evolved down to our time and currently also in evolutionary changes. In many important ways, the scientific picture in our time is a grand cosmic narrative. But for this systematic philosophical theology, science is not the ultimate cognitive frame, only one of the several more proximate cognitive frames. The principal arguments for this are given in Part III.

II. NARRATIVE OF THE PEOPLE

The consideration of divine narrative as the ultimate cognitive frame reflects the concerns of chapter 6 to the effect that certain elements of reality push the symbols of ultimacy toward greater transcendence. The concerns of chapter 7 were with those elements of reality that push the symbols toward greater intimacy. Among those elements were the concerns of individuals and communities to attain an existential religious identity. A special version of this concern for existential religious identity is the development of and adherence to a narrative that defines oneself and one's community in an ultimately significant narrative. Sometimes this narrative is attached to an ultimate cosmic narrative, such as the creation and redemption, or the expansion of the universe from the Golden Egg (hiranya garba) to which it will in due time contract. But the concern of the present section is with those narratives that define a people or person intimately and existentially, that is, as defining their ultimate identity.

The classic example among the Axial Age religions is Judaism. The first eleven chapters of the Torah, Genesis 1–11, are about the creation and the fortunes of universal humanity, ending with the story of Noah's flood and the repopulation of the world. From Genesis 12, which begins the story of Abraham, through the rest of the Hebrew Bible, the entire text, save Job, Esther, Ruth, and Jonah, and perhaps some passages of Wisdom literature, is about the relations between Israel and God. The center of those relations is the narrative of the Exodus from Egypt under the leadership of Moses and the revelation of the covenant at Sinai. That center defines both the pre-story starting with Abraham and the subsequent history of the kingdoms of Israel and Judah, with the disastrous encounters with Mesopotamian empires, the exile, return, vassalage, the destruction of the Second Temple, and diaspora. This narrative defines the Jewish people. In contemporary Judaism, literal belief in God as supernatural agent of the Exodus, as the Covenanter, and Redeemer of Israel, is not necessary for Jews to identify with that story. The story for them has an ultimate quality to it, the defining element in many Jewish sacred canopies. For a great many Jews, throughout the period of the diaspora, a part of their ultimate identity has been the affirmation that they too are part of that narrative, including the victimization of Jews in the Christian and Islamic worlds (and beyond).

For Christians and Muslims, the narrative of the Hebrew Bible is recontextualized and altered in significant ways, and each of those religions attempts to universalize the story. Whereas Jews tend to emphasize that Gentiles have their own different stories, and may not be worse for all that (although some Jewish sources are profoundly committed to Jewish superiority), Christians and Muslims have tended to say that everyone should adopt their respective stories. To be sure, many Christian and Muslim versions of their stories have been told, with different claims to universal applicability. Still, to be a Christian or to be a Muslim is to adopt some Christian or Muslim story as one's own. That is what it means to be a "member" of those religious communities, although the implications of adopting the narrative vary considerably.

Judaism, Christianity, and Islam emphasize being a member of a religious community more than many other traditions. Hence their stories have relatively more powerful existential bite. Nevertheless, in the other traditions there have been sectarian movements, all of which need to have a narrative to separate themselves from the mainstream. In the South Asian religions, Buddhism, Jainism, and Hinduisms of many sorts, the tradition of the guru defines a person's or community's narrative. The Mahabharata and Ramayana are narratives of epic proportions that contain cultural encyclopedias by which many South Asians define themselves. Daoism evolved powerful traditions that require initiation into a community with a narrative heritage.[6] Confucians identify their story as serving the political and cultural world of their time and place, and so existentially define themselves in terms of the historical needs of their situation. Even in those attenuated senses of narrative, having to do with guru lineages and political movements, one's place in such a narrative can be an important existential way of taking on an ultimately important identity.

The problem with defining oneself or one's community with a narrative is that there are always other ways of "telling the story." The Exodus looks much different from the standpoint of the Egyptians or the Canaanites. The Christian story of spreading the love of Christ across the globe looks plainly hypocritical to the Jews who have been so long persecuted by Christians. The Protestant Reformation, which tells its story as one of purification and renewal, is also a significant historical event in the narrative of the development of Christian anti-Semitism. The Buddhist narrative of spreading the healing powers of release from suffering is nothing but social irresponsibility in the Confucian narrative of finding Heaven's Dao in affairs. All in all, the religious move of defining one's ultimate identity in existential terms by signing on to a religious narrative is extremely complicated, in ways that will be explored in the subsequent volumes. The next section, however, analyzes difficulties with narrative itself.

III. THE SYMBOLIC FALSEHOOD OF ALL NARRATIVES

The symbolic falsehood of all narratives, particularly those that involve ultimate realities or personal ultimate concerns, is that they are abstractions that are almost inevitably abused. Consider the following. Within the 13.6 billion years since the Big Bang, the last fifty or so thousand years of human existence with the possibility of human narratives is a very tiny part. The universe now is about 156 billion light-years wide and still expanding. It contains hundreds of billions of galaxies each of which might contain many stars of the right size and heat, with planets the right distance away, to develop something like storytelling human beings. How can we hold fast to symbols of an ontological creator of that vast cosmos while also symbolizing that creator as a player in a human drama, relating to an individual's career, or to the history of a tribe or nation, or to the specific evolution of human beings on Earth? Or to put the point the other way, how can we remember that a creator who communicates specific plans for an individual's career, or supports one nation in territorial claims against another, or who produces human beings on Earth whose purpose is to worship the creator, is really the creator of the immense cosmos? To be a player within a narrative is to be something like a person, and yet personhood, the capacities for intentional thought, action, and interpersonal relationship, is a very late and tiny kind of evolved reality within the cosmos. How is it possible to image the creator as a person-like player in a narrative with human beings without that being a lie about the real character of the creator of the cosmos?

Or consider the depth of nature within which human beings live. Our concrete reality is to occupy existential positions in an incredibly dense network of natural physical and biological conditions. Our individual identities are very much our participation in biological processes, playing roles in metabolic chains, hosting swarms of microbes, modifying ecological niches. Of course we also have our narratives, those defining our families and peoples, those defining our careers and economic roles, those that we would call our own individual stories. But these stories are a very thin part of the much richer biological and inorganic nature that we embody and in which we participate. In the larger picture, what difference does it make who controls Jerusalem, or Sri Lanka, or Tibet? What difference does it make whether one group is rich and the other poor? What difference does it make whether one group lives with a dignified narrative self-identity while another is consigned to oblivion? In all these kinds of agonistic narratives the differences that make a difference to the larger reality of nature's depths are those with outcomes on the environment. How important can human narratives be? Conversely, how can the creator who is the ground of nature's depths be a specific player in human narratives?

Human history has long been thought to have a narrative form, and most of the great historical writings develop their information around stories, inquiring into the causes and consequences of decisive events. The Annales School of historiography, however, has shown that particular events are often not as important for what happens in a region as geography, climate, and the migrations of animals, including germs and people. The understanding of an historical situation includes much more than a narrative story; it includes grasping myriads of underlying social as well as natural factors. Narratives with religious significance such as the Mahabharata and the history of Israel in the Hebrew Bible presuppose but do not express a whole host of conditions that are more determinative of what happens in the story than what the story says. The story itself might greatly exaggerate something rather minor in determining what happens while minimizing the more important determinants.

More particularly, in a narrative there are episodes that take meaning from their roles in the story line, and give meaning to one another within that story line. But each episode is also an episode in many other narratives that are suppressed or hidden in the narrative at hand. Each person in the episode has his or her own story, or in fact a great multitude of stories. The episode in the Exodus narrative when Moses confronts the Egyptian pharaoh is told from the standpoint of the story of the Israelites. But it also is an episode in Egyptian history, and an episode in the life of the Pharaoh who, according to the Exodus story, was manipulated by God to cause the death of all the Egyptian firstborn children. That encounter was again an episode in the life of Moses as a husband and father, and in the changing status of magicians in Egypt. The narrative of the Exodus story pays precious little attention to the fact that the Egyptians had taken in the Hebrews as a massive welfare case a couple of centuries earlier in the time of Joseph, according to the last chapters of Genesis. All these alternative narratives can be inferred from the Exodus narrative in the biblical text. What is the narrative significance of the fact that Egyptian historical sources give no indication of the acceptance of the Hebrews in Joseph's time (or of the existence of Joseph as a major administrative figure), nor of the encounter of Pharaoh with Moses resulting in devastating plagues and the massive deaths of firstborns, nor of the defeat of an entire Egyptian army at the Sea of Reeds, nor of the loss of a significant number of working resident aliens? To be sure, the Egyptian historical records reflect their own political and cultural conditions, and are not historiography in any modern sense. Yet the whole Exodus story might have been fabricated centuries after its alleged occurrence.

In what sense is the narrative believed to be true (a different question from whether it is true in a modern meaning of historicity)? If the narrative is religiously significant, as the Exodus narrative is, it defines something ultimately important for the people whose narrative it is, something ultimate about their identity relative to ultimate realities. If the narrative were historically accurate in the modern sense it would be a symbol of ultimacy referring iconically and would be true as such. If it is historically inaccurate it would be iconically false. But then, many narratives are clearly legendary and fanciful, and are often known to be such by those who identify with them. Think of the stories of the Norse gods, or the Mahabharata and Ramayana, or the accounts of the birth of the Buddha, or the Babylonian creation story in which Marduk kills his grandmother Tiamat, or the variant of that in Genesis 1 of the Hebrew Bible. These narratives refer indexically as well as iconically; iconically they are false, and indexically they are true if they carry over something about ultimacy into the interpreters, in this instance, those who identify themselves in the narrative. As *Philosophical Theology*, Part I, argued, whether they are true indexically can be determined only by independent examination of whether the carryover is accurate.

The narrative form for a symbol for ultimacy is inherently problematic even when it is true iconically or indexically. This is so because of the ways in which narrative excludes other dimensions of the events it recounts. A narrative is abstract in ways that hide, marginalize, or deny those things that are not part of its story. When a religious narrative is cosmic in scope, as in Barth's creation and redemption narrative, all other religious approaches in principle are excluded as false or unimportant; people and communities, as well as cultural traditions that do not play a role in his Christian creation and redemption narrative, are not registered. Therefore, people who identify with or believe Barth's narrative believe those others to lack ultimate significance. To be sure, it might be that all those others indeed have no ultimate significance. But this would have to be shown by good arguments. The narrative itself obscures the need to show this by good arguments. Arguments that would justify the exclusions in any cosmic religious narrative would constitute a metaphysical structure rather than a narrative one as the ultimate cognitive frame. A narrative needs a systematic metaphysical case in order to justify its exclusions. Otherwise it arbitrarily excludes by its very form as a narrative.

A narrative such as that in the Hebrew Bible that gives identity to one people among other peoples does not have the same difficulty as a cosmic religious narrative, for it allows that the other peoples might have their own narratives of ultimate connection with ultimate realities, perhaps different ones. Nevertheless, it introduces a decisive distinction between those to whom its narrative applies and all those others, the in-group versus the out-groups, in this case the distinction between the Israelites or Jews and the Gentiles. The in-group/out-group distinction, of course, was very important in the evolution of human beings in conditions in which family or tribal groups competed against one another for scarce resources and security. Pre-Axial Age religions heavily reinforce such distinctions. But does that distinction deserve any kind of ultimate status? Given the common tiny experience of humanity on this small planet in a vast cosmos, and given the common human interactions with nature's depths, the in-group/out-group distinction seems absurd if regarded as ultimately significant. More than absurd, it is pernicious if it leads to restricting justice and compassion to one's in-group. Moreover, it leads people in the in-group to not pay attention to those in the out-groups, to not observe their diverse narratives and conditions. In important ways, identifying in ultimate ways with narratives that apply only to one's own group treats the others as insignificant people; and it leads to the neglect of those elements of nature that are not part of one's in-group narrative.

When individuals identify themselves with an ultimate narrative defining their ultimate concern and connecting them with ultimate ontological realities, it is quite possible, and almost necessary, to suppose that other individuals have their own ultimate narratives. Everyone has their own story and getting to know other people includes learning their stories. At the individual level, one can get to know the ultimate narratives of people who are not in one's in-group as well as those who are. Comparative narratives are ways of noting individuating differences among people, which are important grounds for respect. The most significant drawback to individual narratives of ultimate connection is that they obscure the vast commonality of individuals through nature and their conjoint existential location in the cosmos. When we think of ourselves in terms of our stories, and tell others those stories, we hide far more than we reveal.

All in all, narrative as a form of symbolization of ultimacy lends itself to the obscuring of many dimensions of life that are also of ultimate significance. The justification for obscuring those things cannot itself be another story.

IV. LIVING WITH BROKEN NARRATIVES AND HUMANIZED TRANSCENDENTS

Nevertheless, the human need for intimate connections with the ultimate realities that might be depicted in sacred canopies means that we cannot do without ultimate narratives of some sort and some kinds of anthropomorphic symbols of ultimate realities (II, 9, i). What is to be said about this theologically?

All religious symbols of ultimacy must be broken symbols if they can be claimed to be true theologically. Even the most abstract metaphysical representations of ultimacy, as will be developed in Part III, are at best only hypotheses that are justified according to the best we can know in our situation. Symbols of ontological creativity might be given anthropomorphic form, although we know that anything that has form is created, and is not the creator apart from creation. The ultimate significance of the places and times of our lives might be symbolized with spirits and supernatural beings even though we know that Jack Frost symbolizing the cold of winter and Santa Claus symbolizing generosity are mere personifications of what is not a person.

Part of the theological task is to trace out the exact ways in which symbols that indexically might be true and ultimately important are to be broken when understood against a more nearly literal symbolization of their objects. How can we live with broken symbols?

It is common to think of folk religion as guided by unbroken symbols, symbols that are taken at face value with "first" naiveté.[7] Surely many religious communities exist in which individuals think of themselves as taking their sacred canopy at face value. They might insist on this when the unbroken character of their symbols is challenged, particularly by outsiders. Yet hardly any community is wholly unaffected by the critical thought that comes with global communications. Even if one lives in a strongly homogenous religious culture, the Internet brings alternative interpretations of one's symbols, and alternative symbols overall. Moreover, folk culture itself is skilled in metaphorical interpretation, never confusing God for a rock or the Dao for a river. In any community, some people will be more canny than others at grasping how symbols are broken. Yet in communities of folk religion, even where canny people might be found, little explicit understanding exists of the limitations of a religious metaphor. And so such communities are prone to in-group/out-group bigotry and very difficult problems with theodicy in which God seems to be punishing the sick and unfortunate.

In the ancient world, it was assumed that social classes are fixed and that religion simply had to accept class differences, as it did slavery. For instance, in his letter to the Corinthians (chapter 8) Paul wrote about the problem in their congregation with people who believe that eating meat sacrificed to idols is sacrilegious and who take offense at fellow Christians who eat such meat. In that culture all meat was ritually sacrificed at temples—the temples were the butcher shops. Paul wrote to his sophisticated literate readers that *they* all know that the idols were just statues, not real gods, and that there is only one real God (who no longer requires his worshippers to keep kosher). But some of the other people firmly believe that the temple idols are real gods, alternative to the Christian God, and hence are offended. Paul's counsel to the literate people was to abstain from meat in contexts where it would offend the superstitious, even though in reality there was nothing wrong with eating the meat per se. It simply did not occur to Paul to recommend educating the superstitious people so that they no longer believed the idols were gods and so would feel free to eat meat.[8]

Today we understand that people are not locked into the particular consciousness of a class but can be educated. Education transforms class boundaries. One of the principal contributions of modernity to all the Axial Age religions is the idea that cultures can be improved with education. This raises the question of education for the religious leadership that has to deal with people across a spectrum from folk religion to the most sophisticated. Clearly the theological mandate is to interpret the strengths and limitations of religious metaphors and symbols. The limitations are difficult to judge without stepping outside of the first naiveté of a religious community. Therefore, the religious leaders need to lose that naiveté and grapple with the problems of interpreting the symbols of their group, or inventing new symbols, as might be relevant to the concrete contexts of their people. No such thing is possible as a set of symbols that is true for every cultural context, even within a single tradition such as Advaita Vedanta or Christianity. Cultural contexts are much too broad. The contexts in which truth is to be measured are particular indeed. What is false, because only referred iconically in one's youth, might become true because functionally referred indexically, in later life.

Because of their functional relevance to conveying the ultimate in intimate terms that connect with individuals' ultimate concerns, narratives, and anthropomorphic images frequently will be required in broadly public liturgies and common rhetorics. Nevertheless, one of the constant offices of theology is to sustain a public breaking of these symbols, indicating their limits and prophesying against their harms in being taken literally. Given the harms that come from certain genres of symbolic interpretation, especially those of narrative, proper theology needs to be in a steady critical, demythologizing relation to first-order religious thought and practice.

Nevertheless, the point remains that the truth of symbols of ultimacy is contextual relative to the interpreters, because such symbols are true or false only when actually employed in symbolic engagements. Those actual symbolic engagements need to be understood in terms of the individuals involved, with their own readiness to employ the symbols, in terms of the modes of reference involved, and in terms of the practical implications of the symbols in their semiotic systems. A Daoist might live ever more richly under the conviction that behavior that conforms to the forces of nature leads to harmony and happiness; yet that symbolic engagement has frustrating consequences when a debilitating and deadly disease process is among the relevant forces of nature. Contrary to popular (though not textual) Daoist hope for individual happiness, the harmony of forces of nature works on the cosmic scale that includes death and destruction as much as flourishing, and not on the scale of human affairs. A monotheist might live in ultimate existential gratitude and prosecute a lifelong career of personal spiritual development with symbolic engagements of ultimacy that employ personal images of God with whom the theist pursues a personal relation. But if good intent is ascribed to the personification of God, and bad things happen, the symbolic cognitive dissonance can be devastating. One of the principal jobs of religious leadership is theological interpretation of just how certain symbols employed with great contextual truth also are broken and should not be allowed to foster false implications that come from the respects in which they are broken.

The fear of the brokenness of symbols of ultimacy, particularly those involving narrative and anthropomorphism, should not lead theology to reject such broken symbols altogether, however. For with what symbols can people grasp ultimate matters in the intimate details of personal and communal life? All those symbols are broken. All are false in some contexts. Yet the genius of religion in all its traditions is that it has provided symbolic means by which people can engage ultimate matters in ways of great existential power.

Part II

Summary Implications

The purpose of Part II was to explore how realities common to the human situation exert pressures on religion to symbolize ultimacy in various ways. These pressures show up in all religions that have reflective depth. They determine that symbols of ultimacy are of various kinds in response to the pressures exerted by the universal realities.

Chapter 5 argued that one of the fundamental distinctions regarding ultimacy is between ontological ultimate realities and anthropological ultimate concerns or quests. The latter fall on a continuum from very mild acceptance of ultimacy as represented in one's worldview (should the worldview contain ultimacy representations at all) through serious questioning about ultimate matters for which symbols of ultimacy need to be able to provide priorities and decision points for life, to ultimate concern that is to conform one's life to what really and truly is ultimate. The conclusions regarding ultimacy from this discussion are at least three. Ultimacy, including ultimate realities and the ultimate dimensions of mundane elements of life, needs to be symbolizable in ways that fit into a sacred canopy that can be part of a worldview. Ultimacy also needs to be symbolizable in ways that order priorities for people seeking to define their lives in terms of ultimate meaning. Ultimacy finally needs to be symbolizable in ways that allow it to be grasped, albeit apophatically, as what it is regardless of projections relative to human needs for ordering life. The sacred canopies of the Axial Age religions contain symbols of all these sorts; or perhaps said more subtly, they contain networks of grammatical connections between symbols of ultimacy that allow them to function in these three ways, acknowledging that these ways blend together and mix in the continuum.

Chapter 6 argued that at least four real elements exist that press for ever more transcendent symbols of ultimacy on the intimacy/transcendence continuum. The scale of the universe in whose boundary conditions ultimacy consists is so vast that any symbol of ultimacy seems to be within the cosmos rather than at the boundary. Identifying anything within the universe as its boundary condition is idolatry, and so the finite sides of the finite/infinite contrasts often seem to be too finite to bear up in the contrast without idolatry. Cognitively, the ultimate boundary conditions are supposed to explain everything else within the dimensions of reality they bound, and themselves not to be in need of further explanation. But most symbols of ultimacy seem themselves to call for more transcendent explanation. Human experience, as it is shaped by more and more ultimate concern, seeks more transcendent symbols of the ultimate to match those concerns. What is wrong with idolatry is not just cognitive error but existential error of defining oneself by a false god. Because of the pressures toward ever more transcendent symbols of ultimacy, there is ineluctable need for a kind of metaphysical dialectic that articulates relative distinctions of transcendence.

Chapter 7 explored the opposite pressure, namely, to make symbols of the ultimate more intimate to human life. To begin with, ultimacy is as internal to human beings as it is external in the vast scale of the cosmos. Human beings each, and together, embody the depths of nature. The boundary conditions of nature and human society are implicit in each person, and so need to be symbolized in ways that define the person. Moreover, daily life for many people is filled with experiences of otherwise mundane matters being touched by ultimate conditions in uncanny ways. Sometimes symbolized as supernatural agents, these uncanny things also can be symbolized in other expressions of the uncanny, but always in terms that bear on the familiar, the sacred streams and grottoes, the divine lightning, the holy changes of seasons. Yet another pressure toward intimate symbols of ultimacy comes from the search for meaningfulness in life. This has many dimensions in all of which ultimacy needs to be symbolized in ways that connect with anything that is supposed to be meaningful. Perhaps most important is the pressure to symbolize ultimacy in ways that might offer correction to the brokenness of human life, to its sufferings, sins, illusions, and conflicts. These symbols need to be able to be related to the specific predicaments of individuals and groups.

Chapter 8 raised the question of the bearing of reality on one particular kind of symbol of ultimacy, namely narrative, in comparison with an ontological ultimate framing of theology. Narrative is extraordinarily felicitous for being able to relate ultimate realities to individual human existential needs. It is a common frame for religious thinking as such, and is expressed in narratives of creation and the intervention of gods in cosmic history. It is also expressed in narratives of people with whom individuals can identify. But narrative runs afoul of reality because it is so abstract, selecting out only certain elements of the cosmos or an individual's life for narrative connection and also hiding, obscuring, or denying the elements that do not fit into the narrative tale. This leads to neglect or denial of those elements of reality, including people, who do not fit one's story. Narrative, by its very form, exacerbates the in-group/

out-group distinction that so much of Axial Age religion means to transcend.

These are not the only aspects of reality that universally exert pressure on symbols of ultimacy. These are the aspects that get expressed through human concerns about ultimacy. Part III explores aspects of reality that universally exert pressure on symbols of ultimacy that transcend human interests (although not human cognition).

An important implication of the argument of Part II is that it is possible, as claimed earlier, to discuss religion as such, illustrating the discussion with networks of symbols from various religions. This is a different enterprise from the approach to religion of Mircea Eliade. Eliade was a phenomenologist who studied many religions, especially pre-Axial Age religions, and made inductive generalizations across religions. He has been criticized for imposing his own categories on the phenomena, a criticism that in principle has to be right. The argument here, however, is that structures in nature and semiotic realities are such that every religion has to respond to them. The categories are derived, not by induction from different religious traditions, but from philosophical analysis of nature and symbolic engagement. The plausibility of the categories is increased if they can indeed be illustrated widely in different traditions.

The kinds of discussions in Part II illustrate the more general claim that theology is not just the study of doctrines but rather the study of symbolic engagement of ultimacy. How are ultimate realities engaged? By means of symbols that reflect various conditions of human life for which ultimacy might have bearing. The next step in the argument is to investigate ultimacy on its own terms, to the degree this can be done.

Before moving to Part III, however, it would be well to note how the considerations of Part II reflect the new aesthetic of our age. The cutting edge of theological reflection on religion has moved beyond the twentieth-century aesthetic of grief at the passing of Christendom in North Atlantic cultures and the parallel grief over the destructive effects of colonialism on other religious traditions. It also has moved beyond the postmodern reaction to this grief, namely to hunker down into micro-perspectives because of the evils of logocentrism. Postmodernism remains preoccupied with the failures of Christianized Western thought. The aesthetic of theological reflection in our own time views all religious traditions as relativized so that they need to be deliberately affirmed to be effective. The effectiveness of religions is the topic of *Philosophical Theology Two*, Parts II and III. For theology, that aspect of religion presenting itself for analysis and affirmation is religious worldviews and their symbols. Religion in the current aesthetic is a matter of symbolic engagement, not first and foremost belief or practice.

Therefore, Part II has looked at conditions for engagement in the nature of reality common to all religions that are sufficiently expansive in their engagement. In an ironic shift from twentieth-century thinking, what is "concrete" in religion is not specific religious practices but rather the array of issues having to do with engagement of the ultimate as such. Specific practices and beliefs, as would characterize a person getting "deeper" into a tradition, are themselves somewhat abstract from the broader and more concrete set of issues of symbolic engagement. Following a religion is a somewhat abstract way of being religious.

This makes evident the importance of making good on the claim that we can have some philosophical purchase on ultimacy that is truer across cultural contexts than the claims of specific traditional symbols. The arguments in Part II about reality setting the agenda for religious symbols and their interpretation have drawn on illustrations from many traditions in no particular order of priorities. The arguments of Part III need to come from their own internal dialectic which is part of the contemporary aesthetic for understanding religion theologically.

Part III

Ultimates Demonstrated

Part III

Preliminary Remarks

The purpose of Part III is to provide arguments for the philosophy of ultimate reality on which *Philosophical Theology* is based. A consistent theme of Parts I and II is that the cognitive control on symbols of ultimacy comes through metaphysics. *Metaphysics*, as the term is used here, and as an interpretive generalization of the great philosophic traditions of civilizations, is the development of hypotheses that attempt to articulate as nearly literally as possible "the generic traits of existence," to use John Dewey's phrase.[1] In this context, the metaphysical question is what to say about ultimate realities.

Metaphysics in the sense intended here is the development and defense of hypotheses about two interconnected topics. One is the question of being: What does it mean to be, and why and how are there beings rather than nothing at all?[2] In deference to some primal traditions in Western thought, this can be called *ontological* metaphysics because of its derivation from the Greek word "to on," being. The other topic is the question of the transcendental or universal traits that define being something, or determinateness: being this rather than that or nothing at all. In deference to parallel Western traditions this can be called *cosmological* metaphysics because it explores what a thing must be in order to be anything at all. The cosmological dimensions of metaphysics are presupposed and employed in various ways in the ontological discussions because the questions of what it means to be are dependent on a theoretical understanding of being "something," or being determinate. Conversely, the questions of cosmological metaphysics presuppose and employ ontological metaphysical hypotheses about the questions of being. Dialectical metaphysical argumentation sorts its way back and forth between the ontological and cosmological questions and hypotheses proposed to address them. *Philosophical Theology* identifies the ontological ultimate reality with the singular creative act through ontological metaphysics, and identifies the four cosmological ultimate realities through cosmological metaphysics, noting the interpenetration of the two. Chapter 9 is mainly about ontological metaphysics and chapter 10 is mainly about cosmological metaphysics.

Cosmological metaphysics is related to philosophical cosmology or philosophy of nature, and frequently is appealed to in metaphysics to provide illustrations of the more abstract hypotheses about what it is to be determinate. "Philosophical cosmology," as Whitehead called it, or philosophy of nature, is more obviously empirical than metaphysics, less general and more concretely involved with cultural concepts of the world.[3] At the imaginative level that functions as a resource for contemporary philosophy, philosophical cosmology draws on many root cultural constructions, such as the substance philosophy of Aristotle in the West contrasted with Plato's process philosophy, or the movement of changes through eons and alternative worlds in South Asian philosophies, or the conceptions of change, yin and yang, and the emergence of things in the Dao in East Asian philosophies. Contrary to what is commonly thought, images such as these have been interacting with and influencing each other for millennia. In Western philosophy, cosmology or philosophy of nature in late modern times has been reduced to science and philosophy of science for many thinkers. But the natural sciences and philosophy of science have been constructed so as to exclude value from nature, which is a mistake obvious to common sense and to awareness of the responsibilities of life (*II, 1; III, 9*). Whitehead's philosophical cosmology took pains to set science and philosophy of science in a wider empirical philosophy of nature than includes value.[4] The cosmological metaphysics of chapter 10 reflects a value-laden concept of nature in philosophical cosmology.

These preliminary remarks sketch the overall metaphysical argument for the theory of ultimate realities employed throughout *Philosophical Theology* (summarized again in *II, pt. 1, pr; II, 16, i; III, 4, ii*). The argument is complex enough that it bears repetition from many angles: Say what you are going to say, say it, and then say what you have said. The sketch here asks a series of questions that add up to a complicated but integrated argument and then indicates the hypothesis and subhypotheses to be elaborated in answer. The technical meanings of many of the terms can only be brought out in the argument itself, which approaches them from several angles. These remarks can serve as a prospectus of the argument as it progresses.

What can be said metaphysically about ultimate reality? The dialectical entrance to this question is through the ontological question of *being*, framed relative to the problem of the one and the many. What is being? What is it to be? What is it to be something? Heidegger famously articulated this "ontological question" in the twentieth century in his early *Being and Time*. But it was Thomas Aquinas in the thirteenth who made the classic identification of being with God.[5] This was not wholly his original invention, based as it was on Aristotle's theory of actuality. Moreover, Plotinus and the Neo-Platonic tradition in late-antique Paganism, Christianity, Judaism, and Islam affirmed something of the sort in the claim that being is the one that is prior to determinateness, and that all determinate things participate in the one through its emanations. Important strands of both Confucianism and Daoism affirm that the many things, comprised of yin-yang patterns, arise from a source that is nondifferentiated, although they tend to call it non-being rather than being. Unless being has some particular determinate character itself, being and non-being are equivalent.

Chapter 9 takes up the question of being. Regarding being, the first question is whether it is possible for being to be the one for the many beings by virtue of which they can be different and determinate with respect to each other. Some philosophers say no. Paul Weiss, for instance, argued in his *Modes of Being* that there is no overarching one for the many but that each of the many is a sufficient one for the others; this argument is analyzed in detail and rebutted. If being, whatever that is, is a possible one for the many, is it so in either an analogical or univocal sense? If being is analogical, as Thomas Aquinas thought, it cannot be the one for the many because it itself is not one, being something different for each thing that has being. The chapter will argue that being cannot be analogical. If being is thought univocally, however, is it determinate or indeterminate? Several possibilities for the thesis that being is determinate are considered and rejected. Being must be univocal and indeterminate, therefore. What can it be? It can only be defined in terms of its function as the one for the many determinate things in which guise it is called the "ontological context of mutual relevance" in which determinate things can be together and determinate with respect to each other.

Chapter 10 then introduces a new line of inquiry. What is a metaphysical account of determinateness such that we can understand the nature of and reason for the context of mutual relevance of determinate things? What exactly does it mean to be determinate? Determinateness at this level of the argument is the greatest possible abstraction because it applies to anything that has some identity over against something else or nothing. An account of determinateness should apply regardless of what kinds of determinate things one's philosophy admits, and any philosophy, true or false, should illustrate the account. The account here hypothesizes that to be determinate is to be a harmony.

What is a harmony? Harmony is analyzed in two modes. One is the mode of having (1) conditional components whereby a harmony is connected with other harmonies so as to be determinate with respect to them and (2) essential components whereby the conditional components are integrated into the own-being of the harmony. The other mode for analysis consists of the transcendental traits of all harmonies, namely form, components patterned together, existential location, and value. The conclusion is that being, as the ontological context of mutual relevance, needs to enable the harmonies to be together with their respective essential components, a possibility not contained within the network of conditional components. The ontological context of mutual relevance cannot be determinate because, if it were, it would require a deeper ontological context of mutual relevance to connect it with the determinate harmonies. This reinforces the previous argument that being cannot be determinate.

What can the ontological context of mutual relevance be? Chapter 11 argues that the only thing that can be the ontological context of mutual relevance is an act of creation *ex nihilo*. What is the logic of creation *ex nihilo*? The act is analyzed in terms of its product or terminus, its existential creativity, and the condition of its absence, nothingness. This ontological creative act is the ultimate reality on which all other ultimate realities depend because they are determinate. It has no nature in itself, save what it gives itself in creating the world. The concept of the ontological creative act is a symmetrical concept, interdefining its elements; but it is the concept of an asymmetrical making.

How does the ontological creative act differ from all the cosmological acts within the created world? Chapter 12 articulates the eternity and immensity of the ontological creative act, and its relation to temporality, spelling out some of the radical implications of the concept of the ontological creative act. This is the abstract expression of the ontological ultimate reality. It is so abstract, in fact, that it is the metaphysical reality for which the symbolic networks of consciousness and spontaneous emergence have been developed in non-monotheistic cultures, and even to some extent within the monotheistic ones. The language of a "creative act" might seem to have greater metaphoric affinities with the metaphoric system of personhood understood as an agent, even an intentional agent. But the indeterminateness of being as the ontological creative act is a decisive rejection of any determinate nature of the creative act save in what it creates; hence there can be no literal sense of agency in some creator. Moreover, the eternity of the ontological creative act has close affinities, although not literal ones, with the atemporality of purified consciousness and the arbitrariness of the act has close affinities with the metaphors of spontaneous creativity.

The rhetoric of the chapters in Part III differs radically from that of the rest of *Philosophical Theology*, being more terse, controlled, dialectical, and concerned to turn vague notions into well-formed logical formulas. Just as the theological aesthetic of our time involves some comfort with being able to speak the languages of many religions and many disciplines involved in the study of religion, it also involves dialectical philosophy.

Chapter Nine

The Metaphysics of Ontological Ultimacy

1. ULTIMATE REALITY, BEING, AND THE PROBLEM OF THE ONE AND THE MANY

What is the best strategy for developing a proper metaphysical conception of ultimate reality? Reflection can begin on the phrase itself. Ultimate reality is the reality that is ultimate or last in the seeking out of conditions, that which is presupposed by other things but has no presuppositions itself. Furthermore, ultimate reality is not merely accidentally last in the sequence of conditions but is ultimate because it has to be last, because there cannot be some further condition behind it. This formal definition of ultimate reality was given in Chapter 1, Section II, in terms of the theory of finite/infinite contrasts. The ultimate condition by itself would be the finite side of such a contrast, and the fact that there is no further condition behind it would be the infinite side. The contrast involves both sides together and can be felt as such.

Now the question is not about the formal definition of ultimate reality but rather about the "material definition," the candidate conceptions of ultimate reality. All the great philosophical traditions have candidates in the sense of fundamental ideas or metaphors that have been variously developed in many schools. The East Asian traditions point to non-being as the ultimate condition, as in Wangbi and Zhou Dunyi. Non-being is always referred to in relation to the Great Ultimate or some other representation such as the Dao that can be named of that which is pregnant with determinate things. Non-being is the really ultimate condition, however, because it lacks all potentialities that might need some antecedent explanation. Fundamental to Daoist and Neo-Confucian non-being is the function of determinate things spontaneously emerging from it. The South Asian candidates for ultimate reality are framed in the metaphors of consciousness: Behind my conscious life is my consciousness and behind that is atman in which the consciousness of all things is identical; behind that is Brahman with the qualities of being the unconditioned reality, and behind that is Brahman without any qualities whatsoever. The West Asian philosophical theologies of Christianity, Judaism, and Islam take their key from Greek philosophy, especially Plato, Aristotle, and Plotinus for whom the candidate ultimate reality is being. All three associated being with unity, the one for the many. Plato pushed the connection between being and value, Aristotle the connection of being with actuality and completeness of actualization, and Plotinus the transcendence of being over all differentiation. As Heidegger pointed out, the Western dialectic of being is inseparably associated with determinate beings.

Our argument here develops a dialectical account of ultimate reality through the metaphoric system of being, mainly in order to take advantage of positions and standard moves likely to be familiar with readers of English. In principle, the same dialectic could be developed through the metaphors of non-being and Brahman.

What is being? This extremely complicated question unfolds as our inquiry proceeds. The strategy is to associate the question of being with the problem of the one and the many, a pervasive philosophical problem that arises in nearly every philosophical context. In the context of the question of being, it is the problem of how being is the one for the many beings. What is being, such that everything that has being has it? Or if the metaphor of "having" being is too biased, we can ask, What is it to be, such that everything that is, is? Resolutely vulnerable, the inquiry should begin by considering some doubts about the strategic topic itself.

First, some people will say that to inquire into the question of being is inappropriate in two ways. On the one hand, the question of being is so abstract as to be metaphysical in the bad sense supposedly refuted by Kant. The answer to that objection is that metaphysics is hypothetical, contrary to Kant's view (I, 2, iv); it can deal with abstract questions as well as more concrete ones. The metaphysics of being is difficult, but there is a long history of it in the world's philosophic cultures, including the East and South Asian as well as the Western.

On the other hand, inquiry into being can be thought to be inappropriate *for theology* because its object is abstract and the object of theology is ultimacy, which has to be concrete. This is to say, there is no proper motive for *theology* to inquire into being. The technical answer to this objection is that the concept of being is the most abstract concept possible, but what it conceives being to be does not need to be abstract. Being might well be beyond the distinction between abstractness and concreteness, and indeed beyond most metaphysical distinctions. To force the Chinese dialectic of *wuji* (non-being) and *taiji* (the great ultimate being) (I, 12, i), or the Indian dialectic of Brahman with and without qualities (I, 6), or the Western distinction between being and determinate being, into the distinction between the abstract and concrete is to do them an injustice. Moreover, the ultimacy of being in its conceptual abstractness might well be a strong clue to ontological ultimacy, for reasons given in chapter 6. Theology in its metaphysical moment attempts to find the most nearly literal conception of ultimacy, and ultimacy has been associated with being as the ultimate finite/infinite contrast in most of the world's philosophical traditions. So the inquiry is perfectly legitimate, even if its conclusion turns out to be that being is not interesting with regard to ultimacy. This will not be the conclusion here.

Second, some people might object to insisting on the problem of the one and the many in the theological context. Suppose, as is argued here to be the case, that the best solution to the problem of the one and the many precludes some favorite conceptions of ultimacy. In point of fact, this chapter argues that being, as the one for the many, cannot be determinate. If it can be shown that being as the one for the many is the most ultimate reality, then conceptions of God as literally determinate are ruled out, however God might be metaphorically referenced. We cannot say that God (or Brahman, or Shiva, or non-being, or the Dao, or Heaven, etc.) apart from identification with the many is good, true, unified, or beautiful (to use a standard list of transcendentals). Much less can we say that God has intentional properties as a person. This is a lot for some people to give up (*I, 14*). So they might say that theology should hold first to some primal determinate identifications of God (for confessional, revelatory, or just plain intuitive or aesthetic reasons) and decline to include inquiry into the one and the many in theology. After all, not everyone has a taste for the kind of metaphysics involved in the one and the many.

Obviously, we should admit that inclinations of taste do determine a theologian's agenda. All theological enterprises are a function of the historical, social, and especially intellectual location of the theologians, and most operate out of a particular theological community. Theologians very well might have the taste to avoid the problem of the one and the many. But when someone sometime somewhere does address the problem of the one and the many in reference to their theology, and it has the outcome just mentioned, then the theologians would have to admit that their conceptions of the ultimate as determinate are just plain wrong. Why not face that challenge earlier? Why not address the problem of the one and the many up front in theological inquiry and see whether or not it provides reasons to eliminate a goodly number of traditional hypotheses about the ultimate for free? At any rate, perhaps as a matter of taste, the systematic philosophical theology developed here addresses the question of the one and the many straight on.

Third, some people might object to setting up the problem so that being is identified as the one for the many. Perhaps the objection reflects a general distrust of the interest in unity or oneness supposed in the question. William James famously objected to what he took to be a philosophical obsession with unity.[1] In point of fact, the metaphysical position to be developed here agrees with James' preferential option for pluralism. The unities of things are only the fitting together of the components of harmonies. Many things are not much harmonized with one another. The cosmos has pockets of order that we can detect, but vast reaches of minimal order, or disorder. Part of the meaning of the claim, to be defended here, that being as the one for the many cannot be determinate is that it does not impose a determinate unity on everything. How much and what kinds of unity the cosmos has *de facto* is an empirical matter. The question of the *one* for the many is not the same as the question of the *unity* of the many, as is elaborated in this part.

The logic of the dialectic of being that is pursued here can now be stated. Being, as the most ultimate reality, is either determinate or indeterminate.

Suppose that being is determinate.

1. If it is determinate, being is either one for the many determinate things or many in the sense of being a function of each of the many things.
2. But being cannot be many (Section II).
3. Therefore being is one for the many.
4. If being is one for the many, it is either analogically or univocally one.
5. But being cannot be analogically one (Section III).
6. Therefore being is univocal.
7. If being is univocal and determinate, it is either what things have in common, or what unifies them as a totality, or is the dynamic of dialectical change (Hegel).
8. But being cannot be a determinate common property, nor a determinate totality, nor the determinate dialectic of change.

Therefore being cannot be determinate and must be indeterminate. With this as the outline, we can move into the argument itself.

II. WHETHER BEING IS ONE OR MANY

In addition to the question of taste for unity or plurality, we can ask whether being is the one for the many or whether there is *no* one for the many, only the unities that each of the many provides for the others of the many and itself. Begin with the latter. This is metaphysical pluralism regarding the problem of the one and many. Alfred North Whitehead in *Process and Reality* sketched the position in his claim that every actual occasion (his term for a real thing) is a unification of all the other actual occasions that are in its world; with the coming-to-be of each unification, a new one is added to the many, and so yet another actual occasion must arise to unify that new many. For Whitehead, there is no unification of the many that is not just another one adding to the many.² His position was a somewhat muddled version of metaphysical pluralism, however, because his doctrine of God held that God completely unifies all things within the emerging divine being, with no possibility of leaving anything out.³ Most Whiteheadians interpret this to mean that past things have no residual reality except insofar as they are taken up into subsequent occasions, and God takes them up totally. If all past occasions are wholly contained within God and have no external reality, then there is only one real thing, God; hence there would be no plurality to incite further actual occasions to come into being as unifications of what had not been unified before. A better development of Whitehead is to say that past occasions retain their own achieved reality regardless of whether they are taken up in subsequent occasions, and hence every new unification creates a new one, which makes for an enlarged many, which in turn incites a new unification. Whitehead's texts are ambiguous with regard to how they are to be interpreted in this way.

But Whitehead's student, Paul Weiss, the most original systematic American philosopher of the last half of the twentieth century and now unduly neglected, was not ambiguous in his development of the pluralistic metaphysics of the one and many.⁴ In his *Modes of Being*, he developed such a metaphysics in a technical way that exhibits with great clarity many dimensions of the problem of the one and the many. If we are going to say that being is the one for the many, then we have to refute his pluralist possibility that there is no one for the many, only enough unifications of the others in each of the many to solve the problem of the one and the many. Weiss's pluralistic theory is worth careful study.⁵

Although Weiss had an elaborate theory of four modes of being of which all things are composed—actuality, ideality, existence, and God, for our purposes "modes of being" can be taken to be his general term for things. "Any single mode of being would be radically indeterminate were it not over against some other," he pointed out. "To be determinate is to be opposed to and opposed by."⁶ A universe could not be made of purely simple modes. If there were two modes in the universe, x and y (to use his language), then the nature of x would have to be 'x and not y,' and the nature of y would have to be 'y and not x.' The 'x and not y' can be interpreted in two ways, according to Weiss. On the one hand, the x must be contrasted with y as something over against it (Weiss symbolized this interpretation as x,y, "x comma y"). This contrast, however, can be made only from a point of view where x and y are merged together in a common ground. This merged togetherness (symbolized as $x.y$, "x dot y") is the other interpretation of 'x and not y.' It cannot be pointed out that the x and y are merged except from a position wherein they are initially contrasted. Therefore, the x,y can be characterized only from the standpoint of $x.y$ and vice versa.

The two togethernesses, the x,y and the $x.y$, themselves constitute a many; How are they united? The unity of the two forms of togetherness,

Weiss argued, is supplied by the very modes they unite, the x and the y. Hence, there are two ways in which the forms of togetherness are united, an x way and a y way.[7] "The relating of the ways of togetherness is via the items which are related; they mediate these ways just as these ways relate the beings to one another."[8] But *how* does each of the items relate the two ways in which it is together with the other? Each item is a unity of what it is in itself, thus as contrasted with the other (x,y), and of what it is as present to and for the other, thus as merged with it $(x.y)$. If it were not the unity of these two things, it could not mediate them. Thus, it seems necessary that there is a division within the unitary items, a division acknowledging the distinction between x,y and $x.y$. This is similar to our distinction between the essential and conditional components of a harmony, to be explained in the next chapter. How is this division unified in each item?

Weiss argued that there are not two but rather four irreducible beings or modes. Each mode has some conditional components that come from its relations to each of the other modes.[9] And each mode has some essential components of its own that are not shared with the other modes. That the conditional components come from the other modes is internal to a mode by means of the x,y. That the conditional components are themselves internal to the mode is constituted by the $x.y$. The essential components of the mode unify the x,y and the $x.y$ within the mode. If each mode unifies the ways by which it is together with the others, then each mode is a one for the many others. As many modes, or things, as there are, that many ones there are. There is not a single one for the many but many ones. Yet if the modes are what is real, and their togetherness is to be accounted for in terms of the modes' components, then there is no context over and above the modes for which a unity of the many ones is to be sought. This is Weiss' metaphysical pluralism. It has three main difficulties, however.

First, if the components of an item are themselves determinate, as they must be if they are distinguished as essential and conditional, then they too must be unified as both merged and contrasted with one another; and the components of the components are the same way, down to an infinite regress. The difficulty is that the unity in each case is again reduced to a *de facto* unity or mere togetherness. The unity of x is simply the togetherness of the components of its nature, and the unity of each of the components is again the togetherness of their own component components, and so on. The togetherness is only acknowledged; it is not accounted for as a genuine unity. The argument in the next chapter will elaborate the togetherness as a fitness of the components of a harmony, and it will have to give an account of the genuine unity of a harmony.

Second, the fact that each item unifies the various ways in which it is together with the others is not sufficient for that mode to account for the being and the unity of those others, which it must do if its own being depends on those others to supply its conditional components. In the first place, it does not account for the unity of those others of the ontological many, for each of those others unifies the many in its own way. That way may be reflected in the conditional components of the first mode, but the reflection loses the immediate presence of the other mode's unity in the reproduction. Moreover, the way the other mode unifies its ways of togetherness is distorted and qualified when it is integrated with the things that must be unified in the first mode's way of unity. In the second place, the fact that each mode unifies the various ways in which it is together with the others of the ontological many does not account for the being of those others. The one for the ontological many must not only unify the ways in which the presence of the many modifies it; it must also account for the unity of the being of the others. This is the inexpugnable insight in the view that being must be common to the many in order to unify them, a thesis to be examined below. But on a pluralistic view such as Weiss's, it is precisely this commonality that is denied in favor of an independence in being of each mode or determination from the others.

The third difficulty with the pluralistic view is that it exhibits a different locus for the ontological unity of the many than the one it advertises. However lacking in rational explanatory power a mere *de facto* unity is, it still is *a* kind of unity that demands an explanation. To acknowledge a *de facto* unity is at least to acknowledge a problem yet to be solved. Pluralism of Weiss's variety claims that the locus for the unity of the ontological many is in each one of the many, that is, that each thing or mode unifies all the others in its own unity. But not only is each a determinate *de facto* unity, the whole of the things constitutes a *de facto* unity; this is the very meaning of pluralism. If each of the many is the one for the many, then there are many ones, each unifying the whole; where there is a many, there is a one; therefore, there is at least a *de facto* unity of the many ones. This last *de facto* unity is the one that goes beyond what the pluralistic theory takes itself to explain. But the unity of the plurality of unities is surely an ontological unity, in fact the most basic one. Therefore, pluralism of this sort exhibits a *de facto* unity that it does not even try to account for. Metaphysical pluralism fails to be satisfactory.

The point of the argument here against Weiss is not yet to push beyond the *de facto* character of the unity to some explanation but only to see what is involved in the *de facto* character itself. An element is involved over and above the specific determinate things unified. Minimally it can be called a "context of mutual relevance." This is the context wherein the things are contained as mutually determinate with respect to each other. The context would have to contain both modes of relevance, x,y and $x.y$, for all the things within the context and their mutual conditionings and independence. The determinate relevancies are, of course, constituted by the really distinct things, but such mutually relevant things presuppose a unifying context for the relevancies, that is, conditional components. The context, in its turn, presupposes the determinate things that bear the mutual relevancies, for it would not be a context unless it were a context for something. The *de facto* unity of the many things in their one context is the kind of unity that itself presupposes a plurality to be unified. But it is in the context of mutual relevance that the many things find their ontological unity. Therefore, we should expect to find the character of being as the ontological one for the ontological many manifesting itself in some close connection with that context. This is the point to which we return in chapter 11.

Now we have rebutted the objection to inquiring about being as the one for the many that comes from metaphysical pluralism that says that there is no one for the many, merely many unifying ones. Can we then say that there must be an ontological one for the many? Yes, but not without ambiguity. For the unifying one might be either analogical or univocal. To resolve this ambiguity is the next step.

III. WHETHER BEING IS ANALOGICAL OR UNIVOCAL

The European medievals said that being is "the first object of intellect." By this they meant that, no matter what an intellect thinks about, it thinks about it as being what it is. This is true about thinking of physical things, philosophical objects, mere ideas, dreams, fictions, and falsehoods. To think of a thing, such as a perfect island (the example in the famous debate between Anselm and Guanilo), that it does not exist is still to think of it as *being* a perfect island that does not exist. This supposes that being is one thing, unified, and that we speak of it univocally when we say it is the first object of intellect.

Suppose instead, however, that being is not univocal but analogical, as Thomas Aquinas claimed.[10] The medievals distinguished among (1) univocal concepts, those that are used in a straightforward single sense, (2) equivocal concepts, such as "bank" meaning both the financial institution and the boundaries of a river, and (3) analogical concepts that are equivocal but have some manageable connection between the various senses. Aristotle, on whom the medieval defenders of analogy drew, said that "healthy" as an analogical concept refers to a person, to the person's diet as a cause of health, and to the person's urine as a sign of health. If being is analogical, then physical objects have being in one sense, ideas have being in another sense, dreams yet another, and the same with fictions, falsehoods, and every other kind of thing. Every kind of thing has being in a sense appropriate to its kind. The motive behind Thomas Aquinas' doctrine of the analogy of being was to be able to say that God has infinite being and everything else has finite being. Yet the claim that being is analogical is not persuasive on the face of it. To say that physical objects differ in kind from ideas, dreams, fictions, and falsehoods is to assert that they have different natures, but in the same sense of "having different natures." They cannot be said to be different without saying that they *are* different. Here is the sense in which being is the "one" that allows for differences to be possible.

Let us consider Thomas' argument further, however, in the case of "God," Thomas's term and metaphorical construct for ontological ultimate reality. He was not unusual among theologians in saying that we use analogies to speak of the ultimate. Like many others he said that, just as human beings have some limited goodness, wisdom, power, truthfulness, and personal unity, so God has those virtues in unlimited, infinite, ways. Keith Ward is one of the latest Christian philosophical theologians to defend this sense of analogy.[11] Behind this list of analogues was a deeper one for Thomas. We are persons with intentions, looking and acting as subjects relative to a world of objects. But the separation or differentiation of us as subjects over against the world as objects, a distinction of our "formal reality" over against the separate "formal reality" of the world, is a limitation that God does not have.[12] God is an infinite person, according to Thomas, who has no other, who does not intend anything other than the divine self; even within the divine self-intention there can be no actual-potential differentiation of the sort that characterizes finite intentions.[13]

But what can infinity mean in this context? It makes sense to call a human being good only in contrast to evil or the less good, wise only in contrast to foolishness, powerful only in contrast to inability, truthful only in contrast to mendacity, unified only in contrast to incoherent. People are virtuous only because they have the potential of lacking those virtues. As persons, the very meaning of personal intentionality is in the finite relation to a potential other. God, for Thomas, has no potentials other than what is always fully actualized in the divine nature. So it would seem that all these virtues, and the very definition of personhood, are utterly meaningless in God's case, and that the analogy does not carry: God for Thomas is infinite act, and not finitely anything. We learn absolutely nothing about God by saying that God is perfectly virtuous and personal in analogy with our imperfect virtue and personality.

This frustrating negative conclusion follows, however, only on the assumption that the being of God and finite creatures is being in the same sense, and that the difference is only in the natures that they have respectively, infinite in the former case, finite in the latter. Thomas' genius was to say that it is not only the natures of God and creatures that are different, but also the senses in which they are or have those natures. The senses in which they are, or have being, is different. In fact, we are to understand the differences in nature, with respect to infinity and finitude at least, in terms of the different senses of being rather than in terms of the properties of their respective natures. Because their respective senses of being are only analogically connected, and because we can understand that analogy of being, we can understand their natures to be analogically connected without losing the meaningfulness of both sides of the analogy. Thomas knew that he had to develop an analogy of being, not just of natures, such that by knowing the finite side we could infer without losing meaning in order to know the divine or infinite side. The analogy of being needs to allow for inference from the finite to the infinite in order to give rise to knowledge of the infinite. The finite needs to be an analogue for the infinite as analogate. The analogate is to be known through the analogue.

From Aristotle and the Aristotelian tradition that had become so lively for him, Thomas drew two forms of analogy, the "analogy of proportion" and the "analogy of proper proportionality." In the analogy of proportion an analogical term is one used in two ways; the ways are different in some respects, alike in others. As Thomas said, such a "term is predicated according to concepts diverse in some respect and in some respect not—diverse inasmuch as they entail diverse relations, but one in that these diverse relations are all referred to some one term."[14] This "one term" referred to functions in the analogy of proportion in the following way: "There exists a certain conformity among things proportioned to each other because of a mutual determinate distance or some of determinate relation between them, as two is proportioned to one by being the double of one."[15] The rub, however, is that in analogy this "determinate distance" or "one term" is what is *not* known. Or if it is known, the result is a completely univocal system with no real equivocation whatsoever. The example of "healthy" cited previously is really a univocal set of relationships having to do with health, not an analogy at all except in rhetoric. Thomas realized this and rejected the analogy of proportion. "It is impossible for anything to be said of God and creature," by the analogy of proportion, "for no creature has a relation to God such that, through it, the divine perfection could be determined."[16]

The analogy of proper proportionality, on the other hand, claims not to depend on the distance being determinate between analogous things. Rather, the two things have similar proportions within themselves. Proportionality is a "mutual conformity of two things between which there is no determinate proportion, but rather a mutual likeness of two proportions."[17] For instance we can know that 36 is to 72 as 2 is to 4 without knowing anything about the relation between the two ratios. Accordingly, although we have no knowledge of the distance between God and human beings, we can nonetheless know, for instance, that God's intelligence is proportioned to God's being as our intelligence is proportioned to our being. This is the significance of the analogy of being, not of natures.

The description of proper proportionality is ambiguous, however, and neither side is satisfactory. On the one hand, the analogy of proportionality could be taken to assert, in the above example, that God's intelligence, like all the divine powers, is appropriate to the divine kind of being as our powers are appropriate to our kind of being. But because we do not know the distance between us and God, we do not know what God's kind of being is and so the analogy gives no information about God or God's intelligence. On the other hand, the analogy of proportion could be understood to assert that the proportions in the analogous things are indeed similar. God's intelligence is related to the divine being similarly to the way human intelligence is related to the human kind of being. But this is clearly false: Human intelligence is discursive and God's is immediate (on Thomas's view). We appeal to analogy instead of to univocity precisely because of the differences, not the similarities. And on this interpretation of proportionality, it is just the respect in which things are said to be analogous that similarity is to be denied.

But this last argument might be too simple. God's intelligence is immediate because God's being is simple. Human intelligence is discursive because human being is discursive, that is, played out in parts. As simple being is to immediate intelligence, so composite being is to discursive intelligence. This is a perfectly coherent proportionality, and given any three terms, the fourth could be worked out. The difficulty with this is the old one, however: To begin with any three of the terms is to know the determinate distance between the divine and human. We have to know that God's being is simple in order to make the analogy work. Thus, the analogy of proper proportionality reduces to the analogy of proportion that claims to know the determinate distance between the two sides of the analogy. To speak of the divine being at all is already to have some notion of the divine nature and hence of the determinate distance between God and creature.

To see that a claim about God is analogous, and not simply univocal, something like the determinate distance must be known. John Duns Scotus put this point most succinctly: "Every denial is intelligible only in terms of some affirmation . . . if we deny anything of God, it is because we wish to do away with something inconsistent with what we have already affirmed."[18] Analogy of being presupposes some non-analogical knowledge of the "determinate distance" between analogue and analogate in order to say that the analogy is only an analogy. It cannot be the case that the analogate is known only by the analogue, and if there is any reason at all for speaking analogically at this point, it cannot be to infer from what is known to something that is not known.

If it is true that any analogical predication of a term must have a univocal or non-analogical ground, both for asserting the analogue in the first place and for showing where it is only an analogy, somewhat equivocal, then God and creatures cannot be said to be in different senses. No univocal concept is able to ground an assertion that there is an equivocation in the respective senses in which two things are, for if "being" is not predicated univocally of two things, then no concept can be predicated univocally of them. If things differ not only in what they are but in the very sense in which they are what they are, then no concept can be applied to them univocally. Hence, no univocal knowledge can ground the claim that being is predicated of two things analogically.

This conclusion is stated in terms of the predication of concepts, following the medieval argument; but it can be restated in first order terms of determinate things themselves. Although two things can differ in what they are, that is, their determinations, they cannot differ in the sense in which they are what they are: to be different with respect to each other, they must be or possess their determinations in the same sense. If two things do differ in the sense in which they are what they are, then in no way can they be said to be alike. Not even in analogy. Hence, however the determinations of being differ, being must be one.

Our original conclusion coming from the discussion of metaphysical pluralism was that being is the one for the many determinate things. To this, it was objected that there is an ambiguity in the sense in which being is the one, namely that it might be analogically one or univocally one. Being cannot be analogically one and therefore must be univocally one. Now this objection has been removed. We can return to the question of what being might be in order to be the one for the many.

IV. WHETHER BEING IS DETERMINATE OR INDETERMINATE

If being is the one for the many, it is either determinate or indeterminate. This section explores possible concepts of being as determinate and concludes that being cannot be determinate and is therefore indeterminate.

One hypothesis for claiming that being is determinate is to say that it is a property common to all beings. When it is said that all beings have being, on this hypothesis what is meant is that there is a property or attribute of being that is a component of all beings, a trait they share in common. This is probably what most people think of when they think of the being of beings. On any hypothesis about being, to be sure, it must be possible to say that all beings have being in some sense or other. What is distinct about this hypothesis is that the being they have is a determinate property alongside of or on a par with other properties.

The claim that being is a property common to all beings can be vague with respect to just what kind of property is involved. The property might just be a surd, a "simple non-natural" quality as G.E. Moore thought value is, something that is merely recognized. Being has a kind of qualitative mysteriousness that lends itself to this kind of interpretation. On the other hand, the property might be something like "presence to consciousness." The phrase, "being is the first object of intellect," lends itself to this interpretation.

Whether a determinate surd, or a determinate quality that can itself be further characterized in terms of other things, the common property hypothesis says that being is determinate as a property that all beings share and is on a par with anything else that is determinate. Any being has many properties, including being; beings differ from one another by having different properties except for the fact they all have being.

This interpretation of being as a determinate property beside others founders on a fundamental dilemma of ontology: If being is a property, what is the ontological status of the other properties? The other properties, by virtue of being other, contrast determinately with the property of being. But to contrast with being, they must have an integrity or being of their own over against being. If being is one of many properties, then those other properties also must be, on their own and in contrast to the property of being. Then the properties other than being would have a higher sense of being than that of the determinate property of being.

Perhaps it might be said, in defense of the common property hypothesis, that being is one property among others and that the others "are" only in the event that they have the property of being. After all, many properties contrast with each other and yet by their natures entail the others; for instance, "red" is not the same as "colored" and yet entails it. But what is at issue is not whether one property can participate in another, even to the point of necessary entailment. The issue concerns the ontological status of those characters of properties by virtue of which they contrast. If a property is other than being, even if it has being, then that by virtue of which it is other than being must have an ontological status. The contrasting elements must be over and against being. Red may be a color, but it is not the same as "color" because it is different from blue, which is also a color. As "redness in contrast to blueness" is over against "color," so the contrasting properties that have being are over against being. Otherwise there is no point in saying that being is a determinate property. But if this is so, then they have being over against being, which is a contradiction.

Perhaps, then, it might be said in defense of the common property hypothesis that only substances have being and that properties "are" only when they are properties of substances; the Aristotelian tradition supposes an interpretation something like this. To speak of properties having being, on this interpretation of being as a common property, is merely a confusion. Substances have being, and being is a property of substances. On this interpretation, it would be a distorting abstraction to speak of the property of being; one can speak of being as a property had by substances, but to isolate it and call it a determinate property by itself is an unwarranted hypostatization. Needless to say, this interpretation only occasions more difficulties of the kind that beset the previous argument. If substances contrast with being, what is their ontological status insofar as they contrast? And even if properties are only to be found in substances, how do they contrast with the property of being? If it is said that to be is to be a substance—that this is just exactly the property that being is, again, how does a substance contrast with its other properties? Its other properties are either exactly identical with it, all substances being alike, or they contrast: If the other properties differ from substantial being, whatever in them is other than being must have some ontological status, must have being of its own. That is the same contradiction noticed previously.

The difficulties of the common property hypothesis exhibit a basic metaphysical principle that can be called the "principle of the ontological ground of differences." It is that two differing determinate beings presuppose a common ground in virtue of which they are relevantly determined with respect to each other and from which each delimits for itself a domain over against the other. Although both differing elements must *be* in the same sense (univocally) in order to be comparable, and thus must have being in common, at the same time they differ according to their individual integrities or natures and therefore each must have its "own" being, or "own-being." Being must be such that each being can delimit it and possess its own domain.

The error of the interpretation of being as a determinate property is that it emphasizes the commonality in the principle of the ontological ground of differences while it pays insufficient attention to the sense in which each side has its own being. Consequently, the interpretation acknowledges the latter side unreflectively by construing the relation between being and the beings as that of universal to particular or of genus to species. Put in this bald way, it is readily seen that neither of these models can suffice. As Aristotle saw, neither the universal nor the genus properly bespeaks the components that differentiate their instances or species from the other; yet these distinguishing components have their being too, over against the universal or genus. The conclusion of this phase of the argument is that, if being is determinate, it cannot be determinate as a property common to beings.

On the supposition that being is determinate, the hypothesis opposite to that of the common property hypothesis is that of being as the determinate completion or totality of the ontological many. This hypothesis is associated with absolute idealism. Two points in this hypothesis should be emphasized. First, in order to be a determinate totality, not an adventitious massing or de facto collection, being in the totalizing sense must be a highest principle or category. This highest category cannot be exhibited fully by any limited number of the beings of the ontological many but must be exhibited by them all together, a super-category that integrates the many and gives a determinate place to each. Second, the many beings included within the totality are in themselves only partial or abstract expressions or embodiments of being. They might be real, concrete, or capable of exercising brute force, but still they are abstract in relation to the fullness of being.

The totalizing hypothesis for interpreting the claim that being is determinate founders, however, on the same fundamental dilemma of ontology that struck down the common property hypothesis, the dilemma of giving being a positive characterization. Being as the highest category must be determinate. If so, it needs a significant contrast category. How can the determination that unifies all other determinations determinately be what it is and not some other thing? Two answers are possible.

Suppose the highest category does not have a significant contrast term. But then it can have no determinateness uniquely its own whereby it internally relates, as a "third term," the abstract categories and beings it encompasses. For, to have a significant determination of its own over and above the abstract determinate things that it contains, it must have a significant contrast, contrary to the totalizing hypothesis. To put the point another way, in virtue of what does this highest category unite its contents? The answer must be, in virtue of its own determinate nature. But, to be determinately what it is, the highest category must contrast with what it determinately is not. Otherwise, it would contain the encompassed things as a box indifferently contains a miscellany of things; even this analogy begs the question, since a box has a determinate principle of ordering space in virtue of which it unites its contents. The highest category, if not determinate over against a contrast term, could not of itself give an interpreting order to its contents, nor could it even be said to be anything more than the uncollected sum of its parts. And, at any rate, if it has no significant contrast and hence is not determinate itself, it cannot be an interpretation of the claim that being is determinate.

Suppose, then, contrary to the previous supposition, that the highest category does have a significant contrast term. What can that be? Again, two answers are possible: The contrast term could be one or all of the categories or beings contained within the highest category or it could be absolute non-being. Suppose the former. Although the highest category would be a significant contrast for any one of its abstract parts because it would contain the other determinations, the contrary does not hold. The abstract part has no determination over and above the whole of which it is a part, that is, the highest category; for, the highest category must wholly integrate its parts and hence all of its parts are completely internally related to it. The abstract part cannot be a significant contrast for the highest category unless its limitations make it sufficiently less than the highest category. But the limitations of an abstract part are nothing more than the totality of the rest of the abstract parts. Thus, an abstract part together with its limitations is the same thing as the highest category because they must be unified within and by the highest category. Then the totality of parts is the same as the highest category. Otherwise the parts could not be "totaled," and a thing cannot be a contrast term to itself.

Suppose then the second answer to the question of what the contrast term to the totalizing category might be, namely, absolute non-being. Now, by definition non-being cannot contrast with the highest category by some determination of its own, because if non-being had a determination it would be something determinate, not non-being. Then, the contrast must be that non-being has absolutely no features, whereas being does have determinate features. But if this is so, absolute non-being cannot be the contrast term for that specific positive determination in virtue of which the highest category unites its parts; and it is the highest category's peculiar inclusive determinateness that needs the contrast, not determinateness as such.

These difficulties with the totalizing category hypothesis about the claim that being is determinate, like those with the common property hypothesis, exhibit a basic metaphysical principle, which can be called the "principle of the ontological equality of reciprocal determinations:" if two determinate thing are contrast terms for each other, then they must be on the same ontological level and the categories descriptive of them must be on the same logical level. Of course, if the contrast is not reciprocal, the determinate things need not be on the same ontological level.

The basic difficulty with both the common property and totalizing category hypotheses about how being can be determinate is that they accept a meaning of "determinate" that requires that being have a contrast term. Yet there is nothing on the same ontological level with being with which it can contrast. Nor is there anything on the same logical level in the order of varying degrees of abstractness with which it can contrast.

So, if being is to be the one for the many, and if it is to be determinate in order to be so, then it cannot be either a static common denominator or a static totality of beings. The next step, a short one, is to consider a more dynamic conception of being as determinate, that of Georg Hegel.

Hegel conceived the Absolute to be the dynamic dialectical process by means of which that which is abstract or partial externalizes itself to have something with respect to which it can be determinate, in turn causing a further dynamic growth to unify the things external to each other, which again in turn requires something further with respect to which it can be determinate, and so on. This dialectic takes place in terms of sheer logic, in the progress of temporal history, and in the successive stages of integration of logic and history that constitutes the life of Absolute Spirit itself. Hegel was fully aware of the dialectical difficulties with the common property and totalizing category hypotheses. If two stages of the dialectic are external to one another, then a third stage is needed to unify them. That third stage has to be determinate in order to add something unifying to the otherwise external things, and it is determinate with respect to the first two stages that it contains. But those contained stages are not on the same ontological level as the unifying stage, and so the unifying stage still needs something other external to itself in order to be properly determinate. In fact, the dynamism of the dialectic consists in the fact that a unifying stage cannot be itself to do the unifying job without giving rise to its own negation with respect to which it can be properly determinate. Hence, the dialectic is always driven forward seeking further determination in order to secure the partial determinations that unify previous stages.

Our minimal question for Hegel, whose theory is far richer than can be explored here, is whether his conception registers being as the one for the many as determinate or indeterminate. In one sense, a unifying stage is determinate insofar as it unifies the preceding stages. But in this sense it is exactly the same as the totalizing category hypothesis, and is subject to the same difficulties: For the third stage to be determinate, and related to the determinate preceding stages, there has to be a context of mutual relevance uniting them, and the position reduces to a bad infinite regress (Hegel called this a "bad infinite"). Precisely for this reason, Hegel thought the determinate unifying stage necessarily gives rise to its own negation as the ground for the determinateness it needs to unify its predecessors; then it and its negation need a further unifying. To read Hegel as saying that the earlier stages of the dialectic are actual and are producing more actuality through negation and synthesis is mistaken. Rather, the earlier stages are abstract and incompletely real except insofar as the later stages make them real. The problem for the Absolute is that at no stage in its dialectic is it fully real. No last stage can exist because that would reduce immediately to being as a highest category. In this sense of the infinite growth of the Absolute, the process of unifying many stages is *in*determinate, or at least always incompletely determinate. Incompleteness does not mean that the details are not all filled in. It means rather that such determinateness that the Absolute has through its dialectical stages is incompletely real. At no stage is the Absolute determinate enough to be the one for all the many. On this reading, Hegel's theory amounts to saying that being, as the one for the many, is not determinate. Of course, we might not agree that Hegel gives the best account of indeterminacy in being. But he does not provide a viable hypothesis, different from being as a highest category, for saying that being is determinate.

At this stage in the argument, we can say that being, in some sense yet to be found, must be the one for the many things that are, because the attempt of ontological pluralism to say that there is no such many, that each of the many is a one for the others, fails. We also can say that being as the one cannot be so only in an analogical sense, not a univocal sense, because the attempt to defend analogy within being fails. Finally, we cannot say that being as the one is determinate, for if it were, it would be one more of the many. To be sure, there might be more hypotheses defending the determinateness of being as the one, but those we have considered, the main ones, have failed. The bottom line of the discussion so far is that, if being is the one for the many and is determinate, there must be some deeper "one" that connects being as the one to the many. If that deeper one is determinate, there must be an even yet deeper one that connects the deeper one to the one and the many, and so on infinitum. Therefore, we can conclude with considerable plausibility that any hypothesis that says that being as the one for the many is determinate is mistaken. We need instead to find an hypothesis that accounts for an indeterminate sense of being as the one for the many. This is an unusual claim, but the one at the heart of the metaphysical hypothesis of *Philosophical Theology*.

Certain things have already been learned about the conditions for that indeterminate one. The consideration of various hypotheses about being in this chapter has elicited two general principles. The first is the "principle of the ontological ground of differences," namely, that two different determinate things presuppose a common ground in virtue of which they are relevantly determined with respect to each other and from which each delimits for itself a domain over against the other. Yet that common ground cannot be yet another determinate thing. The second is the "principle of the ontological equality of reciprocal determinations," namely, that, if two determinate things are contrast terms for each other, then they must be on the same ontological level and the categories descriptive of them must be on the same logical level. This is to say, if a thing is determinate, it is determinately itself and not some other thing; it needs the contrast with the other thing to be determinate itself. The other thing in the reciprocal contrast cannot be simply a proper part of the determinate thing, because then it would not be other than the thing. To deny the principle of the ontological equality of reciprocal determinations is to deny genuine multiplicity or plurality. It would be to deny that there is real "otherness" in reality. The religious significance of this is that it would deny real "otherness" in other people, allowing them to be related to us only insofar as they are encompassed wholly within our own experience (II, 3, 7).

From the dialectical background of this chapter, the combination of these two principles yields the hypothesis that being as the indeterminate one for the many is an "ontological context of mutual relevance." The principle of the ontological equality of reciprocal determinations says that determinate things are really different from one another, and that they have to be different in order for any to be determinate with respect to one another. The principle of the ontological ground of differences says that such different things need a context in which they can be mutually relevant without being reduced or merged into the same thing. The ontological ground is better called a "context" because it should not be suggested that the ground is determinate.

In contrast to the determinate beings, being is that which allows the beings to be determinate with respect to one another, the ontological context of mutual relevance. Being is not a determinate thing, which would make it one more of the many. The nature of the oneness or unity of the one is whatever kind of unity the ontological context of mutual relevance might have.

The question for our argument now is, What can be the ontological context of mutual relevance? The term *context* is still radically underdeveloped in the argument here. The context cannot be something determinate itself. It must encompass the determinate things in their mutual relations and also in their reciprocal otherness that cannot be reduced to their mutual determinations. What might satisfy these conditions? Can we develop a metaphysical hypothesis about an ontological context of mutual relevance that makes sense of the requirement that being as the one for the many is indeterminate? To do so requires a shift of topics in the argument to study determinateness itself, the plot for the next chapter.

To take stock here briefly, it is safe to say that in today's climate of philosophical theology, most of the questions studied in this chapter are of little interest. Most thinkers do not worry about how to understand the unity of fundamental plurality, the problem of the one and the many. Most do not care whether plurality or unity is primary, or how to balance them. Most would not be interested in the question whether being might be analogical in Thomas Aquinas's sense rather than univocal as Scotus argued. Most would not be concerned about whether being as the alleged one for the many is determinate or indeterminate, or motivated to examine the candidate conceptions for being as determinate in any detail. Fair enough. For most thinkers there is no need to understand and assess the arguments of this chapter with much exactness. Nevertheless, it is very important to decide about the conclusion that being cannot be determinate, which is a very important conclusion indeed. For, it entails that no conception of ultimate reality, of God, Brahman, Heavenly Principle, Dao, or any other such can be the conception of a determinate thing. For theists, this means that one cannot say that God is personal, has intentions or agency, or is even good; the point holds for process theology as well as those theologies that say that God creates the world from nothing. Most theists want to resist this conclusion. But then they need to go back and study the arguments of this chapter carefully. The arguments cannot be dismissed later just because of a late recognition that they prohibit some favorite theological conceptions. The ontological context of mutual relevance, which is the ultimate reality within which determinate things are possible and actual, cannot be determinate. This is the ontological metaphysical hypothesis backed by argument.

CHAPTER TEN

The Metaphysics of Cosmological Ultimacy

I. DETERMINATENESS AS HARMONY: ESSENTIAL AND CONDITIONAL COMPONENTS

Before we can be more exact about what might constitute the ontological context of the mutual relevance of determinate things, it is important to develop a formal theory of determinateness. In several of the previous chapters it was asserted that to be determinate is to be a harmony of essential and conditional components. Now this needs to be explicated as a proper metaphysical hypothesis.

To be a thing is to be determinate, to be something rather than something else or nothing. The hypothesis to be advanced is that to be determinate is to be a harmony of at least two kinds of components. The conditional components of a thing are those by virtue of which it is related to other things, conditioned by them or conditioning them. The essential components are those by virtue of which the harmony integrates the conditional components so as to have its own-being.

Note at the outset how abstract this point is. Many kinds of things exist, stable things and changes, ideas and physical objects, past, present, and future things, contradictions and counterfactuals, totally determinate things and infinitesimally determinate things. The analysis of determinateness must be abstract enough to apply to anything. Furthermore, the analysis of determinateness must be abstract enough to apply to any and all philosophical theories about what it is to be a thing, to Aristotelian substance theories, Platonic theories of the ideal, Neo-Platonic theories of emanating things, Cartesian, Leibnizean, Spinozistic, Hobbesian, Lockean, Humean, Kantian, Hegelian, Whiteheadian, and all other Western philosophical theories. Of course, to be properly abstract, the analysis of determinateness should apply to Chinese conceptions of yin-yang changes, South Asian theories of nondual things, and

Buddhist theories of empty dharmas rushing pall mall in *pratitya samutpada*. The level of abstraction involved in analyzing determinateness needs to allow that any and all of these more specific theories might be true. These theories are not compatible with each other, but we do not have to sort or evaluate them to see well enough that they ascribe determinateness to things that fall under their analysis.

The abstractness of the hypothesis about harmonies of conditional and essential components is so great that it is almost impossible to explicate without calling to mind specific examples of conditional and essential components. Those examples would already be couched in some more specific languages, such as those mentioned in the previous paragraph. As indicated in Chapter 9, Section I, we can distinguish the strictly metaphysical theory of determinateness as harmonies of essential and conditional components from philosophical cosmologies of various sorts that illustrate it. Even when they contradict one another or are in such different languages as not immediately to be comparable, all the philosophical cosmologies must illustrate it if the metaphysical hypothesis about determinateness is properly abstract. Charles Peirce would say that the kind of abstraction involved that contains contradictories within it is "vagueness."

Although it might seem a disadvantage for the theory of determinateness to be so abstract as to apply to all possible kinds of determinations, a compensating advantage also holds. The abstract metaphysical hypothesis has the power to ask questions and reveal limitations of the more specific philosophical cosmologies that illustrate it. In the consideration of those cosmologies, we can ask how they deal with the question of determinateness, and judge whether their account is sufficiently full, consistent, coherent, adequate, and applicable to all possible determinate things.

Consider the following. Without conditional components, things would be such atoms as to have no relations whatsoever. Strict philosophical atomisms have always been a difficulty, because most such theories say that there is a space–time receptacle with intrinsic properties of motion that impose external relations on the atoms. That receptacle is determinate, but is not another atom; and therefore determinateness as such cannot be defined atomistically. Moreover, although the receptacle might impose only external relations on the atoms with reference to one another, it must itself be internally related to the atoms in order to contain them and move them about. For atoms to be in space–time, they must have some internal space–time dimension of their own, and hence have characteristics of the receptacle internal to their natures as atoms. Leibniz' theory of monads, in his *Monadology*, was perhaps the most ingenious Western attempt to hold to a philosophical atomism. He argued that, internally, the monads have no space–time dimensionality, only the unfolding of perceptions in succession. But those perceptions are mirrors of the space–time dimensionality of all the external monads, where space–time dimensionality means how other monads are mirrored in the interior of any given monad. For Leibniz, there would be no sense in which the monads are really in space–time were it not for God creating each monad eternally actually to mirror the other monads. The commonsense implausibility of such divine correlative behavior led Whitehead to construct his "cell theory" of actual occasions according to which each cell becomes an actual part of subsequent cells, and itself contains previous cells as its own actual parts.[1] Whitehead saw that strict atomism is impossible and developed a theory in which things are conditional components of other things by virtue of being prehended by them, or anticipated by them. If things were only atoms and not internally related to each other in any way, they would not be different from one another in any respect. Wholly atomized, unrelatable, things would not be determinately what they are rather than being some other thing or nothing.

Without essential components, on the other hand, things would be reduced to their conditional components, which in turn would be impossible because there would be nothing for other things to condition or be conditioned by. As F.H. Bradley showed, if there are only relations and no terms related, then all determinateness disappears with the absence of plurality.[2] However things are internally related to one another by possessing conditional components from one another, they need also to be external to one another in a strict enough sense as not to be reduced to just one thing. Bradley's conclusion was that only one thing exists, the Absolute, which is totally indeterminate because it contains no distinctions within itself; nor is it determinately distinct from anything else. But there are determinate things in experience. Even to be wrong about determinate things is determinate. Therefore there must be essential components in addition to conditional components. In Whitehead's cosmology, the past things prehended into an emerging actual entity are integrated by various subjective processes of creativity internal to the emerging entity. Those subjective processes are the essential components that make the emerging entity something new over and above all the past things that are its conditions.

Essential and conditional components are both equally necessary for determinateness. "Essential" should not imply greater importance or necessity than "conditional."

To say that things are *harmonies* of essential and conditional components is to say that their components simply fit together. They are not components of some underlying substance, although some harmonies might have properties like substances. The harmony itself is the determinate entity. The fitting together of essential and conditional components in a harmony is not derived from a higher integrating principle, although some harmonies are possible only because they exist within larger harmonies, like heart and lungs working together in a human body. The ontological reality of the harmony is just the fitting together of its components, which must include essential and conditional ones.

The reason to call things "harmonies" rather than "substances" comes from this fact that harmonies just fit together. The hypothesis here is closer to Plato, for whom aesthetic balance is metaphysically deeper than substantial integration, than it is to Aristotle, the substance philosopher. Aristotle argued that there is a sense in which the form of a substance integrates all the formal properties involved. In another sense, he said, the material substratum or material components integrate the forms by embodying them. In another sense, the purpose, telos, or value of a thing integrates its parts. And in another sense the efficient cause integrates the parts of a substance by putting the forms together in the matter. These four senses of integration, Aristotle said, work together in the integration of a substance. This is to say, they just fit together. No one integrates the others. Aristotle, however, did not give an account of just fitting together, as Plato did in the Philebus, for instance. Plato argued that substantiality is just the reality of those things fitting together. We return to his kind of argument in the next section. Here we note that harmonies simply are the fitting together of their components, conditional and essential.

Correlative with the fitting together of components in a harmony is the point that the recognition of a harmony as a determinate thing is an aesthetic judgment. Or, more subtly, many ways exist of interpreting and relating to determinate things, and they all involve some version of grasping the things as harmonies of things. Aesthetic or value judgments are involved in all those ways. At least four families of aesthetic judgment need to be recognized, those in imagination, interpretation, theorizing, and the pursuit of responsibility. These are spelled out in this *Philosophical Theology* as needed (III, 9).[3]

If everything determinate is a harmony, then the components of harmonies are harmonies, both the conditional and essential components. Considered as components, these components themselves are harmonies with components, which in turn are harmonies with components. Thus, each harmony is infinitely deep in a sense. It would take a philosophical cosmology to explain how this is possible in an intelligible way.[4] But suffice it to say here that there are no simples. Simples, in fact, would be atoms, and hence not determinate.

A final point is to be made about this stage in the argument. Determinate things are determinate with respect to one another, and hence must be both mutually engaged and also in some sense external to one another, not reducible one to the other, as claimed in the principle of the ontological equality of reciprocal determinations (I, 9, iv). Things that are determinate with respect to one another must somehow be other than one another. The elementary metaphysics of otherness is the following. From the standpoint of harmony A, harmony B is other if and only if harmony A contains some components of B as conditional components of A, but does not contain some of the essential components of B as any components of A. A and B share some conditional components, and therefore are together in some kinds of relations. If they did not share any conditional components, they would not be together in any kind of relation, and thus would not be determinate with respect to each other. On the other hand, if harmony A contains B's essential as well as conditional components, then A wholly contains B, which is thereby not other than A. B's otherness depends on B's essential components not being subsumed wholly within A. This becomes extremely complicated when sorting different ways in which determinate harmonies can become components of other harmonies with respect to which they are determinate. Before proceeding to this point, however, another level of analysis of harmonies helpfully can be given, an analysis that was used in Chapter 1, Section III, to organize fundamental human problems defining ultimacy.

II. TRANSCENDENTAL ELEMENTS OF HARMONY: FORM AND COMPONENTS

Four transcendental traits of any harmony exist: pattern or form, components formed together, existential location, and value. They are transcendental because they are found in any determinate thing, any harmony. Thus, they are constitutive universal traits of anything at all. This section treats the first two because they are so intimately interdefined, and are intelligible mainly within the limits of the harmony itself. Existential location and value-identity are traits of a harmony by virtue of its connections with other harmonies and are treated in the following two sections.

Form

Form is the pattern of components as they fit together in a harmony. The components do not fit together because of the pattern, but the pattern exists because the things fit together. The form provides formal unity to the harmony; components that do not fit together cannot be formally unified. If form were not relative to components to be unified, it would be wholly pure formal unity, and as such would be indeterminate. Plato had this in mind when he said that the Form of the Good by itself is beyond determination.[5] But any form, as determinate, is a harmony with pure formal unity as its essential component and the determinate things to be formed into a harmony as its conditional components. A form's determinate pattern is how the determinate components might be unified.

This can be illustrated with a philosophical cosmology of time's flow that is elaborated in detail in chapter 12.[6] The future is a temporal mode that constitutes formal possibilities. The possibility structure of any date in the future is relative to the temporal modes of the past and the present. The past consists of all the things that have been actualized and the present is the temporal mode in which past things are responded to, reconfigured, added to, and integrated into the new present reality. When that present moment of creative harmonization is finished, the result is a past actual thing. The future provides the possibilities for a present moment of creative harmonization relative to the past things with which it has to work. The present moment of creative harmonization, it should be said, might be very destructive of past things and also lead to disastrous consequences; "harmonization" should not be assumed to be beneficent, although it always results in something of value, however destructive, as is seen later. So, the pattern of possibilities at a future date, say a year from today, is relative to the diverse things that are actual today, and also to the decisions made today. Today's decisions shift the possibilities for a year from now, perhaps significantly or only slightly. Thus, the form or possibility structure of any future date is constantly shifting as the decisive present moves on from moment to moment making new actual things to be the components from which the future possibility structure takes its harmonic form. Form as future possibility is extraordinarily dynamic.

As the future date approaches a decisive present, its formal structure is still universal; that is, it is a pattern that could integrate any set of components that had the same formal nature, not just the actual set it will have to integrate. Moreover, the possibility structure of the future date might well contain alternative possibilities for actualization, so that the deciding future moments will have to choose which possibilities to actualize and which to reject. When the future date becomes present and the possibilities are being sorted, with some actualized and others rejected, the universals are instantiated with a thisness: this actual embodiment of a universal. Duns Scotus wisely called universals "common natures" that achieve thisness, or "haecceity," in being actualized. This allows us to acknowledge that different things share common natures, whereas each embodies them in its own unique ways. Haecceity is an extremely complicated concept. But the analysis of its formal dimension is that the common nature is vague with respect to various ways it might be instantiated, and that the decisions of present creative moments resolve the vagueness so that it is specified with complete and formally consistent determination. Thus, the actualized possibility is real as both vague, allowing for discussions of common natures, and as formally completely determinate in its haecceity. Once an erstwhile future possibility has been actualized, it constitutes part of the structure of the past. That structure embodies both the common natures of the form and the specific haecceities. Because of the reality of common natures in actualized things, representative knowledge and interpretation are possible. Because of the haecceities, deference is necessary.

Another dimension of form as temporal possibility needs to be indicated, a dimension that applies to any determinate form per se, not only forms as possibilities for actualization. This is form's value dimension, which is discussed in more detail with reference to human choice in *Philosophical Theology Two*, chapter 1, and given a theoretical elaboration in *Three*, chapter 9. Any form has the value of getting its components together in that pattern in that existential location relative to other patterns. There would be a different value if the components were arranged with a different pattern, or if the same pattern were used for somewhat different components, or the thing were located differently. This point supposes that components that are patterned together themselves have value so that the alternative results of their patterning would have different values.

The antecedent value in the determinate things to be patterned together in a harmony can be explicated with the following consideration. The just-fitness of things in a harmony (e.g., the harmony of a determinate form) has two elements: complexity and simplicity. Complexity is the differences among the things harmonized; if the things were not harmonized, complexity would be mere manifoldness. Simplicity is the integration of the manifold with unifying forms; if the things were not harmonized, simplicity would be mere unity. Harmonies can have minimal value in two ways. If there is maximum complexity with minimum simplicity, the harmony tends toward mere conjunction: this and that and that other. . . . If there is maximum simplicity with minimum complexity, the harmony tends toward mere unity: homogenization. Value increases as both complexity and simplicity are maximized together. This means that the pattern of a harmony simplifies some of the manifold with certain unifying forms, other parts of the manifold with other forms, on and on. Then the unifying forms are simplified with more unifying forms, on up in a hierarchy to the point where, at the top, as it were, only a very few forms fit together. The danger to value in such a hierarchical tower of unifications is that complexity will be lost. Therefore, to maximize complexity, the higher order unifying forms should not block or lose the complexity in the manifold they unify. The mid-level and top unifying forms should retain the complex manifold and allow the diverse things to be together precisely because of the simplifying structuring. Value is thus increased as the density of being is increased: More diversity is crowded together with more intensity of unifying contrasts. "Contrast" was Whitehead's term for value, which he construed this way, as the use of simplifying forms to allow greater diversity to be together and make an impact, each thing on the other.

For a given set of components, there might be many different ways of maximizing complexity and simplicity, some ways with more complexity, others with more simplicity. Moreover, many alternative unifying forms might be used in the hierarchy of a harmonic pattern, so that the different possible structures are not merely quantitative alternatives for maximizing complexity and simplicity. Therefore, we should not speak only of degrees of value but also of kinds of value.

Every future possibility thus is a possible value. If it contains alternatives, it contains alternative values. The decisions in the present shift the values in future possibilities and, when that future moment comes, decide which of the values will be actualized. The past is thus filled with the values that have been actualized, and its structure is such that alternative values could have been actualized but were not.

Therefore, the already actualized components that give determinate structure to future possibilities each embody values. This is why it is important to say that every future possibility has the value of getting its components together with that pattern; each of the components brings a value that will be retained, diminished, or enhanced by the role of the component in the pattern. Moreover, the future possibility itself needs to be understood as modifying the values of its components by its own structure of complexity and simplicity. Everything possible has a value, perhaps alternative values. Everything being actualized in present decisive creativity is being given a specific value, perhaps selected among alternatives. Everything actual has the value of the form it has in its common natures and haecceity. The temporal world is shot through with value because of the form it has in its temporal modes.

This theory of value is by no means universally accepted.[7] A powerful tradition of science in Western modernity says the temporal world is to be understood simply in terms of facts, not values; for this tradition, values are human projections onto the natural world. Taken at face value, this tradition of modern science is a great lie concerning value, however, because the differing values of things in the world are so obvious. What is more potent in human experience than that we are often wrong in our evaluations? We can only be wrong about something that is real. Nevertheless, we can reject the fact-value distinction in the modern scientific worldview only if we can develop an alternative worldview that acknowledges the other things in reality about which science is right. Therefore, we need a philosophical (and theological) cosmology that shows both how scientific mathematical analysis and properly disciplined valuations of things can be true.[8] This cosmology would provide a justification for the theory of value here.

Short of that, however, its experiential plausibility can be illustrated. In moral analysis, for instance, we routinely imagine alternative scenarios that provide different possibilities for resolving critical tensions in the situation. In morals, we tend to keep the complexity factors steady, attempting to be responsive to all the interested parties; so we imaginatively play with different arrangements of simplicity. In this part of moral analysis, we employ aesthetic judgments to discern now to resolve the situation with maximum simplicity in light of the given components. In artistic endeavors, by contrast, we can vary the components as we please, deciding, in a painting for instance, which colors to use, how to bound areas, and the like. If some component is difficult to work with, it can be eliminated, unlike the moral situation. Mathematicians follow not only the logic of their arguments but adjudicate between equally valid arguments on the basis of their elegance, an aesthetic mode of valuation that attempts to judge how much (complexity) can be gotten by the most economical (simple) means.[9] Whereas the commonsense metaphysics of modern science might say that there is no real value in things, in practice we make critical value judgments all the time.

It would take an entire philosophical cosmology to describe the various kinds of form that are possible for harmonies. A quick list, however, can convey something of the variety. Some forms are synchronic, like a static pattern of things at a moment, others are diachronic, such as a piece of music played out in time. Some forms are tightly integrated, others are very loose. Some are enduring and capable of adjusting to change and others are evanescent. Forms are possibilities for things to fit together in harmonies. As such, they are ideals in the sense that they are the possible achievements of value that would come from getting the components together in that form.

From the standpoint of human beings, formal possibilities bearing values determine human beings to be obligated. We have some control over the outcomes of our decisions, and these outcomes differ in value. To choose the better outcome is to make ourselves the better chooser, and vice versa. The values, it should be remembered, are distinguished not only in quality, as in better and worse, but also in kind. So we make ourselves this or that kind of moral (or immoral) person. To be under obligation is to be in a position of choice with moral weight to the possible outcomes. The general virtue of righteousness comes from the obligation we have to put the "right form" on the things we affect.

COMPONENTS

The components of a harmony are other harmonies, each with its own essential and conditional components, and each with its forms, components to be formed, existential location, and value-identity. Thus every harmony is infinite in its components. Some components can be completely contained within their harmony, which is to say that their essential components as well as conditional components are wholly internal to the harmony in question. Other components can be contained within the harmony only in conditional ways; in this instance, these components are others to the harmony of which they are components. Yet other components move in and out of harmonies; for instance, iron in a rock might leach into soil where it is taken up into a plant that is eaten by an animal with the result that the iron becomes part of the animal's blood; when the animal dies the iron returns to the soil, which might become compressed into rock. The career of the iron puts it into several larger harmonies in sequence. A melody is in a composer's mind, then on a sheet of music, then in a performance, and then in the experience of the audience. The relations of the essential and conditional components of components internal and external to the containing harmony constitute the existential field, about which more is discussed later.

A harmony is grounded in its components in the sense that it is made up out of them. Although the harmony adds something to the components by virtue of getting them together with its value-laden form, the components are the ground out of which the integrating harmony arises. This spatiotemporal metaphor is best illustrated with spatiotemporal issues. If a harmony arises as an integration, in a present moment, of antecedent actual conditions, which are its causes, its actuality is grounded in those antecedent actualities. The antecedents provide the potentials for the new actual harmony. By the same token, a future possibility is a harmony whose grounding components are the actual things in the past, constantly being added to by present decisions. The harmony, which is a past state of affairs, is not only grounded in its own antecedents, but also in the subsequent things that are actualized that might change its meaning and value.

In these examples from spatiotemporal flow, it might seem as if the components of a harmony are identical with its conditional components, and that the essential components of a present decisive moment are exclusively the novel contributions of the emerging harmony. But the essential components are components too and need to just fit together with one another and the conditional components. For instance, in the responsible decision making of a human being, some essential components are in the spontaneity of creative harmonization of the present, others from past decisions for which the person is responsible in the present, and yet others from the future that is being determined in part by the present decisions.[10] Otherwise, responsible moral character would not be part of the identity of the person emerging in each moment of decision.[11]

From a human perspective, developed in *Philosophical Cosmology Two*, chapter 2, the fact we are grounded in our components means we need to comport ourselves toward them with some deference. On the one hand, the more important components have a reality and value of their own that we should acknowledge and appreciate. On the other hand, those important components give us our being and identity as something that is not only ourselves. They are our connections with the rest of reality. Deferential comportment is acknowledgment of the nature and value of those things we take up and possibly modify in ourselves and actions and at the same time is acknowledgment of our debt to them. Whereas righteousness has to do with right form, deferential comportment has to do with how we make ourselves whole out things that are not entirely ours.

III. TRANSCENDENTAL ELEMENTS OF HARMONY: EXISTENTIAL LOCATION

Existential location is the matrix of a harmony constituted by the relations of otherness with determinate things relative to the harmony. Insofar as a harmony has components that are other to one another, there is an existential field within the harmony. Insofar as the harmony has antecedents and successors that cause and are caused by it, such that the antecedents and successors have essential components external to the harmony, the harmony has a finite time in a temporal field. Insofar as the harmony is conditioned by and conditions contemporaries, it is in a place in a spatial field. Modern physics makes the extensive relations between space and time much more complicated than these common sense remarks suggest.

Harmonies, of course, are not only spatiotemporal things. Fictional stories are harmonies, and the things in the story have fictional existential location relative to one another. Formal structures, as in logic or mathematics, have formally defined elements that are existentially located relative to one another. Human meanings have existential location relative to the spatiotemporal location of the people but are not limited to that kind of extension. The heart and the lungs are external to one another in the body, conditioning one another but with different essential components; one body is external to another body with which it dances, even though they share conditional components in the dancing. With regard to most harmonies with which human beings have to deal, the spatiotemporal existential field constituted by their physical relations within and external to one another is basic to the larger existential field defined by their relations with those harmonies. This is not to say that the particularities of the physical spatiotemporal field are always important to those other harmonies. A philosopher developing a theory over time is always located somewhere physically. But the resulting theory has a structure to which it is largely irrelevant whether the philosopher was at a desk or sitting in a reading chair when various thoughts occur—largely irrelevant, but not entirely so: Continuity of logical thought is dependent on continuity of body states.

From the perspective of human beings, our existential location is subject to misinterpretation and denial. Within limits, we can imagine ourselves to be existentially connected with different things from our real connections, in a different time and place, connected to different individuals from those of real life, and hence with different (or no) responsibilities. Our components, especially our conditional components, constitute us as connected in all sorts of biological, social, and interpersonal ways, and the relations among these constitute the existential field within which we exist. But within limits it is possible to deny this. Often, it seems very desirable to deny some of these existential connections—to do so might make our obligations to righteousness and deference to our real groundedness much easier to fulfill. Denial is especially effective with regard to our mistakes regarding righteousness and deference. The possibility of denial defines the virtue of engagement, or what Tillich called faith.[12] Faith is the acceptance of our existential location, with all the obligations of righteousness and deference this entails. Because we have existential location, the pictures of us as harmonies actualizing possibilities and integrating components need to be supplemented with a picture of us engaging, or failing to engage, the harmonies with which we are existentially connected (II, 3).

The existential location of any harmony derives from its conditional components connecting it with other things. The existential locations of many things in mutual connection with one another constitute an existential field. An existential field is simply the mutual togetherness of the harmonies located within it insofar as this is determined through conditional components. But most fields have structures themselves that are over and above the structures of the harmonies within them because of the dominant characters of certain kinds of harmony. For instance, a physical existential field is dominated at a basic level of organization by those harmonies that have mass, gravitational pull, and so forth. An existential field that includes people dancing still has the basic structure of its gravitational characteristics, with the result that the human harmonies have to be careful not to trip and fall down.

This point about existential fields being constituted by their components is not philosophically innocent. It sides with Leibniz and Whitehead over Einstein with respect to the question whether space–time is a container for events or just the extensiveness of the events themselves. The arguments for it need not be given here.[13] But the general point is one of simplicity: the existential field is a function of the harmonies that are its components, and is itself a harmony: Its conditional components are the harmonies in the field and its essential components are whatever allows those harmonies to be together with the essential components each has that the others do not contain (the ontological context of mutual relevance, in other words). This theory does not require a distinction between the extensiveness of the field and the things that lack extension but can be located in the field so as to gain extension, a difficult distinction to conceive.

The physical existential field is an obvious example of an existential field constituted by harmonies with dominantly physical properties. Contemporary physics is extraordinarily complicated in its speculations about what the physical field might be, entertaining theories of the spread of space-time from the Big Bang, or the possibility of many physical existential fields each with its Big Bang and minimal or no contact with one another. The cosmos within which we live might be unified by certain laws and histories of light energy. But it also has pockets of higher order, as on planets with ecologies, that are not uniformly spread throughout, for instance between planets.

Moreover, because anything determinate is a harmony, and thus has existential location, there are many kinds of existential fields, perhaps not much connected with one another. Human imagination can construct parallel universes in literature. A field of imagined possibilities as in mathematics might not have much embodiment in a physical field. The field of memories of college that people share at a class reunion has some reference to the physical field but also has many other kinds of harmonic connections that give it a different dominant structure. The examples can be multiplied.

Discussions throughout *Philosophical Theology Two* and *Three*, particularly focused on engaging other things within one's existential field, flesh out the concept of location in an existential field with human, especially moral, implications.

IV. TRANSCENDENTAL ELEMENTS OF HARMONY: ACHIEVED VALUE-IDENTITY

The fourth transcendental trait of any harmony as a determinate thing is that its identity has value, actually, many values. Roughly put, the value of a harmony is the value of getting its components together in its form in its existential location. The components of a harmony have value, which consists in their own components being together with their forms in their existential location. A harmony inherits the values of the past harmonies that are its conditioning causes, and passes on its value-laden harmonization of them to the extent that it conditions succeeding harmonies. The value of a harmony, then, is not just a function of its essential components but of how it puts all its components together in establishing the existential location it has in the vast web of conditioning relations among harmonies. Value is a dimension of form in the sense discussed previously, and the value of a thing can be traced through its forms. But value is also a dimension of the grounding components of a harmony. In the case of spatiotemporal harmonies, these grounding components include the actual components that are haecceities and whose integration in space–time is another haecceity. Because of its existential location, the value of a thing consists not only in its own harmonic structure as containing its components but also in what it does to fulfill, modify, or destroy the values of the past, and the value-impact it has on subsequent things. Because of conditional components, each harmony affects the values of other harmonies to the extent it conditions them, or allows the values in what conditions it to be sustained, attenuated, enhanced, or changed in kind. Given the ways in which form, components, and existential location define the value of a thing, the sum of those constitutes the thing's cumulative value identity. "Value-identity" is an awkward phrase, and would not be necessary if we commonly understood the identity of things always to bear value. Because our scientifically influenced culture has taught us to think of identity as a matter of fact not including value, however, the laborious phrase is helpful. When speaking of human beings who achieve their identity over a lifetime, the phrase becomes "achieved value-identity."

We identify harmonies in a great many ways, often meaning only to distinguish one harmony from another. We can do this by citing some aspect of form, some component, some location, or some pertinent value. But *ultimate* identity is the sum total of a harmony's identity, what it adds up to or, to draw out its theological connotation, what the harmony is in absolute perspective. Cumulative value-identity is the identity of the harmony as registered in all the finite/infinite contrasts that should be recognized in a truthful sacred canopy. Because of the limitations of our understanding of what should be in a truthful sacred canopy, as discussed in Part II, it is impossible fully to know the cumulative value-identity of anything. Nevertheless, it is important to understand what cumulative value-identity is. This is especially important for the identity of human beings. The cumulative value-identity of human beings is who we are in ultimate perspective. Sometimes this is symbolized in terms of divine judgment, or as sub-specie aeternitatis, or as a role in the Dao, or a divine narrative, or as merged with ultimate reality. The implications of these symbols are discussed in *Philosophical Theology Two* and *Three*, although the metaphysics for those discussions is sketched here.

The *cumulative value-identity* of a given harmony includes forming its components together in its existential location: the harmony of these components, here, in this particular pattern. A harmony has form, components formed, existential location, and the cumulative value resultant from this. The value of a harmony should not be identified exclusively with the value of the elegance of its form, nor with the sum of the values of its components as these are enhanced or inhibited by their patterning together, nor with the roles the harmony plays in the other loci of value in the existential field. All of these count. Counting them all together is the cumulative value of the harmony.

Four basic modalities of value exist, which together help articulate the many kinds of value that make up ultimate and proximate identity deriving from form, from components, from existential location, and from identity.

The modality of value deriving from form has to do with what is achieved by putting components together in patterned relations. In any form or pattern, certain things are subordinated to others, compromises are made, new kinds or levels of reality are made possible by patterned combinations, and so forth. When the harmony at hand is a society, for instance, the formal modality has to do with issues of justice, balancing rights, organizing economic systems, using resources for education, and so forth. When the harmony at hand is a personal individual, the formal modality has to do with how the person's life is organized, his or her physical, mental, and emotional well-being, development of competencies, and so forth. In our culture we have a sense that a large harmony including nature as well as societies and individuals should be understood to have ideal formal patterns within which eco-justice can be articulated, although we don't have good models for this yet. Plato in the Republic treated the modality of formal value as justice in society and paralleled in the soul.

The modality of value deriving from components is not the value that components have in terms of their roles within the larger formal pattern—that is a matter of their *formal* value relative to the inclusive harmony. Rather the modality of *component* value is how a harmony is determined by the summary or cumulative value-identity each of its components has. The value of a family includes the component values of its members. It enhances the members in various ways, especially during infancy and growing up, and it inhibits, frustrates, and hurts its members in various other ways. The enhancement and inhibition of the family members is part of the cumulative value of the family as a whole. A dysfunctional family has a definite value, positive in some respects doubtless, but negative in ways that family values should not be. Remembering that many harmonic forms are discursive through time, the value of a family is constantly changing, from time to time, although adding up to a comprehensive or cumulative value-identity. Whereas the virtue associated in human life with the modality of formal value is something like justice, the virtue associated with the modality of component value is piety, a kind of deference to the components that get shoe-horned into a larger harmony. Surely, for the sake of justice in human well-being we should eliminate or contain the HIV/Aids virus, which is very harmful for the human community.[14] Nevertheless, it is an astonishingly elegant virus with uncanny self-protective components of evolution, and should be regarded with natural piety.

The modality of *existential location value* is the ways a harmony conditions the values of other harmonies. This includes how a given harmony repeats, enhances, diminishes, or changes the values of other harmonies that it includes as its conditional components, and also how the given harmony contributes to the value of harmonies that it conditions. The modality of existential value includes as well how a harmony passes on values in harmonies that condition it to other harmonies that it conditions, functioning as a mediator. Summarily put, a harmony's existential value is how it reflects and affects the values of the harmonies in its existential field. Put in more traditional terms, a harmony's existential value is the value-difference it makes in the existential field of actual and possible harmonies.

The modality of *cumulative value-identity* is the sum total of all values pertaining to a harmony as exhibited in eternal immensity, as is discussed in chapter 12.[15] By "eternal immensity" is meant the nontemporal togetherness of all the modes of time plus the nonplaced togetherness of all dimensions of spatiality. Space–time, as argued above, is a construction of the things within it, of harmonies. We should bear in mind that our commonsense notions of past, present, future, and spatiality may not be fully emblematic of the curious complexities of existential dimensions that are important for physicists, but they will have to do for the time being. The general metaphysical hypothesis for eternal immensity, anticipating the following two chapters, is that it is the ontological context of mutual relevance in which harmonies can be together, each constituted by its essential and conditional components. Within the existential field, harmonies condition one another and are together that way through mutual conditioning. But for them to condition one another, and still be distinct with their respective own-beings, their respective essential components need to be together in a deeper ontological context than the cosmological existential context of conditioning. It is argued in the next chapter that the only ontological context that can do this is a nontemporal, nonplaced act of creation that produces everything determinate. The dynamic modes of time are thus created and, within the existential field, time flows.[16] At any given place or moment, some harmonies have been actualized determinately, other remain possibilities, and yet others are dynamically unfolding. Nevertheless, at any given place or moment within the existential field, there is no satisfactory position from which the summary value, the whole value, the cumulative value, of a given harmony can be registered. This is because other harmonies have essential components in other places and moments that might contribute to the harmony's value or benefit from it, and those essential components are disconnected from the given harmony save through conditioning causation. Only the ontological context of mutual relevance connects the essential components of separate, mutually conditioning, harmonies.

Now the ontological context of mutual relevance, which the next chapter argues is the nonplaced act that creates all determinate things together, that divine eternal immensity, has great religious and metaphysical interest. It is the only context in which a harmony's values in all modes are registered together. This sheds light on the biblical wisdom that we should not judge one another but leave judgment to God, who alone has the perspective in which any one has ultimate value, to personify the metaphysical argument. All other perspectives or positions of value are partial because of the otherness of the essential components of other things. In ultimate perspective, all values are commensurable.

But the ultimate perspective is of little help when we try to balance values that are incommensurate and perhaps incommensurable from our local positions within the existential field. So what do we do? As to the modality of form, we are obligated to affect the patterns of things influenced by our actions so as to pattern things together with as much justice as possible. Formal integration requires subordination and coordination, enhancing but also inhibiting harmonies by ordering them. As to the modality of components, we are obligated to respect and defer to the formal, component, existential location, and cumulative values of things that play roles in the harmonies we affect, but that are not exhausted by those roles. This is an obligation to piety and can be in strong tension with subjecting harmonies to larger orders, however just. As to the modality of existential location, we are obligated to care for the difference we make to existence, what things we continue or extinguish, the transformations of actuality. This difference is reflected in different forms that we influence, and in the ways by which we are deferential, but it is not exhausted by them: It is a difference made to actuality. The virtues of form are righteousness. The virtues of components are piety. The virtues of existential location are effectiveness in being, having the courage or faith to act. These are often at odds, and incommensurable.

From a local standpoint in the existential field, perhaps the best we can do is to balance the demands of these virtues temporarily, optimizing their harmony but without a stable, justifiable form for integrating them more than for the moment. The perceived limits of the justification's moment are when we sense that the modalities of the values we are subordinating for the sake of other values at some point come in danger of being lost. So, on the one hand, we can integrate competing modalities of value only when we have a kind of metaphysical love that appreciates each for what it is and does not allow any to be reduced to the others, or neglected. On the other hand, we can integrate competing modalities only with the utmost metaphysical humility. The best that we can do is limited to but a tiny perspective within an eternal immensity where alone all the harmonies with all their values in all their modalities are together. Usually, the best we can do is to juggle while falling, perhaps graced with a glimpse of the contrast of ecstatic excellence with its cost in irrevocable desolation, but mainly just hoping, ruing, doing our best, regretting, trying again, grieving, and then leaving.

A summary statement of the hypothesis about value-identity is that it involves two kinds, subjective and objective. The subjective value of a thing, especially of a person, is the value of all the elements that are included within the thing's own harmony. The objective value of a thing is the multitude of values in other things that it causes or influences, even when those other things determine how those values are integrated within their own identities. This is especially important for human beings whose most important values so often consist in how they influence or affect others.[17]

This chapter presented a formal hypothesis about determinateness as harmony, involving conditional and essential components, and as having four transcendental traits: form, components, existential location, and cumulative value-identity. Now the argument returns to the consideration of how determinate beings exist.

CHAPTER ELEVEN

Proof of an Ultimate Ontological Creative Act

The metaphysical question for this chapter is how it is possible that there is a world of many beings. This question is answered in four ways. The first section presents a dialectical argument that such a pluralistic world is radically contingent and that the only thing on which it might be contingent is an ontological creative act that functions as the ontological context of mutual relevance. The second section rebuts arguments that an ontological creative act can explain nothing. The next section explicates further the conception of the world as the terminus of the ontological creative act, thereby defining the nature of the act in the only sense that the ontological creative act has a nature. The final section analyzes the asymmetry in the concept of creation in terms of the symmetry of the explanatory concepts of the act itself, its terminus, and the nothingness that would obtain if the act were not actually creative.

The discussions of chapters 9 and 10 developed the conception of the many for which being is proposed to be the one. The conclusion of chapter 9 was that being as the one for the many determinations of being cannot itself be determinate. Nevertheless, it must perform two functions in and for the determinate beings so that they are possible: Their possibility requires the principle of the ontological ground of differences and the principle of the ontological equality of reciprocal differences. The former says that determinate things must be in a context in which they are mutually relevant so that they can differentiate themselves from one another. To be determinate at all is to be determinate in respect to something else, this and not that. The latter says that within the ground that allows for their mutual differentiation, they still need to be real as other than one another. Together these principles define the function of what has been called the "ontological context of mutual relevance."

Chapter 10 developed a more detailed theory of determinateness than was supposed in chapter 9. It argued, first, that to be determinate a thing is a harmony with conditional and essential components and, second, that a harmony has the transcendental traits of form, components, existential location, and value-identity. These notions are used throughout *Philosophical Theology* as the philosophical structure for the analysis of ultimates and human religiosity.

I. RADICAL CONTINGENCY AND THE ONTOLOGICAL CONTEXT OF MUTUAL RELEVANCE

The distinction between conditional and essential components of harmonies is most relevant for understanding the radical contingency of all determinate things individually and together. The conditional components are those that express the mutual determination of harmonies such that they are differentiated as determinately different from one another, as required by the principle of the ontological ground of differences. The essential components are those that give the harmonies their own-being such that they are ontologically equal as reciprocal contrasts, that is, other than one another. The ontological context of mutual relevance, whatever that might be, needs to be the context in which things that are genuinely different, but mutually conditioning, can be together.

Each thing is a harmony of both essential and conditional components. If a thing were only its conditional components, it might very well be totally together with the things it conditions or that condition it, with no remainder. But then, there would not be different things, only one thing, the set of mutual conditions, which in turn would not be able to be determinate in the first place and so would be impossible. So the ontological context of mutual relevance must allow things to be together with their essential as well as their conditional components. This hypothesis, derived from the dialectical analysis of different things each with both essential and conditional components, requires further explication.

The importance of the *ontological* context of mutual relevance is to be seen in comparison with what, in parallel, might be called the *cosmological* context of mutual relevance. The cosmological context of mutual relevance is the matrix of connections among things constituted by their conditional components. Things are cosmologically relevant to one another by the various ways in which they condition one another. The argument so far has shown that harmonies can condition one another with respect to their four transcendental traits: form, components, existential location, and value. The further explication of these four kinds of conditioning enriches the hypothesis about the cosmological context of mutual relevance.

Existential location is the most obvious dimension in which things condition one another. Using the illustration of temporal flow introduced in chapter 10, the past conditions the present by providing potentials for integration into a new thing; the future conditions the present by setting formal limits of possibility for integration. The future conditions the past by providing the possibilities that have become the actual structures of the past; the present conditions the past by continually adding new actualities, thus shifting both the meaning and value as well as the historical character of the past. The past conditions the future by giving it determinate things that structure the future's determinateness; the present conditions the future by creating new actualities that require new structures of possibility. Or consider spatial relations in conjunction with time: Distant things cause subsequent close things which in turn cause elements in what is here; and in reverse, actions here lead to distant consequences. We know from physics, for instance in the phenomenon of entanglement, that the characters of the harmonies that make up the space–time field are far more complex in minute detail than the kinds of Euclidean-like examples discussed here.[1] Existential location has many dimensions besides those of the space–time field, as discussed previously. The cosmological context of mutual relevance contains as their bases all existential fields in which harmonies might be located.

In addition to existential location, the components in which harmonies are grounded also constitute a dimension of the cosmological context of mutual relevance. In the swirl of spatiotemporal processes, lines of causation come together for a while, forming harmonies, and then go their own ways, dissolving those harmonies, perhaps entering into others. Thus, harmonies are grounded in causal processes that extend far beyond themselves but that become components for a while. Some harmonies, like melodies or human lives, take time to play out, and thus at any moment have changing relations to their other moments. But many things that enter into such a discursive harmony are not from the harmony's own past but from the past of other processes that enter only temporarily into the harmony as components. Science studies the causal patterns and histories of the components of harmonies.

Forms are modes of conditioning in that they distinguish components (common natures) that make things determinate with reference to one another. Because common natures can be defined in terms of one another we can describe the differences resident in different things. Moreover, forms for harmonies have a hierarchical structure, with internal forms unifying forms that unify forms and so on, exhibiting complexity and simplicity (*II, I*; *III, 9*). Because of this, things have value. Because the forms distinguish harmonies relative to one another, their values are distinguished relative to one another. So part of the cosmological context of mutual relevance is the array of values bearing on one another due to the distinctions of forms.

Harmonies also have cumulative value-identity, and that cumulative value-identity is an extraordinarily complex harmonization of the values internal to the harmony with those that are external and affect and are affected by it. So there is a cosmological matrix of value that, temporally mirroring what is fully real only in eternity, exhibits the ultimate values of things in relation to one another insofar as temporality allows a perspective on them.

In all these complex ways, the cosmological context of mutual relevance exhibits the togetherness of all determinate things, such as it is. Pockets of intense order exist in a vast ocean of minimal mutual determination. But there is a *de facto* set of determinations with various kinds of unity of the four sorts discussed here. The cosmological context of mutual relevance is constituted by the countless ways in each of these four dimensions that harmonies condition one another.

Here is the argument that proves the radical contingency of the world:

1. For the harmonies to condition one another, they must be real in the sense of having their essential as well as conditional components. Their essential components function *de facto* in the cosmological context of mutual relevance.

2. But the essential components of one harmony *cannot be included as conditions of another harmony* without being swallowed up in the other. All the conditioning relations presuppose the essential independence of different things that are determinate in reference to one another.

3. In the cosmological context of mutual relevance, the togetherness of the essential components of different things is exhibited, but cannot be given an account, because only conditional components function in the cosmological context of mutual relevance.

4. Therefore, the very possibility of a cosmological context of mutual relevance presupposes an ontological context of mutual relevance in which the essential components of different things are together in noncosmological ways.

Or to put the point more exactly, there must be an ontological context of mutual relevance in which harmonies that necessarily include both essential and conditional components can be together. Otherwise, no real thing would be able to condition another real thing, because real things require both essential and conditional components. Now the problem is to find out what the ontological context of mutual relevance might be.

The hypothesis is that the ontological context of mutual relevance is an ontological creative act that creates all of the determinate things, the harmonies, together. This act functions as the ontological context of mutual relevance in that the determinate things just fit together, each with its essential components and all with the mutual implications of their conditional components. The act is not something determinate over and above the things created. Rather, it is a sheer making, the terminus of which is the world of determinate things together with just the kinds of connections, unities, and separations that they have. How can this hypothesis be made plausible?

II. PROOF OF AN ONTOLOGICAL CREATIVE ACT

The argument takes the form of seven considerations arising out of the previous discussions that add up to the conclusion that only an ontological creative act can be the one for the many, the ontological context of mutual relevance.

The first consideration is that a multiplicity of real determinate things exists. This is asserted because of a kind of common sense obviousness. The world appears this way, and we want to save the appearances in our explanatory accounts. Of course, there are theories that reject this assertion despite its commonsensical base. Shankara's Advaita Vedanta rejects any kind of dualism as ultimately real: Ultimate reality is Brahman and Brahman is without qualities. Nevertheless, Shankara had to explain why the world appears to be so dualistic, especially why people think that they are actors or agents doing things.[2] The determinate distinction between the way the world appears and the way it really is as nondual is enough to get our assertion of multiplicity off the ground. The Advaita theory of Brahman is discussed throughout *Philosophical Theology*. One might also take F.H. Bradley's theory that all relations are internal, and hence that there are no terms external to one another, to conclude with the result that everything is one and undifferentiated.[3] But then Bradley's view also fails to save or account for appearances to the contrary.

A second consideration in the argument is that the multiplicity is determinate because things are at least partly determinate with reference to one another if they are different from one another: this and not that. Things do not have to be completely determinate, and not all things have to be determinate with respect to all other things. But to the extent that things have determinate identity, this identity consists in them being themselves in distinction from being something else. The analysis of determinateness in chapter 10 provides terms for expressing mutual determination. Determinate things are harmonies with essential and conditional components. They cannot do without conditional components, for then they would not be in relation to anything else and so could not be different or the same. They cannot do without essential components, for then they would not have their own-being so as to sustain conditions given by other things and to cause conditions in other things.

A third consideration is that the possibility of harmonies determining one another requires that the harmonies be together in an ontological context of mutual relevance. This ontological context is distinguished from a cosmological context that is constituted by the web of conditional components connecting determinate things: The cosmological context is not possible without the ontological context. The arguments for this premise were given in the previous section.

A fourth consideration is that some account of the ontological context of mutual relevance must be given in order to solve the problem of the one and the many. That problem is to account for how the many determinate things can be many while being determinate with respect to one another. The argument of the previous two chapters has transformed the conception of ultimate reality into the question of being, and the question of being into the question of the one for the many, and then that into the question of the ontological context of mutual relevance. Ultimate reality in the first instance is the ontological context of mutual relevance, whatever that is. Of course, one can decline to consider the problem of the one and the many, leaving it unsolved. But when someone does come along and addresses the problem of the one and the many, the results of the solution given are likely to have immediate consequences for the rest of one's theory of ultimate reality.

A fifth consideration is that the ontological context of mutual relevance cannot be a multiplicity of perspectives, identical with the multiplicity of determinate beings. As seen in the discussion of Paul Weiss in chapter 9, the perspective in which one thing grasps another thing does not grasp that other's essential components, or if it does, it reduces the other to itself, denying independence.

A sixth consideration is that the ontological context of mutual relevance cannot be an analogical ground in the sense that determinate things are determinate in different senses. For, then they would not determine one another. Moreover, there would be no univocal ground for saying that they are determinate in different senses. They are determinately different from one another because of their differences, not because of their senses of being with those differences. Chapter 9 argued this case.

A seventh consideration is that the ontological context of mutual relevance cannot be determinate. For, if it were there would have to be a meta-ontological context of mutual relevance to make possible its determinateness with respect to the other determinate things. And if that meta-ontological context were determinate, there would have to be a meta-meta-ontological context, and so on. Chapter 10 argued this case, building on the argument in chapter 9.

The conclusion, therefore, is that the only thing that can be the ontological context of mutual relevance is an ontological creative act, the terminus, result, or conclusion of which is any and all things determinate. The act itself is not determinate except in what it produces. Yet its production sets the things together in the ontological context in which they are mutually relevant to one another: They are created to fit together in just the ways they do.

The remainder of this chapter begins to flesh out this hypothesis to make it plausible, although the whole of *Philosophical Theology* contributes to the task. The overall argument of this chapter is that, given the reality of a multiplicity of mutually determinate things, and all the other premises rehearsed here, there exists an ontological creative act that is being or the "most ultimate" ultimate reality.

The ontological creative act is a sheer making, with no potentials antecedent to the making. Any potentials would have to be determinate, at least in being something rather than nothing, and on this hypothesis all determinate things are created. Premise seven rules out determinateness for the ontological context of mutual relevance.

This concept of sheer making seems counterintuitive to some people because the philosophical concept of creation seems to be an extrapolation of our understanding of human creative activity. We do make new things, but always out of previously given things, raw materials, as it were, including among those "potentials" our own powers, talents, habits, and intentions. So it would seem that the ontological creative act would have to make the determinate world "out of something." Thomas Aquinas said, *ex nihil, nihil fit*, out of nothing, nothing is made. He had in mind an Aristotelian model of causation according to which all of the "act" or reality in the effect must somehow already be present in the cause or causes. Thus, Thomas thought that all the finite reality of the created world of determinate things is just a delimitation or finitizing of the infinite Act of To Be, nothing new. The world arises, on Thomas's account, from the Act of To Be's introduction of negations so as to finitize the infinite divine nature of Pure Act. The Act of To Be, which Thomas identified as God, does not create anything new, or *ex nihilo*, only the negations that delimit the infinite Pure Act. Thomas's is, thus, an extremely attenuated view of divine creation for a Christian theologian, with the world containing nothing new save delimitations of infinite Being, creation *a deo* rather than *ex nihilo*. But if there is nothing new in creation, then there is no positive change from God alone to God plus the world. Or, to put the point in the temporal terms of our own creative processes, unless we add a little bit of novelty to what is given as resources, there is no change in the effect from the resources by themselves prior to the creative act: that is, nothing is created that was not there before. In human creativity, at the very least there is novelty in the integration of things that were unintegrated before.

So the analogy with human creativity can be reversed from what is supposed by Thomas and his Aristotelian tradition. Just as, within time, we add a bit of novelty, at the very least to effect a rearrangement of what was there before, so the ontological creative act is the making of total novelty. For us, there are many antecedent resources to which we add only a little novelty. For the ontological act, there was nothing there before. Everything is new. This is the mark of the transition from complete indetermination, or nothing, to whatever determination exists in the world.

Moreover, to continue the analogy with human creativity, we do have some intuitive feel about what it is to make something new in our limited, finite way. Some people have peak experiences of creativity, and most of us have inklings of being creative. Everyone has the experience of shock in the sudden realization that we have done something freely that has consequences. But whereas we are only relatively free, the ontological creative act is absolutely free in this sense. We are bound by our resources, and free in the little we can do with them. The ontological creative act is bound by nothing. But just as we add at least a little bit to the resources that were there before in order to get our new creation, the ontological creative act adds everything, and has no resources with which to cope.

The ontological creative act creates the determinate harmonies to be together in the ways required for the essential components of different things to be harmonized with those things conditional components, such that the things can condition one another. Thereby the different harmonies can be determinate with respect to one another. Included among the determinate things are the cosmological relations of the mutual conditioning. But the ontological creation itself is of the entire field of mutually determinate things. The act of creation is the ontological context of mutual relevance in which things have their being together without being reduced to conditional components of one another and without being wholly unrelated so as not to be determinate with respect to one another. The following sections detail some of the radical implications of this element in the concept of the ontological creative act.

Apart from creating the determinate world, the ontological creative act is not determinate. To be sure, given the creation of the world, the act has the determinate character of creating this world. But the "nature" of the act results from its creating. The ontological act of creation is not a determinate thing over and above the determinations created. Therefore, it does not fall prey to the argument that the one for the many, the ontological context of mutual relevance, cannot be determinate. If there were no ontological creative act, there would be nothing.

But there is the determinate world, whatever it contains, according to the first consideration presented earlier. Therefore there is the ontological creative act, which has created itself (in creating the world) to be the creator of the world. This is the nature of sheer making: It is what it does. This is what was to be proved.

III. THE DETERMINATE WORLD AS THE END OF THE ACT

How can we understand what the ontological creative act does? It creates everything determinate. Among the determinate things is intelligibility itself. The nature of intelligibility is a vast problem, which is explored only in selective problems in *Philosophical Theology*. At its most abstract, however, it is what Plotinus called the dyad, sheer difference, otherness, distinction. Actually, the grasping of difference requires noting difference in some respect, and so Plotinus went on to write that the dyad immediately generates the world soul, which connects the differences.[4] On the other side of the ancient world, the Chinese philosophers grounded intelligibility in the difference between yang expansion and yin contraction, but went on to say that these are intelligible as being in patterns, for instance the hexagrams of the *I Jing*. The patterns are made up exclusively of yang-yin alternations, but in reference to one another.

Some thinkers, Leibniz, for instance, are scandalized at the thought that intelligibility is created, which Descartes had claimed.[5] For these thinkers, God the creator, as they identified ontological ultimate reality, is conceived to be perfectly intelligent, knowing all possibilities in choosing to create the world. Intelligibility thus is resident in the divine nature before creation. This view is in trouble, however, if the creator cannot be determinate because intelligibility would have to be indeterminate, which is unintelligible.

Other thinkers have said that the creator apart from creating is simple and internally undifferentiated. For them, intelligibility in the sense of understanding the natures of things in terms of their differences is created. Thomas Aquinas would hold to this view, for instance, although he also agreed with Aristotle that God is thought thinking itself and added that this "thought" is the pure Act of To Be simply being itself. Thinkers in the Neo-Platonic tradition, and its global variant the Perennial Philosophy, believe that intelligibility is scaled to levels of being.[6] Ordinary intelligibility is the discrimination of things in common experience; higher levels of theorizing conform or expand the mind to grasp the higher principles of things. Beyond the first principles, however, is sheer being or the One that transcends intelligibility except insofar as the trajectory of ascent by itself is intelligible.

Yet if intelligibility itself is created, then we have a problem with the intelligibility of the ontological act of creation, to which we return in the next section.

Because space–time is determinate, however complex and nonintuitive to our commonsense habits of thought according to contemporary physicists, space–time is created. This means that the ontological act of creation does not take place at a time. Rather, the whole temporal unfolding of events is created together, although of course not "at the same time." This must be the case, because events that are earlier and later, nearer and farther, are different from one another, and determinate with respect to one another at least insofar as they are temporally and spatially different. Therefore, the earlier (and nearer) events harmonizing their essential and conditional components must be together ontologically with the later (and farther) events harmonizing their own essential and conditional components. Those earlier and later events are not together at any time, obviously: they are different in time. So their togetherness is in the ontological context of mutual relevance, which is the ontological creative act. The ontological creative act should be called "eternal," to contrast it with the temporality of most determinate things; the hypothesis of the ontological creative act contrasts with all views of creation of the world within time. The ontological creative act also should be called "immense," that is, not locatable with a measure, to contrast it with the hypotheses of divine spatiality of in many views of the creation of the world as the filling of a primordial space.

This point about the creation of space–time is extremely abstract, and vague in the technical sense. The space–time plenum might actually have a first moment, as in some interpretations of Big Bang cosmology. Or it might be an infinite cycling of expansions and contractions, as in other interpretations of the Big Bang and in ancient South Asian cosmologies. Or a unique Big Bang might expand forever until the things expanding are so distant from one another that space and time become meaningless. Or the space–time plenum as we know it now might at some point be radically transformed as a further development of creation, as some theologians such as Wolfhart Pannenberg believe who are committed to a consummatory eschatological reality.[7] The point at this stage in the argument is that all of this is created.

Hence the entire determinate world unfolds in space–time. To the extent the philosophical cosmology sketched earlier is true, events take place in the mode of present time, creatively integrating the resources of their past to make new realities. The new realities they make add to the actual past. The present events are constrained by the possibilities defining future moments. Some of those possibilities are decided upon by present moments of creative integration and become the structure and value of the past. Some present moments are highly constrained by the past actualities that are their potentials for integration, and by the future possibilities, with minimal freedom for innovation. Other present moments are structured by the past and future so as to have momentously important options. Most present moments lie between these extremes.

Because all events are matters of harmonies, the transcendentals of form, components, existential location, and cumulative value-identity define part of the nature of the ontological creative act. In the monotheistic traditions that call that act God, the transcendentals sometimes function as Wisdom or Logos.[8]

Because the nature of ontological ultimate reality is constituted by the act of creation, it is interesting to ask how much more we can tell about that nature. We know the ontological creative act has the vast extensiveness of the entire plenum of space–time, and that it has the infinite intensive depths of nature within each human being, given the infinity of components in harmonies; we have some emerging scientific understanding of both the expanse and intensive structures of nature. But our sample of the cosmos is so small it is hard to generalize to many other traits of the ontological creative act.

The determinate world is part of the ontological creative act, its terminus. It has no existence apart from that act, because the act is the ontological context of mutual relevance in which that world exists. We cannot imagine that God, Brahman, the Buddha-mind, *wu-ji* (the Ultimate of Non-Being, in Wing-tsit Chan's translation), or the Dao is a determinate being who makes the world as an array of other beings independent from its own being. No medium exists independently of the ontological creative act and the created world in which the world might be set apart from the creative act. Thus the ontological creative act is immediately present in the very being of each determinate thing, as structured by the determinate character of that thing in reference to other things. Because determinate things are mutually defined, the ontological creative act, as the context of mutual relevance, grounds the togetherness of the determinate things.

Some similarity exists between this conception of the determinate world as the terminus of the ontological creative act and Spinoza's conception of *natura naturans* giving rise to *natura naturata*.[9] For Spinoza, God is the only substance and, having no peer, is indeterminate with respect to anything else. But God does have an infinite number of attributes that are determinate with respect to one another, of which we know only mind and body. Yet God's being those attributes, *natura naturans*, "nature naturing," achieves determinateness only in *natura naturata,* "nature natured." The similarity between Spinoza's conception and the conception of the ontological act of creation does not go too far, however. He would say that *natura naturans* does not make anything new, only that it expresses the divine attributes in determinate form as *natura naturata*.

A similarity also exists between the conception of the ontological creative act and Ramanuja's view that the world is the body of God.[10] The act of God being God is the bodily manifestation of the world. Yet a dualism remains in Ramanuja's view between us (the world) as the divine body and the mind of God, Brahman, a dualism asserted over against Shankara's nondualism. This dualism does not obtain in any distinction between the ontological creative act and the determinate world that is its terminus.

The ontological act of creation can be explicated from many perspectives. This section has explicated it from the perspective of the terminus of the act, treating the world as the created product of the act and the act's only determinate nature. The next section explicates the act from the standpoint of the asymmetry in the very notion of making.

IV. ABYSS IN THE ACT: SYMMETRY OF THE CONCEPT VERSUS ASYMMETRY OF WHAT IS CONCEIVED

The *concept* of the ontological act of creation is determinate. The concept arises as an hypothesis out of a careful dialectical consideration of the problem of the one and the many. That consideration included the development of an hypothesis about harmony with the elaboration of technical distinctions between essential and conditional components and between the transcendentals of all harmonies: form, components, existential location, and value-identity. Included in the background of the concept of the ontological act of creation is the elaboration of an hypothesis about determinateness and of the being of which determinate things are determinations. Although all these hypotheses are hypotheses, nothing deduced from first principles, they have a plausibility that has been indicated in the discussion so far and that will be embellished in the use of these hypotheses in subsequent discussions. In fact, if they were deduced from first principles, that would be insufficient, because we have seen that intelligibility itself, the first principles, are not really "first." They are created. So the plausibility of all the elements of the argument comprising the background for the concept of the ontological act of creation arises piecemeal from the many different angles taken on its steps.

The concept itself is *of* an asymmetrical act of creation. From nothing, the ontological act creates the somethings of the world. This is an unusual concept. Most of our concepts of "making" have to do with taking an assortment of things in some pattern and rearranging them into some other pattern. Aristotle gives four versions of this, each of which yields a kind of intelligibility.[11] Formally, it is the replacement of one form with another. Materially, it is the actualization of potentials in the original things to exist in another pattern that might change their natures. Teleologically, the change is understood to be for a purpose or for the achievement of the value of having the later form. Efficiently, it is understood in terms of the action of rearrangement, employing the act in the cause to reduce the potentiality in the effect to act. The ontological creative act is not the replacement of one form with another, only the creation of the forms as transcendental elements of the end-product of the act. The ontological creative act is not intelligible as the actualization of antecedent potentials because all determination is the result of the act. The ontological creative act is not intelligible as the realization of some purpose or intention of creating value, although every harmony created has a value. The ontological creative act is not intelligible in terms of action by an agent that applies antecedent actuality to potentials to bring them to actuality, although the end result of the act is a world that includes actual things with potentialities (as well as many other kinds of determinate things). No, the ontological creative act is intelligible as a making of something new. A similar contrasting argument could be made with, say, Kant's idea of causation, namely, the rule that alterations of type A are always followed by alterations of type B; Kant had no use for the notion of power in the cause, only of the regularity of the causal law. The ontological creative act has no antecedent types and creates all regularities.

Asymmetrical as the creation of novelty is, the *concept* of it is symmetrical. That is, the concept is defined in the relation of three terms: the nothing that would be the case were there not the creating of the world, the act of creating itself, and the product created, which is the terminus of the act. After all the dialectical discussion here there is nothing mysterious about these terms and the ways by which they define the ontological creation of the world out of nothing. "Nothing" is not a stuff or resource out of which things are created, only the absence of all determination. Of course, if one insists on a different idea of causation, say, Aristotle's, then much is mysterious in the concept of the ontological act of creation. If the form of the consequent is to be derived from the form of the antecedent, for instance, and there is no form of the antecedent, the form of the ontologically created world is absolutely arbitrary, however intelligible in itself. If the material definiteness of the world is supposed to be the actualized potentials of previous material, then the novel material reality of the created world is absolutely arbitrary. If the formed material of the world is supposed to reflect some purpose or previously intended value, then the ontological creation of the world which has no purpose is absolutely arbitrary. If the power to create the world is supposed to derive from the power or actuality resident in the cause, then the ontological act of creation is absolutely arbitrary because the act has no power except in its exercise. All these Aristotelian approaches to causation (and the case can be made for many other philosophical cosmologies of causation) assume that there has to be some antecedent reason for why there is a world, and this world, at that. But all of these approaches deny that creation is the creation of novelty. The ontological creative act, however, makes all things new.

Some might think it possible to make the ontological creative act intelligible as symmetrical rather than asymmetrical by giving it an internal genetic process. That is, it might be possible to conceive the act as beginning with infinitesimal determinateness and then by stages, understood in symmetrical ways, unfolding to the complete definiteness of the world. This was Whitehead's ploy in attempting to explain creation of novelty within time. For him, an actual occasion within time has a "genetic" structure, as he called it, that begins with the past occasions as felt, proceeds through stages of sorting and integrating of these feelings of past actualities, and resulting in a completely definite actual entity. This genetic process is not itself temporal. It has stages of integration related as logically before and after, but not earlier and later. Whitehead said that this genetic process is not itself actual. What is actual is only the completed actual occasion that has some actual spatiotemporal thickness, joined with the spatiotemporal properties of environing actualities. Although Whitehead used the processive language of concrescence, "becoming concrete," to describe the genetic structure, when he spoke carefully he said that the genetic structure is a mode of analysis of how a new occasion arises rather than a symmetry of stages. On Whitehead's account everything in an actual occasion that is added to the initially felt past occasions is novel, not contained in the past but arising spontaneously in the coming to be of the present occasion.[12]

The concept of the ontological creative act, however, cannot appeal to past actual occasions so as to construct stages of concrescence or genesis. Everything in the ontological creative act is novel. It has no stages. Perhaps we can say that the ontological creative act is "immediate," although we should beware of the connotation that it takes place in an instantaneous now without duration. All "nows" are the end product of the ontological creative act. No temporal, albeit nondurational, medium exists within which the ontological creative act plays out. No proto-space exists within which the ontological creative act creates the world of spatial things; the act does not take place in any there—there is no "there" there until the act creates the world.

But then how does it explain anything to say that the world is created by an absolutely arbitrary act of ontological creation? If explanation does not mean deriving what is to be explained from something antecedently understood, what does it mean? What does it add to the determinate world to say that it is created by an ontological creative act that is indeterminate apart from creating?

The previous section said that intelligibility at its most abstract lies in the dyad, difference, otherness, and then said that (in Plotinus' account) this means difference in some respect. Determinateness always involves difference in some respect. But something is glossed over in the rush to define difference in terms of some respect of difference. Charles Peirce understood these matters in terms of his three categories of Firstness, Secondness, and Thirdness.[13] Firstness is the quality of being wholly isolated in itself, with no character or relation of difference or opposition to any other thing; Firstness is pure chaos and is unintelligible; firstness does not need an explanation because there is nothing to explain. Secondness, for Peirce, is sheer opposition, difference without a respect in which things are different. Secondness is pure positivity, pure surprise (put in psychological terms). His illustration was this. Imagine you are in a hot air balloon drifting above the city in the dead of a cloudy night—no sound or sensation at all: suddenly a factory whistle goes off! The shock of that is Secondness; as soon as you realize what it is, you have interpreted it as being determinate in respect of being a factory whistle. But the sheer sudden positivity of the whistle is Secondness. Thirdness is mediation, and in this instance is the respects in which the transition from silence to sound is mediated by the circumstances of the factory whistle. Peirce criticized Hegel for thinking intelligibility lies only in the mediations of thirdness. There is a brute insistence to things, Peirce said, that is part of intelligibility.

What the concept of the ontological act of creation adds to the world as understood is the articulation of its bruteness, its sheer positivity, its absolutely arbitrary being-hereness. As a concept, of course, it is made up on what Peirce called Thirds, the concepts we have been discussing. In fact, the concept cannot be separated from its background of the dialectical analysis of the one and many, being, determinateness, harmony, and the rest. What the concept does, as framed against this background, is to point our attention to the radically contingent, arbitrary, sheer being of the world. The sheer being of the world is not some inchoate positivity: it is rather the being of determinate things together, mutually determining one another, with their essential and conditional components together in the ontological context of mutual relevance. The being of determinate things together in the ontological context of mutual relevance is nothing other than the being of the world. The concept of the ontological creative act is an index of that being.

This point can be put another way. In understanding ordinary things, we note their changes of patterns, actualization of potentials, and all the rest of the Aristotelian vision. We explain things in part by showing how what we note illustrates higher order theories and principles. Set a metaphysician loose on the hierarchy of principles and the result is a theory of first principles, principles that do not allow of contradiction. Philosophers such as Charles

Hartshorne have argued that first principles do not themselves have to be explained because they are necessary on their own terms.[14] But consider, we also explain things in part by noting the decision points in causal processes at which a future that allows of alternatives is resolved into an actual and completely definite set of affairs. In fact, any complex thing, composed of many parts, is to be understood in terms of locating all the decision points in its own actualization and in the actualizations of its antecedents that gave rise to its complex contents. Whitehead called this the ontological principle, namely, that every complexity is to be explained by the actual decision points that put it and its parts together.[15] Although there is a kind of intelligibility in seeing the changes that transform the past complexities into the current complexity, and those changes can be formulated in terms of a hierarchy of principles (to the extent the world is regular), how the complexities actually got to be the way they are is the result, Whitehead said, of decisions of actual entities creating novel realities. Or as Peirce put it, order explains some things, but the existence of order itself is the thing that most needs explanation. Chaos needs no explanation. Order does. Thus the first principles of a metaphysics (or science) most want an explanation, and the explanation is that something just made them the way they are.

So there is a priority in intelligibility of a kind of empirical grasp or perception of creative novelty-making taking place. The principles of knowledge help us locate the decision points in temporal matters. The dialectic of the one and the many, and related notions, help us locate the creative act by which the world of beings is constituted. In subsequent chapters we discuss the sense in which this is an actual mystical vision (I, 15, 16, II, 11, 12, and III, 15, 16). Here it is only necessary to note that the dialectic of concepts culminating in the concept of the ontological act of creation is an index that turns us to the right elements in the world so as to perceive the force of its being. Thinking it through, with or without the deep spiritual trappings of mystical vision, we can say, Aha! I see it. The dialectic is what allows us to engage being. It allows us to engage the reality of the world in its ultimacy. The symmetrical concept of the ontological creative act is not an icon of the act, because the act has no determinate nature to model apart from its product. The symmetrical concept is an index of the act; or rather, the concept with the dialectic developing it in relation to determinateness is an index. It is the comprehensive metaphysical symbol that most literally allows us to grasp what is ultimately real. Or at least, this is the hypothesis of *Philosophical Theology* (I, 14).

This chapter has woven a multiplicity of arguments into an hypothesis that says that everything determinate is radically contingent on an ontological creative act that creates all determinate things together, with whatever connections and unities they might have. The following chapter expands the plausibility of this hypothesis by discussing some of its implications.

Chapter Twelve

The Ontological Ultimate
An Act of Creation

1. THE NATURE OF THE ULTIMATE ACT AS CREATED

According to the concept of the ontological creative act, the act has no nature except that which comes to be in its creating the world. This affords the greatest intelligibility to the question of why there is a world at all. For, the concept of the ontological creative act starts within nothing, which needs no explanation. It moves through sheer making, productivity, creativity of novelty, immediately to the determinate world in which things have natures. The nature of the ontological creative act harmonizes four metaphysically distinguishable components: first, the brute facticity of its creating the world; second, the act as the ontological context of mutual relevance for the multiplicity in the world of determinate things with essential and conditional components; third, the determinate creatures as harmonies all of which bear the transcendentals of form, components, existential location, and value-identity; fourth, the *de facto* particular characteristics the world has cumulatively that determine the particular kind of creator the ontological act is—the creator of this particular world.

The ontological creative act is the most ultimate finite/infinite contrast that should be in a theologically acute sacred canopy (I, 1, ii). The finite side is the brute facticity of the creation of the cosmos, which in this facticity is radically contingent and arbitrary. The finite side is also elaborated in terms of how the creative act is the ontological context of mutual relevance for all the determinate things, the one for the many, the being that grounds all determinate beings. The infinite side is the absolute nothingness that would hold if it were not for the ontological creative act creating the world. The sheer arbitrariness in the ontological creative act is the guarantee of the fact that this is the most ultimate finite/infinite contrast. Absolute nothingness is not some infinite fullness that awaits a finitizing move to create the determinate world. It is just nothing. And this finite/infinite contrast is intelligible in the concept of the ontological act of creation.

The complex ontological act of creation of the world, including the world in all its dimensions as its terminus and absolute nothingness as its alternative, is the most ultimate reality that can be symbolized in sacred canopies. What is determinate about that act is not the whole of the act itself, only the nature of the act which is itself the product of the creating. Therefore, no determinate symbol can be applied literally to the act itself. Determinate models of the act, such as emergence, personhood in gods, and consciousness, need to be "broken" so as to indicate that they apply in iconic senses only to the produced nature of the act, not to the act of making itself.

Numerous symbol systems exist in various traditions to symbolize different aspects or emphases of this. For instance, on the emergence model in East Asian philosophical theology, the Daodejing distinguishes the Dao that can be named from the Dao that cannot be named but is the mother of the Dao that can. The Dao that can be named is the world that the East Asians understand in terms of the philosophical cosmology of yin-yang philosophy. It has a particular moral flavor that is differently accented in Daoist and Confucian writings. The Dao that can be named is radically contingent on the Dao that cannot be named. This Daoist motif was influential on Wangbi (226–249) who introduced the thesis that non-being is the most basic ground of all other things. Wangbi in turn influenced Zhou Dunyi (1017–1073), the father of Neo-Confucianism who wrote:

> The Ultimate of Non-Being and also the Great Ultimate (*T'ai-chi*)! The Great Ultimate through movement generates yang. When its activity reaches its limit, it becomes tranquil. Through tranquility the Great Ultimate generates yin. When tranquility reaches its limit, activity begins again. So movement and tranquility alternate and become the root of each other, giving rise to the distinction of yin and yang, and the two modes are thus established.
>
> By the transformation of yang and its union with yin, the Five Agents of Water, Fire, Wood, Metal, and Earth arise. When these five material forces (*ch'i*) are distributed in harmonious order, the four seasons run their course.
>
> The Five Agents constitute one system of yin and yang, and yin and yang constitute on Great Ultimate. The Great Ultimate is fundamentally the Non-ultimate. The Five Agents arise, each with its specific nature.[1]

In the yin-yang cosmology, the determinateness of the five basic substances comes from different vibratory patterns of yin-yang alternations. The alternations are like waves, which can differ from one another in frequency and amplitude. Determinate things have specific vibratory patterns that are related to the other vibratory patterns around them, all constantly shifting somewhat. Strictly speaking, there is no process of time in this philosophical cosmology until the yin-yang alternations are organized in patterns of change, involving the five elements. So it is not that there are earlier stages of unorganized yang movements and yin retreats to tranquility. Rather, at every moment of change in time there is a vertical stack of conditions, as it were, reaching down to yin, to yang, to the Great Ultimate, and to the Ultimate of Non-Being. The Ultimate of Non-Being, *wu-ji* (literally, "having no characters") gives rise to the Great Ultimate, which is the ontological context of mutual relevance in which yang and yin can distinguish things while relating them. Other traditions have their own symbols, reflecting of their philosophical cosmologies and other factors. Chapter 6 traced some of the South Asian concepts of ultimacy that illustrate, each in its own way, important aspects of the ontological act of creation. The discussion of the Dao and of the metaphysics of Zhou Dunyi illustrates the way spontaneous emergence can be developed as a model for the ultimate act of creation.

The question arises how the ontological act of creation, as the ultimate reality in a theologically acute sacred canopy, squares with the idea of God. The root model for most ideas of God is that of the person or personality, suitably made both transcendent and intimate. In most Buddhist and East Asian cosmologies, altogether too many gods are believed in to be serious competitors for ultimacy. In many South Asian cosmologies, conceptions of God that in popular religion have personal characteristics in more esoteric or sophisticated forms of religious thought have transcendent characteristics that can register the dependence of the determinate on the indeterminate required for symbolizing the ontological creative act. But in these transcending modes of reflection, the personal model of the God, say Shiva or Vishnu, shifts over to the model of consciousness, first as the consciousness had by the God and then as consciousness per se as in Brahman. Of course, consciousness itself is transformed from ordinary consciousness or "purified" as it is the model for Brahman. In most South Asian religions, any *person*, even the person of Shiva or Vishnu, is subject to the law of karma, and hence cannot be truly ultimate.

But in West Asian religions, both polytheisms of Persia, Greece, and Egypt and the developing monotheisms of Judaism, Christianity, and Islam, the term "God" has a strong personalistic history. Gods were special humans, super-humans, wielders of power over nature and creators of worlds who were conceived to have purposeful intentions. Far from having their "natures" result from creating all determinate things, these gods (or God) were interesting precisely because of their natures in the sense of capacities. Because their actions were thought to proceed from their natures, it was religiously imperative to attempt to know that inner nature: would this God fight for us against our foes, punish us without remorse, or be filled with mercy? Because of the need to deal with God as the ultimate force in the universe, or as the controller of human destiny, or as one with whom we can interact out of personal concerns, a popular conception of God is of a person with a (contested) personality. Just as some Buddhists pray to Guanyin for success and healing, so the ancient Greeks prayed to Apollo for wisdom and to Ares for martial strength, and Christians, Jews, and Muslims pray to God for help, or at least mercy.

Does the concept of the ultimate as the ontological act of creating the world of determinate things, whose nature comes from the creating, do such violence to the rhetorical matrix of the idea of God that the ontological act cannot be called God? It certainly cannot be called God in a literal sense, just as it cannot be called emergence or consciousness in a literal sense. But does it have metaphorical viability as a "broken" symbol? Many obviously say yes. But others, such as Tillich, claimed that the personal conceptions of God are idolatrous and advocated instead belief in the "God beyond gods."[2] He advocated this for Christians as the best expression of the Christian gospel. Tillich had in mind the great Christian traditions of Neo-Platonism and Thomism for which God is not a person but in fact is simple and indeterminate apart from the world, as grounds for the orthodoxy of his own belief.[3]

The position taken in *Philosophical Theology* is that the term *God* is indeed legitimately used to refer to the ontological act of creating the world, bearing in mind the need to break the literal application of the model of the person in reference to the ontological act. The ontological act of creating the world is singular. Although not within time or space, it is the one act creating all the determinate things and their changing interactions. Its singularity is eternal and immense, as spelled out in the next sections. It can be referred to as "*an* act," as "*the* act," singular. Much of what is at stake in theism is the singularity of God, however God is conceived, as is discussed at length in chapter 13. Thomas's Act of To Be is singular. So is the Neo-Platonic One. If the ontological act were a principle rather than an act making the world, it could not bear metaphorical carryover from the model of a person. If the ontological act were really a series of acts within time, each moment being a new creative act, the act itself could not bear the metaphorical carryover from the model of the person—rather an agent behind the many ontological temporal acts would have to be postulated, which is denied in the conception of the ontological act of creation. The ontological act of creation can be addressed and engaged as a singular, although not as a being apart from or as participating temporally within the world.

If the emergence and theistic models plausibly can be applied to the conception of the ontological act, is the same true of the consciousness model? The consciousness model lacks the strong causality imagery of emergence or agential action. Nevertheless, it very much connotes the dependence relation of the contents of consciousness, including the objects of conscious and unconscious intention, on the ground of consciousness. From the time of the Samkhya philosophy onward, in all the traditions affected by yoga, the discipline of coming to true consciousness has to do with learning to distinguish the contents of consciousness from the pure gaze or intention of consciousness itself. Consciousness comes into its own through disciplined meditation (of various sorts). In most traditions that ontologize consciousness, consciousness itself is the source of the objects of consciousness, their substrate: Things are construed as modifications of consciousness. Sometimes, as in Samkhya, objects of consciousness are allowed as having their own reality, but are experientially significant only when held as objects of consciousness, rightly or wrongly. Most forms of Buddhism emphasize the intentional aspects of consciousness, with the religious problematic having to do with identification with the objects. Yogacara forms of Buddhism emphasize the dependence of the arising and ceasing of forms on the emptiness of consciousness itself.[4] Madhyamika forms of Buddhism emphasize that even the substratum of consciousness is not real, and the experience of pure consciousness is itself a mistaken identification with consciousness as an object. Hindisms of the Vedantic schools emphasize the identity of personal consciousness with the universal underlying Brahman. The Advaita Vedanta school says that the very appearance of separate things in consciousness is a misplaced imposition of ontologizing on the flow of consciousness; the other Vedantic schools account for the otherness of the objects of consciousness in terms of a deeper underlying consciousness. That deeper source is symbolized sometimes in theistic terms with the notion of the God Ishvara. But Isvara is a manifestation of Brahman, conceived to have qualities as the source of the world's creation, and conceived better to be beyond qualities as consciousness is beyond its objects. In all versions of the consciousness model for the ontological act of creation, the conceptual and experiential "approach" to the act involves retirement into the deeper recesses of consciousness away from the play of figures across consciousness.

All three general models of the ontological act—emergence, theistic persons, and consciousness—have expressions of the terminus of the ontological act. Each has symbols in their associated sacred canopies for the mutual determination of determinate things, with some version of the distinction between essential and conditional components. This is the ground for piety of the most profound sort, expressed in terms of love or compassion, relating to other human beings but also to all beings. The ontological creative act is manifest as the ontological context of mutual relevance in this ground. Moreover, the transcendental traits of all harmonies, form, components, existential location and value-identity also need to be symbolized within a sacred canopy, especially as they address human problems of facing possibilities with obligation, attaining wholeness, exercising compassion, and finding meaning, as discussed in chapter 1 and developed thematically in *Philosophical Theology Two*.

In sum, the terms *Brahman* and *Buddha*, parsed with the imagery of consciousness, *God* parsed as person, and the arising of distinction and flow parsed as spontaneous emergence legitimately can be used as models for the concept of the ontological act of creating the world as the ultimate reality, bearing in mind all the other elements of ultimacy involved in the background dialectic for that concept that also are to be found in a good sacred canopy, and all the dimensions of ultimacy that a good worldview might find in the mundane matters of life. The critical limits of such symbols are that they always must be treated as broken when drawing inferences from them. Part IV draws out these limits at length.

II. THE ETERNITY OF CREATION

One of the most unusual elements of the concept of the ontological act creating the world is its recovery of the concept of eternity.[5] The reason the concept of the ontological act requires the concept of eternity is that temporality is manifold and determinate, with different times distinguished and related to each other in various ways. As determinate, temporality in all its modes is created. The ontological creative act includes the temporal world as part of its terminus. Giving rise to the whole of temporality is part of the created nature of the ontological act. But the ontological act itself takes place at no time. It is eternal. "Eternity" is a place-holder for a concept of an act of making that is not temporal, at this stage in the argument. The rest of this chapter explicates that concept.

Strictly speaking, the ontological act creates space–time, the whole extensive continuum.[6] The ontological act no more takes place in a spatial place than it takes place in a time. It creates all determinate (and determinately indeterminate) extensiveness. Therefore, as mentioned earlier, the ontological act should be called "immense" in the sense of being not measured by either time or space.

The nature of the extensive continuum is extraordinarily complex and not what our commonsense image assumes about space as three dimensional and time as a linear progression of present moments through the unchanging dimensions of space. Late-modern physics has shown, for instance, that the nature of space–time is affected by the speed of light, with the result that the simultaneous "presence" of an event at any date with the rest of the cosmos has been rendered problematic. "Presence" is relative to the speed of light and the mass of bodies lying in the way of light and always relative to a perspective. Space–time is not a neutral container that defines simultaneity apart from the things in it; rather it is constituted by the things that are in it as they are determined with regard to one another by their conditional components, perhaps most relevantly here by the character of the movement of light. A theologically interesting consequence of this follows for some conceptions of God modeled on personhood. Some people conceive of God as a temporal being who is immediately present to all other temporal things as time unfolds; often they conceive of God as presently conscious of other things. But this cannot be if there is truth in relativity theory. Whitehead was acutely aware of this consequence of the newly discovered, non-commonsensical character of space–time. He argued that God is a temporal being, but was careful to say that God has causal connections only with regard to what is past and future, never with anything simultaneous to a divine moment. In fact, what is simultaneous to any divine moment, for Whitehead (and his follower Charles Hartshorne), is precisely that which has no being for God at that moment. What is simultaneous to God at a moment is negatively defined as what God cannot feel as past relative to that divine moment and cannot in that moment influence as future. What is simultaneous to God at a divine moment is absolutely nothing for God. Although God can interact with the world in causal fashion, being affected by what is past and affecting what is future, according to Whitehead, in the "present moment" of God or any other temporal thing all things are absolutely alone and not present to anything except themselves.[7]

Although *Philosophical Theology* does not have to accept Whitehead's conception of God, and indeed cannot because for him God is determinate and would therefore be less ultimate than the ontological creative act, he did draw out the right consequence for theologies that claim that God is temporal. If God is temporal, God is not present to any other things. If God is identified with the eternal ontological act of creation, however, then God is immediately present to all determinate things as the act that gives rise to them in their ontological context of mutual relevance, present in their own being (essential components) and in their mutual determination (conditional components). Thus, the hypothesis that the ultimate is the ontological act of creating the world is closer to the pervasive religious intuition of divine presence, closer to us than we are to ourselves, closer to us than our jugular vein, than would be possible on any hypothesis that the ultimate is a temporal being, however exalted.

For most religious purposes the complexities of late-modern physical theories of space–time can be ignored because most religious issues arise within the commonsense worldview of space–time. An important exception to this is the development of theologically responsible and scientifically chastened images of the ultimate as creator of the extensiveness of the cosmos (I, 6). That aside for the moment, we can focus on issues of temporality and eternity, suppressing the complications of the interactions of temporality with spatial extension.

In contemporary theological reflection, eternity is not an easily accessible notion, however popular it has been under various symbolic forms in the past. In East Asian thinking, for instance, the emphasis in understanding nature has been overwhelmingly on temporality and process. To be a thing is to be a change, not a substance that endures with a relatively fixed nature. As seen in the previous section, a change is a function of the interactive alternation of yang-extension and yin-return to the tranquil matrix, passing through patterns of yin-yang alternations. In Daoist thought, the superiority of water to harder things is that it flows through changes with less impedance. The most virtuous action is non-action (*wu-wei*) that does not try to sustain a nature but allows the forces of change to accomplish its purpose. In Confucian thought, the focus is on perfecting relationships, especially with other people but also with nature, and the scale of attention is often large enough to apprehend the actions required to sustain and perfect institutions in a changing environment. To be, in the East Asian motifs of thought, is to be a change and to be coming with changes. Yet, as we also saw, quoting from Zhou Dunyi, accompanying the yin-yang dynamism of processes is an ontologically thick set of levels of reality reaching down through the Great Ultimate to the Ultimate of Non-Being. Every change in the harmonic process of changes is what it is because of that ontological thickness that embodies the finite/infinite contrast of Ultimate Non-Being and the Great Ultimate. That contrast is not temporal in the way changes are, but is eternal (in ways to be explicated).

South Asian thought has too many myriads of ways of accounting for temporal flow to allow of such generalizations as are (barely) possible for East Asian thought. Think of the direct opposition of the Hinduisms that affirm, according to one theory or another, that there exists a self or ultimate Brahman that remains unchanging beneath changes to the Buddhisms that deny such continuities. Vaguely common to most of them, however, is the sense that temporal change is problematic. For the Buddhisms, the arising and ceasing of things prompts a clinging to some forms of continuity from which suffering arises; the continuities are illusions, strictly speaking. For the Hinduisms, the temporal changes are, if not illusions as the Advaitins argue, at least less real than the continuities. To be sure, the contrast between change and continuity is wholly a temporal notion. But on some theories, at least, continuity is itself grounded in that which is not temporal, for instance Brahman.

West Asian thought has been deeply influence by Plotinus' Neo-Platonism. Plotinus was one of the great culminations of Pagan thought and was influential in Christian, Muslim, and Jewish kabalistic theology. He held that eternity is the state of the One/Dyad/World Soul that contains an infinite dynamism. Only with the creation or emanation of the temporal world is that dynamism played out part by part, with the parts being externalized with reference to one another.[8] Neo-Platonism was quite friendly to notions of eternity. The same was true of the Aristotelian influence on Paganism, Christianity, Judaism, and Islam: The divine is that which is all actual with no potency. Therefore it cannot change and is eternal. The unchangeableness of God was a fixture of ancient and medieval theology in those traditions. Later modern theology in Christianity and Judaism, and perhaps to some extent in Islam, often has rejected the desirability of unchangeableness or eternity in God. In response to pressures for intimate connections with God, much recent theology has emphasized divine temporality and interactive presence. The deficit in those later conceptions of the malleable God, as has been argued, is that the malleable God, being determinate, is not ultimate and, being in time, is not really present to other temporal things in the sense of simultaneity.

The real hostility in the West to eternity, however, comes from an interpretation of modern science that found its epitome in Immanuel Kant's philosophy. For Kant, the possibility of objective scientific knowledge based on a priori principles requires that all objects be inscribed on the transcendental structures of human knowing. In particular, this refers to what he called inner sense, which has the form of time. He defined existence as occupying a place in inner sense.[9] Therefore, by definition all existing things are temporal. Kant did not want to say that God is temporal, or that God does not exist. But he did say that God cannot be known, at least not in the objective way that science knows by "determining objects." Therefore, theology is impossible in any cognitive sense. And what can be known is temporal. Some theologians influenced by Kant sometimes do want to say that God is temporal so that God can be known, although others have found some way of circumventing his strictures against knowing nontemporal things.

The result of Kant's influence for Western theology is that eternity is a hard case to make. *Philosophical Theology* is not Kantian in its epistemology. But it does have to construct a plausible theory of eternity to make out its claim that the ontological creative act is eternal. That theory begins with a theory of temporality.

III. TIME AND ETERNITY IN THE THREE MODES OF TIME

Bearing in mind, although setting aside for the moment, the complexities of space–time mentioned above, temporality has three modes: present, past, and future. Some of the characteristics of these modes were discussed in chapter 10 as illustrations on the level of philosophical cosmology of the transcendental traits of harmonies. The discussion here focuses on the modes at the metaphysical level of being determinate.

Here is the hypothesis about temporality. In order to account for the flow of time, it is necessary to define present, past, and future in terms of one another. This is to say, each has essential components of its own, and receives and contributes conditional components to the other two. A brief explication of this is necessary in order to understand time's flow.

The essential components of the present mode of time have to do with the spontaneous (relative to the past) creative integration that makes up a new entity. The present is the becoming of something actual. Whitehead called it "concrescence," becoming concrete.

The essential components of the past mode of time have to do with being actual and fixed. The past is what it is, except in the sense that it is continually being added to. The actuality of the past offers resistance to anything in reality or imagination that would try to change it.

The essential components of the future mode of time have to do with formal unity and value. In a purely formal sense, the essential components of the future are like the One and the Form of the Good in Plato. Of course, the essential components of the future are impossible without the conditional components it gets from the past and present. So the future is not pure undifferentiated unity or goodness.

The present receives conditional components from the past and future. From the past it receives actual things as potentialities for integration in its spontaneous creativity. The present integration needs to add something to the actual past as given in order to give rise to a new thing. At the very least the present adds a new "unit" of space–time, mainly of time, to what was given before. More than that, however, the present combines and recombines the potentials given by the past with new forms. It is the actual past things that are given to the present moment as conditions, not representations of the past. Thus, real continuity exists from the actual past to the actualizing present. Whitehead noted that this means a rejection of what he called the "doctrine of simple location."[10] That doctrine is that a thing has its location only in its proper space–time locale, and that it can enter into another thing, somewhere else or later, only by a representation of itself, not by its own reality. To the contrary, the character of space–time is such that things have multiple locations by being actually present in other things that define a new space–time locale.

The present receives as conditional components from the future the possible forms its spontaneous creative integration might take. These forms determine what consistent pattern might be actualized in the integrative process. The forms very well might allow for alternative consistent actualizations. Surely the forms in the distant future allow for many alternative ways of being actualized. The spontaneity in the present decides which of the alternatives relevant for its integrative process will be actualized. It is to be remembered that the forms possible for actualization bear value, in two ways. Each form has the value of getting the components (the potentials) together according to its pattern and relative to the existential location of its actualization related to other actual and possible things. And each form adds to the values of its components the additional values (or disvalues) of its hierarchical layerings of complexity and simplicity, characteristic of its particular pattern. These two points are coalesced if the layerings of complexity and simplicity are acknowledged to be part of the pattern of the form (*III, 9*).

The past receives as conditional components from the present the decisions determining just which possibilities are actualized. The full integrative process of the present ends with the actualization of the potentials in a new definite pattern, all other possible alternatives having been eliminated in the present's spontaneous creativity. This complete determinateness is the conditional element provided to the past by the present. The full actualization of the integration is the creation of the actuality of past things. As soon as a present moment resolves the last alternative possibility, this is actual and past. The present must be a process of integrative changing; the past cannot change. The newly decided actualization is the continuity between present and past. Each present moment adds something to the actuality of the past, so that the past is always growing, as it were.

The past receives as conditional components from the future the forms that the present has actualized for it. Thus the past has determinate structure. It is what it is and is not another thing. Among the implications of this is that the past in a peculiar way bears its own counter-factuals. The actual past is what it is and is not what it could have been. So in the actual past is not only mutual determination of one past thing by another past thing, as is involved in actual structure, but also the mutual determination of what the past actually is and what it could have been had different present decisions been made. Because the forms from the future also bear value, the past has a rich texture of value. Various things in the past have value relative to one another because of the mutual determinations of the harmonies contained therein. They also have the value they do have in contrast to the value they might have had, were their forms different. Moral responsibility requires both that the past have differential value and that its counter-factual values are also real (as unactualized, something traceable to the relevant deciding present moments). Einstein was a great creative genius in part because he chose to work on problems in mathematical physics instead of choosing to be only a clerk in the bureaucracy in which he was employed.

The future receives from the past the determinate differentiations that constitute the specific multiplicity that it must unify formally as possibilities. If there were not the multiplicity of specifically different actual things requiring unification in present moments of spontaneous creativity, the future would have no structure. By virtue of the actual things, the future offers structured possibilities, all of which have formal unity, that constitute its possibilities that it offers present moments. Among the diverse structures of the past are alternative potentials for integration. This means that several different present acts of spontaneous integration can arise from the same past. The consequence is that the future has the possibility structure of a field in which many contemporary present decisive events might take place. Each present moment receives from the future a possibility that includes a field in which its actualizations must be consistent with what other actualizing processes might do. A structured future is relevant not only for a single creative present but for all the creative contemporary present acts. The internal possibility with alternatives that each creative moment faces must be compatible with what other creative acts might be doing, and this compatibility constitutes a field of possibilities. Existential location is not only actual location but possible location relative to a field. The structured field of possibilities is temporally deep in the future, with possibilities of the field for today being correlated with possibilities for the field tomorrow, depending on what happens today. Because the structured possibilities all bear value, the structured possibilities of the future constitute a shifting field of differential values. The structure of possibilities derives from the multiplicity of past actualities requiring formal patterns in order for unity and value to be achieved.

The future receives as conditional components from the present the steady changes to its formal structure that come from present decisions being made. Each present moment results in an actual effect that alters the possibility structure of the future. The possibility structure for a week from now is altered by everything that happens between now and then. Because the structured field of possibilities is temporally deep in the future, the whole future field of possibilities is shifted by every present decision made. The existential field is not only the field of future possibilities but that as connected to the interconnected structures of the present and past.

The dynamism of the present is its spontaneous integration of potentials given by the past according to possibilities given by the future as decided by the creativity of the present. Thus each present moment, when fully actualized, triggers a new present moment to integrate the past with its new actual elements. The dynamism of the past is that it is constantly being added to by present decisions. This means not only that new things are actual but that the structural and value implications that had previously been actual are changed. Sometimes what looked like a good idea at the time turns out to be a disaster in its sequelae. Who would have thought that the storm of expanding gasses ten minutes after the Big Bang would lead to Shakespeare's plays and sonnets? The dynamism of the future is that its possibilities are constantly changing structure and value with each new present decision. Although we are inclined to think of only the present as dynamic, the past and future are dynamic as well in their own senses.

Time's flow consists in the interaction of the three modes of time as each actualizing present moment shifts to a new date of present actualization. If time were just actualization, with the past dropping out of reality as soon as it is actual and the future not being real because it has no actuality, time would not flow. Some South Asians have argued that this is indeed the case, that time's flow is unreal. But for common experience, time does flow. Flowing means that the present spontaneous moment embraces both the past within it, as conditional components providing potentials, and the future within it, as conditional components providing consistent possibilities. Flowing means that the past is continually rolling on, with new things constantly being actualized by present moments that have structure and value derived from future possibilities. Flowing means that the future provides structures with value that steadily roll into actuality and in turn is readjusted to provide new possibilities for new decisions.

Thus, the present, past, and future need to be together for time to flow. That togetherness obviously cannot be a temporal togetherness. Rather it is eternal togetherness, for that is the ontological context of mutual relevance in which each mode of time can be together with the others, each with their essential as well as conditional components. How is this so?

Consider that each happening has a "date" when it is a present moment of integration or harmonization. The date has a fixed nature insofar as the creative present results in definite actuality and that date is then fixed as past actuality relative to other dates. The meaning of "date" depends on the character of temporally present happenings in the field with their past and future. Given the complications of simultaneity in that extensive field, relative "dating" might be different from commonsense imagination. For the sake of easy illustration here, however, let us assume that by date we mean a day in a calendar of years. Suppose that a present moment of creative spontaneous harmonization results in a day's worth of space–time novelty.

Consider a long-lived person, for example, a woman with a hundred years of days or dates. Every one of those dates has the mode of being of future. Every one has the mode of being of present happening (which names the date). And every one has the mode of being of past fixed actuality. Within the temporal flow, at the age of five, the first five years of dates are past actuality and the next ninety-five are future save for the present day of the 5-year-old. At five, the woman's past is extremely formative for her future identity but is largely not her own responsibility; the distant future of the 5-year-old is extremely vague, that is, open to contradictory possibilities. By the age of thirty-five, however, she has exercised much more responsibility for whom she has become and what she has done. Her past is extremely rich and her future is much more determined by the circumstances in which she has become individuated and the commitments to which her choices have led her. A person at forty-five usually has a life densely determined by commitments in many directions, to family, career, roles in society, and so forth. "Middle age" is a time of ubiquitous obligations. Her future developments are still fairly open, given a tolerant historical environment, but the main channels of her future have been roughly set by her decisions and situation. At seventy-five, however, she has actualized most of the important elements of her life's situation, being now largely determined by her own choices and the actual happenings of the history through which she has lived. In one sense, given good health she is at the height of her long-cultivated powers for creative life, although these are in deep channels of her actualized character, commitments, and individuated circumstances. Her future is fairly narrowly defined in terms of the kinds of things she can do in her circumstances. By the age of ninety-five, chances are that most of her important decisions are in the past. The circumstances for her last five years might well be beyond her control if her historical situation is not responsive to the preparations she had made earlier. Life at ninety-five has few interesting expectations but is a deeply rich field for reflection on the meaning and value of her previous years, given a still-sound mind. The *temporal* identity of this woman depends on which day of her life we pick as the present, the perspective of which determines which dates are her actual past and her possible future.

Living within time, her life flows from one day to the next, each day involving decisions that add to her actual past and reshape her future for every day of the rest of her life. This temporal flow of life is possible only because at each present date her past and future are together with the present creativity. The past and future are not temporally present with the present. On the contrary, it is because they are other than the present that they can contribute the conditional components of potentials and possibilities, respectively, for present creative integration. The past and future dates have their own essential components that give them determinate difference from the given present date. Therefore, the present, past, and future dates are together in the ontological context of mutual relevance, as the ground of the possibility of their being together cosmologically in the passing time of temporal flow.

In this sense, then, the real identity of the person is the *eternal* one in which all of her dates are future, all present, and all past. There is no time, no single date, at which this eternal identity exists. At any single date within her life, some of the dates are past and others are future. Even on the last day of her life, all her dates save that one are past and none is future. Only in the eternity of the ontological context of mutual relevance is she concretely real. The determination of her life within time is an abstraction from the concrete reality of her identity within the eternity of the ontological context of mutual relevance that makes the temporal flow of her life possible. Suppose that she has lived and died. Who is she? What is her real identity? Is she the decrepit, senile person of her last weeks? Yes. But she is also the one who at the age of five had the whole world ahead of her. She is also the person who at thirty-five was an active responsible player in the world of her family, friends, careers, and historical circumstances. She is just as much the person of deeply focused creativity that she was at seventy-five, and the reflective passive person of ninety-five. Her real concrete identity is her present moments in every one of her dates. She really is the actual achievements of all of her dates. And she is the person who at every present date faced the future structure of form and value in her future dates relative to that. Her real identity is her eternal identity, of which her temporal identity on any present day of her life is a real but abstract part of her concrete identity. The eternity of her identity cannot be contained within any date of her temporally flowing life. At any temporal date, her future is not determined as it will be actualized later, but is open to the kaleidoscope of shifting possibilities; within time there is no predetermination except as resident in the past potentials and the possibilities themselves. Even at dates after her death, when within time she has been reduced to all past actuality, she is not concretely real. Her concrete identity is only in eternity.

Now, this discussion of the individual woman is a great abstraction. Because of her relations to other people and to her environment throughout all her life, by means of the conditional components necessary to any of the harmonic identities of that life, her identity is bound up with all those others. Therefore, her eternal identity is part of the eternal identities of all the other people, events, and places with respect to which she was determinate along the many days of her life. Those other things too are concretely real only in eternity; at any date of their interaction among themselves and with her, they face a shifting field of possibilities, which is part of their larger existential field relating their pasts and present becomings according to such structures of causation as might exist. She and all those other things to which she related during her century of life are mutually determined and different, each harmonizing their conditional relations with their own essential components in the eternal ontological context of mutual relevance. Now expand the scope of attention beyond her and her contextual partners to the entirety of the cosmos, from the Big Bang to, suppose, the Final Dissipation in which things cease to have mutual relevance. At any date within cosmic history, other dates are past and yet others are future. But time can pass within that history only because all of the dates are created together as present, all as past, and all as future. This creation is not at any time. Rather time itself is created with this character of related modes of past, present and future, internally flowing.

So eternity is the togetherness of all the spatiotemporal things in the ontological context of mutual relevance, which is to say that they are created together in the ontological act of creation whose created nature, among other things, is to be that ontological context of mutual relevance. Strange as it might seem to people conditioned to think that only temporal life is real, with the present experience of consciousness being the mark of reality, this temporal flow is only real because of its ontological location within the creative act in which all the moments can be together as harmonies of their own essential and conditional components. The better intuitions are in those people who sense the more concrete reality of eternity behind the fleeting moments of time's flow.

IV. ETERNITY AS ONTOLOGICAL AND COSMOLOGICAL ULTIMATE REALITY

The dynamism of temporal life is a fundamental part of human experience, the underlying condition for many of the basic human problems that call for symbolization in sacred canopies. The introduction to *Philosophical Theology One* took note of several of these basic human problems, all of which are shaped by the dynamism of temporal life. That we have possibilities, a function of the future, gives rise to the fundamental problem of righteousness, of making the right choices and living up to commitments and obligations (*II, 1*). That we integrate our components means we have the fundamental problem of deference or comportment toward those components of life to which we must respond by harmonizing them with a degree of wholeness (*II, 2*). That we have spatiotemporal locations in a dynamic existential field involving future, past, and present, means we have the fundamental problem of living life with compassionate appreciation of the rest of creation (*II, 3*). That to be at all through a lifetime of change means we have the fundamental problem of achieving a value-identity (II, 4). All these "problems" reflect boundary conditions of the human world and need to be symbolized in sacred canopies in connection with ultimate finite/infinite contrasts.

So also sacred canopies need symbols for expressing the ultimacy of temporal dynamism as a pervasive boundary condition of human life. Many common such symbols exist in various forms in different traditional canopies. For instance, symbols mark the ultimacy of the rotation of the seasons and the repetition of the years, sometimes in connection with astrological concepts. Symbols mark the passage of time itself in terms of life and death, building and destruction, growth and decay, effort and loss. Ecclesiastes in the Hebrew Bible is about the vanity of permanence, achievement, and status in a world of flowing time; surely that book reflected ideas from Buddhism![11] The symbolic systems around Shiva have to do with his dancing the passage of time, creating and destroying, guaranteeing death so that new life is possible. Now we have in *Philosophical Theology* a metaphysics of temporal dynamism that can function as a control on the rich symbols of time's passage in sacred canopies. And we can insist that this metaphysics finds adequate symbolic expression.

The argument of this chapter, however, is that the dynamism of time's flow is dependent for its determinate ontological reality on the eternity of the togetherness of the modes of time in the ontological creative act. Temporal dynamism is an abstract part of eternal dynamism. Eternity embraces all moments (and places) together as present, all as future, and all as past. In the eternity of the ontological creative act, every moment is the spontaneous creativity of present harmonization, every moment is the shifting kaleidoscope of future possibilities relative to the sequential march of the present, and every moment is the rich actualization of value as a past state that is constantly altering in meaning and value relative to subsequent actualizations. Only because the modes of time are together ontologically, with the integrity of their different harmonic contrasts of essential and conditional components, is the temporal flow we experience in time possible. Thus, this eternity of the ontological act of creation is a fundamental aspect of ultimate reality and needs symbolization in sacred canopies.

Symbols of eternity are perhaps more complex than the symbols of time's passage. Perhaps most common are symbols of "another time and place" for an afterlife where the effects of time's flow are somehow nullified. Such conceptions of "heaven" symbolize the fulfillment of righteousness and justice that seem so elusive in temporal life. They ground heavenly life in paradisiacal circumstances, however the particular culture understands paradise. They perfect all the social and natural connections that time and space ruin, reuniting loved ones, settling people at home. They accept the cumulative value-identity of people as beloved and rewarded. Of course, such conceptions of heaven are impossible to think out in detail because they still have the symbolic trappings of temporality. How old will a person be in heaven? How old will parents and grandparents be? The friends of late life?

If everyone is thirty-three (Augustine's suggestion, based on the supposed age of Jesus when he died), your grandparents would be younger than you ever knew them! You would love to be reunited with your mother as the young woman of your infancy, as the responsible career woman of your youth, and also as the elderly grandmother of your children—which shall it be? So long as such eternity is symbolized with the frame of temporality, "another time and place" that nullifies the effects of time's flow, such paradoxes will arise. In eternity, of course, all people are together at all dates of their lives in the present, past, and future modes; but this togetherness does not have the frame of temporality.

Not all conceptions of the afterlife nullify the effects of time's flow. Many, to the contrary, suppose a karmic reality within the afterlife in which a person faces similar fundamental problems, with moral consequences, to what are faced in "this life." In these conceptions of "another time and place," eternity is symbolized by various conceptions of getting out of the karmic round, stopping the wheel of rebirth, making this death final. The symbols for escaping the karmic round and all aspects of time are extremely various. Some symbolize identification with this or that unchanging reality. Others symbolize change as ultimately illusory. Yet others symbolize the self as having only momentary and unchanging reality. Such conceptions find friendly reception in many of the religious movements of South Asia, but have had currency in West Asia and East Asia.

Yet other ways of symbolizing eternity have to do with mystical ascents that aim at visions of the togetherness of things where the limitations of temporal togetherness are set aside, transcended, or trivialized. Sometimes, as in various versions of the Perennial Philosophy and in this *Philosophical Theology*, the conceptions of the metaphysical structure of time and eternity are used as symbols for eternity. They can be used as symbols for engaging the ultimacy of eternity, as discussed in chapter 15.

Notice how complex the metaphysical argument of this part has made the workings of a theologically acute sacred canopy. Something is ultimate about determinateness as such. Something is ultimate about mutual determination with others. Something is ultimate about the ontological context of mutual relevance. Something is ultimate about the ontological act of creation. Something is ultimate about the fundamental structures of the world created, especially about the transcendentals of all harmonies: form, components, existential location, and value-identity. Something is ultimate about the temporality of the world. Something is ultimate about the eternity of the ontological creative act that makes temporality possible.

All these aspects of ultimacy need expressions in the symbols of a sacred canopy according to which one can live. But there is an ordering of ultimacy among them. The fundamental ultimate reality is the ontological act creating the world. The other ultimate realities are boundary conditions for life within that world, all aspects of that fundamental ultimate reality.

The ultimacy in practical religion is not limited to the sacred canopy, understanding it, or engaging ultimate reality through its symbols. Rather, practical religion involves worldviews that connect the ultimate realities symbolized in the sacred canopy with various other parts of life. By virtue of these worldviews, those mundane domains of life take on dimensions of ultimacy. Because worldviews provide orientation structures for those mundane domains, just how those domains ought to be oriented to ultimate reality is an open question for theology. Not all worldviews provide orientation that is in accordance with what is ultimate. Hence, not all worldviews can shape the anthropological ultimates of people with adequacy. The anthropological ultimates are the ways in which all the domains of life are oriented to what is ultimate. The metaphysics of ultimacy provides an anchor for addressing the theological problems of worldviews, which are engaged in *Philosophical Theology Two* and *Three*.

Part III

Summary Implications

One purpose of Part III was to develop a set of metaphysical ideas about ultimate reality that can serve as a kind of orienting control on the symbols of ultimacy discussed in Part II. Many of those metaphysical ideas were introduced in Parts I and II, but not developed and defended. The main purpose of Part III was to provide a detailed defense of the metaphysical elements in the hypothesis about ultimate reality that undergirds the whole of *Philosophical Theology*. Part III has the form of a dialectical argument so complex that its Preliminary Remarks said what the chapters were going to say, chapters 9 through 12 said what the dialectical argument is, and these Summary Implications are a resaying of what has been said.

Chapter 9 opened with the identification of ultimate reality as "being," a classic identification, especially in Western philosophical theology. All beings have being. The way into the analysis of this is through the problem of the one and the many. How is it possible that there can be many beings that are different from one another? Something one must exist that allows them to be related enough to be distinguished and distinct enough as to be different.

But perhaps there is no one "one," only the unifications of all the others from the standpoint of each of the many. This position of ontological pluralism in the form presented by Paul Weiss was examined and found wanting because none of the many could unify itself with the others without encompassing them within it without remainder. This would eliminate the real differences between things. So there must be some one "one."

But perhaps the one "one" is not univocal, not being or one in the same sense, but analogical, as Thomas Aquinas argued. Thomas' theory of the analogy of being was examined and found wanting because differences in the senses in which beings are being, or are one, cannot be asserted without a more basic univocal sense of being. The analogy of being does not hold.

Then we asked whether being, as the one for the many, is determinate or indeterminate. As something common to all beings, being could not be determinate, because something more basic would have to be common to it and the other beings. As something perfecting or integrating the beings, totalizing being could not be determinate, because something higher and determinate would have make it possible to relate the array of beings to their determinate integrating principle. A similar difficulty holds if the perfecting principle is dynamic and laid out in time, as in Hegel's view. So, being as the one for the many cannot be determinate. In the process of this complex argument we articulated two principles. The principle of the equality of reciprocal differences says that different things must be equal in the ontological status of having their own essential components over against each other. The principle of the ontological ground of differences says that being must be a unifying ground in which differences are possible. The junction of these principles is the problem of identifying an ontological context of mutual relevance, which is what being has to be in order to be the one for the many. And this cannot be determinate in the senses considered in chapter 9.

Chapter 10 recognized that the problem of finding an indeterminate context of mutual relevance has no traction without a more detailed metaphysics of determinateness. A metaphysical hypothesis was presented to the effect that to be determinate is to be a harmony with essential components of its own and conditional components that relate it to the other harmonies with respect to which it is determinate. Harmony was analyzed as the "just fitting together" of the various components, understood in terms of a theory of form, of components formed in harmony, of existential location, and of cumulative value-identity. An analysis of value was given as a function of complexity and simplicity in form. With regard to temporal harmonies, form has the mode of future possibilities, of selective decision making in the present that resolves alternative possibilities, and of past realized actualities that bear the values given in their actualized structure. The problem for identifying the ontological context of mutual relevance, then, is to find that togetherness in which different harmonies, each with their own essential components fitting with their conditional components, can be together.

Chapter 11 distinguished the ontological context of mutual relevance from the cosmological context in which things are made mutually relevant by their various conditional components. Causal relations are all cosmological and would not be possible without the more basic ontological togetherness in which causes and effects have their being together. What can be the ontological context of mutual relevance? Only an ontological creative act that creates all determinate things can be the ontological context of mutual relevance. Apart from creating, the act is wholly indeterminate. In creating the world, it creates its own determinate nature as creator, which is among the determinate things created. The ground of all determinations, including the determinate nature of the creative act, is the ontological act itself that simply makes the determinate things of the world together. The ontological creative act is the one for the many, the ontological context of mutual relevance. The determinate created world is not separate from the act, but rather is simply its terminus. The ontological creative act is not something separate from the world of determinate things, but rather is the world's ontologically unified depth. That ontological creative act is singular, however, not some vague depth behind determinateness. It is creative of time and space, and hence is itself not in time and not in space. From within time, the future is partly indeterminate and is made determinate by present decisions, date by date. The nature of the creative act is to be the ontological context of mutual relevance for the things created, to exhibit the transcendentals of all harmonies, namely form, components, existential location, and cumulative value-identity, and to be the creator of the particularities of the world, of which we have only a small sample.

Chapter 12 analyzed the contrast between the temporality of the created world and the eternity of the ontological act of creation. A detailed philosophical cosmology of the three modes of time was elaborated, couched in the language of the essential components of the present, past, and future respectively and of the conditional components each contributes to the other so that those three modes are understood as harmonies. Their togetherness makes possible time's flow. That togetherness itself cannot be temporal—they are not together at any time, rather, their togetherness constitutes time and its flow. The togetherness of the modes of time is the eternity of the ontological creative act. Therefore, it was argued that the concrete reality of determinate things such as human beings is not limited to their temporal lives. Rather, it is the togetherness of all the dates of their existence as all future, all present, and all past, a togetherness that constitutes their part of the ontological creative act. Despite the strong bias toward privileging temporal experience, symbols also exist by which people can understand and engage their eternal existence.

It remains for this metaphysics of ultimacy to be related to ultimacy as definitive of religious experience and guidance.

Part IV

Ultimates Known

Part IV

Preliminary Remarks

The philosophical theology of ultimate reality has been built on three layers of argument. Part I presented tools for the analysis of religion, including a theory of symbolic engagement according to which theory can deal with first-order questions about ultimacy. Part II examined elements common to religious life in the real world that put pressures on symbols of ultimacy, including those for ultimate concern, for ever more transcendent symbols, for ever more intimate symbols, and for narrative and its limits. Part III developed an elaborate metaphysical theory of ultimacy and argued for it dialectically. That theory has both positive and negative consequences that are explored in Part IV.

The positive consequences are what we can know about ultimacy, discussed in chapter 13. The negative consequences are rejections of many positions concerning what we can know that cannot be true, especially those having the wrong commitments to determinateness in ultimacy, discussed in chapter 14. In theological life, theology itself constitutes a symbol of the ultimate and enables experiential engagement of ultimate reality. Theology thus can be part of religious life, as discussed in chapter 15. But in the end, theological expressions of ultimacy, even when given metaphysical generality and attempted literalness, break on the wildness of ultimacy. Chapter 16 discusses the apophatic turn of mystical adepts.

CHAPTER THIRTEEN

What Can Be Known about Ultimacy

Given the abstractness of the conception of the ontological ultimate arising from an analysis of bare determinateness, and the explicit denial that the ontological act of creation has a nature of its own over and above its products, what of religious importance can be known about it? This chapter articulates what positively can be known and the next draws negative inferences about what cannot be known.

Chapter 12 opened with a brief argument that the ontological act of creating the world legitimately can be called "God" but just as legitimately can be named in the metaphors of consciousness and spontaneous emergence. The first section of this chapter conjures with the fact that the metaphors surrounding "creation" are biased toward the language of God and divinity. The ultimate reality that determines ultimacy in all its varied dimensions is the ontological act creating the world and this can be understood in part through dialectical arguments such as those given in Part III. But that dialectical argument is a very difficult "symbol" of ontological ultimate reality for practical religious orientation, having mainly indexical reference. In practice, religions and religious peoples have developed models of the ultimate.

I. THE ULTIMATE AS MODELED: GOD, CONSCIOUSNESS, EMERGENCE

Strictly speaking, the ultimate ontological creative act cannot be modeled. A model asserts some kind of isomorphism between the model and its object, as, for instance, a mathematical equation models a natural set of relations, or a machine models a natural structure, or a set of theoretical assumptions models a social reality, or a Dickensian description models life in London. Strictly speaking, a model refers iconically, in the sense described in Chapter 3, Section III. But the ontological creative act cannot be modeled, or be a part of a model of the world, because it is not determinate. Only determinate things can be in isomorphic relation with the determinate elements of a model. This is true not only of the creativity of the ontological creative act. Creative processes within the natural world also cannot be modeled, strictly speaking. What can be modeled are their stages but not the power or creative emergences involved in causation as such. Experiential elucidations of creative emergence have to do with indexical referencings of things felt, not modeled.

Nevertheless, certain things within the world, which themselves can be modeled with various conceptual and symbolic schemes, have been developed within the world's varied religious consciousnesses as fundamental symbols, or thematic motifs of thought, that can be used practically as signs for the ontological ultimate reality. These thematic motifs then are construed as models of ontological ultimate reality, although strictly speaking they are not. The suggestion in *Philosophical Theology* is that the most common, although not only, basic models for ultimacy are personhood, consciousness, and emergence. Everyone knows persons, is aware of consciousness in reflexive ways, and interacts with emergent things. Thus, these motifs tie in to intimacy when used as signs of ultimacy. In the major religious traditions the motifs are developed in various ways so as to transcend various aspects of their finite inadequacies so as to be more nearly true to the peculiar indeterminateness in the ontological act of creation.

The model of personhood is likely universal across all the world's cultures from the Paleolithic Age to the current Paleogalactic Age. Perhaps this is because there seems to be a biological developmental stage at which all children attribute agency to a wide range of things that extends far beyond living beings that really are intentional agents.[1] Once the distinction is made between the naturally intentional things and the rest, attribution of agency to the nonintentional things seems to be an affirmation of supernatural agents. Mountains, storms, and extreme natural phenomena, dead people, especially ancestors, as well as some animals, are modeled as persons with intentional agency. For many cultures, including popular cultures in the modern world, the "natural world" contains a host of "supernatural" elements. For the most part, these supernatural elements are not taken to be ultimate, only beings to be coped with in the course of life, and sometimes as mediators of the unknown. In many South Asian traditions, all persons and personified life forms are taken to be subject to the laws of Karma, and hence cannot be ultimate. Even the high gods are construed as subject to Karma, although there are dialectical ways of limiting this subjection.

In the instances where supernatural agents are conceived to be superior to human beings and in control of some or all of the conditions of human life they are construed as gods. Sometimes a certain god is construed as superior to all others. In China, before the first millennium before the common era, the storm god Shangdi was taken to be the ruling god, rather like Yahweh in Israelite religion of approximately the same time. In the religious revolutions of the next thousand years the anthropomorphic conception of Shangdi as God was decisively rejected by the intellectual elite in favor of the explicitly nonpersonified conceptions of Heaven, Earth, and Dao, in Daoism, Confucianism, and most of the other schools. Nevertheless, even during the high Neo-Confucian period an important concept was the "mandate of Heaven," a holdover from the intentionality of Heaven or Shangdi. South Asian thought conceived a wide spectrum of life forms, from lowly insects through human beings to high gods, sometimes with the assumption that a given soul could pass through many of these life form, including demons and advanced gods. Some of the high Gods, such as Vishnu and Shiva, are conceived in very transcendent personifying terms, often in connection with avatars of various sorts, as Krishna is a chariot-driving avatar of Vishnu; these personified Gods are also construed as images of that which is beyond personification, for instance, Brahman.

The West Asian monotheisms developed through a complicated history of competing gods who were high Gods of different groups, of the benevolent God fighting against divinely personified forces of evil as in Zoroastrianism, to some notion or other of an exclusive personified God who creates all things. A personified monotheistic God is conceived according to many motifs of personification. Some are clearly intended to be metaphorical, as when the 23rd Psalm in the Hebrew Bible calls God a "shepherd" and people "sheep." Other references to God as a king and to the world as a kingdom are perhaps less self-consciously metaphorical in their personification of the creator. Personification is difficult to sustain when the natural created world is conceived to be as extensive and intensive in its natural, non-human, orders (I, 6-7). Although Moses was said to have seen God's backside and Isaiah the hem of His garment, by the first century of the common era, the monotheistic God is Israel was conceived to be so transcendent as to be known only through angelic messengers, or co-creating Wisdom or Logos, or through a divine Son, Jesus Christ, who was the first visible sign of a totally invisible, that is, indeterminate and inconceivable, God (Colossians 1). The many variations on the motif of personification in the monotheistic traditions have often been inconsistent and even mutually contradictory; but they have functioned as motifs of symbolic elements for engaging ultimate reality. Much Jewish and Christian theology of the past two centuries has been preoccupied with whether and to what extent personifying imagery for God can be reconciled with modern science.[2]

Another model of ultimate reality taken from the human sphere is consciousness, with an implicit distinction between consciousness as such and its objects or contents. This motif has been particularly important in South Asian thought where it has developed in relation with the personification motif, sometimes as an alternative, sometimes as the "true interpretation" of personified images, and sometimes just independently. A deep motif in South Asian thought is that wherever there is diversity, plurality, or change, there must be an underlying unity. Sometimes, although rarely, that underlying unity is construed as an objective thing, such as matter. More commonly it is thought to be something like consciousness that is itself no matter what objects appear within it. Sometimes, as in Samkhya philosophy, the physical world is thought to be a nature of its own independent of consciousness, with a task for consciousness to understand its own nature as consciousness apart from the physical world. Sometimes the objects of consciousness are thought to be functions of consciousness itself, without much independence. Sometimes consciousness itself is construed as a reality that provides continuity through time, or that is timeless. It is Atman, which is identical with Brahman, a deeper form of consciousness, a prominent position in the Upanishads. Sometimes consciousness is thought to be nothing other than its contents, arising and ceasing, as in various forms of Buddhism, giving rise to the denial of the self or Atman. In the famous contest for the Patriarchate in Chan Buddhism, one candidate said the mind is like a mirror whose contents are like dust that should always be cleared away. The winning candidate asked "What mirror?"[3]

Pure consciousness is wholly indeterminate, like the ontological act without creating, and the determinate things of experience and the world are functions of consciousness. Pure consciousness cannot be conceived or experienced, however, without the dialectic of removing its determinate objects. So, like the dialectic in Part III, the transcendent-consciousness motif reveals consciousness to be the ground for any determinate connection between things, a ground which disappears into nothingness except for the memory of intentional consciousness when the determinate contents are removed. Only some versions of this motif would attribute causal powers to pure consciousness for the creation of its contents. But the ontological creative act, modeled here as consciousness, itself comes to be with its creation of the world: So consciousness in relation to its objects (in whatever variant of that idea is at hand) is gratuitous, arbitrary, undeserved by anything in the world, and surprising, a pure "suchness," as most Buddhists would say.

The West Asian monotheisms generally have not developed consciousness as a metaphysical motif. Nevertheless, they have a variety of mystical traditions aimed to develop consciousness of the ultimate reality with something approaching immediacy. The mystic's consciousness is aimed to approximate the reality of the ultimate act of creation, which thus is modeled on something like an immediate content of pure consciousness. Although the more active creationistic metaphors are rarely absent from the Western mystical traditions, the immediacy of mystical consciousness is a persistent theme (I, 15, 16; II, 11, 12; III, 15, 16).

East Asian religions since the first millennium have been much influenced by Buddhism with its motifs of consciousness. Apart from that influence, which has been thorough and broad within both Daoism, especially the Shanqing school, and Neo-Confucianism, there has been little appeal to the motif of consciousness for symbols of ultimate reality.[4] The closest connection is likely to be the emphasis on sincerity or transparency in Confucianism. A human being embodies the Dao best when in relation to other things in the world such that they are apprehended as they are with the values they have and responded to appropriately according to those values.[5] This is not a transcendent Dao but an embodied Dao.

The motif of emergence is far more prominent in East Asian thought than personification of the ultimate or consciousness as ultimate. Acutely sensitive to nature's movements and the emergence of novelty out of inertial processes, the ancient yin-yang cosmologies stressed emergence as the prominent component of reality. Reality does not consist of "things" as much as it consists of "changes," that is, emergences. The opening lines of the Daodejing point to a double meaning of emergence. "The Dao that can be named is not the true Dao." The Dao that can be named, that is, described, is the emergence of things within time from the past, with tendencies and impulses toward the future. But that temporal Dao itself emerges from a deeper fecundity that gives rise to the temporal process itself, something not temporal, although present at all moments connecting them in emergent ways. Emergence has both a horizontal temporal dimension and a vertical nontemporal or eternal dimension, with both dimensions capable of being apprehended at any moment.[6] The passage quoted earlier from Zhou Dunyi illustrates this position. Meditative strains within both Confucianism and Daoism foster the abilities to become aware of and take advantage of this duality of dimensions of emergence.

Emergence is not thematized so broadly within South and West Asian traditions. In the former, it is perhaps most prominent in rituals of sacrifice in which the act of sacrifice produces an emergent condition of a world-divinity connection.[7] In the latter emergence is prominent in nature mysticisms as well as sacrifice rituals. The Abrahamic monotheisms generally have not construed the sacrifice rituals to be the constitution of divinity, however, as in many Hindu traditions, only of a renewed good connection between God and the people.

Each of these models of ultimacy has generated an astonishing array of symbols and metaphoric strategies for interpreting the ultimate dimensions of life across worldviews. These arrays have interacted with one another and with secular modes of thought, and have developed in particularized contexts that sometimes seem inconsistent with one another when brought together. But none of them models the ultimate ontological act of creation, strictly speaking. When personified symbols of God are made so transcendent as to be indeterminate, they hardly remain models of personhood. When apprehensions of consciousness are made so transcendent as to be indeterminate as the ground of all difference, they cease to be consciousness rather than anything else. When motifs of emergence are tracked down to that which cannot be named, the Ultimate Non-Being, emergence ceases to be different from just arbitrary surprise. The validity of using these models for engaging the ontological creative act must be assessed according to whether they carry over what is important in that act into the experiences of the people who use them, context by context. Their reference in this way is indexical, not mainly iconic.

Philosophical Theology develops its categories with awareness of these models and of their influence. In principle, it should work equally with developing categories from each of the motifs, and in many instances it does show how its categories relate to the different metaphoric systems. But overall in practice, its responsibility for developing consistent categories puts pressure on accountability to equal time for all models. Moreover, the aim here is never to show that the theology in *Philosophical Theology* is valid because it is reinforced by many or all traditions, although this is one strand of argument. So it is to be admitted that the categories here derive from the metaphorical base of theism however much that is purified, and the limits of this must now be explored.

The ultimate ontological act of creating the world is not to be construed as personal in any literal sense, however much contexts might arise in which personification is legitimate. The reason for this, we have seen several times, is that, as the ontological context of mutual relevance, the ontological act of creation cannot be determinate except as what it makes itself in creating. Chapter 14 explores some of the religious implications of this in detail. But for the purpose of this chapter we need simply to highlight the point that the term *God* when put to use in *Philosophical Theology* does not necessarily imply personhood, or any determinate characteristics.

Once again it should be stated that this nonpersonal God is not an innovation in the monotheistic religions, recalling both the indeterminate One of Neo-Platonism and the simple Act of To Be of Thomism. Thinkers in these traditions also tried to reconcile these nonpersonal conceptions of God with biblical personifying language, by means of theories of rhetoric or analogy or symbolism. *Philosophical Theology* tries to do the same. More recently, however, Tillich has been explicit in saying that God is beyond all gods who might be called personal, and his own theory of symbolism translates the biblical symbols rather radically before connecting them with his conception of God as the Ground of Being.[8]

Ultimate reality as the ontological act of creating the world, explained according to the metaphysics of Part III, is a vague category that has been specified by deep ontological symbols other than God. For instance, it has been symbolized in Chinese religion as the Dao and as Heaven (and sometimes Earth in combination with Heaven). The categories in Zhou Dunyi's metaphysics—the Ultimate of Non-Being, the Great Ultimate, yang, yin, the five elements, and so forth—together articulate something very like the metaphysics of the ontological act of creation, and yet none of his categories carries many of the basic connotations of God, save perhaps the

Great Ultimate. South Asian thought exhibits many kinds of theism, but often as distinguished from the most ultimate of realities such as Brahman without qualities.

Although attempting to balance at least these three basic models for the ontological ultimate reality that cannot be modeled, *Philosophical Theology* exhibits a philosophical dialectic that arises in response to the Western theistic dialectic that moves from personal imagery to what is transcendent and determinate beyond theism. Some crucial elements in the metaphysics of the ontological creative act fit easily with this Western dialectic that are not conveyed so easily by the other conceptions.

The most important of those elements is the singularity of the ontological creative act. As noted in chapter 12, the ontological creative act is singular in the sense of creating all determinate things together. As the ontological context of mutual relevance, the act gives rise to each determinate thing together with all the other determinate things with respect to which it is determinate, in the respects in which they are determinate through their conditional components. These determinate things include temporal things whose determinate natures unfold in time through temporal decision making. By no means is everything determinate with respect to everything else in every respect, and the dynamism of determining a partially indeterminate future is particularly interesting. So it would be inappropriate to say that the ontological act of creation is totally unified. It does not imply any totality to the determinate things created, if that means some inclusive principle that integrates them. The determinate things have their *de facto* unities and the unity exhibited by the ontological creative act is the array of *de facto* unities, which of course is itself a *de facto* unity.

The ontological creative act is singular, however, not because of its unity but because it creates *this de facto* world. Whatever variety of harmonies this world contains, however connected they might be, the same ontological act that creates any one or several of them creates all of them insofar as they have any connections whatsoever. For, the very being of things with essential and conditional components, if they are different from one another, requires that they be created together with one another.

It might be tempting to say that the singular ontological act of creation is individual—singularity and individuality are related. But individuality suggests that the ontological act is *an* individual, which would require it to be among the determinate things. The determinateness of the ontological act consists only in its being what it is as creator of what it creates, and what it creates are mutually relevant individuals (and other determinate things). As Thomas Aquinas said, God is not in a genus, and hence is not a being.[9] Nor is God the highest genus, and hence is not a category. God, for Thomas, is the peculiar singularity of infinite actuality, with no limits or potentials. Similar to this in one respect is the claim in *Philosophical Theology* that the ontological creative act is singular.

Singularity is one of the most important connotations of the term God. It is not a strong connotation of Dao, or Heaven, or even the Great Ultimate. Brahman, in Advaita Vedantic thinking, has no other, but it does not connote singularity. Of course, we can begin with the metaphysics of the ontological act of creation and read singularity in to these non-theistic symbols. The symbol God brings the point immediately to mind, however.

The symbol "God" has a peculiar logic in the monotheistic traditions. On the one hand it is a common noun, signifying the embodiment of divinity (whatever that might mean—try "ontological act of creation"). The limitation of this reference is why Thomas Aquinas hurried to say that God is not in a genus or even a genus itself. On the other hand, "God" is a proper name, naming *the* ontological act of creation. Given the singularity of the ontological act of creating the world, there is something appropriate about naming it. In fact, as chapter 15 argues, the dialectical, metaphysical theory of the ontological act of creation is as much a name for God as a description.

Closely allied with singularity is the eternity and immensity of the ontological act of creation. Most of the conceptions of ultimate reality in East Asian, South Asian, and West Asian thought (counting Islam as originally a West Asian religion) are responsive to the needs for transcendence discussed in chapter 6. But they rarely press the point of the eternity and immensity of ultimate reality as contrasted with the spatiotemporal realities of the created world. The metaphysics of Zhou Dunyi does not claim that time flows or that spatial differentiation exists before yin and yang alternate; so the Ultimate of Non-Being and the Great Ultimate are not temporal or spatial. Nevertheless, the sequencing of those levels of reality in his theory is something like temporal order. The distinction between eternity and temporality is not measured in intervening levels but is immediate with the creative act. The transcendence of Nirguna Brahman is such that time's flow is not only trivialized but denied, at least in Advaitic thought. The term *God* as creator of a genuinely temporal world better conveys the metaphysical point about the ontological act of creating the world. The conception of the ontological act of creation in its way is nondual: The act is not some determinate thing in contrast with the temporal flow of the world. But the conception does argue for the reality of temporal flow and of mutually determining dualities within the created order.

Perhaps most important about the symbol "God" is that it readily expresses the freedom or arbitrariness of the ontological creative act. Not all conceptions of God do that, of course. Those that affirm that a divine nature precedes the divine creating, and that God creates a world that necessarily expresses that divine nature, cannot allow for divine freedom and cannot acknowledge the fundamental arbitrariness of the created order. But that divine nature must be a wee bit determinate, if there is to be meaning in asserting it as a nature of God apart from or ontologically prior to creation. If it is determinate, it cannot function as the ontological context for mutual relevance and a deeper such context is required to relate the divine nature to the potential finite natures of things in the world.

One of the legacies of the conception of gods as persons is a possibility of emphasizing freedom in creation, and an acknowledgment of the arbitrariness of the world. Purge those conceptions of all traces of a divine nature behind the exercise of antecedent freedom, and the result is the conception of an absolutely arbitrary act, as required by the conception of the ontological act of creating the world. That act is arbitrary in its creating a world at all, since nothing in the *nihilo* apart from creation could be a potential for creating, let alone an explaining necessity. It is also arbitrary in creating the world we have. The symbol of God as an arbitrary free agent well expresses the arbitrariness in creation. God is wild, absolutely wild. That character of the created divine nature will be very important for the analysis of religion in the next two volumes.

As Part III argued, the understanding of ultimate reality involves a trinity of interlocking notions. Without the ontological creative act there would be nothing. With the ontological creative act there is the determinate world as the terminus of that act. The act itself is the absolutely arbitrary act of making the world, which we must affirm because there is a world of plural determinate things that requires the act as the ontological context of mutual relevance. The arbitrariness of the ontological creative act would be lost if the act were not defined in terms of the nothingness that would obtain without the act. Furthermore, some mystical disciplines move imaginatively from the determinate world through the depths of their creation point to the nothingness as the abyss from which the creative act arises. The nothingness is the source of the ontological creative act, not in the sense of being the resource, the potential, but in the sense of being the starting point, the condition that would obtain without the act. Even that minimal intelligibility of nothingness, however, is possible only because of the creation of intelligibility.

This trinity of source, act, and terminus, all making up the ontological act of creating the world, is not to be confused with the Christian Trinity. Rather, the metaphysical realities to be associated with the Christian Trinity, at least at the philosophical level, are something like this. The First Person of the Trinity, the Father, is the ontological act of creation, which is as arbitrary as the Bible depicts Yahweh to be. That biblical First Person of the Trinity includes the whole of the philosophical trinity of source, act, and determinate terminus of the creative act. The Second Person of the Trinity is the Logos, or set of transcendentals that constitute the characters of harmony.[10] These transcendentals are resident in the determinate things, including temporal ones, and of course themselves are determinate. They are both created but also that in and which all determinate things, as harmonies, are created. The Third Person of the Trinity, the Holy Spirit, is the force of temporal process that continually builds up harmonies and tears them down. The Spirit blows where it wills! The Second and Third Persons together constitute the way by which the eternal act of creation proceeds within time from date to date.

The Christian notion of the Trinity is far richer than this metaphysical isomorphism, to be sure. For instance, Jesus is conceived to be the human incarnation of the Logos. What does the Logos mean for the direction of peculiarly human affairs? A specifically Christian concept of the Logos means the righteousness of finding the right forms of life, the piety of being appropriately grounded, the faith to engage one's existential location, and the hope that one's value is ultimately worthy. Christians can understand Jesus as one who did all that right, however ironic and complicated this is in light of the crucifixion.[11] Most Christologies cannot make much sense of the claim that Jesus is the incarnation of the Logos, and hence in some sense is the Second Person of the Trinity.

Similarly, the Holy Spirit is more complicated than the creative force of building up and destroying harmonies, in Christian theology. The Holy Spirit, among other things in Christian theology, is the spirit of Jesus that ideally animates Christians in their congregations, the counselor guiding Christians by interpreting Jesus to them in diverse situations. The Jesus to be interpreted is, on the one hand, the Logos: So the Spirit guides in righteousness, piety, faith, and hope. The Jesus to be interpreted is, on the other hand, the historical figure of Jesus: So the Spirit constitutes both the distance from and connection with the historical Jesus. But the metaphysics of ultimacy, even at this stage in the argument, has brought important knowledge of God that is religiously significant for Christian theology.

II. ULTIMACY AND THE TRANSCENDENTALS: FORM, COMPONENTS, EXISTENTIAL LOCATION, VALUE-IDENTITY

Another level of what can be known about ultimacy derives from the transcendentals of harmony, in and through which all harmonies are created. All harmonies exhibit form, components formed, the existential location in which the components are formed (which exists in an existential field connecting harmonies insofar as they condition one another), and the value-identity achieved by getting the components together in that location as organized by the form. What we can know of ultimate reality as the ontological creative act includes that act's nature as creating a world of harmonies.

With regard to form, it must be emphasized repeatedly that apart from creation the ontological creative act has no form, nor value which is a function of form. But with the creation of the determinate world of harmonies, the act is the creator that establishes the world with possibilities. The possibilities are formal unities that might integrate actual things in the process of time. They also achieve value in the ways by which they are patterns of possible integration, achieving some degrees or other of complexity and simplicity in harmonies that just fit together as contrasts.

Because form is itself a harmony bringing together pure unity with the contingent diversity of actuality and decisive present moments, the ontological creative act creates a world that is transcendentally oriented to order. Because form constitutes possibilities in future time, and receives complete definiteness in present decisions, and is resident as haecceity and common natures in past actuality, the world future, present, and past has an order to it. Although it is an extraordinarily complex topic not to be entered into here in any detail, we can understand mathematics as the study of forms that might be ingredient in the world. Mathematical science, in principle, should be able to explicate the forms of future, present, and past realities, of the existential field, and of all process. This point gives expression to the claim made by Whitehead and others that the possibility of science comes from the rationality of God as creator. Usually that rationality was interpreted as a rational mind of a personal God apart from creation. That interpretation cannot hold here. But its interpretation here is that the formal rationality of the world is a transcendental trait of every created thing. So the ontological creative act is the ground of the rationality of the cosmos and the possibility of mathematical science. Mathematics is not the only medium through which form is understood.

The pure formal unity that is the essential component of formal possibilities is united in contrast with the diversity of the actual world to give rise to the determinate structures of possibilities. Without the diversity of the actual world, pure formal unity would be indeterminate. The actual diversity of the world is fundamentally arbitrary. To be sure, everything actual has its rational form. But that form also is a contrast of pure formal unity with antecedent (in some sense of "antecedence") diversity. The ontological act of creation could not have created a world of determinate harmonies without the absolutely arbitrary diversity coupled with pure formal unity in a world that is both arbitrary and rational. The diversity of the world in the ontological act of creation cannot be deduced from formal rationality. Structured formal rationality requires an independent and arbitrary, from the standpoint of form, diversity.

Because form always conveys value in its patterns of complexity and simplicity, by a parallel argument the ontological creative act is the ground of value in the world. In fact, because value in form is a transcendental, everything created has its value. In this sense, the ontological act creates a good world. Nothing can be totally without value: To be determinate is to be a harmony which is to be good. Of course, the goods of some things are in disastrous conflicts with the goods of other things. The creator is the source of the destructive elements, from the perspective of the things threatened, as well as of the constructive elements. Christians tend to tame the Holy Spirit too much. Shaivites know that Shiva is the destroyer as much as the creator.

To say that the ontological creative act is the source of value in the world is not to say that the act is good or valuable apart from creation. Nor is it to make a summary judgment that the ontological creative act's creation exhibits the just and merciful providential care associated with conceptions of God as a benign creator. To the contrary, we know that the harmonies constituting plate tectonics cause earthquakes and tsunamis that wreak vast suffering. The history of the evolution of our Earthly animal species is red in tooth and claw. The more accomplished villains are at doing evil, the more evil they do. In contrast to the religious claim attractive to some that God is benign, the better summary judgment is that the ontological creative act is simply wild, and that the harmonies, all of which have value, are often in conflict. Nevertheless, we can say that ontological act is good in the sense that it creates a world in which to be at all is to bear some goodness.

Because human beings have some control over their lives, the formal possibilities that give human beings options and the different values that lie in each of those options mean that we are created under obligation to do the better. We cannot say from this that the ontological creative act personified as God antecedently intends us to be under the obligation to do good, as if that intention were a determinate nature in the act prior to creation. But we can say that the ontological act creates us in a normatively binding context. This is the ground for all the symbols that say that, in ultimate perspective, we are under judgment.

With regard to components, considered within the spatiotemporal flow as the past actualities that constitute potentials for present creativity, the ontological creative act is not to be conceived as the antecedent reservoir of infinite actuality that gets finitized in the world. But the act is to be conceived as the creator of a world that, for any creature, especially for human beings, contains actual resources for harmonization. The transcendental trait of harmonies having components in which they are grounded makes the ontological creative act the source of the grounding. Part of the nature of the ontological creative act is to be the source of the actualities of our world. Attending to them with proper piety and gratitude, we acknowledge the ontological act through the power of actuality. The actual past is a fixed structure with haecceity, thisness. The ontological act is the creator of haecceity. Because the past has form, it also has value. Therefore, we are given a world of actualities that all bear value. Moreover, although it sounds strange in light of the arbitrariness of the actual past, the past given to us has a formal rational structure that allows us to deal with it in the slim ways we can. Perhaps most of the religious piety in traditions that employ symbols of divine creation is directed at creation as the gift of actuality. The arbitrariness of the actual past is the source of our own uniqueness and individuality.

With regard to existential location, the world does not exist in the ontological creative act, nor is the world's time set within a divine time. But the act is the creator of the existential field, through creating extensive harmonies, and thus gives us our place. The existential field is as vast as the entire creation, a point explored in the last section of this chapter. Vast as that extensive creation is, it gives particular existential location to any harmony within it. For human beings, this means that the ontological act creates us in our place. Our place has perspectives and coordinates formed by the extensive nature of the conditional components that are important for our existential location. Given the vastness of the cosmos, most of the cosmic extension is so distant as to be trivial in our location. Unbeknownst to us, however, distant factors might be highly determinative of our situation, and what we do with seemingly local consequences might have far more important distant consequences. The current concerns for environmental causation are causing people to re-examine what they had presumed to be important for their existential location.

Because existential location is constituted by the conditional components connecting extensive harmonies, and the conditional components are among the components of the harmonies, the harmonies are grounded in their existential field. For human beings, this groundedness calls for a kind of piety. The existential field, however, is not only the field of past actualities. It is also constituted by the field of future possibilities relative to any moments of present creativity and thus also coordinates the structures of simultaneity of those present moments. The dynamism of the existential field, involving present and future as well as past, makes our present existential location dynamic. In this sense, the ontological creative act is the creator of the existential field in which we live and have our being, day by day.

With regard to cumulative value-identity, this consists in the values achieved by having the components of a harmony integrated with the form that bears complexity and simplicity in the existential location of the harmony. The achieved values include those components received by the harmony from other harmonies and the components the harmony contributes to other harmonies. Thus the value of a harmony is not to be understood exclusively in terms of the pattern of its integration of its own essential and conditional components. Rather, the value of the harmony consists in that plus the values of the other things with which it is mutually determinate insofar as those things contribute to or are determined by the harmony. The cumulative value of a harmony requires that it be in a context of mutual relevance with the other things whose values are relevant to its own.

For human beings, cumulative value-identity requires the ontological context of mutual relevance in at least two related ways. First, human beings are discursive individuals that live through time. Hence, our temporal harmony is a harmony of the many dates of our lives. As chapter 12 argued, because the dates are temporally external to one another, their real differences require that they be in the eternity of the ontological context of mutual relevance, each date as future, each as present, and each as past. The value-identity of a person is not merely the accumulation of achieved actual values of the person's moments as past, although it includes that. The peculiar value of human beings, who have some responsibility for how we handle our times, is the togetherness of the values of our dates in all three modes.

Second, human beings are together with things that are external to their discursive identity through time, being environing elements and processes. As pointed out in chapter 12, some things are external for a while, become internal components of a discursive harmony, and then perhaps re-emerge as external. The cumulative value of a person thus includes what the person does with conditions coming from the outside and also how the person conditions consequences external and perhaps distant. Factor this set of "environmental values" with the multiple modes of temporal extension throughout the life of a person and the complexity of harmonic relations in the ontological context of mutual relevance becomes apparent.

The ultimate value of a person exists only in the ontological context of mutual relevance which consists in the ontological act of creation. This is to say, we have cumulative value-identity only within the ontological creative act. From no place within the spatiotemporal continuum can a person's cumulative value be registered, only those non-ultimate values that appear within finite perspectives. The ontological creative act is the only location in which we have ultimate cumulative value-identity. But then, that ontological act is not a location. The ontological context of mutual relevance cannot be determinate save in terminating in the *de facto* harmonies of the created world. So the ontological act does not have a determinate perspective within which our ultimate value can be registered in a determinate way. The ontological creative act is not a super-harmony, an *ens perfectissimum*. On the contrary, the ontological creative act is simply the coming into being of the determinate things together so that they can be different with mutually conditioning components as well as their essential components. Hence, the closer we come to imagining our ultimate value, the more our value identity slides into the ontological act of creation itself. This is the fundamental insight in those theologies that say that individuals merge with the ultimate, losing the importance of their determinate identities. In our ultimate value-identity we ultimately lose our selves. This is not to say that our identities dissolve as a drop in the ocean. Every character of our lives is what it is in eternity, as possibility, act, and actuality. Nevertheless, the ultimacy of that identity, especially that identity as an achievement of ultimate value, *consists* in the singular ontological creative act that creates all things, and our lives are nothing but the ontological creative act terminating in us and other things together. Because of that ontological creative act, our ultimate identity and value is a finite/infinite contrast.

III. ETERNITY AND THE DIVINE LIFE

The nature of the ontological creative act as constituted in the creation of the world can be summed up as "divine life," if we can take the rhetoric of divinity from the theistic traditions. Selection of theistic language for this point introduces an asymmetry into the parallelism of the personal, consciousness, and emergence models for the ontological creative act. But the language of divine life does capture an internal dynamism to the ontological act for which there seem not to be parallels in the other models save when they themselves move toward personifications, as Brahman becoming Shiva. The symbolism of life for the ultimate is not universal, of course. In East Asian thought movement is more basic than life and ontological generation is more basic than movement. The Dao that can be named moves, and the Dao that cannot be named generates it. Yin and yang constitute movement, and the Great Ultimate generates them. In South Asian thought many diverse opinions are held, with no easy way to summarize them. Perhaps the simplest metaphor for the ultimate is that of consciousness, without the contents of consciousness that might move. Is that pure consciousness "life"? Perhaps, although not life in the sense of temporal change. But then, eternal life is not temporal change either. The richness of the symbol of divine eternal life recommends it as ordering symbolic references to the ontological act of creation.

The eternal togetherness of the three modes of time constitutes the eternal life of the ontological creative act. The three modes are themselves dynamic within eternity, which justifies calling them together "life." All moments with any spatiotemporal extension have a present reality in which they are creative integrations of components into actual harmonies. All moments also have the mode of future possibilities and thus, in any moment relative to present time, are changing in the patterns that would be relevant to integration. All moments have actuality in which they have fixed achieved value and structure and that actuality grows as subsequent moments are actualized, adding to the value and structure of what had previously been actualized. Within time, the present moment flows from date to date, transforming future possibilities, actualizing new realities, and adding to past achievements of definiteness and value. This temporal flow is possible only because the ontological creative act constitutes an ontological context of mutual relevance in which temporal differences and connections are together. The eternal togetherness of the modes of time is the divine life with its three related but different modes of dynamism.

The picture of the divine life is far more complicated than this, however. All temporal change involves the transcendental traits of harmonies, as indicated in the previous sections. So the divine life, as the product of the creation of the world, combines the wholly arbitrary creation of diversity with the necessary drive toward formal unity. This combination is exhibited in any temporal moment of the created order and manifested throughout the dynamic depth of the future, the dynamic creativity of present spontaneity, and the dynamic depth of the past. Moreover, the ubiquitous combination of arbitrary diversity and the press for formal unity is also the formation, actualization and completion of value, exhibited in all things. The divine life is thus the eternal transformation of goods. Given the wildness of the divine life, we should remember that the transformation of goods does not always lead to better goods, but only to different ones, which might be of less value than those in some previous temporal situation.

Some thinkers are tempted to say that the combination of arbitrary diversity with the pull of formal unity in the created divine life is a fair analogue for intentionality, and thus would lay the groundwork for saying that the ontological creative act is a person. Whitehead, for instance, laid the basis of intentionality in the character of actual occasions that seek definiteness in their concrescence or becoming, a definiteness guided by the search for intensity of value.[12] Those actual occasions include intervening logically ordered but nontemporal stages in their concrescence, and that concrescence is like thinking ahead intentionally, although the thinking ahead is not earlier. Whitehead held God to be an actual entity like others in this respect. But the ontological creative act cannot be a determinate actual entity. Within the divine life there is no moment of divinity that thinks ahead about the future because that would make the ontological act of creation an action within time. Rather, there are only finite created things that might be so organized as to think ahead and thus be intentional. The analogy of intentionality to the divine connection of diversity and formal unity is misleading if taken too seriously. This point is re-examined in the next chapter.

In addition to having the transcendental trait of form relative to the to-be-formed, the divine life also has the infinite depth of the components of the created order, each functioning in others in various causal or conditioning ways. Thus, the divine life can be said to be infinitely deep. This infinite depth is all at the level of the terminus of the divine creative act. A different sense of depth would be involved in reaching from the determinateness of the terminus of the act back into the act itself. But because the act is immediate, with no mediations distinguishing absolute nothingness and the created world, the metaphor of depth is not well suited to describe the act "prior" to its terminus in the created world. Rather, the created divine nature, concomitant with creating the cosmos, has infinite depth because of the composition of components in harmonies. Similarly, the divine life has extensiveness coextensive with the cosmos, a point elaborated on in the next section.

The value of the divine life is the togetherness of all the things created, including the values of all the things passing through temporal dynamics. For those harmonies that are haecceities, the value of each is unique. The togetherness of all the things created in the divine life has a value over and above that of any of the things. This togetherness has a pattern that exhibits many kinds of complexity and simplicity with infinite depth, and so the divine life has a value of its own. But that divine value does not stem from any higher determinate principle in the divine life, such as that all things be reconciled with no suffering. The divine value is simply the value of having all the things that are determinate together. This is a *de facto* harmony and value, the simple result of the ontological creative act creating the world. Because the determinate things in the world are constituted by their essential natures and their conditional togetherness, the togetherness of all determinate things is not more than the determinate things together. The ontological creative act has no value other than the values of the things it creates.

IV. ULTIMACY IN EXTENSION AND INTENSION

Several times earlier it was claimed that the symbols for ultimacy need to be controlled by the philosophical considerations that are intended as nearly literally as possible. So, for instance, whereas there might be circumstances when it is perfectly appropriate to engage the ultimate symbolized in a personified form, perhaps as having a personal relationship with a community or individual, the inferences to be drawn from that personified symbol need to be criticized by the logic of the more philosophical symbols. In particular, it was claimed that insofar as we understand ultimate reality to be the creator of all determinate things, the metaphysical symbols of ultimate reality need to express the extensiveness of the created cosmos as well as the intensiveness of nature in all things, especially human matters. Now it is possible to express the extension and intension of the determinate terminus of the creative act with clearer categories.

Regarding the extension of the cosmos, the vast age and size of the universe dwarfs any symbols of the creator as being finitely involved in human history. As remarked earlier, the historical development of ideas of God grew from local deities to larger and larger conceptions, relative to the growing ideas of the extent of the cosmos. Cosmic imagination unbridled by intimate ties with local kings came early in South Asian, particularly Aryan, religious thought. The cosmic imagination of the East Asians might have always viewed China as the "center," yet as early as Zhuangzi contained an ironic acknowledgment of the relativity of standpoints: When the cosmic fish leaps from the ocean and flies over the continent, the sparrow in the bush does not notice.[13] West Asian biblical thought tied its conceptions of God very early to an historical divine agent who intervened in the history of Israel, and then in the history of Israel plus the Gentiles, and then in the orientation of the Islamic march to the establishment of a divine political order. Although more transcendent conceptions were added to these, the rhetorical center was much affected by the early conceptions of God creating special programs for communities and individuals through political activity. Our current understanding of the extension of the cosmos relativizes those symbols of local divine activity.

In an empirical scientific sense, we know that the cosmos is vast, although our sample of its vast character is miniscule. In an empirical sense of philosophical cosmology, the hypothesis defended says that the extension of the cosmos is that of all determinate things that are determinate at all with respect to one another. The spatiotemporal extension of the cosmos includes all dateable moments in all three modes of time as future, present, and past. For religious purposes, we often symbolize the extension of the cosmos from the perspective of our finite existential location within it—how old it is, how large, how long it will last. The ontological creative act is the creator of all that including our own small place within it. "Heaven is my father and Earth is my mother, and even such a small creature as I finds an intimate place in their midst. Therefore that which fills the universe I regard as my body and that which directs the universe I consider as my nature."[14] Our metaphysical and cosmological argument, however, also has given us to see that the extension of the cosmos can be expressed in terms of the eternal immensity of the ontological creative act. In that eternal immensity, all places and times are together, in all modes of time, with whatever bizarre and counterintuitive (from a commonsense viewpoint) structures and relations they might have. That togetherness is not just "very big." It has the internal complexity and depth of the dynamism of the eternal immensity.

Regarding intension, the affairs of human life consist of harmonies that rest atop a vast ocean of biological, chemical, and physical processes. We can say that these processes are components of the harmonies of human life, in the many senses through which we have traced the conception of components. Human affairs are not grounded only in the actual past and anticipated future of human affairs, but also and far more richly in the intensive levels of nature. Human affairs are important as understood at their own semiotic levels. *Philosophical Theology Two* and *Three* deal mainly with human affairs. But the historical development of the semiotic systems for articulating human affairs has tended to cut off recognition of the intensive depths of nature. A theologically acute symbol system needs to reverse this and indicate that, from the standpoint of the creator, the intension of the components in which we are grounded is through the complexities of nature far more than those of human social organization. The developments of the understanding of human nature and society within evolutionary biology and psychology are responsive to this need.

What we can know about ontological ultimate reality in light of considerations of the extension and intension of the creation can be summed up in the term *depth*. The metaphor of depth was made popular in Western theology by Tillich. He spoke of the "depth dimension" in human experience and this metaphor was reinforced by his concept of God as the ground of being, and by his close interest in depth psychology. We can give that metaphor some further precision. Beginning any place in finite reality, the locus of that place bears the depth of the ontological creative act in its extensive connections with things in other places, temporally as well as spatially distant, and in its intensive complexity, its groundedness in its components. This is to say, we can engage things for many human purposes and ordinarily we let those purposes set the pragmatic limits of what should be attended to in the engagement. So limited, these are mundane engagements, however important they might be. At the same time, any one of those engagements can be a sacred engagement of the depths of the ontological act of creating the world. A theologically conditioned engagement of anything can reach into the depths, mediated as best as can be by our understanding of the conditions of extension and intension.

More than just depth, however, is the value in the depths. Our account of form as containing value in its complexity and simplicity has shown how all future possibilities are patterns for the achievement of some value, how all present creative decisions are selections of what value shall be achieved and what excluded, and how all actual states of affairs have structures with complicated patterns of value. The depth dimension of this is that every layer of the intensive organization of components itself has a dynamic history of value-embodiment (and exclusion) that is as extensive as the spatiotemporal field of the cosmos.

The depth patterns of value in the determinate nature of the ontological act of creation are wild. This is to say, they are not organized, so far as we can tell, by an intention to achieve a human-like purpose, or to reward good and evil behavior, or to organize the cosmos with justice. So many valuable things conflict with other valuable things. So many processes involve decisive events that exclude the greater value and actualize the worse. Law-like patterns of value-actualizing order are of such differing scales as to be indifferent to the actualization of the better values in each other—plate-tectonics is indifferent to the people living along the fault lines.

Yet in all the wildness of the divine nature as the terminus of the ontological creative act, every interplay is an interplay of value, to be celebrated from the perspective of each value achieved. Although not nice, not domesticated by human values, the divine nature is glorious. This can be known.

CHAPTER FOURTEEN

What Cannot Be Known about Ultimacy

I. THE ULTIMATE HAS NO INTRINSIC NATURE APART FROM CREATION

Apart from the ontological act of creation, and its termination in the determinate things of the world, nothing is to be known of ultimate reality. This is affirmed explicitly in the Hindu notion of Nirguna Brahman, Brahman without qualities. As discussed in chapter 6, the move to greater transcendence involves a dialectic that ends with denying any traits to Brahman as ultimate reality, albeit Saguna Brahman, Brahman with qualities, is ultimate as the source of creation. Although a quite different rhetorical system is involved, in the Chinese Neo-Confucian case of Zhou Dunyi, the Ultimate of Non-Being is explicitly without qualities and unknowable like Nirguna Brahman. The Great Ultimate is without determinate qualities except for being pregnant with determinations in the form of yang and yin, somewhat like Saguna Brahman. Like Nirguna Brahman, the Ultimate of Non-Being is "known" only in the dialectic of ontological origination in both traditions that says that the quality-less, the order-less, the chaotic, is the only thing that does not need explanation by something else. In Platonic Paganism, the Form of the Good, which Plato says creates the world of knowable things, is known only as it is a kind of normative measure for the plurality, rather like the account given above of the form of pure unity. In itself, the Form of the Good is not good; only when schematized to things to make them harmonious is the Form of the Good good, and then only as ideal for what it measures. The West Asian monotheisms have had many conceptions of the transcendence of the ultimate that put it beyond knowable traits. In the ancient world this occasioned moves of various sorts to introduce divine intermediaries between the ultimate monotheistic divinity and the determinate world with religious imagination. Strains of rabbinic Judaism have held that the Torah is complete within the transcendent God, just as strains of Islam have held that the Qur'an is similarly resident in the divine as a determinate mediation to the human sphere.

One major version of the Christian doctrine of the incarnation claims that the Logos, that in and through which the world is created, is a determinate word or wisdom that became flesh in Jesus of Nazareth. Colossians, one of the more metaphysical New Testament writings, says of Jesus that:

> He is the image of the invisible God, the firstborn of all creation; for in him all things in heaven and on earth were created, things visible and invisible, whether thrones or dominions or rulers or powers—all things have been created through him and for him. He himself is before all things, and in him all things hold together. (Colossians 1:15–17)

Thrones, dominions, rulers, and powers are angels native to ranks that exist within the created natural order but above the plane of the Earth with its earthly causal properties, according to first century Mediterranean thinking. Jesus, or the Logos of which he is the embodiment—ideas combined in Colossians, is the ground of the creation of the angels with their levels along with the rest of nature, that ontological context of mutual relevance in which they and all other things are together. Jesus is the first visible image of the invisible God, according to Colossians. This does not mean, most likely, that God is invisible because of a spiritual ghostlike quality that is hard to see; rather it means that there is nothing determinate about God to be imaged at all. Jesus is the first imaginable or knowable image of the transcendent God. Apart from such mediators, the Western monotheisms include dominant strains that say that God cannot be known. The ontological creative act is not something knowable apart from creation.

Before we deal with the seeming paradox of this claim, it is important to attend to the fact that in biblical religion, God is never treated as apart from creation. Not once in the Hebrew Bible, the New Testament, or the Qur'an is God mentioned out of relation to creation. If anything, the biblical traditions bend over backward, perhaps too far, to make God relevant to creation and to human affairs in history.

So what then prompts some theologians devoted to personifying models of God to think that the ultimate has a nature in the divine aseity that might be known? First, they hold to the assumption that the creator must be a being that creates out of its own nature. This is a substance conception of what it is to be a thing. Although it has become common sense in much of the West, the substance conception has alternatives and always has had. The substance conception is that a creator makes things out of the raw materials around and with the actualized powers of the creator's own nature. This is pretty much true of finite creators such as artisans (the Genesis 2 story of God making a clay model of Adam and then breathing life into the doll treats God as an artisan potter). But as we have seen, even in the case of finite creators, at least a modicum of spontaneous novelty is involved in making something. An alternative to the substance model of creation is the one developed here, with classical precedents in the West, that the nature of an agent comes from what the agent does; without doing anything, an agent is not even an agent. The contrary idea, that the agent has to have potentialities before doing or making anything, undermines the very idea of the making of novel things.

To be sure, the argument given in Part III is that ultimate reality cannot be determinate because it is the one for the many determinate things of the world. It has to be the ontological context of mutual relevance within which genuinely different but mutually determined things can be together. It is this ontological context simply by creating them together in the ways discussed. If ultimate reality were determinate in any way as a reality connected to the determinate world, a deeper ontological context of mutual relevance would have to exist to make that connection possible. As the ontological act of creation, ultimate reality is determinate only as the result of creating the determinate things. So, ultimate reality cannot be known apart from its function as creator of the world. What can be known of ultimate reality are its characteristics as creator (I, 13).

A second reason exists, however, why some theologians look to posit and know a nature in God or ultimate reality prior to or apart from creation. As mentioned earlier, there is an existential interest in predicting what God might do, what might be created, what might be demanded of human beings, how rewards and punishments work, and what to expect eschatologically. Perhaps these are less than transcendent interests. As concerns they are not fully ultimate concerns, as understood in chapter 5, because they still require the conception of ultimate reality to be related to human interest, rather than turning human interests around to be ultimately concerned with ultimate reality. Nevertheless they have more transcendent counterparts in the concern that ultimate reality be good, ultimately lovable, fair and just, beautiful, wondrously unified, balanced, whole, symmetrical.

For this reason, some theologians have agreed on the one hand that ultimately transcendent reality is indeterminate in the sense of having no finite traits that can be known, but on the other hand have argued that ultimate reality is the fullness of being that remains at the core of finite things when the negations of finitude have been introduced. Both the Neo-Platonic One and the Thomistic Act of To Be are like this, both conceived as the indeterminate ground of determinate being but also as the fullness that carries over into finite things. Finite things are actual because of the pure infinite act in their divine causal ground. Perhaps more important, finite things are good, beautiful, and endowed with other excellences because they participate in the divine being that has these excellences in infinite ways. To be sure, these excellences are identical with one another in God. But because finite things derive from the divine being, the excellences become determinately distinguishable when expressed in finite things.

This conception of creation from the fullness of being does not seem to be an economical hypothesis, however. First, if the excellences in God, including actuality itself, are not determinate, then there is no pragmatic difference between affirming them and affirming that there is nothing in God's aseity. Second, the only difference between the infinite fullness of God and finite beings is the introduction of negations that delimit portions of the otherwise infinite divine being. How can divine creating consist only in the bringing into being of negations? Does there not have to be something positive to justify negations? It is far better to say that the creation of finite things involves giving them essential components as positive own-being so that they also can have the negations that make them determinately different from one another. Third, the fullness-of-being hypothesis supposes that there is no creation of novelty. The whole being of things is in their antecedents in God, and the creation is only a diminishment of reality in a certain sector, the extensive continuum of the world. The surprising freshness of determinate reality, ontologically understood against the background of the ontological context of mutual relevance, suggests that it is novel in the face of what would obtain were there not the creation. On the fullness-of-being hypothesis, it would not be novel in the face of what would obtain were there not the creation, because what would obtain would be the fullness of being.

So, our first conclusion regarding what cannot be known about ultimacy, in light of the metaphysical considerations of Part III, is that nothing can be known of ultimate reality apart from creation. Nothing is there to be known. We can know this, by the dialectical considerations of Part III. Nothing is mysterious here in any ultimate reality apart from creation. The great ultimate mystery lies exclusively in the arbitrariness of the ontological act of creation itself.

II. THE ULTIMATE AND OTHER POSSIBLE WORLDS

Does the freedom or arbitrariness of the ultimate ontological act of creation mean that it could have created a world different from this one? Yes and No.

Yes, in the sense that from the perspectives of present moments within the temporal flow, sometimes the available future possibilities allow of alternatives. Where there are alternatives, all but one must be excluded for any one to be actualized. If the alternatives were real possibilities, then the ontological creative act could have actualized one of the excluded ones instead. For most things within the temporal flow, the decisions among real possibilities in moments of present creativity are simply chance events, spontaneous selection of one among the possibilities.

For responsible beings such as persons, however, certain moments of present decision making set the spontaneity within the larger context of the person's life. Values in the distant past will be affected for better or worse by the present decision, and among the things in the past are the person's own previous choices and commitments. Furthermore, because of their semiotic complexity, persons can frame their choices in terms of distant future outcomes that differ in their values. So, in addition to the essential spontaneity of a present moment there exist essential components from the past and future that define responsibility and obligation, such that the outcome of the present decision making in part determines the person's moral identity. Because human decisions can sometimes control important outcomes, human beings are responsible decision makers. The course of a molecule in a rock might have many spontaneous present moments; but its possibilities are extremely limited and it carries no moral freight from its past and bears on very little beyond the next moment. We would not think to call the present moments in the career of a molecule in a rock the actions of an agent the way we do human decisions. In a universal and largely trivial sense, the ultimate ontological creative act is the source of spontaneous decisions in all present moments, including human ones and rock molecules. But the complex cross-temporal structure of human beings makes at least some of those human decisions the morally relevant responsibility of the human beings.

All this is from the standpoint of human beings within time, which is something of an abstraction from the concrete reality of the eternally created world. In the ontological act of creation, all things are eternally and immensely together. Moreover, in the eternal act of creation every moment is present, every moment is future, and every moment is past (I, 12). From within time, it seems as if a different world might have been created if different alternative possibilities had been realized. But within the eternal creative act, the singular togetherness of all the moments in all the modes of time simply is what it is. All the moments are past, to be sure, and this would make it seem as if the creation is wholly deterministic. Yet all the moments are also present, with creative decisiveness. Thus in eternity it is always the case that a particular morally freighted moment is open for decision. And in eternity every moment exists as future, and its shape is different relative to every other preceding moment as present. So if the question of whether the ontological act of creation could have created a different world means a world different from the actual one, and by the actual world is meant all the moments as actualized past, the answer is No. But if the question means whether events might have gone differently from the way they did, and by events is meant all the moments in their present decisive state, the answer is Yes, always. From the standpoint of any present event, the future cannot wholly be known, only its possibilities (as limited by our abilities to know). From any present standpoint, the future might be different from what it turns out to be.

Nevertheless, the ontological act of creation is singular, and the created world in its eternal and immense concreteness simply is what it is, and there is no knowable reason for why it is that way.

Or perhaps the question of whether the ontological ultimate could have created a different world means to ask whether a different creation could have a different metaphysical structure, not "harmonies" or "determinate things." Of course, it should be stressed at this point that the theory of harmonies and determinateness is itself an hypothesis. It has been presented and defended here as a true hypothesis, but with full consciousness that hypotheses rest only on the strength of their arguments and their plausible usefulness, and are never certain. But suppose that the abstract account of determinateness is right so far as it goes. Determinateness defines possibility. An alternative world that is not determinate is not a determinate possibility. What would it mean to create a nondeterminate world? How would that be different from nothing? No reason exists why the ontological act of creation should create a determinate world. All reasons lie in the product.

Perhaps then the question whether a different world might have been created means that, although any created world would have to be determinate (harmonies with essential and conditional components), possible worlds could have different cosmologies. For instance, instead of a world with a spatiotemporal continuum of changing harmonies, there could be a world with no change, no time. Whitehead subtitled *Process and Reality* "*An Essay in Cosmology*" to indicate that the structures he depicted might obtain only for our cosmic epoch. We can, of course, imagine this, working within the structures of intelligibility that would obtain for any determinate world. In this respect, then, we can say that the ontological creative act could have created a determinate but otherwise cosmically different world. This is why the creation is arbitrary.

In summation, we cannot know why there is any determinate world at all. We know only that there is our world and, if the arguments in Part III are more or less correct, that this means that it is created. Otherwise, it could not be a world of different mutually determinate things. Apart from the ontological act of creation exists no potentiality or motive for creation.

Within the world, we can in fact know why many of the details of the world are the way they are because we can locate the present decision points that made them this way. This is how we understand human choices and the building of moral character for better or worse. It is also how we understand processes that are not human and to which we would ascribe no moral weight (although all choices determine value). In all cases, we understand a present decisive moment in terms of its past conditions and future possibilities, and we observe, note, and accept, the elements of the decisions that spontaneously render the vague future with alternative possibilities into the haecceity of the past. Where the future is open and the past allows of different outcomes, the decisions just happen and are to be observed. There is no more "reason" to be found behind them. They are part of the spontaneity of the ontological creative act.

Have the general cosmological conditions of our epoch evolved from different antecedent conditions? Possibly. And it might be possible to identify those antecedent conditions and the various decision points in natural history that changed them into our cosmic epoch. Nevertheless, whether attending to the array of spontaneities in the moments of temporal presence or to the singular eternal ontological act of creation itself, the making of determinate novelty is always spontaneous. Thus creativity is not to be understood wholly in terms of past conditions and future possibilities in the case of temporal spontaneity, nor in terms of any determinate factors in the case of the ontological act itself.

In reference to itself, ultimate reality is absolutely free. In reference to any possible motive, it is absolutely arbitrary. In reference to our expectations, it is absolutely surprising. The only sense in which it is to be known is that we observe it, identifying the ontological decision point with our dialectical philosophical theology and identifying the temporal decision points with our many forms of interpretation. In the face of this freedom, awe is due. The great themes of the freedom of God in theistic traditions reflect this ignorance of constraining causes, because we know there can be no constraining causes.

III. THE ULTIMATE IS NOT A PERSON

This brings us to the point that has been made many times before, namely, that the ultimate, even when called God, is not a person. Therefore, God cannot be known as a person might be known. Let us sum up this important argument, because it runs against the metaphysics of much popular religion, and not only in the West.

First, given the possibility of alternative cosmologies, it might well be the case that the ontological act of creation has given rise to a cosmos like Whitehead's that contains what Whitehead called God, performing the functions of integration and valuation that Whitehead described. If this were so, such a God would be a creature, a part of creation, and not ultimate. In fact, many religions believe in super-human beings, sometimes of cosmic proportions, that are not ultimate but that perform important functions. Some interpretations of Vishnu and Shiva affirm this. Many process theologians such as John B. Cobb, Jr., and Marjorie Suchocki would like to attribute personal qualities to Whitehead's God, although that is hard to do. Whitehead himself used poetic language to describe God as the ever-present companion, the fellow sufferer who understands.[1] On most interpretations of process theology, God is ascribed the intentions to be just and bear suffering with sympathy.[2] Whitehead himself knew too much of the vast expanse and natural depth of the cosmos to relate God's cosmic function to the scale of human affairs in any but the most poetic senses. Yet, suppose the analogy to human personhood can be carried through, even still God so conceived would not be ultimate. A theologian who accepts the idea of the ontological creative act, who still likes a Whiteheadian cosmology complete with the process God, and who employs Christian symbology might very fruitfully consider Whitehead's God to be the Logos, that through in and through which the cosmos is created. In

Philosophical Theology, however, the term *God* is reserved as a broken-symbol model for the ultimate reality of the ontological act of creation.

Second, no intentionality can be ascribed to God as the ultimate apart from the ontological act of creation. Apart from that ontological act, there is nothing, no God, nothing ultimate or determinate in any sense. Therefore, it is pointless to ask why God decided to create the world, or to create just this world. If any answer were given, that would be proof that we were not speaking of the ultimate and that a deeper ontological context of mutual relevance would have to be found to identify with the ultimate.

Third, no nature or moral character can be ascribed to God apart from the ontological act of creation, for the same reasons: If that nature is determinate, the God who holds it must itself be a creature of a deeper ontological creative act. Thus, we cannot say that, apart from creation, the ultimate is (purely, infinitely) good, (purely, infinitely) one, (purely, infinitely) wise, (purely, infinitely) beautiful, (purely, infinitely) balanced, symmetrical, or any other such positive quality. To be sure, relative to creation we might say that the ultimate is good because the creation is good, one because the creation is unified, wise because the creation is intelligently ordered, beautiful because the creation is beautiful, and so forth. But so far as we can tell, the creation contains good things but in such conflict that much evil is done, the creation is partially unified and somewhat dis-unified, intelligible but also random, beautiful but also ugly, and so forth. Apart from creation, however, the ultimate cannot be any of these excellences.

Fourth, no intentionality can be ascribed to God *within* the ontological creative act. If that act were discursive, with stages, it might be represented as first the divine contemplation of possibilities, then the choice of which ones to actualize, and then the actualization of them, something like Leibniz' story. That would be a fair analogy to intentionality. But the act of creation cannot be discursive because there is no such thing as a medium between nothing determinate and something determinate. There can be no infinitesimally determinate early stages that gradually become more robustly determinate. A (slightly) determinate early stage would have to be determinately different from the (robustly) determinate later or final stages, and that mutual determinate difference would require the whole ontological context of mutual relevance from the "beginning." So the ontological act of creation cannot be internally intentional.

Fifth, it might be thought that, just as human persons are most interesting because of what they do with the conditions given them, so God, the ontological act of creation, is most a person because of what is created, that which concludes the creative act. Surely God's nature, as argued here, is the result of creation. Is that nature enough like that of a person to ascribe personhood to God? What could that mean? Perhaps it means that a person is an intelligent designer, and that God is the supreme intelligent designer. But the arguments have not been successful that have aimed to prove that the world has an order that could not have come from natural but not especially intelligent processes. The world contains a lot of unintelligent disorder. Perhaps saying that the world is what a person would create means that it exhibits some personal traits such as gratuitous kindness, justice, or mercy. But the world is too wild for that. Perhaps, in accord with previous arguments, the world is arbitrary just as a willful person might be an arbitrary creator. But a creator who makes things through will has to have stages of choosing and doing, otherwise it is just making pure and simple. The ontological creative act is a "just making," pure and simple, not an act of a willing intentional agent. So there is not much ground for saying that God is a person because of the character of the created world.

Sixth, it might be said that the ultimate might turn out to be a person if we only knew the whole of creation. As it is, we know such a small sample of the cosmos that we do not have a fair picture. The sample we have mixes goodness with evil but still might be the best of all possible worlds; it mixes unity with confusion and irrelevance but still might exhibit a higher unity; it has rational order but also unordered elements that might be in a higher order; it has beauty and ugliness but in toto might be wholly beautiful; it has symmetries and asymmetries but in the whole might be perfectly or most basically symmetrical. Surely we cannot generalize too much from our small sample. But why presume that a larger sample would support a more ideal view of the world? Only if we had a prior commitment to the view that ultimate reality creates a cosmos as a super good, unified, wise, beautiful, symmetrical person might do? That commitment cannot be made on the basis of a prior intention in the ultimate ontological act of creation, for the reasons just given. The point of the larger sample is to see, when more things are considered, whether the act of creation produces something that is what a perfect person would produce and that the act of creation thus has a personal form: The act of creation creates itself to be a person. Of course that is conceivable. But it is highly unlikely, given even our small sample.

The result of all these considerations is that the ontological act of creation, as the ultimate reality, should not be conceived literally as a person. Hence, the personal connotations many people have with the term *God* should be carefully expunged from philosophical theology. Of course, there might be situations in which highly personified symbols of ultimacy are well used for engaging ultimate reality. These symbols would not be literally true in a theological sense. But they might be interpretively true in the sense that they carry across what is really valuable or important in the ultimate into the interpreters in their context and with their purposes and states of symbolic readiness. The force of the metaphysical dialectic of Part III was to arrive at symbols for ultimacy that can be taken as literally as possible. This is in response to the pressures for transcendence in symbols of ultimacy. The next chapter discusses the senses in which these nearly literal symbols are functional in engagements with ultimacy. As chapter 7 argued, however, pressures also exist for intimacy in symbols of ultimacy, and these personifying symbols might very well involve iconically false but indexically true interpretations.

The great traditions modeling the ultimate on consciousness and emergence do not have the same temptations to ascribe some prior determinate character to the ultimate. There does not have to be an agent who is conscious, only consciousness itself—agency falls away with the expunging of the determinate contents of consciousness. Emergence does not have to be from any thing, only from no thing (which has not emerged).

IV. THE ULTIMATE AND INTELLIGIBILITY

Underlying the issues about what can and cannot be known about ultimate reality is the issue of intelligibility itself, which has been broached at least obliquely several times in this study. Part III claimed that intelligibility itself is created with the creation of determinate things. The discussion so far has led us to mention four forms of intelligibility in conjunction with the transcendentals of harmony.

The most common kind of intelligibility, and the least controversial, is the knowledge of a thing's form by means of a formal representation. A formal representation is taken to refer to its object iconically. A mathematical formulation refers to relations in its object that it mirrors. A map, including a map in mind like a taxi driver's knowledge of the streets, is a form that refers to some aspect of form in the territory: to the territory's streets, its natural contours, its elevations, its distribution of population or vegetation. The form of the representation need not be so abstract as mathematics or mapping. A story has a form that iconically represents certain forms of events. A "realistic" painting depicts its subject matter. A verbal description has complex symbolic forms that refer to what is described. By means of formal symbolic representation, knowledge of one part of the subject matter can lead to inferences about other parts of the subject matter. The more complex the form in the symbolic representation, the more detailed inquiry can be into other aspects of the represented material. Aristotle argued that knowledge is most basically the obtaining of the form of the object in the actuality of the mind, leaving the matter in the object behind, save as that can be redescribed as form. The dialectical development of the complex hypothesis about being as the one for the many, which has to be an ontological context of mutual relevance and that can only be an ontological act of creation, is the creation of a complicated formal representation that aims to be as literally iconic of ultimate reality as possible. Some people think that formal intelligibility is the only kind.

A second dimension to intelligibility, however, lies in the groundedness of the components that make up knowers. Whitehead said rightly that there is a vector feeling of force in symbolic reference.[3] Representational symbols are not only projected onto objects in acts of interpretation. The acts of interpretation themselves arise as ways of taking in and organizing the components that make up knowledge. Peirce said that this dimension of intelligibility is indexical in the sense discussed earlier (I, 3, iii). On the one hand, we say that the representational symbol "points" to its object in such a way as to establish a causal relation between the object and the interpreter, so that the interpreter can register what is important in the object. On the other hand, that same process can be described as the object coming into the interpretive experience as a component that needs to be harmonized by the interpretation. That "coming into" is a natural causal process that has weight to it even as it is transformed into semiotic kinds of interactions. As Peirce said, there is "Secondness" in interpretations. Whereas it might be possible to think of the formal iconic dimension of intelligibility in terms of abstract, free-floating representations or propositions, the component indexical dimension of intelligibility is inexorably bodily. The feeling of the weight of the world is often an unnoticed but all pervasive element of interpretive experience. Many religious traditions have cultivated special disciplines for improving sensitivity to this body-knowing.[4] Things become intelligible in a way when they are felt indexically.

A third dimension of intelligibility is the orientation or placing of things in context in some kind of existential field, as having an existential location relative to the knower. Many kinds of existential fields exist, not only the spatiotemporal one discussed at length here. Anything that can provide a context is such a field. Orientation involves the formal dimension of intelligibility, but is not reduced to it. In fact, insofar as formal representation is iconic with its object, it neglects the context. Or if it enlarges attention to include the context in formal iconic reference, this larger view might be in still larger contexts; or the larger view might be unoriented. Most ordinary human events are oriented within worldviews, the intelligibility of the event is enhanced by the worldview's orientation even when the worldview operates unconsciously. To develop a theory of worldviews and locate an event within a particular world is to give a formal iconic analysis of event-plus-worldview. Orientation often involves naturally grounded elements, as components come through the existential field. This is always so when the orientation of the act of interpretation is to spatial and temporal location.

A fourth dimension of intelligibility is the aesthetic appreciation of value. This can be merely through the appreciation of complexity and simplicity in form. It also can be feeling the value in which the interpreter is grounded through components. Orientation combines the value of the object represented or felt with the values in its context. These can be enhanced and integrated as interpretation comes closer and closer to appreciating the ultimate value of a thing in the ontological context of mutual relevance.

So at least these four dimensions of intelligibility are possible, that of formal iconic reference of representations, that of groundedness or the vectoral feeling of components, that of orientation, and that of value. Wise people learn to seek out all four dimensions.

How, in these terms, can the ontological creative act be intelligible as ultimate reality? The metaphysical conception of the ontological act is a formal theory, aiming to be as iconically literal as possible. Chapter 15 argues that the theory plus the dialectical case for it allows for the ontological creative act to be felt as the master grounding component of a certain kind of religious experience. The dialectical theory surrounding the problem of being and the one and the many provides an intelligible context for the conception of the ontological creative act. Moreover, the illustrations of symbols for the ontological creative act in various religious and philosophical traditions provide a different sort of context. The appreciation of the value of the ontological creative act in its product constitutes the aesthetic element of intelligibility, often described as awe, or glory, or bliss, depending on the orientation of the interpreter. To make ultimate reality intelligible is to achieve proper formal analysis (the right form, the best hypothesis), sensitive piety, engaged orientation, and receptive appreciation.

Some people demure to all of this and argue instead that intelligibility consists in seeing how things to be understood exhibit some first principles of metaphysics. Like a hypothetico-deductive system in science, a metaphysical system for understanding ultimate reality has first principles that provide the intelligibility of all else, according to philosophers such as Charles Hartshorne.[5] The first principles themselves are intelligible because their denials are self-contradictory, or close to it. To the argument that the first principles are created, Hartshorne would reply that this is unintelligible. The whole idea of creating *ex nihilo* is unintelligible, he argued. To say that something is "simply created" is to add nothing to the created things. Only some determinate first principles could add an explanation to the unexplained determinate things.

In one sense Hartshorne's argument has been answered already in the dialectic of Part III. The *de facto* togetherness of the determinate things of the world exhibits an ontological togetherness that cannot be accounted for by the conditional components that constitute cosmological togetherness. The ontological togetherness cannot be enabled by another determinate thing because that would have to be together with the other determinate things in a yet deeper ontological context of mutual togetherness. The only thing that could function as the ontological context of mutual relevance is the creation of the things together *ex nihilo*, which therefore does add something explanatory to the *de facto* array of things to be explained.

In another sense, however, the disagreement has not yet been addressed. The claim of rationalists such as Hartshorne is that an act of making is simply unintelligible. As a process philosopher, Hartshorne affirms a kind of creativity in the process in which decisions are made that were not wholly determined beforehand. But for him the decisions are not intelligible. Intelligibility in process consists only in identifying the antecedents, the possibilities, and the outcomes. Therefore, any divine creativity is intelligible only if any given act of divine creativity has antecedents in the world, possibilities in the divine nature, and outcomes in completed moments of divine concrescence. The freedom of God, for him, is highly constrained; its arbitrariness is unintelligible per se, but is so minimal that the divine nature is still highly intelligible. For Hartshorne, the divine nature includes all the metaphysical principles as abstract but necessary and completely intelligible components. In his eyes, a conception of an ontological creative act creating all determinate things *ex nihilo* is in principle unintelligible because it has neither antecedents nor possibilities and its outcome is wholly arbitrary.

Behind the several dimensions of intelligibility, therefore, lurks the question whether an act of making something new is intelligible apart from antecedent potentials and future possibilities. Rationalists such as Hartshorne would deny this kind of intelligibility because, for their deep intuitions, intelligibility means intelligible connections between determinate things, "ratios." For empiricists of a certain sort, however, the deepest intuition about intelligibility is that it is the locating of the makings that give rise to complex things, those decision points where the indeterminate that does not need explanation gives rise to the determinate. Ultimate intelligibility, from this empirical point of view, is locating those decisions. The dialectic of the one and the many in Part III is a map for locating indexically the ultimate making that in turn makes the world and makes it intelligible.

Interestingly, Whitehead was an empiricist in the sense of this contrast with rationalism. His very important "ontological principle" says that the "reason" for any complex thing lies in the decisions that collectively gave it its determinate character.[6] He had in mind that any actual occasion within time has its reasons, first, in what it creatively does with the objects it includes as components and, second, in all the subjective decisions made in the past by those objects in their own concrescence, plus the subjective decisions in their prior components, ad infinitum. For Whitehead, instead of the intelligibility of process lying in the antecedents, possibilities, and outcomes, it lies instead in the array of decision points. Deciding is the ultimately intelligible factor. Whitehead did not apply the ontological principle to the explanation of the complexity of the metaphysical principles in his philosophy, nor to the complexity of his Category of the Ultimate, namely the conjunction of creativity, many, and one. But the metaphysics of Part III here does apply the ontological principle to the most abstract kind of determinate complexity. We need not distinguish first principles from any other determinate thing to grasp the argument about determinateness in diversity requiring an ontological context of mutual relevance. Nevertheless, our argument does account for the creation of the "first principles" in the dialectic of the one and the many.

Perhaps at the deepest level, the intelligibility of the ontological act of creation as ultimate reality depends on the intuition that decision points of the creation of novelty are intelligible. The dialectic of the one and the many locates the decision point at which all determinateness is created so that things are ontologically as well as cosmologically together. What we cannot know about ultimate reality are any antecedent potentials for the ontological creative act, or possibilities, or stages of intentional choice. But we can know why these things cannot be.

CHAPTER FIFTEEN

Symbolic Engagement as Praying the Ultimate

I. THEOLOGICAL UNDERSTANDING AS A SIGN

The metaphysical theory of ultimacy developed in Part III and from which consequences about the knowledge of the ultimate were drawn in chapters 13 and 14 stands as an hypothesis. It was drawn up in light of analyses of how ultimacy figures in people's worldviews, both as more or less directly symbolized in those portions of worldviews we called sacred canopies and as the worldviews relate the sacred canopies to certain other more mundane contexts within them. The hypothesis is about what ultimacy might be such that it can be symbolized in sacred canopies and understood as providing ultimate dimensions of other parts of life. Some of the arguments for the hypothesis are internal dialectical ones arising from the consideration of the classic metaphysical problem of the one and the many, treating being as the putative one for the many and identifying being with ultimate reality. Other arguments for the hypothesis come from its responsiveness to the constructions of ultimacy in sacred canopies and their larger worldviews. Yet other arguments for it are in the process of being made to show its fruitfulness for the development of a systematic philosophical theology, and these arguments continue throughout *Philosophical Theology Two* and *Three*. Laying out the overall plausibility of the hypothesis is a complicated task, more like binding many fibers together to make a rope than creating a chain made of independently standing links.[1]

An interesting element of the plausibility of the hypothesis is revealed when we temporarily set aside the concerns for its truth and examine some of the ways the hypothesis itself can function in the engagement of ultimacy. Chapter 3 sketched an epistemological theory of symbolic engagement.[2] The primary contention of that theory is that the real object of symbolic engagement itself is involved in the engagement. Whatever ultimacy really is, it is directly a part of the interactions involved in theological symbolic engagement, however mediated that engagement is by the symbols. A symbolic engagement is a transaction, a causal interaction, of the interpreter with the interpreted, shaped and guided by means of the interpreting signs.

Some actual symbols of ultimacy are necessary for any such interpretive engagement with ultimate reality to take place. Although religious and philosophical traditions have developed myriads of symbols of ultimate realities and the religious dimensions of things, not all of them are adequate to effect a genuine symbolic engagement of ultimacy. In part, this is because the semiotic, cultural, and existential contexts of the interpreters have to be ready and fit to use those symbols in a genuinely engaging way.[3] Symbols from someone else's tradition might leave the ultimate inaccessible. Or symbols that were effective in earlier times might lose their potency under new cultural or personal conditions. Surely many aspects of ultimacy cannot be engaged now because no one yet has imaginatively constructed symbols that can interpret them in appropriate respects.

Symbols of ultimacy must first be engaging, making an interpretive connection between the ultimate object and interpreters. But then again they should also be true. Truth in this context means that, when they are employed in actual interpretive engagements, the symbols carry over what is important in ultimacy in the respects in which the symbols stand for ultimacy. By itself, the interpretive engagement bears its truth, if it has it, but it cannot tell whether it is true. The assessment of the truth of such an engagement needs to take place around the engagement in various ways that can identify what is important about ultimacy with some independence and check to see whether this in fact is carried over properly into the engaging interpreter. In this regard, all of the assessments of plausibility mentioned above are relevant to identifying ultimacy. In addition spiritual discernment is important for understanding the engaging experience on the personal level.

The hypothesis to be defended here is that the theory of the ontological creative act, whether metaphorized as Brahman, Emptiness, God, Heaven, the Ultimate of Non-Being or some other appellation, can itself serve as a symbol for engaging ultimacy. The theory itself is to be understood as a complex sign that functions as an engaging symbol. According to the epistemological theory of symbolic engagement, certain conditions of the interpreters and their contexts and intentions must obtain for actual engagements to take place. These are discussed in more detail in Section IV of this chapter and in the following chapter. This and the next two sections discuss some elements of the logic of the symbolic engagement of ultimacy.

Symbolic engagement involves three kinds of reference, it will be recalled from chapter 3. Iconic reference supposes that the object to which reference is made is something *like* the referring sign. Because the theory of the ontological creative act is a metaphysical theory, it aims to be as iconic as possible, although many other symbols of ultimacy might not be very iconic and there is indexical reference also in thinking with the metaphysical theory. Indexical reference establishes some kind of causal connection between the object and the interpreter, which is the ground for genuine engagement. Conventional reference is how the signs involved in the symbolic engagement are connected and defined in semiotic systems so as to refer to other signs, which in turn might be used iconically and indexically to engage relevant matters.

The iconic element in the theory of the ultimate ontological creative act is complicated. The theory says, in mutually defined determinate and symmetrical terms, that the creative act brings all determinate things into being out of nothing, and that this act is asymmetrical. Although the form of the theory, in order to be determinate, is symmetrical with concepts interpreting concepts, what it asserts is the asymmetry of the ontological creative act. Thus, the assertion describes iconically at least the asymmetry of the act of making determinateness. This is the first level of iconicity.

With regard to its indexical reference, the theory is surrounded by the dialectic of the one and the many. Although that dialectic most often has other philosophical positions as the objects of its engagements, collectively the elements of that dialectic serve to point engaging attention to the reality of the creative act. Whereas interpretively engaging physical objects can take the orientation of its attention from elements in the existential spatiotemporal field, the interpretive engagement of ultimacy has a much more difficult time locating the ultimacy to engage. A symbolic engagement is an interpretive act that selects or orients itself to the object it engages. To the extent the theory of ontological creation is true, its object is not an object in any kind of sense that puts it in an orienting field for attention. The dialectic of the one and many is the intellectual creation of a dialectical orienting field that turns the interpreter in "the right direction." Chapter 14, Section IV, spelled out at length the kind of intelligibility that comes with locating a decision point so as to encounter a decisive creative act. The dialectic of the one and many works to locate that ultimate decision.

Indexical reference in a symbolic engagement, however, also constitutes the interpreter as in some sense *a causal product of the object*. In the case of symbolic engagement of the ultimate, this means that the material qualities of the engaging symbol must include the feeling of being created as one among the many. The intellectual signs of the theory and the surrounding dialectic might be understood only in terms of their network meaning as defined by relevant semiotic systems. But they need also to be transformed into content meanings so that the vectoral force of their indexical reference can be felt. This is a deeper meaning of indexical reference than the mere orientation of attention. It means that through indexical reference the interpreter is being transformed by the object, in this case the ultimate ontological act of creation of all determinate things, so that the object itself enters the interpretive engagement as something felt. That feeling is the material quality of the sign or symbol used, in this case the intellectual thinking of the theory of the ontological act.

Thus, the task of engaging ultimacy requires giving the signs of the theory not only their intellectual network import but also the material import of bearing the causal effects of the ontological creative act. This is not mysterious, because the theory itself says that every determinate thing, including theological interpreters, is the product of the ontological creative act. We literally are the ontological act itself in its determinate result in our portion of the created world. So the development of the material quality of signs that effectively index the ontological act is just coming to interpret ourselves (together with others) as creatures of that act. It means feeling our creatureliness, our radical contingency. Nevertheless, this requires extraordinary achievements of spiritual growth, for we are generally not very close, interpretively, to ourselves as creatures. The next chapter details something of what is required to develop the material qualities of signs to feel ourselves as creatures within the ontological creative act.

At this stage in the argument, we can make the suggestion that a spiritual life of prayer, in many of the senses of that term, can employ the metaphysical theory of the ontological creative act to engage the ultimate. This assumes that the theory is true in the crucial senses in which it effects the engagement. In a rough sense of "prayer," to be parsed into several more precise senses in the next chapter, the metaphysical theory of the ontological act of creation, with its surrounding dialectic, can be used as a "name of God," as Muslims might say. As Muslim theology has suggested, in a variety of not entirely consistent ways, the names of God are separate from God in some sense, but also identical with God in some other sense. So, engaging the ultimate with prayer, using the metaphysical theory as the complex of signs in the prayer, or "name of God," does not exactly refer the complex of signs to some "other object." Rather, there is a close identity of the signs and ultimate reality, a close causal connection in which the act creates as part of its singular but plural product its own prayerful interpretation. The symbolic engagement through the metaphysical theory thus seeks less to access the ultimate by means of the theory than materially to think the theory which is at the same time to be embracing the ultimate act. All this supposes that symbolic engagements are not mere logical propositions but rather interpretive acts by concrete interpreters in actual contexts. The existential elements of symbolic engagement are discussed shortly.

II. MULTIPLE SYMBOLS ALONG THE SOPHISTICATION/ POPULAR RELIGION, TRANSCENDENCE/ INTIMACY, AND SACRED/MUNDANE CONTINUA

Before discussing the existential elements of symbolic engagements using iconic metaphysical symbols that are as literal as possible, we should reflect on the locus of these symbols in worldviews. Worldviews, chapter 4 argued, are best understood in terms of certain analytical continua. Three of those continua are important to elaborate here, that of sophistication and popular religion, that of transcendence and intimacy, and that of the sacred and mundane.

The discussion of the metaphysics of the one and the many, of the ontological context of mutual relevance, and of the ontological act of creating multiple harmonies with essential and conditional components, is at the extreme sophistication end of the spectrum with popular religion. For many thinkers, the extremity of the abstract argument illustrates the point that sophistication is not always a good thing. Surely, they would say, nothing religiously useful is to be found in the dialectical worry about how an other can be known without reducing its essential components to components of the knower. The previous section made an initial rejoinder to that claim: The metaphysics itself can be used as a prayerful symbol. But the overall critical point is well taken. For most people, excepting perhaps only prayerful metaphysicians, the sophisticated categories have no bearing on religious life.

Such sophisticated thinking has been present in the major religious and philosophical traditions, however, and most have had strains that understand the many as arising out of the one, or the nothing, which the one would be apart from the many. Many different and conflicting conceptions of God have been held within Greek and Roman Paganism and West Asian monotheistic religions, and some of their sophisticated arguments have been mentioned here. The positions most akin to the ontological act of creation have not always been dominant. For instance, in Islamic philosophical theology, the Mutazilites, who are closest to this position, have been subordinated in the hierarchy of orthodoxies to the Asherites who ascribe determinate characteristics to God apart from creation in order to take scriptural language more literally than the Mutazilites wanted. But the debates, and therefore the careful definitions of the issues, have been extremely sophisticated. Not all forms of Hinduism accept the dialectic of the transcendence of Saguna Brahman over the creator Isvara, or the transcendence of Nirguna Brahman over Saguna Brahman; but those that disagree have done so with great sophistication in many instances. Similarly, the debates among Daoists, Chinese Buddhists, and Neo-Confucians about just how empty Emptiness or the Ultimate of Non-Being is have also had extremely sophisticated expressions.

In all these traditions, however, those concepts and the various symbols for them also were loosened up in order to be religiously available. This means that their nearly literal metaphysical iconicity was allowed to take on considerable metaphorical distance; they became less iconic and depended more on their indexical references. The purpose, of course, was to allow those symbols to relate to people's existential religious concerns in terms of everyday life, including everyday religious practices. Perhaps the South Asian traditions have the easiest time with allowing the sophisticated symbols to take on increasingly more popular forms. Their default strategy is to say that there are multiple ultimate beings like gods with more and more anthropomorphic and narratively defined identities that still are in some sense identical with each other along the sophistication-popular religion continuum. Other traditions have found it difficult to multiply ultimates in avatar-relations to one another along the continuum, and have tried instead to give the "right" definition. Rightness might not consist in approval from the authority of the most sophisticated extreme in the continuum but rather concerns about the proper running of the community that has to deal with popular religion, as in the outcome of the historical dominance of the Asherites over the Mutazilites.

The sophisticated terms of the metaphysics also stand at the extreme transcendence end of the transcendence/intimacy continuum. These symbolic terms in different ways have been translated down that continuum toward more anthropomorphic and domesticated versions in order to respect the pressures for intimacy in symbols of the ultimate. Where the sophistication/popular religion continuum is weighted in the middle by concerns for making religion relevant to the various affairs of life, the transcendence/intimacy continuum finds the weight in its middle by virtue of concerns for existential relevance to personal understanding and orientation. One of the most common modes of this is connecting to the ultimate by one's own story: If the ultimate can be related to one's situation by becoming a part of one's own life narrative, for instance intervening to answer particular prayers, then the ultimate is intimate.

The sacred/mundane continuum serves to relate domains of a worldview that orient many or all of the acts and events of life, and sometimes that orientation makes the sacred canopy in the worldview bear on otherwise mundane acts and events. The dialectic of the one and many, and the conception of the ontological act of creation, are about the ontological ultimate reality per se. How do they bear on, say, diet? Are all things acceptable to eat because all food is created? Or should dietary prohibitions that serve to define one's in-group be observed in order to preserve the essential differences of one's group against others?

As we consider symbols of the ultimate that have very sophisticated, transcendent, and ultimate-oriented forms like those in our metaphysical theory, we need to keep in mind a background analysis of how those symbols have been moved along the three continua so as to function in daily religion, in existential needs, and in indicating how many or all of the affairs of life have ultimate dimensions. This is necessary in order respectfully to understand the use for religious purposes of those symbols of ultimacy that have sophisticated formulations but that also are used in unsophisticated, anthropomorphic, and mundane ways. Is the following a joke?: Thomas Aquinas said that God is the pure Act of To Be, utterly simple, related to nothing else because nothing else could limit pure act, lacking all potentials of acting, incapable of intending any finite objects, and that the Virgin Mary is His mother. All but the last are sophisticated responses to the problem of the one and the many. The last seems an absurd trait to associate with the others. But there is a well-trod theological continuum for Thomas that relates the pure aseity of the simple God to the otherness of relations within the divine Trinity, and then to the scriptural and liturgical identification of the Second Person of the Trinity with Jesus, and the scriptural-liturgical Jesus to liturgical-legendary accounts of Mary. In the background is a debate preceding Thomas about whether Jesus is divine, which was argued through in reference to the formula of whether Mary is the mother of God or only of the human element of Jesus. In Thomas' liturgical world, individuals should pray to Mary for divine interventions. Considerations like these relocate the Act of To Be along the middle of the three continua in question, and the list of traits of God is not a joke.

What is at stake in these symbols that can be given metaphysical formulations that are as nearly literal as possible but that in fact are moved along the continua to have only metaphorical reach? The reason for moving those symbols along is to attain greater practicality in popular religious life, to gain greater intimacy in existential concerns, and to integrate many aspects of life relative to ultimate dimension. But the symbols when operating in the middle of the continua often are silly, or wildly counterintuitive, or plainly contradictory when interpreted literally. How can God as the pure Act of To Be have a mother? Does the literal silliness of those symbols count against them? The answer to that question has to do with ascertaining their truth in context: However inconsistent literally, do they function to carry across what is ultimately important into the interpreters in those mid-continua contexts in the respects that they really represent what is ultimate?

III. SYSTEMATIC THINKING FOR CONTROLLING SYMBOLS

The answer to this question depends on whether, and if so how, theology can control for the truthful versus false, and sometimes demonic, function of those symbols. Because theology in many, but by no means all, religious traditions often has taken itself to define theological truth in iconic propositional terms, the alternative view stressed in the theology of symbolic engagement needs to be stressed here. To be sure, in theological contexts, the carryover of what is important should end up in forms that can be debated and analyzed critically. Hence, the push toward sophisticated language. But interpretive symbolic engagement should be true in all contexts, not only intellectual ones. Interpretive symbolic engagements of ultimacy define much of the important character of individuals.[4] Who we are is how we interpret our world and act on that interpretation, which of course is a further symbolic engagement.

Hence, how true people are to the ultimate depends on how their worldviews connect their attention to ultimacy in their sacred canopies with the rest of their lives. Many variables determine the worth of a worldview. Any event or aspect of life that is not oriented to the rest of life is a sign that the worldview is inadequate. Worldviews should be able to orient everything. Worldviews make all kinds of orienting associations across life's panorama, and some of those associations are bad, for instance those fostering bigotry. Worldviews, of course, are themselves complex signs of the world's realities relative to experience. They have reference of various sorts and employ semiotic symbol systems. And of course they should be true, although the truth of worldviews is even more complicated than the truth of symbols of ultimacy: Philosophy as a whole is the critic of worldviews.

With reference to ultimacy, vital truths ride on how ultimacy is attached to mundane matters. In a given context, for instance, it might be extremely important that the distinction between one's in-group and the out-groups be fixed, obvious, viscerally internalized, and pervasive. In this circumstance, there might be truth in attaching ultimacy to the mundane markers of the in-group, for instance diet, racial and ethnic characters, speech, clothing and adornment, and so forth. Certainly, this was the view of the exiles returning to Jerusalem under the leadership of Ezra and Nehemiah who promulgated the Holiness Code (Leviticus 17–26) and draconian laws about marriage. Yet that historical viewpoint was contemporary with the burgeoning universalism of the Axial Age religion of the late Hebrew prophets who advocated universal justice and charity and the concern of God for all people.[5] Most historical contexts since the Axial Age have emphasized the importance of minimizing in-group/out-group rivalries for the sake of universal justice, care, and peace, so that giving ultimate sanction to mundane matters that in themselves merely indicate different conditions and customs would be false (*III, 10*). It would be false in the sense that the value it would carry over from what is ultimately important into in-group markers asserts an ultimacy to those markers that they should not have. The ultimate created status of different people acknowledges differences but does not make group inclusion and exclusion ultimately important, if the Axial Age movement is right. *Philosophical Theology Three*, chapter 2, defends the Axial Age on this point. Cultural disputes of the significance of, say, diet might very well have to do with the alleged ultimate dimension of that matter. So the symbols of ultimacy need to be elaborated beyond their sophisticated literal forms, appropriate for the sacred canopy as deployed by theologians, to working network symbolic connections with the mundane affairs of life. The truth or falsity of those ultimate symbols as connected with the mundane affairs lies in how they actually shape those affairs. How can we tell whether this reworking is appropriate and true?

Similarly, individuals and communities need to find ways of connecting their deep, perhaps ultimate, concerns to what is really ultimate, as discussed in chapters 5 and 7, along the transcendence/intimacy continuum. But not every way of letting ultimacy shape existential decisions leads to a true existential embodiment of ultimacy. When tragedy threatens, as with a seriously ill child, hope is sustained through prayers for intervention to the ultimate, and hope is a good and true constitution. But when the tragedy occurs, should the image of the ultimate as a petitionable intervener lead to the inference that God intended the death of the child? Was that intention aimed to punish the parents? Was it an indication of divine anger about some other issue, as some Christian evangelicals blamed 9/11 on God's anger at American feminism and support for gay rights? Existential responses to deep crises are true or false depending on how the ultimate is engaged in those crises. How can we tell when those existential symbolic engagements are true or false in the concrete context?

Similarly with the sophistication/popular religion continuum. Both of the other continua need to embody truth carried from the ultimate into the ways of living out publicly the religious dimensions of things. Not all popular religion is true, even when it involves popular expressions that are true in certain contexts. How can we tell whether popular religion carries over ultimate truth into its practitioners from context to context?

No simple answer exists to determine the truth of symbols of ultimacy when they are transformed along the continua of worldviews. But the problem defines a task for *practical* theology. Systematic practical theology addresses the issue of determining whether symbolic engagements are true context by context. That is, do the symbolic engagers in those contexts have in their practical lives the truth of ultimate reality? To determine this, practical theology needs to understand the contexts. It needs also to understand the symbolic interpretations in terms of the symbols involved and their functional network semiotic connections. It needs to understand their iconic referential dimensions, articulating just how the likenesses hold or do not hold. It needs to understand the indexical references involved, which are often very different from what the iconic references would suggest. It needs to understand the personal ways by which the individuals and groups are ready or unready for accepting the symbols in a true way. But in order to do any of this, systematic practical theology needs to hold on to the most sophisticated truth possible about what ultimate reality really is. Systematic philosophical theology is a crucial component of systematic practical theology.

The practical function of the metaphysics of ultimacy as the ontological creative act is that it sets limits to the metaphorical reach of symbols of ultimacy. In the case of facing the potential of a health crisis for one's child, it ultimately is important to have hope in the face of the possibility of disaster. Not to have hope is to abandon one's engagement with the possibilities at hand, dire as they might be. This is especially so when a good outcome is a long shot. Having a false hope is better than having none at all as an attitude toward engaging bad possibilities. Consider the great wisdom of King David in having hope when his illicit son by Bathsheba was ill:

> The Lord struck the child that Uriah's wife bore to David, and it became very ill. David therefore pleaded with God for the child; David fasted, and went in and lay all night on the ground. The elders of his house

stood beside him, urging him to rise from the ground; but he would not, nor did he eat food with them. On the seventh day the child died. And the servants of David were afraid to tell him that the child was dead; for they said, "While the child was still alive, we spoke to him, and he did not listen to us; how then can we tell him the child is dead? He may do himself some harm." But when David saw that his servants were whispering together, he perceived that the child was dead; and David said to his servants, "Is the child dead?" They said, "He is dead." Then David rose from the ground, washed, anointed himself, and changed his clothes. He went into the house of the Lord, and worshiped; he then went to his own house; and when he asked, they set food before him and he ate. Then his servants said to him, "What is this thing that you have done? You fasted and wept for the child while it was alive; but when the child died, you rose and ate food." He said, "While the child was still alive, I fasted and wept; for I said, 'Who knows? The Lord may be gracious to me, and the child may live.' But now he is dead; why should I fast? Can I bring him back again? I shall go to him, but he will not return to me."[6]

The biblical writers interpreted the child's death as the will of God in punishment of David; David seems not to have bought that interpretation. But he did have hope until the end that God might save the child: not to have done so would have been to betray his love for the child. When the child died, David re-engaged the next set of possibilities. His belief in a sometimes-merciful God was his symbol of the ultimate in that circumstance that gave him hope. Had David inferred from that symbol, however, that God was out to punish him, this would have made the symbol false. We know from the concept of the ultimate as the ontological creative act that God does not have intentions.

Metaphysics can tell us when a false inference is being drawn from an anthropomorphic symbol of divinity. Anthropomorphic symbols are not the only kind that for good reason are sometimes stretched into a metaphoric reach far distant from the defensible iconic significance. Popular Daoism, for instance, suggests that the pulse of the Dao is more attuned to human affairs than it is. And it suggests that the Dao, through the heavenly bureaucracy, can be manipulated by human beings. All this might well be helpful in providing orientation regarding difficult possibilities for living. But there are circumstances in which the symbols of the domestic and manipulable Dao are false and dangerous.

This and the previous section have dealt with practical circumstances in which the theological metaphysics of ultimacy has a public critical role with regard to engagements with ultimate matters across life. But now the discussion should return to the topic of using the metaphysics to engage the ultimate directly.

IV. THINKING THE ULTIMATE

To understand the ultimate is the work of a system such as *Philosophical Theology*. This work is astonishingly complex because of all the indirection involved. As the work has been performed here in *Philosophical Theology One*, it begins by engaging several aspects of the nature of religion, initiating a theological theory of religion, a topic that is engaged in greater detail in *Two* and *Three*. The work engages in a critical analysis of some of the major ways of identifying and studying religion and develops the epistemology of symbolic engagement. The work then labors through an analysis of how human concerns engage the ultimate. The work looks at how various aspects of reality press sacred canopies to develop transcendent symbols of ultimacy, and also how other aspects press for humanly intimate symbols. The work looks at the special strengths and limitations of narrative as modes of connecting human beings with ultimacy. In all these studies in Parts I and II, the direct object of engagement is something other than ultimacy or ultimate realities, except insofar as remarks are made to provide heuristic definitions of ultimacy and to anticipate later direct engagements with ultimacy. Part III is indeed an intellectual engagement with ultimacy, but again mainly indirect. The work of the argument enters the study of ultimacy by examining some aspects of the philosophical concept of being, which eventually is identified with the ultimate. What is directly engaged, however, is the philosophical argument about the analogy of being and then the problem of the one and the many. Regarding the one and the many, the argument works around the position that claims that each of the many is a one for the others, with no underlying ontological one. This leads to setting up criteria for an ontological context of mutual relevance that would make a many possible, but again only indirectly looking at ultimacy. The manifold of the many requires determinateness, and so the next part of the work is the development of a theory of determinateness in terms of harmony, essential and conditional components, and the transcendentals of form, components, existential location, and ultimate value or identity. All these again are indirect approaches to ultimacy. Only in chapter 11 does the work of understanding ultimacy deal directly with ultimacy through the hypothesis of the ontological creative act of creating the determinate world. That hypothesis is mediated by all the preceding discussions but it does have as its direct topic, the ontological act as the ultimate. To add to its complexity, chapter 12 turns to understand the ultimate act in terms of its being the home for human beings in time and eternity. The chapters in Part IV draw out the generalized implications of the symbols involved in understanding ultimacy.

The work of *Philosophical Theology* so far has been to engage with ultimacy by developing an hypothesis about it. But the point of a theology of symbolic engagement is that the "hypothesis about" is a complex sign or symbol by means of which ultimate reality itself is engaged. However long and discursive a process "thinking the hypothesis" is, thinking this hypothesis is "thinking the ultimate." As the first section argues, the elaborate indirect work is necessary to direct the attention of the engagement to the place where the ultimate reality, the ontological creative act, acts. The indirect work also provides a variety of checks on the hypothesis as engagement of ultimacy because the theory of the ontological act itself needs to be examined from the outside, as it were, regarding whether it carries what is important in ultimacy over into the engaged interpreters.

The symbolic engagement of the ontological act of creation itself has to be a concrete interpretive act carried on by actual interpreters in actual contexts of engagement. In that concrete interpretive act, the distance between ultimate reality and the interpretation of it is bridged. The interpretive experience is not about ultimate reality, as if the interpretive engagement were a sign for something else. The interpretive experience rather is having the ultimate within the experience, as the symbols represent it. The symbols of the theory of the ontological act of creation represent the ultimate only in certain respects, in this case defined by the dialectic of the problem of the one and the many. Within the limitations of those respects, however, the hypothesis of the ontological act effects the direct albeit mediated experience of the ontological act itself, to the extent the hypothesis is true.

Now, the truth of the hypothesis consists in the carryover of ultimacy into the interpretive experience *as mediated by the biology, culture, and semiotic systems of the interpreter (I, 3)*. So, the ultimate enters into human experience only in forms that can be thought by meat brains. The ultimate is related to human beings as the object of a concern that is mediated by our culture, particularly here the culture of those who are both intellectually and existentially concerned. The ultimate is limited to what can be represented, through the hypothesis of the ontological creative act, in the semiotic systems of all those aspects of the work of *Philosophical Theology* just rehearsed, as well as a symbolic context drawing up world religions. The point can be summed up by saying that *the ultimate as engaged by Philosophical Theology can be thought*. Many ways besides thinking allow for the symbolic engagement of ultimacy and, as argued here, these sometimes stand in a critical relation to thinking ultimacy.

What can the act of thinking ultimacy be? A review of the various parts of the argument? Yes, but more. Holding the complex structure of the theory of the ontological act of creation in mind at once? Yes, but more. The act of thinking ultimacy must also intend ultimacy. Like addressing a person, the singular ontological act of creation must be intended in order to be thought. Part of intending is turning attention to the right thing, and all the indexical references in the hypothesis of the ontological act of creation serve to direct attention that way. But another part of intending the ultimate is forming the act of intention so that the interpretation is fulfilled by the grasping of the ultimate, in the shape given by the hypothesis. Developing that intention is not easy.

First of all, this kind of intention requires a context. Most human contexts are defined in large part by human purposes having to do generally with the avoidance of harm and the flourishing of the good for persons, environments, societies, and civilizations. As has been argued, the ultimate enters as a dimension of many of the affairs of human life regarding which purposive interpretive contexts exist. In these contexts, however, although the ultimate is involved, it is involved indirectly. The grasping of the ultimate itself is not the purpose in those contexts. To intend the ultimate in thought means to be concerned about the ultimate itself. Chapter 5 argued that a continuum of concern exists, running from concerns about many things, although not ultimate things, through a concern to order one's life's priorities according to what is ultimately important, to abandoning concerns about life's priorities and one's self in order to be ultimately concerned to grasp and conform to the ultimate itself as well as possible. To intend the ultimate in order to find priorities for life is a genuine intention of ultimacy. But it adds to the limitations imposed by our biology, culture, and semiotics those particulars of our own life that need prioritizing. Properly to think the ultimate is to intend it for its own sake, in its own nature, which is, according to the hypothesis, the ontological act of creation.

Very few contexts of life allow for this kind of focus of attention. Obviously, it requires a kind of spiritual maturity to make the move from thinking the ultimate for the sake of guidance to thinking the ultimate for itself. Most human contexts do not allow that much abandonment of concern for the self's proper priorities. The contexts for thinking the ultimate thus are embedded in larger contexts of spiritual development.

The contexts for thinking the ultimate also need to allow for the assembling of the thinking required, a certain kind of education and intellectual practice. These are privileged contexts. This is not to say that people in less privileged contexts cannot engage the ultimate. They can do so with symbols that very well might carry over what is true. But they would not be thinking the ultimate with the symbols that are as literal as possible so as to allow an iconic identification in the intellectual interpretive act.

Part of the maturity involved in thinking the ultimate is the spiritual transformation of the concepts involved from their network meanings to having content meanings. The network meanings are those that symbols have by virtue of their definitions of one another in syntactical and semantic ways; these are the meanings that function in dialectical arguments. The content meanings of the symbols are those that allow the higher-level symbols to order the lower-level symbols they contain without distortion, so that through the many layers of conceptual meaning the object is carried into the interpreting experience without distortion. The object is carried by means of the symbolic representations, but the representations are open to the objects themselves. So often with religious symbols, the associations of the symbols block any real experience through them. Spiritual work needs to be done to overcome these blocks. Concrete symbols are more problematic than abstract ones such as in the hypothesis about the ontological creative act. For instance, people who have been brutalized by their father are likely not to be able to symbolize the ultimate with content meaning as a father; they can know the network meanings, and correct the symbolic distortions that would come from construing God as a father in the wrong sense, but they cannot grasp God through the symbol of father. To do that, they would have to overcome their childhood experience of abuse. So many concrete religious symbols are filled with distortions that prevent them from functioning with content as well as network meaning. These are not likely to be found in the abstract statement of the hypothesis about the ontological act of creation. What is required for content meaning with that hypothesis is the development of an ease and familiarity with the abstract reasoning involved, something that does not come naturally to many people.

All this is to say that the right context and the right intellectual and spiritual development is required for symbolic engagements that actually intend the ultimate for its own sake and fulfill that intention with the grasp of the ultimate. Or, as argued in Section I of this chapter, the engaged person needs to develop the material quality of the symbols that can bear to be the causal effects of the ultimate as creator of the interpreter in context. Chapter 16 studies some means to do this.

Chapter Sixteen

Mystical Engagement

The purpose of this chapter is to explore paths of spiritual cultivation that make possible and promote the development of concrete, materially constituted, acts of symbolic engagement of the ultimate understood as the ontological act of creation. This preliminary exploration is supplemented from many other angles in *Philosophical Theology Two* and *Three*. These paths of spiritual cultivation are defined by goals of spiritual virtuosity that are beyond most people but that are known and somewhat understood in larger communities within which the virtuosi live. The vague term *mysticism* has been applied to them all. Chapter 5 argued that ultimate concern runs along a continuum from mild interest, which has little serious religious significance, to stronger interests often triggered by crises that involve serious participation in religious life that sets priorities for personal and social order. Sometimes, although rarely, ultimate concern moves beyond the concern for priorities for the self to concern only for what is ultimate. Toward the last stages on the continuum, religion, like the self, is relativized, even trivialized, in the face of giving oneself over to the ultimate. Concerns for self and religious prioritizing of life are not necessarily left behind (although sometimes they are). Rather they are simply turned into proximate concerns. Often, accomplished virtuosi are marginalized in those communities they treat as trivial, or at least as proximate in importance. Or the virtuosi are even perceived as threats. The degree of their engagement with the ultimate moves them to the edges of, and perhaps beyond, the sacred canopies that roughly are taken to be normative by religious communities. Each of these spiritual paths is thought to be "mystical" in some senses, often in senses peculiar to the path itself.

The material quality of the signs (as analyzed in *I, 3, i*) that are used in virtuoso acts of symbolic engagement of the ultimate is important because it goes beyond the "meanings" of those signs, at least beyond the network meanings. Given the syntactic and semantic structures of semiotic systems, the network meanings of signs, whereby they refer to their objects in a certain respect when employed in interpretive acts, possibly can be carried by any number of different kinds of tokens. For instance, a linguistic sign can be expressed in English, German, Latin, French, Italian, Spanish, and Romanian—the languages are different tokens for a common meaning that is not much affected by differences within this fairly close family of languages with a history of intertranslation. The sign also can be expressed in English, Sanskrit, Arabic, Finnish, and Chinese, although the structural differences among the languages are great and begin to make a material difference. Some language or other has to be acquired, however, for any verbal sign to be employed in an act of symbolic engagement; without any language, no linguistic sign could be employed. In the case of the spiritual adepts, the linguistic, artistic, musical, and other signs common to many people need to be supplemented by extra signs in order to give material reality to concrete virtuoso acts of engagement of the ultimate. The spiritual paths aim at the cultivation or achievement of these extra signs.

In addition to the network meanings of the signs, these virtuoso acts of symbolic engagement of the ultimate need signs that effect the intending of the ultimate. In the intellectual dimension, as chapter 15 argued, the dialectic of the one and many serves to direct the attention of the interpretation to the real locus of ultimacy so that it can be included within the interpretive experience as intended. This means that the signs can come into interpretive practice only insofar as the habits of that practice are triggered to intend the ultimate by the signs. This intending function is connected with the material reality of the signs.

Closely related to this is that the material reality of the signs must also identify and steady the context in which the acts of symbolic engagement take place. So, cultivation of the material reality of the signs involves in addition the cultivation of the contexts of the virtuoso engagement, for instance in practices of prayer, postures of meditation and contemplation, activities of devotion such as singing or spinning, abstinences such as from food or sex. At the beginning it might seems as if the context comes first, such as learning to sit in a proper meditative posture. But enhanced cultivation is not externally related to posture; only with rich engagement of the ultimate does it begin to be possible to sit just right, or be properly celibate.

All four of the paths of spiritual cultivation studied in this chapter aim to engage the ultimate so as to be "unified" with it in some sense. As the previous chapter argued, the engagement finally is not "about" the ultimate but is a way of grasping the ultimate, or having the ultimate itself indexically form the interpretive engagement. Nevertheless, each of these paths engages the ultimate only in certain respects as determined in part by their intentions and the material reality of their symbols. Other respects exist in which the ultimate might be engaged, and therefore each of these ways is partial. Sometimes recognition of that partiality is built in to the spiritual path itself. Even cumulatively, however, these respects are only certain respects among possible others. Therefore, it can be known that there is much that is not engaged regarding ultimacy. Moreover, it can be known that the limits of the respects in which spiritual adepts engage ultimacy cannot be known within those respect themselves, and so the symbolic engagements in these virtuoso paths might in the end be other than they seem. In this sense, they all are apophatic, signaling their inability to contextualize and therefore understand even themselves.

The four paths identified for preliminary analysis here come from ways of relating to the transcendental traits of harmony. Thus, the distinction between the four comes from philosophical considerations and can be illustrated by various spiritual techniques from different traditions. Actual spiritual practices can combine elements from the paths distinguished here. Perhaps in some sense the ideal adept follows all the paths.

The paths, with almost arbitrarily defined names, are those of meditation aiming at experiencing the ultimate as the creation of unity in diversity; of contemplation aiming at experiencing the ultimate as the creation of diverse things such as they are; of the mystical abyss aiming at experiencing the ultimate as the creation of an extensive world from nothing; and of love or devotion aiming at experiencing the creation as the ultimate act of value-making.

I. THE PATH OF MEDITATION: NONDUALISM

The path associated with meditation and aiming at experiencing the unity of the radically contingent creation is extremely broad with many interweaving wagon tracks. One track is intellectual with both epistemological and ontological interests. With regard to the former, part of meditation is to understand what meditation is. The meditative practices of yoga, for instance, long have been associated with the Samkhya philosophy of purusha and prakriti, with its analysis of consciousness, mind, will, identification, and the like that provided the terms for the long traditions of debate about meditation in South Asian conversations.[1] Neo-Confucians, with great moral urgency, debated with Chinese Buddhists about meditation. The epistemology for meditation in this *Philosophical Theology* is a naturalistic account of causal perception giving rise to intentional fulfillment, elaborated in *Philosophical Theology Two*, Part III. With regard to the ontological interests in meditation is the development of metaphysical theories about the nature of ontological unity. Perhaps the most famous, most elaborate, and most discussed is the Advaita Vedanta theory of nondualism elaborated by Shankara and developed in many subsequent ways. Whereas the yogic traditions of meditation involve long years of sitting in special postures with controlled breathing and exercises for the focusing of attention, the Vedantic practices emphasize more the long years of sitting with a guru commenting on texts. The "aha!" moments of Vedantic understanding change the material qualities of meditative symbolic engagement just as do the long years of yogic meditation. The argument of this *Philosophical Theology* is that the intellectual side of meditation is best served by the cultivation of the thinking of the ultimate as the ontological act of creation, as described in Part III and chapter 15.

The point of the meditative path is to be able to feel the unity of things as positive, in light of the finite/infinite contrast in which there might be nothing at all. Cultivation practices of feelings of unity are extraordinarily diverse, as are the ways of fitting of such feelings together. Nature mysticism is important in many forms of meditation, as is face-to-face communing with other people. But so also is the feeling of one's body: Often, nonadepts feel their bodies as distractions from meditation, a jarring cacophony of feelings. This is why meditation is sometimes associated with practices of martial arts, or the asanas of yoga.[2] Feeling oneself as whole and unified is a difficult accomplishment. The development of effective material symbols, based in one's context, body, and interpreting feelings, constitutes many more tracks in the meditative path. Consider the following extraordinary account of a meditative experience by an anonymous writer:

> I am about to describe an experience I had while rowing one night on Lake Washington. Understand, in reading it, that this sort of "thing" would occasionally happen to me. The history of my life has been an ongoing attempt to understand and to reproduce this experience. Attempting to symbolize this experience, as well as repeating the experience itself, are endeavors that have given my life meaning.
>
> I was preparing for the 2000 Olympics in Seattle. If, where, and when I wanted to row, I rowed. My life was utterly monastic; everything I did was organized around rowing. I knew exactly how many hours my body needed to rest before I could work out again, and so I would sometimes work out at night, as my physical cycle would prompt a workout at two, or three, or four in the morning. No drinking, no social life, just the rhythm of my training, the rhythm of the boat, the rhythm of my breathing, year after year after year.
>
> It was time to practice. It was around two in the morning, late spring, and it had been warm in Seattle, so the night air was just right for rowing. My boat was very fine, 28 feet long, 18 inches wide, fiber glass, about 29 pounds, an object with great esthetic appeal. Sitting in it I am about eight inches off the water, with but the needle-like stern of the boat reminding me that I am not somehow myself, floating over the water. And at night, the boat is difficult to see, and my eyes look far over the water; sweat and fatigue blur my vision.
>
> I'm alone. I head out, through Portage Bay, through Union Bay, and into the massive and uncharacteristically still expanse of Lake Washington. I've pulled my rowing gear off and am naked now, which is how I row whenever I can get away with it. Not a boat around, most of

the houses on shore dark and, in any case, far, far away. And everything is okay because I'm all breath now, and rhythm, and my eyes half shut, but in no way sleepy: focused, concentrating, relaxed. And I row.

And I row, and there is *nothing* of my life in this place, there is nothing in this place, and I've forgotten myself; my consciousness is mixing with the darkness and I become unsure of where I am and where I am not. The dark water and the dark sky hide the horizon and the whole world is colored deep grey-black. I have no sense of direction, as a man lost at sea without land to teach him his position. Time is an endless instant, meaningless.

In this place that is my floating breath, in an emptiness without any center or limit, I am beset, if I can use that word, by the utterly overwhelming weight of infinite blackness around me. I am filled with an intensity of feeling that is agonizing; a feeling too intense for me to contain. The sense of it is all things at once: power, insignificance, exhilaration, dread.

And on I row, choking, fascinated and afraid. It quickly becomes more than I can bear, and I find myself weeping, and groaning, and crying out. I am madness, my sense of exhilaration beyond measure, my fear of annihilation a welcome relief and yet a dread to me, a sense of omnipotence that was not for any-body to have to hold. The infinite abyss had taken me up, and I was all the world, and I was nothing. All words fall away.

I stop rowing some time later. Was it five minutes? Twenty? I am crying now, just crying. Not sad, but wrung out. Crying because it helps sooth the aching in me; and I am grateful that it is over. The row home was forgettable. Dulled and numb, I don't think as much as peek around the corner of the memory my body still holds. I return home and am ill at ease for the rest of the night and confused and worried the next day as I struggled to symbolize and make finite what had happened. I feel unhinged, and overwhelmed, and yet utterly passionately alive.[3]

To people who are not elite athletes, the material quality of the rower's meditative engagement is not easily accessible, although it is perhaps no more physically unusual than the practices of mountain-top ascetics. The experience was set in a life of ferocious physical and emotional discipline, "monastic" he calls it, in its single-minded and all-consuming focus. The darkness and calm water helped still the situational distractions. The physical act of rowing, with all that practice, helped bring unity to his sense of body and intentionality. Since college, the rower had been a student of philosophy and psychology, both depth psychology and cognitive psychology, and thus had words such as *power, insignificance, annihilation, dread* with which to hold the experience (not the vocabulary of many athletes). He understood at some basic level that his life, including its athletic training and competition, was a kind of spiritual quest, and recognized that the transcendent sense of intensity and dislocation in the experience was an extraordinary juxtaposition of agonizing death and omnipotent life. He cultivated experiences like these before and after this episode, continuing for years with daily extensive yoga practice and meditation as well as rowing practice. So the material quality of the experience itself was intentionally and contextually oriented toward engaging the ultimate.

But in the rower's experience, the ultimate was not something toward which the experience *pointed*. That experience was not "about" anything. It was only itself. But included within it was the ultimate insofar as it was grasped by the experience taken as a sign. The rower was experiencing, not the world as created, but the fact of creation in his unified being, with the exhilaration of its power and the threat of annihilation in its radical contingency. The value of the ultimate was carried over into his being, exhausting and numbing him, but making him passionately alive.

Aristotle said (about contemplative, not meditative, experiences in this sense) that one swallow does not make a summer. However life transforming, such virtuoso experiences as the rower recounted come and pass, needing to be sought again, perhaps by other means. The path of meditation involves the cultivation of intellectual/physical/emotional signs of unity (in which disparateness disappears) that can bear the actual causal power of the ontological creative act. Many such signs, and acts of using them, seem to be required in order to make the meditative engagement of ultimacy a habit.

The spiritual path of meditation, in its various tracks, aims at unity. Looking toward the future, unity lies in possibilities, and so does the value that unity always has in the unifying patterns with their complexity and simplicity. As we have seen, the unity is not only in trivializing environmental distractions and unifying the sense of bodily singleness, but also unifying one's sense of being with others. The distinction between self and other falls away in advanced meditation, as does orientation to others in existential fields. The aim of the meditative experience has something to do with attaining an immediacy of unity. But that immediacy is in the material quality of the adept's achieved complex symbol that embraces both the real object, ultimacy, and the contextualized interpreter. The engagement itself is highly mediated by all the tropes of unification, beginning perhaps with feelings of unity with nature and deep communion between persons, and moving through the construction of layers on layers of signs that arrange the network and material qualities of the intellectual, emotional, and brutally physical signs that together constitute the unified engaging experience, as in the rower's transcendent moment. Tropes of unification, as in facing possibilities, guide the whole of multifarious tracks in the path of meditation as understood here.

II. THE PATH OF CONTEMPLATION: SUCHNESS

The path of contemplation takes a somewhat opposite direction. Instead of being oriented to unification, it is oriented to the components of harmony, or of life, explicitly attempting to set aside the task and effects of unifying the components. The path of contemplation aims to deconstruct the self in ways that compensate for the fact that usually the components of the contemplator are biased and modified by virtue of being harmonized within the contemplator. The aim of contemplation is to attend to the things of creation such as they are, without the bias of the contemplative perspective. The ultimacy in this is that the ontological act of creation creates the determinate things just as they are, just fitting together.

Of course the basic fact exists that we do integrate our experiences to a great degree, as indeed we must in order to be at all attentive on any spiritual path whatsoever. Ordinary life means that we subordinate many of the contents of our lives to its overall shape and purposes, most of which are legitimate. We need safety, nourishment, associations, and love. Economic work is necessary, as is the political activity of organizing social institutions from friendships and family to communities and nations. Purposive activity is necessary and requires adept habits of keeping ourselves and our relationships balanced and harmonious. So it is unrealistic to say that we can become adept at contemplating the components of our lives without integrating them and changing them in the integration. The ordinary truth of things is that we relate to them perspectively from a more or less centered sense of self and purposeful direction.

This is not unlike the ordinary truth that any meditative path toward unity or nondualism still admits that the unity is always of a plurality of diverse changing things making up our lives. Facing the future's possibilities is always to have in hand the diverse potentialities that must be integrated in the future. The immediate act of virtuoso meditative engagement also is mediated by the path that brings an individual into a capacity to focus on unity without distraction, feeling that the body's multiple tugs are made into a singular effort, that other things are ourselves, and that the singularity of the creative act is determinate only because of the plurality of determinations created. The spiritual path of meditation is to subordinate the plurality into the rich unity that is comprised of their just fitting into a singular engaging experience.

Similarly, the contemplative spiritual path aims to subordinate the unifying or harmonizing directions of experiencing things to every enhanced appreciation of the things as they are themselves, harmonies in their own rights. Basic elements of the contemplative path have to do with the cultivation of a lack of selfishness. Much of the preparation for contemplation is the settling of one's life onto a relatively selfless take on things. Most spiritual traditions of contemplation put the attainment of a degree of moral selflessness at the beginning of the path. The fourth of the Fourfold Noble Truths of the Buddha does just that: learn to live without harming or distorting others before undertaking the more esoteric forms of contemplation.

Like the way of meditation, the contemplative path is very broad with many crisscrossing tracks. One such track is simply through inquiry into the way things are. Instead of interpreting things mainly in terms of their relation to human interests, or to the place in a cosmos understood as oriented to human interests, people can study things for what they are on their own, in their own terms, following their native rhythms. Scientists often develop virtuosity at contemplative knowing, sometimes to the point of being overwhelmed by wonder. Mathematicians can become ecstatic at the beauty of mathematics so abstract as to be impossible to distort for human interests. Philosophy, theology, literary and critical studies, history and cultural studies can all be undertaken for their own sakes. Knowledge for its own sake is a powerful kind of contemplation, and capable of being pursued only by the most disciplined and humanly modest inquirers. Of course, these studies begin with what we know, and are thus deeply biased by the human perspective. But as they advance, the human perspective can be relativized and the perspective of the things studies made more dominant.

Advancing along the path of contemplation requires some kind or other of systematic deconstruction of the self or ego. Buddhists go right to the ontological heart of this task by claiming that there is no self in the sense of an abiding entity that has a right to force its interests and perspectives on the components of experience. This is a bit ironic in that Buddhists generally and Madhyamikas specifically do not take themselves to be making an ontological argument, thinking that ontology is what misleads us in the first place into believing in too directive a self. But the Buddhist anatman doctrine is the most straightforward denial of the self. Its claim is that the integrative activities of purposive life are in some sense delusory. Of course, the Buddhists accept the conventional truth of having to cope with organized life. But the higher truth is that there is no self and that when this is recognized through appropriate kinds of contemplation the attachments to things that come from the ego can be relaxed, reducing suffering, perhaps completely. One does not have to accept the Buddhist ontological claim about the lack of reality of the integrative self to appreciate the spiritual task of deconstructing that self so that, in virtuoso experience, things can be apprehended rather much as they are, in their suchness.

Many techniques of advanced contemplation exist, including a kind of focusing of attention on watching the contents of consciousness come and go, a cultivation of a lack of attachment or aversion to experiential contents so as to accept them, and shock techniques so as to disorient the ego and let new and more realistic attitudes toward things form. Patrick McNamara even argues that the evolutionary adaptive advantage of ecstatic religious experiences is that it disorients habitual ego structures long enough for new and more realistic ego structures to form, thus making human beings more adaptive to important realities.[4] All major religious traditions have spiritual forms that cultivate virtuosity in contemplation as defined here.

As with the meditative path, virtuosity in contemplation requires building the signs that allow for engaging others more on their terms than ours. This requires actual deconstruction of distorting ego structures as well as acquiring actual contact with and appreciation of the things to be contemplated. On the intellectual side, there is the task of building an epistemology to understand what is taking place in this deconstructed ego experience; some traditions, especially those of South India, attend mainly to an epistemology of consciousness while those of East Asia attend more to an epistemology of harmonious nondistorting response. Most traditions, including the Western ones, employ visualization techniques to take one out of the ordinary mindset.

Having acquired the effective material reality of the signs for contemplation, layered many deep, direct immediate engagement of the ultimate as the ontological act of creation is possible. This interpretive act needs to be intentionally formed so that the ontological act is within it. The ontological act in its way creates the experiential engagement, but only as mediated by the signs with their material qualities. Whereas the meditative path toward unity tends to give great importance to the essential components harmonizing experience, the contemplative act tends to give the greater importance to certain kinds of conditional components. Negatively put, the meditative act finds ways of suppressing without losing the diverse components whereas the contemplative act finds ways of suppressing the essential harmonizing components without losing their discipline.

III. THE PATH OF THE MYSTICAL ABYSS

The way of the mystical abyss embraces signs for the entire existential field, thereby including signs for essential and conditional components alike, and moves to the consideration of the radical contingency of the whole creation, and from the contingency of the creation to the act of creation, and from that act to the absolute nothingness that would be the case were the ontological act not to create. This is perhaps the most familiar kind of mysticism in the West, expressed in Tillich's rejection of (determinate) God in favor of the God beyond gods, in Nicolas Berdyaev's abyss with the fire of creation, in Meister Eckhart's God beyond the Godhead, and in many other mystical writers.[5] The movement from determinate contingency to the creation of that contingent world and then beyond to nothing is not limited to Western mysticism, however. Chapter 6 discussed the dialectic of Ishvara the creator, on to Saguna Brahman, and then to Nirguna Brahman; chapter 12 quoted and discussed Zhou Dunyi's model of the 10,000 things resting on the five elements that are constructed of yin-yang patterns, which arise out of the Great Ultimate, which follow on the Ultimate of Non-Being.

The issue in this section is not the intellectual structure of the ontological creative act. The question rather is how to develop signs with adequate material quality as well as network meanings and intentional ordering so that the ultimate reality of the ontological creative act can be included within an engagement of it in the properly prepared context.

Signs for the contingent world depend on the cultural factors defining the world, of course. Ancient sciences around the globe depicted a world vastly different from what we now understand, and they were astonishingly different from one another. Indeed, our contemporary understanding of the cosmos is significantly different from that of two centuries ago in the West. But the specific images of the world are not so much to the point. The point rather is that they embody a sense of the world as a whole. "Wholeness" here does not mean imagining the world as bounded in some sense, but rather self-contained. However the cosmos is symbolized, the symbols have to include a sense that this is all there is, of the worldly stuff. In the metaphysics of *Philosophical Theology*, this means "everything determinate." In East Asian traditions, it might mean the vast mass of *qi* as patterned by yin and yang; in South Asian traditions, it might mean "anything that might be in consciousness, including consciousness," or the physical cosmos that expands from the Golden Egg to its maximum and then contracts back to the Egg, and then to repeat, or the multiply implicated Buddha worlds of the *Lotus Sutra*. Monotheistic traditions have many images for that which is created by the High God. *Philosophical Theology* interprets traditional symbols of the world as versions of, or alternatives to, the metaphysics developed in Part III.

A main consequence of that metaphysics is that the symbols for the world in the path of the mystical abyss embrace both essential and conditional components in the things defining the existential field. In this respect, the way of the mystical abyss needs to incorporate the emphasis on essential components and unification from the meditative way as well as the emphasis on conditional components and the suchness of things other than the interpreter. This is not to reduce the meditative and contemplative paths to the mystical path of the abyss, or make them incomplete versions of it. But it is to say that the path of the abyss needs to find some of its most important signs, including their material qualities, from those other paths.

To be sure, from no finite spatiotemporal perspective can real other things be engaged in their essential components without reducing those others to the interpreter's finite spatiotemporal perspective. This point is one of the keys to saying that the ontological context of mutual relevance cannot be made up of the finite perspectives that are related only by their mutual conditionings. The world is ineluctably other to any finite knower. Nevertheless, this very metaphysical point provides signs for engaging the world as a self-contained whole. We can develop signs, such as those in the metaphysics of Part III, that articulate determinateness as such. With these signs, we can engage the created order without reducing the actual created things to what we know of them. Although we cannot experience other subjects as nonobjectified in our own experience, we can experience the world as a massive interacting process of subjects, not objects: Each harmony is the subject of its own harmonization.

Although signs of the world as a whole obviously do not in fact embrace all the world, they can very well embrace the contingency of the world. However the world is signified, the signifying symbols need to carry into the engaged interpretive experience a feeling of the contingency of all things. The contingencies of some things on other things, causal processes of all sorts, need to be felt as themselves contingent in the context that allows for the connections and differences between causes and effects. Many images of the world can bear this radical contingency and can be incorporated in the adept mystic as the way of feeling the world.

The mystical path of the abyss does not only require the acquisition of ways of feeling the world as contingent, however. It needs signs for tipping that sense of contingency into feeling the act of creating the contingent. How is this to be expressed? There is some *power* of pure positivity in determinate things. Regarded, not in terms of one thing causing another, but as the whole self-contained world, or array of determinations, or however the world is conceived, existence itself has the quality of being surprising, shocking, unmotivated, just there. The mystical path of the abyss requires learning to attend to what Tillich called the "power of being," that which makes all somethings stand out from nonexistence. This moment in the mystical path has a heightened aesthetic sense of sheer existence.

That tipping from the feel of the world as self-contained to the feel of the power of its existence can be pushed further into the feel of its radical arbitrariness. Precisely this point is what is unsettling to some thinkers who believe that the concept of creation is unintelligible unless there is a nature within the cause that explains the effect. But without the arbitrariness of the sheer power of creation, the making of new somethings, could not be felt.

To feel the arbitrariness, however, invites the feeling of the counter-factual, of what there would be without the ontological creative act. Of course there is no positive feeling of nothingness—nothing would exist to be felt. But there can be the feeling of counter-factuality—the alternative to what is the case. What is the case is the creation, and the path of the mystical abyss involves cultivating and embodying symbols that express the positive making-be of the act of creation, tied to what is made to be. The arbitrariness, not of what is created but of the fact of creation itself, is meaningful only in a finite/infinite contrast with nothingness, albeit a counter-factual nothingness. Therefore, the feeling of the contrast involves the feeling of non-being as well as being. The abyss is what gives meaning to the absolutely free act of creation. Or as the mystics (including the rower) testify, the feeling is of their death as of their life. Often, the operative complex feeling of the ultimate abyss in symbolic engagement is like that of a fall, a free-fall plunge, from the radically contingent expansive world through the immediate fire of creation into the bottomless pit. The material symbolic act is a feeling of falling from any extensional location through the astonishing power of arbitrary affirmation into nowhere. The rower's experience had much of this dimension of moving through absolute exertion into complete dislocation. The mystical fall into the abyss is terrifying and involves confronting and accepting one's own annihilation.

The overwhelmingly powerful emotional tone of the symbolic engagement of the ultimate through the mystical path of the abyss is the razor-sharp and infinitely dense contrast between being and non-being, life and death, joy and terror. But the mystics, like the rower, usually try to come back for more. Perhaps the best name for the contrastive feeling is bliss, something beyond good and evil.

The path of the mystical abyss is a process, with elements of its signs being acquired in diverse ways throughout a significant period of time. The signs need to be acquired in material qualities filled with indices to real things, and each sign is many layers deep. The feeling of the contingency of the world that comes, for some, while lying in an open field in the dead of night staring at the stars is only a small contribution to more robust feelings of radical contingency. One experience of the startling positivity of something in the world needs supplementation by many other such experiences. One experience of plunging into the abyss of arbitrariness is a start but hardly enough. The *path* of the mystical abyss requires the accumulated habitual character of bearing the extraordinarily rich and complex sign that engages the ultimate ontological act of creation as a proper finite/infinite contrast. This sign, developed from parts over time, needs to be able to focus attention so that it is the ultimate that is its object, and not one's ordinary fear of death. Also, this sign needs to be tied to contexts so that actual acts of symbolically engaging the ultimate can be concrete. The signs involved in the path of the mystical abyss, like those in the other paths, mean nothing by themselves except what can be recorded in a semiotic system of network meanings. Their content meaning is only in being used in actual acts of symbolic engagement. If properly acquired, the mystic symbols of engaging the ultimate abyss are the mirror process of the abyss from which the ontological act creates giving rise to the mystic experiencing. The work of the mystical path is to develop the capacity to perceive the ontological act of creation in the respects in which the symbols allow.

IV. THE PATH OF LOVE

The paths of meditation, contemplation, and the mystical abyss correspond roughly with engaging ultimacy through the tropes of the transcendental traits of harmony: form, components to be formed, and existential location in a field encompassing all determinate things. The transcendental trait of ultimate value-identity provides the tropes for the way of love. The path of love is very broad indeed, including all the bhakti dimensions of South Asian faiths, the devotionalism of much Christianity, Judaism (especially in its Hassidic forms), Islam in its Sufi forms, Pure Land Buddhism, popular Buddhist devotionalism (as to Guanyin), the cultivation of the bodhisattva's compassion, and the cool kinds of love in the Confucian cultivation of humaneness or *ren*.

The breadth of the path of love allows not only an astonishingly diverse array of different kinds of love but also many tracks for people who are not adepts at love. Although most forms of love are not easy, societies generally foster love, care, compassion, and concern for others. People need love, and so it is rewarded in most, although not all, of its forms. In Confucian cultures, for instance, love is regarded as arising from and learned primarily within the family, and the forms of love appropriate for friends, neighbors, people in the community, and distant people, are extensions, variants, and diversifications of family love. Confucian love is learned by children from parents. Even when messy and noisy, cuddly infants are easy to love, with instinctive emotions and culturally dense mores of care. Small children require parents to grow in their ability to love, and adolescents provide a steep learning curve for parents. The purpose of parental love is to bring up the children to be virtuous, and the chief virtue is being able to love. But parents do not know whether their children are virtuous until they see them actually loving their own children. This is why multiple generations living together are so important in Confucian cultures: Only grown grandchildren can demonstrate much about parents' success in loving their own children. The obverse of parental love is filial piety, and the highest form of filial piety is to become so virtuous as to set your parents free of the obligation to make you virtuous. Although the Confucian household has variant forms of love respecting siblings, birth order, gender, and other variables such as avuncular duties, there is much cultural support and pressure for everyone to be loving in the sense of nourishing the significant people around according to their needs.[6]

Adepts at the path to the ultimate through love need to master and embody these and many other forms of human love and care, and perhaps extend it to love and care for the natural environment as well as social institutions. But they go beyond that in connecting love with their ultimate identity and value. A person's ultimate identity and value is the sum of the values realized through all the forms actualized in present moments. Because those values include their real effects on other things, and also include the ways the person's life has diminished or enhanced the values actualized in the past, the person's ultimate identity and value can be appreciated only from the standpoint of eternity within the ontological context of mutual relevance. For this reason, a person can symbolically engage his or her own value only by signifying it as having a place within the eternal ontological creative act.

The path of love, arising out of the multitude of ordinary kinds of love and devotion, aims the spiritual person to engage the ultimate as love by becoming an adept lover. These are nonordinary notions of love. How can the ultimate as the ontological act of creation be loving? How can the person's practiced loving become like the ultimate's loving? How can virtuoso loving be the sign of engagement of the ultimate such that the ultimate's creation of the lover is the engagement's perceptual path? To connect loving neighbor and loving God as somehow identical, and to claim that the ultimate is love, are not unusual in the history of religion. But the meanings attending to these senses of love are not ordinary.

The feelings of love for other people, despite their diversity of forms and situations, combine two fundamental elements. One is giving oneself over in emotion, will, and actual practice to enjoying the other, delighting in who the other is, grateful to all powers for the existence of the other. The other element is devoting oneself to the good of the other, however that is relevant to the person. Without the former, devotion to the other's good is only a moral obligation, since we are always under obligation to make things good where we can. Without the latter, delight in the other is only a selfish emotion because of the pleasure in delight. Love requires some elements of both, always scaled to circumstances and the nature of the relationships involved.

The reason sexual imagery abounds in religious language about love is that the delighting in the other needs to be embodied in the material qualities of the signs that carry it. Sex is extraordinarily embodied, and in fact is a steady corrective to attempts to love "at a distance." Of course, sexuality is filled with ambiguities, humiliations, the giving and receiving of hurt, and enough other conflicting elements as to make it a treacherous sign system for love in its adept forms. But those ambiguities are precisely what give sex such body. Love has all those ambiguities too. Delighting in another person can be very painful for the other as well as oneself and those around. Nevertheless, love of even the most elevated kind needs to be embodied in ways analogous to the way sexual love is embodied if the signs are to enable actual concrete symbolic engagement.

Willing the good of the other is even more ambiguous and dangerous than delighting in the other's existence and nature. Who knows what is good for the other? Some kinds of loving relationships, as between parents and children, gurus and disciples, presuppose various kinds of wisdom about the asymmetry of this. The reverse loving in those same relationships does not. Most relationships of love involve constant negotiation about what is good for the beloved. "Do to others what you would have them do to you" works only when everyone is much alike, and even then, who of us knows really what would be good for ourselves that we should foist it on others?

Eventually, however, loving others involves understanding and willing their good in their whole context. Although of course we can never know people and their contexts fully, and although loving relationships are always ritually channeled so as to have some duties and some restrictions, progress can be made in loving relationships toward greater understanding and proper helpfulness. Part of virtuoso loving is cultivating the relationship itself, with a ritual structure, enhanced sensitivities to idiosyncrasy, and patience through uneven times. An adept at the path of love learns to establish many different kinds of loving relationships, ideally so as to be able to love everyone with whom some kind of relationship can be established, even if only through distant and anonymous charity.

Part of being an adept lover is having the character to be patient when love is returned with disinterest or enmity. Although loving means delight and the will to help, often the beloved is not so delightful and rejects help. Jesus' famous injunction to love enemies is radical indeed, although it was a clear expression of the Axial Age principle of loving all people, some of whom are enemies.

Another equally if not more difficult part of being an adept lover is allowing oneself to be loved in return, when that happens. Jesus' equally famous injunction to love your neighbor as yourself (quoting Deuteronomy) supposes that you do love yourself, that you know how to do so and that you actually do. Self-love is very difficult, however, because we better than anyone know how unlovely we ourselves are in so many ways, from the immoral to the disgusting. Much of the spiritual path of love is learning to love ourselves and to let others love us.

Loving other people is one thing (actually, a very great many things). Loving the ultimate is something else entirely. Or is it? For those who symbolize the ultimate in personifying terms, loving God or gods is rather like loving ordinary persons, but perhaps intensified and given no ritualized restrictions. In many traditions, personification of the ultimate is encouraged in the context of cultivating love of the ultimate, which is perfectly appropriate as long as mistaken inferences are not drawn about that which is in fact beyond determination save in creation. Sometimes, love of the ultimate is mediated through avatars such as Jesus or Krishna, the avatar of Vishnu in the Bhagavad Gita. Devotions to Jesus as friend and Krishna as the trainer or seducer are powerful spiritual techniques for cultivating the human capacity to love well enough to love the ultimate. In traditions that do not personify the ultimate, such as the Daoist and Confucian, the language of love is not so commonly used to indicate attitudes or practices toward the ultimate. Nevertheless, love on an ontological scale is still an ideal for human spiritual virtuosity.

According to the metaphysics of the ontological creative act, the determinate reality of that act is the array of determinations created. Therefore, to love the ultimate is to love that array as the product of the singular act of creation, delighting in it and working where possible to enhance it. No one, of course, actually attends to every determinate created thing. The spiritual path of love therefore requires ways of symbolizing the array through more selected components. Like the path of the mystical abyss, the created world needs some symbolic engagement as self-contained and as tipped to reveal the power of the singular creator in it. There can be no such thing as loving the ultimate apart from the determinateness that accrues to ultimacy in creating. Nevertheless, to love the creation as the creative expression of the creator is to love the ultimate directly, because the ontological creative act has its determinate identity in what it creates. Therefore, all the work on the path of love to perfect the loving of people and the other elements of God's creation contributes to the loving of the creator in the creation.

An important difference between loving certain other people, mountains, a town, or one's self, and loving the ultimate is in intentionality. Those finite objects of love are brought into the loving symbolic engagement through the intentions that make them the objects actually engaged. The intention of loving the ultimate as over and above loving elements of the terminus of the ontological creative act is embodied in the signs that signify the creation as a whole as the determinate reality of the creator. For this, signs are necessary to address the singularity of the ontological act of creation despite the temporal, spatial and other forms of distance between determinate created things.

So loving creatures and loving the ultimate together can be expressed this way. To love a creature in a virtuoso way is to love it in its ultimate identity, that is, to love it explicitly as part of the ontological creative act. One need not think about it in those terms, but the symbols employed to identify the beloved need to have the scale of the ontological context of mutual relevance in order to grasp the beloved in all the value ways appropriate to be treasured and helped. To love the ultimate is to love it as the creator of all the creatures to be loved. Different symbols are required to focus intentionality on the singularity of the creative act. But that singularity is the act that creates all the lovable creatures, some of whom the virtuoso lover actually loves. In this precise ontological sense, "loving neighbors and loving God" are the same, and involve each other.

What sense does it make to say that the ultimate, the ontological creative act, loves? It cannot make literal sense to say that the ultimate takes subjective delight in the creation or in any creature, or that it works to enhance the creature. Those traditions that personify the ultimate do indeed represent gods as taking delight and intervening to help (just as they also represent gods as being angry and causing grief). The first creation account in Genesis says that after God created each thing, he "saw that it was good." Setting aside the personifications, which are very misleading when it comes to suggesting divine acts to intervene, how does the ultimate "love"? The immediate ontological act of creation creates the whole being of the harmonies together, each of which is valuable. Ultimate delight symbolizes the goodness of each thing created in mutual determination with the others, even if the goods of some things are destructive of the goods of others. Ultimate helpfulness symbolizes the very giving of being to each thing. The ontological creative act is immediate, so that there is no separation of subjective delight from the objects created. For the same reason there is no separation of a need for help and the being of the helped thing. Female sexual birth imagery symbolizes the novelty and value-making fruitfulness of the ontological creative act. Male sexual ejaculatory imagery symbolizes the immediacy of the creative act.

In summary, to love the ultimate as creator in a virtuoso way is to love the ontological creative act as the loving creator of the manifold of the world, each thing with its own being and value. Acquisition of the symbols with embodied material quality for intentionally direct symbolic engagement of the loving creator in love is an enormously complex process. Such engagements of the ultimate can be viewed as interpretive acts of the virtuoso, or as partial elements of the ultimate's singular act within which the virtuoso turns out to be the adept lover. The virtuoso loving symbolic engagement of the ultimate as love, because it itself is part of the creation, is a perception caused by the ultimate acting on the interpreter through the indexical connections with the creative act.

PART IV

Summary Implications

Part I of *Philosophical Theology One* raised the problem of how to understand ultimacy and suggested the hypothesis of the ontological act of creation, although not exactly in these theoretical terms. Part II set this problem in the larger context of how various dimensions of reality exert pressures on understandings of ultimacy, defined as symbols of ultimacy; in important respects, these pressures are countervailing and thus give rise to tensions among symbols and their interpretations that are felt in all the long-standing literary religious traditions. Part II further contextualized these problems with copious illustrations from religions. Part III developed a metaphysical theory of ultimacy in terms of the ontological act of creating the world. This theory is abstractly formulated and defended on its own terms, although also illustrated by traditional religious ideas. Part IV analyzed how the metaphysical theory can function to allow for the symbolic engagement of ultimacy, restating the problems with knowing the ultimate in the terms of analysis developed since the beginning.

The first chapter of Part I raised the question of how to understand ultimacy in terms of Peter Berger's idea of the sacred canopy as the medium in which people think about ultimate matters, although it developed that idea fairly radically in directions Berger has not taken. It defined ultimacy in terms of a larger theory of finite/infinite contrasts and offered an hypothesis about how world-defining problems are more or less universal and thus exert pressures on all sacred canopies. It concluded by raising various problems with how sacred canopies can be right or wrong, genuine or spurious, about what they represent as true about various aspects of ultimacy.

Part I, Chapter 2, set the whole discussion of how to understand the truth or falsity of symbols of ultimacy in the larger context of how approaches to religion do or do not allow those symbols to refer to the ultimate realities to which they seem to refer, as religious people employ them. Particularly at issue were the limitations imposed on understanding the truth of symbols of ultimacy by reductionisms of various types, particularly scientific reductionisms. The chapter argued that controlling for those limitations is an important office of philosophy, and that it performs that office through the development of metaphysics, a once-despised philosophical discipline. Metaphysics of the sort employed here was described and defended.

Part I, Chapter 3, presented a theory of the symbolic engagement of ultimacy, based on a more general pragmatic philosophical epistemology of interpretive engagement. Within that theory are three related kinds of reference—iconic, indexical, and conventional—that are relevant for reference to ultimacy. This theory was spelled out in terms of the three kinds of reference to finite/infinite contrasts. The result of this is to shift the understanding of ultimacy that theology might provide from the elaboration of doctrine to the study of how symbols of ultimacy do or do not facilitate genuine symbolic engagement with ultimate realities.

Part I, Chapter 4, integrated the previous discussion with a theory of worldviews of which sacred canopies are the parts in which ultimate realities are more or less directly engaged. Those parts of worldviews that are not themselves referring to the ultimate as symbolized in their sacred canopies can still be related to the sacred canopies through the integrating structure of the worldview. Depending on the worldviews in different ways, wherever some mundane part of the worldview is connected with the ultimacy in the sacred canopy, a religious dimension of that mundane matter is made part of the worldview. Symbols of ultimacy all along the worldview, from its most sacred to its most mundane elements, lie along a continuum from the transcendent to the intimate, especially the anthropomorphic, for good reasons. Similarly, a continuum of symbols ranging from the most sophisticated to popular culture ranges along the sacred/mundane axis. Moreover, the ways by which people engage their worldviews lie along continua of sharing or not sharing the worldview with others, of allowing the worldview to define life comprehensively or only in small parts, and with different degrees of intensity of commitment. The theory of worldviews sums up the other analytical tools presented in Part I for the analysis of ultimacy.

Part II examined certain aspects of the reality of engaging ultimate matter and showed how that accounts for the continua of positions in worldviews. Part II, Chapter 5, provided an analysis of concern for ultimate reality, and distinguished stages on a continuum from little or no concern to concern of the sort that seeks ways of giving priorities to life, to concern for the ultimate itself irrespective of life's other concerns. Part II, Chapter 6, analyzed certain aspects of reality that press for greater transcendence in symbols of ultimacy, emphasizing problems of scale, of overcoming idolatry, of finding adequate explanations for the scale of the world, and of doing justice to the depths of the experience of the ultimate as standing behind the vast array of non-ultimate things. Part II, Chapter 7, by contrast, analyzed those aspects of reality that press symbols of the ultimate to take on greater intimacy to human experience. These include the infinite depths of organizational levels of reality resident in a person's own being, familiar things that are uncanny or holy, the need for the ultimate matters to give meaning to human life, and the need to grasp the ultimate as giving correction to human life. Part II, Chapter 8, raised the question of how all these issues of human concern for ultimacy, and of transcendence and intimacy in symbols, affect the attempts to understand ultimate matters in terms of a cosmic narrative in which individuals might find meaningful roles of a cosmic metaphysics in which individuals find right relations with ultimates. Narratives have great power to give meaning. But they also are highly reductive, and can be controlled for only by a larger metaphysical theory of ultimacy and its relations with human life.

Part III aimed to provide that metaphysics. Chapter 9 addressed the fundamental metaphysical problem of the one and the many, adopting the provisional identification of ultimate reality with being, which in turn was identified with the one for the many. If being is analogical, then it cannot be the one for the many; but it was shown that being cannot be analogical. If there is no one one, but as many ones as there are many, each of the many being the one for all the others, then there is no one as being; but it was shown that this ontological pluralism cannot be right. Can being be determinate? Not if it is the one for the many, and something must be the one for the many. Being therefore must be indeterminate if the many things are to be determinate with respect to one another. Whatever being is, it must function as the ontological context of mutual relevance.

Part III, Chapter 10, stepped back to contextualize the problem of being as the one for the many with a theory of determinateness. It argued that to be determinate is to be a harmony with conditional components defining it with reference to other determinate things and essential components giving it is own being. Harmony has four transcendental traits: form, components, existential location, and ultimate value-identity. These are the traits that provide the schema of fundamental human problems in chapter 1. Chapter 10 then argued that the ultimate ground of determinate beings cannot itself be determinate but must be the one in the sense of the ontological context of mutual relevance.

Part III, Chapter 11, argued that the only thing that could function as the ontological context of mutual relevance is an ontological creative act that creates all determinate things out of nothing. The determinate world is not something separate from the ontological act that creates it but is rather the terminus of the act itself. The ontological creative act makes the difference between nothingness and the contingent determinate reality of the world. It is an act that produces novelty. This is a symmetrical conception, with its parts defining one another, of an asymmetrical act of making. The only determinate nature of the ontological created act is what comes in the creation; the nature of the acting creator is part of what is created. This is enough to make the creative act intelligible, and to see how it can function as the ontological context of mutual relevance.

Part III, Chapter 12, analyzed the extensive character of the world as the terminus of the ontological creative act. Because time is created, and all moments of time are created relative to each other, the ontological act of creation is eternal. This can be understood only in terms of the interactions of the modes of time, past, present, and future, that constitute the flow of time. Eternity is the togetherness of the modes of time that itself makes possible the temporal togetherness of things within time. As the ontological context of mutual relevance, the ontological creative act creates temporal (and spatial) things within eternity, while the things themselves, or at least most of them, are temporal. Ultimate reality is eternal and embraces the temporal within it.

Part IV drew out some consequences of the metaphysical theory of the ontological creative act. Chapter 13 elaborated some of what can be known of the ultimate, based on the metaphysics. First, the ultimate is a singular act of creation, not in time or space but creative of time and space. The ultimate is to be understood triadically in terms of the act of creation itself, what is created, and what would be if the arbitrary act were not to take place, namely nothing. The ultimate also can be conceived through the transcendentals of harmony. The ontological creative act is the source of possibility and value through the form in all things, allowing for temporal change to actualize possibilities with values. The act is the source of the components that harmonies harmonize in their time, and thus of the groundedness of those harmonies. The act is the source of the existential location of each harmony in a field whereby it can be connected and mutually determined by other harmonies. And the act is the source and context of the ultimate identity or value attained by each harmony, and of the harmonies together. All of these traits are religiously important, and address the fundamental human problems sketched in chapter 1. Given the dynamism of the relations among the modes of time, their togetherness can be understood as divine life, eternal but embracing the temporal. The concept of the divine life still does not require personifying the ultimate in ways that would make it determinate apart from creation. Finally, the ultimate as the ontological act of creation is to be understood as perceptible in the extensiveness of creation and in the intensiveness of nature in any part of creation. This is quite a lot to know about the nature of the ontological creative act that itself is the result of that act.

Part IV, Chapter 14, detailed some of the things that cannot be known about the ultimate that some people would like to know. First, the ultimate has no nature or reality apart from the creating of the world. This is a disappointment to those monotheisms that are committed to understanding God to have a character on the basis of which the world is created. But if God were to have such an independent character, then there would have to be a more ultimate context of mutual relevance connecting that determinate divine character with other determinate things. Second, because the act of creation is immediate and stems from nothing, it is arbitrary, absolutely free, and nothing can be known about any explanatory motivation. No such motivation can exist. Therefore, we cannot know an antecedent reason for the world, only the act of its making. Third, because the ultimate has no nature apart from creation, it cannot be a person apart from creation, who creates as a personal act. But neither can the ultimate create itself to be a person in any sense deeply analogous to finite creative people as persons. Can the ontological creative act be made intelligible? No, if by intelligibility one means the setting of first principles and the deduction of other things from them. But yes if one admits the intelligibility of the making of novelty as attention is directed to the acts of novelty, including the ontological creative act, by the dialectic of the arguments presented heretofore.

Part IV, Chapter 15, took up precisely this theme, of how the symbolic engagement of the ultimate can make the ultimate intelligible. First it argued that theological understanding of the sort in this *Philosophical Theology* can itself be a complex symbol in an intellectual, but spiritual, act of engaging the ultimate. In religious settings, such symbols must compete with variations along the continua of sophistication and popular religion, of transcendence and intimacy, and of the sacred and mundane. The inner dialectic of the theory of the ultimate ontological act of creation needs to be accessed in order to place critical limitations on the symbols of ultimacy along those continua. When that happens, however, it is possible to think the ultimate in profoundly engaging ways, engaging in the sense that the ultimate is present in the interpretive engagement in the respects in which the symbols guide the interpretation.

Part IV, Chapter 16, pressed the notion of engaging the ultimate through philosophical theology to the virtuosity of mystic adepts (which most theologians are not). The mystical path of meditation cultivates the embrace of form in possibilities so as to overcome dualism and apprehend the ultimate as the singular act of creation of all things as singularly together. The mystical path of contemplation, as this is turned into a term of art, cultivates the embrace of components as real and valuable in themselves without being harmonized in the experience of them, appearing as such as they are. The mystical path of the abyss combines elements from the meditative path of unity and the contemplative path of identifying with the others as such to grasp symbolically the entire existential field of realities as the product of the ultimate act. In all these paths, the adept is required to embody the symbols of ultimacy in material qualities of experience. The network meanings of the symbols are not enough for the content meaning of ultimacy to come through. The acquisition of the rich existential symbols is what makes these mystical paths so long and difficult. They amount to the creation of the mystic as a special bearer of the creation itself, as limited to the respects in which the embodied signs can represent the ontological creative act. The path of love brings all these together in the task of making the adept a lover rich enough to love the ontological ground of mutual relevance in each creature loved, and to love the ontological act of creation as the context in which every other lovely thing is found. A strong analogy exists between virtuoso human love of creatures and the creator, and the divine love in the ontological act of creation itself; in crucial religious ways, the ontological act of creation is love in the most profound sense. As such, the ontological act of love is the reciprocal of the love of the ultimate in the act of symbolic engagement of the ultimate in loving symbols. The limitation of this reciprocity is that the ultimate is engaged by us only in those respects in which our signs, intellectual, emotional, and physical, can represent the ultimate.

This limitation has astonishingly profound consequences. All of what has been proposed here is mostly false about the ultimate in the long run. Everything that has been claimed is an hypothesis about the ultimate, including what has been claimed about various methods and ways of understanding ultimacy. Although this volume defends the hypotheses on many levels, they are only hypotheses and most likely will be amended or rejected by thinkers in the future who can see things not apparent now. Moreover, the hypotheses only articulate ultimacy in the respects in which the signs in the hypotheses can refer to the ultimate. How many other respects are there in which ultimacy should be engaged? This question can never be answered even though we find new signs that reveal more respects for engagement, as we surely will. But if we do not know what other respects there are in which to interpret ultimacy, how can we know the limits of the respects in which we have good hypotheses now? We cannot. We cannot know those limits and therefore cannot fully understand what we think we know through the good hypotheses we have. In this sense, even these complex symbols of ultimacy are to be regarded as broken. Even being is to be known only through broken symbols. For this reason, any circumspect theology is apophatic, finally distancing itself from the steadiness of the best hypotheses.

But the apophatic moment is a mood of humility that should accompany all theological thinking. The best hypotheses surely will be broken, but not yet. When we have good reason to come to doubt them, then their brokenness provides stimulation to do better. Theology is inquiry that is always vulnerable to correction, even in the richest mystical embrace. But until there is reason to amend the hypotheses, the best hypotheses are the best guides to engaging the ultimate.

Despite the complexity of the many-angled approach to ultimacy in *Philosophical Theology One,* the merit of the cumulative argument here can be assayed broadly only through examining the existential aspects of religion, the topic of *Existence: Philosophical Theology Volume Two*, and the quotidian aspects, the topic of *Religion: Philosophical Theology Volume Three*.

Notes

NOTES TO THE PREFACE

1. Philosophy, especially metaphysical philosophy of the sort found here, needs to defend itself in the contemporary situation. Metaphysics is defined from many angles throughout *Philosophical Theology*, but is explained most systematically in *I, 2, iv* and *I, 9, i*.

2. See the bibliographical items below for the author to find the system. A summary of the core tenets, at least in an early version, is "Sketch of a System" in Neville, editor, *New Essays in Metaphysics*. Commentary material is in *Interpreting Neville*, edited by Nancy K. Frankenberry and J. Harley Chapman and *Theology in Global Context*, edited by Amos Yong and Peter G. Heltzel.

3. This conception of the public for philosophical theology is explored throughout these three volumes, but especially in *I, 3*.

4. I am a Christian of the Methodist denominational culture by birth and early training, the Missouri Midwest version, and am ordained in the United Methodist Church. I am also a Confucian by hard learning through comparative theology and practice and for several years have served on the Consultative Committee of the International Confucian Association, as well as being deeply involved in Buddhist theology and some kinds of practice. I am less well versed in the various kinds of Hinduism but the effort to overcome this limitation shows in the frequent treatments of Hindu themes in these volumes. I believe that the separation of Christianity, Judaism, and Islam in the first millennium was a mistaken way of dealing with different emphases within Hellenistic Semitic religious life. Moreover, I was educated in the West with English as my native tongue and for the most part am dependent on English translations and scholarship, although I have taught Sanskrit and studied Chinese as well as several European languages.

5. This conception of theology as including within it all the studies necessary to make cases for its first-order topics is an outgrowth of Paul Tillich's conception of theological system. It stands in contrast to Karl Barth's conception of theology as anti-system whose boundaries are very tight because they all have to do with determining religious (for him, Christian) identity. Barth viewed theology as a confession of Christian identity and that confession was based on a revelational starting point.

Nevertheless, cases need to be made for the revelational starting point in comparison with other revelational claims, in terms of philosophical conceptions of revelation, relative to liturgical and practical uses, with assessments of imaginative appeal, and so forth, so that the whole panoply of a theory of religion opens up.

6. See Keith Ward, *Religion and Revelation*, *Religion and Creation*, and *Religion and Human Nature*. See also T.W. Bartel, editor, *Comparative Theology: Essays for Keith Ward*.

7. See the analysis by William Wood in his "On the New Analytic Theology, or: The Road Less Traveled." His essay discusses the "field" exhibited in some recent anthologies in analytic philosophy, *A Reader in Contemporary Philosophical Theology*, edited by Oliver D. Crisp, *Analytic Theology: New Essays in Philosophy of Theology*, edited by Oliver D. Crisp and Michael C. Rea, *The Oxford Handbook of Philosophical Theology*, edited by Thomas P. Flint and Michael C. Rea, and *Oxford Readings in Philosophical Theology, Vol. 1: Trinity, Incarnation, Atonement*, and *Vol. 2: Providence, Scripture, and Resurrection*, edited by Michael C. Rea. One of the first analytical books was James F. Ross' *Philosophical Theology* in which he attempted to redirect the scholastic philosophy deriving from Thomas Aquinas into new forms provided by analytic philosophy, treating the concept of God, the existence of God, Thomas' proofs for God's existence, omnipotence, divine goodness and evil, and divine freedom in creating. He treated no religions or philosophical theological traditions other than Christianity, with the exception of a footnote reference to Avicenna. He took analytic philosophy's commitment to "justification in terms of consciousness alone" to justify ignoring the philosophical significance of other disciplinary approaches to his topics.

8. See Frankenberry's edited *Radical Interpretation in Religion*, especially her introduction and chapter 9.

9. "Analytic pragmatism" is a moniker popularized by Robert B. Brandom in his *Between Saying and Doing: Towards an Analytic Pragmatism*. In the afterword to that volume, he defends the importance of analytic philosophy in the mix he calls analytic pragmatism. His argument is to make distinctions clarifying criticisms of analytic philosophy as a movement, showing that many of them do not hold. In particular, he says that the ideal of a clear, unified argument in a justified ideal language, the goal of much analytic philosophy, always supposes a hermeneutic context that justifies and contextualizes the ideal language. He says that Wittgenstein and others, whom he also calls pragmatists, made this argument in favor of hermeneutics. For all this, there are many reasons, defended in *Philosophical Theology*, for not resting with the limitations of analytic philosophy even if it is not as bad as some of its critics claim.

10. Richard Rorty is famous for this point, both in his edited volume, *The Linguistic Turn* and in *Philosophy and the Mirror of Nature*.

11. On these points, see Frankenberry, *op. cit.*, p. xiv, and the discussions in *I, 2, 3*.

12. See Brandom, *Making it Explicit: Reasoning, Representing, and Discursive Commitment*, and also Jeffrey Stout's fine analysis of this in Frankenberry's *Radical Interpretation in Religion*.

13. See Francis X. Clooney, SJ, *Comparative Theology: Deep Learning Across Religious Borders*. See also Hugh Nicholson's "The Reunification of Theology and Comparison in the New Comparative Theology" and Reid B. Locklin and Hugh Nicholson's "The Return of Comparative Theology."

14. See Wesley J. Wildman, *Religious Philosophy as Multidisciplinary Inquiry: Envisioning a Future for the Philosophy of Religion*.

15. *III, pt 1* discusses the contributions and limitations of the sciences in more detail.

16. See Justus Buchler's concept of exhibitive judgment and exhibitive query in his *Nature and Judgment* and *The Main of Light*.

17. See Charles S. Peirce, "A Neglected Argument for the Reality of God" in volume six of *The Collected Papers of Charles Sanders Peirce*, pp. 311–339, and in *The Essential Peirce*, volume 2, pp. 434–450.

18. This in fact is argued in *III, pt 1*. Inquiry in the sense of *explanation* of religion in terms of something else gives way to inquiry in the sense of *understanding*, including understanding causal connections of religion with other things.

19. See *I, pt 4, si* for a retrospective tracing out of the modes of argument employed here.

NOTES TO THE INTRODUCTION

1. "Broken Symbols" is a phrase of Paul Tillich's. See Neville, *The Truth of Broken Symbols*, for an analysis of that phrase as a technical term in this system.

2. For a detailed example of this, see the discussion of Abhinavagupta' conception of Shiva as consciousness in *III, 7, Prologue*.

3. For an example of this, see the discussion of Zhou Dunyi in *I, 12, i*.

4. *I, 10, 12* argue that the existential field is constituted by the way in which determinate things condition one another so as to be determinate with respect to each other; it is not an independent field in which things are separately located. Existential location is a function of the ways a determinate thing is related to other things.

5. See Asad's *Formations of the Secular*, and the detailed analysis of "religious situations" in *III, 3–4*.

6. Tomoko Masuzawa has shown how complicated and historically conditioned the very notion of "world religions" is; see her *The Invention of World Religions*. Because *Philosophical Theology* aims to present a viable theology for our contemporary religious situation, it focuses mainly on the Axial Age religions, as discussed in *III, 2*. But even the identity of these religions is distorted by the conventional labels, and the argument here in part is to find another way of thinking about identity in religious traditions.

7. For a fairly comprehensive review of modern Western attempts to define religion, and the historical relations among them, see the first chapter of Walter H. Capps *Religious Studies: The Making of a Discipline*. There he treats the views of Descartes, Kant, Schleiermacher, Feuerbach, Marx, Ritschl, Freud, Bloch, James, Otto, Dewey, Nygren, Barth, and Tillich. See also Gavin Flood's *Beyond Phenomenology: Rethinking the Study of Religion*.

8. All the points about Tillich in this paragraph are to be found in his *Systematic Theology*, volume 1.

9. In addition to volume 1 of his *Systematic Theology*, see Tillich, *The Religious Situation* and *Theology of Culture*.

10. In the third volume of his *Systematic Theology*, Tillich attempted, with some success, to move beyond individual existential ultimate concern to historical and social issues. *Philosophical Theology Two* focuses more on individuals as religious and *Three* more on the social aspects of religion, although both maintain the insistence that religion

is individuals participating in religious groups, not the groups themselves. *II, pt 4* focuses on individuals accessing religion through various dimensions of participation.

11. Mark C. Taylor, *After God*, p. 12.

12. "Religious Situation" is the title of an early book by Paul Tillich. See *III, 3*.

13. See especially Daniel Boyarin, *Border Lines* and Thomas Sizgorich, *Violence and Belief in Late Antiquity*.

14. See Sizgorich, chapter 1.

15. For the secularist point of view, in extreme form, see the writings of the "New Atheists," especially Richard Dawkins and Daniel Dennett. In the new preface to the *God Delusion*, Dawkins explains why he will not identify religion with its moderate and liberal streams in addition to its ultraconservative ones: They are not as bad.

16. See *Strong Religion: The Rise of Fundamentalisms around the World* by Gabriel A. Almond, R. Scott Appleby, and Emmanuel Sivan, p. 17. Italics in the original. This book is a summary of the massive Fundamentalism Project of the American Academy of Arts and Sciences.

17. For a thorough and general introduction of the term *quasi-religions*, see John E. Smith's *Quasi-Religions: Humanism, Marxism and Nationalism*. The analysis of ultimate concerns for *Philosophical Theology* is in *I, 5*.

18. He analyzes the Humanism of thinkers such as Corliss Lamont and Paul Kurtz, Marxism and its critics, and nationalism that takes the Nazi movement as the extreme case.

19. Whitehead's major statement of this is *Process and Reality*. See *III, 9*.

20. Hence, this is a limit to the fruitfulness of Robert Brandom's analytical pragmatic approach, which is fully enmeshed in the logic of propositional functions, although it does wonderfully inventive things with them.

21. The phrase "making cases" was made important in theology by Van A. Harvey in his *The Historian and the Believer: The Morality of Historical Knowledge and Christian Belief*. His development of the phrase derived from Stephen Toulmin's *The Uses of Argument*. Toulmin made the best case for his theory of making cases in his *Human Understanding: The Collective Use and Evolution of Concepts*.

22. See Barth's *On Religion* and the introduction by Garrett Green. Barth, of course, had a great many gripes about religion, but they all had to do with representing the ultimate, God for him, as contained and explained within the web of human reasoning, thus domesticating the gracious arbitrariness of creation. He was rather limited to Christian ways of making this point, however, and often vacillated between limiting all revelatory engagements to Jesus Christ (as he understood him as a Christian theologian) and evacuating Jesus Christ as a revelatory event and person so as to mean anything that is revelatory anywhere. That he recognized this vacillation and called it "dialectical" does not help it as an intellectual strategy.

23. Wesley J. Wildman has pointed out a similar parallel between Barth and pragmatic theological method that denies that God is a determinate entity. Barth attacked the analogy of being, the Neo-Platonic theory of "vestiges" of the divine in nature, all natural theology, and the proclivity to anthropomorphize because these theological strategies fail to respect the infinite otherness of God. From the standpoint of the pragmatic "religious naturalism," as Wildman calls the position he shares with *Philosophical Theology*, there can be nothing determinate in God apart from the world to be analogized, leave traces, conclude an inference from nature, or be morphed into human-like form. Thus Barth's vigorous defense of revelation surprisingly sup-

ports some of the conclusions of Wildman's program of religious philosophy and also *Philosophical Theology*. See Wildman, *Science and Religious Anthropology*, p. 26.

24. A current useful summary of the ways in which neuroscience, cognitive science, evolutionary biology, and physical anthropology contribute to the study of universal characteristics of religion is Patrick McNamara, *Neuroscience of Religious Experience*. For a broader view, see Wesley J. Wildman, *Science and Religious Anthropology*.

25. See, for instance, Talal Asad, *Genealogies of Religion*, and also the measured discussion in Gavin Flood, *Beyond Phenomenology: Rethinking the Study of Religion*. Tomoko Masuzawa, *The Invention of World Religions*, is helpful here.

26. Smith, *Quasi Religions*, p. 1.

27. The phrase "sacred canopy" was invented by Peter Berger in his landmark *The Sacred Canopy: Elements of a Sociological Theory of Religion*. The concept of sacred canopies is developed here in ways Berger did not do. His own particular interest was in the dialectic between externalization—the projection of human concepts or symbols on the world, objectification—the actual construction of physical and semiotic artifacts in the world, and internalization—the reappropriation of that meaning-laden world in subjective experience. He emphasizes the dynamic or shifting qualities in this dialectic as human imagination adds to what is externalized, hard realities shape what can be projected onto it, and reappropriation gives new meaning to the ideas, extending them into new areas and changing circumstances. His analysis, coming as it does from sociology of knowledge, does not focus as much on issues of individual relations with sacred canopies as this *Philosophical Theology* does.

28. This point is well made by Wesley J. Wildman in his "Theological Literacy: Problem and Promise." Wildman distinguishes two types of theology. The first type teaches the symbols of a religious tradition, their logic and practical implications. These are the symbols in a sacred canopy, as worked into a larger practical worldview (in a sense explained later), and knowledge of the working of these symbols constitutes a kind of theological literacy. But sometimes things happen that render some or all of the sacred canopy implausible. Wildman's example was the 1999 shooting of students at Columbine High School, he might have talked about the experience of the Holocaust for Jews, or the Dong Dynasty defeat of Confucianism by Buddhism in the imperial court, or the failure of Jesus to re appear according to St. Paul's time table. The second type of theology is the kind that kicks in when the sacred canopy is rendered implausible or inadequate for the circumstances, recognizing the failure of the traditional religious literacy. Sometimes the old symbols can be patched together again, said Wildman. But in the end, the theologians who do the second kind of theology recognize the limits of all symbols.

NOTES TO PART I PRELIMINARY REMARKS

1. "Vagueness" was first analyzed by the founder of pragmatism, Charles S. Peirce. See, for example, his widely anthologized essays, "Issues of Pragmaticism" and "Consequences of Critical Common-Sensism," which are found in volume 5 of *The Collected Papers of Charles Sanders Peirce*. An analysis of his texts is found in Neville, *Ritual and Deference*, chapter 11; see also Neville, *Normative Cultures*, pp. 62–68. The systematic use of vagueness in comparative theology, along with elaborate philosophical discussions, is in the three volumes of the Comparative Religious Ideas Project, *The Human Condition*, *Ultimate Realities*, and *Religious Truth*, edited by Neville.

2. See "Cooking the Last Fruit of Nihilism: Buddhist Approaches to Ultimate Reality," by Malcolm David Eckel with John J. Thatamanil in Neville, editor, *Ultimate Realities*, chapter 6.

3. See the first volume of his *Systematic Theology*. Tillich's notion of ultimacy is discussed at length in Neville, *On the Scope and Truth of Theology*, chapter 1.

4. See Tillich's *Systematic Theology*, volume 1, pp. 14–17.

NOTES TO CHAPTER ONE

1. *The Sacred Canopy*, p. 19. Berger's theory has been extraordinarily influential. Recent studies such as Mark C. Taylor's *After God* extend it in detailed and highly literate ways.

2. *The Sacred Canopy*, pp. 22–23.

3. *The Sacred Canopy*, pp. 25–26.

4. See his discussion of these alternatives at *ibid*.

5. See Bellah, *Religion in Human Evolution*, Preface.

6. See Barth's negative comments on Tillich in the new Foreword to the Harper Torchbook edition; see Tillich's negative comments on Barth in the first volume of his *Systematic Theology*, pp. 4–5. On the comparison of the two regarding the nature of theology, see Neville, *Realism in Religion*, chapter 1.

7. The *Axial Age*, a term coined and explained by Karl Jaspers in *The Origin and Goal of History*, refers to the period between 800 and 200 BCE when Confucianism, Daoism, Buddhism, Hinduisms, Zoroastrianism, Judaism, and Greek and Roman Paganism were invented; Christianity and Islam, deriving in many ways from Judaism, also count as Axial Age religions. The term will be explained in the texts of the three volumes of *Philosophical Theology*, especially in *III, 2*. Karen Armstrong gives a popular but very thorough and accurate account of the Axial Age in her *The Great Transformation*. The new definitive study is Robert N. Bellah, *Religion in Human Evolution: From the Paleolithic to the Axial Age*.

8. The term *finite/infinite contrast* is developed throughout Neville, *The Truth of Broken Symbols*, especially in chapter 2.

9. See Whitehead's *Process and Reality*, p. 22, where he defines contrast as the eighth category of existence, and pp. 110–129 where he defines contrast as the locus of value.

10. Immanuel Kant, *Critique of Pure Reason*, A 102.

11. For an analysis of the grasping of a harmony, see Neville, *Realism in Religion*, chapter 8. For a philosophical cosmology that accounts for the intentionality of judgments regarding harmonies, see Neville, *Reconstruction of Thinking*, chapters 6–7, and *Recovery of the Measure*, part 4.

12. For the most technical expositions of this theory of harmony, see *I, 10* and Neville, *God the Creator*, chapter 2.

13. This point is argued in detail in *I, pt. 3*.

14. This point, of course, needs to be qualified by degrees of commitment, on which see *I, 4, iv* and *II, 14–16*.

15. This is Berger speaking as a sociologist. He is also a theologian and treats certain elements of sacred canopies as "signals of transcendence," which involves a semiotics of reference. See his *A Far Glory*, for instance.

16. Neville, *On the Scope and Truth of Theology*, is the volume in which issues of truth in theology are laid out in detail as an introduction to this *Philosophical Theology*.

17. It is explained and defended at length in Neville, *Recovery of the Measure*. It is applied in detail to religious symbols in Neville, *The Truth of Broken Symbols*.

18. Coherence, consistency, adequacy, and applicability are the criteria for philosophic systems enunciated and explained by Alfred North Whitehead in *Process and Reality*, chapter 1.

NOTES TO CHAPTER TWO

1. See Carl G. Vaught's study of Augustine in two volumes, *The Journey toward God in Augustine's* Confessions, and *Encounters with God in Augustine's* Confessions, especially chapter 2 of the latter.

2. Malcolm David Eckel, with John J. Thatamanil, "Cooking the Last Fruit of Nihilism." See their related essays, "Beginningless Ignorance" and "With a Great Noise and Mighty Whirlpools the Ganges Flowed Backwards."

3. See Frei's *Types of Christian Theology* and Lindbeck's *The Nature of Doctrine*.

4. This discussion of Kant derives from his *Critique of Pure Reason*. The present point about putting questions to nature comes from the Preface to the Second Edition.

5. See Kant's discussion in the chapter on the Second Analogy in the *Critique of Pure Reason*, beginning at B 232.

6. See, noting the title, subtitle, and preface, Edwin Diller Starbuck's *The Psychology of Religion: An Empirical Study of the Growth of Religious Consciousness*, with a preface by William James. In the preface, James acknowledged his reluctant conversion to statistical approaches to the study of religion. See also Leuba, whom James frequently cites in *The Varieties of Religious Experience* along with Starbuck. For James' interaction with Freud (and Jung), see George Prochnik's *Putnam Camp* and also Robert D. Richardson's *William James: In the Maelstrom of American Modernism*, especially chapter 90.

7. See, for example, the explicit disclaimers about reference and metaphysics in Patrick McNamara's *Neuroscience and Religious Experience*. For further discussion of reductionism in the sciences attempting to understand religion see *III, 1*.

8. Rappaport, *Ritual and Religion in the Making of Humanity*, p. 3.

9. See Tanner, *Theories of Culture: A New Agenda for Theology*.

10. See Emile Durkheim, *The Elementary Forms of the Religious Life*.

11. See Wesley J. Wildman, "The Significance of the Evolution of Religious Belief and Behavior for Religious Studies and Theology" for a comprehensive critical but appreciative analysis of the pros and cons of reductionism in the evolutionary and biological studies of religion.

12. See, for example, the prefaces to the first and second editions of the *Critique of Pure Reason*, which have this as their main themes. Many readers penetrated little further than these prefaces, but still got Kant's main point. For an account of Kant in his intellectual and social situation, see Manfred Kuehn's *Kant: A Biography*.

13. See especially Descartes' *Rules for the Direction of the Mind*, and *Discourse on Method*, and *Meditations*, in *Philosophical Works of Descartes*.

14. See Spinoza's *On the Improvement of the Understanding* in R.H.M. Elwes, *Benedict de Spinoza*, volume 1. See also Leibniz' *Discourse on Metaphysics* and *Monadology* in *Leibniz*, translated by Montgomery. Behind the perhaps exaggerated claims for reason lay an existential problem for Descartes, Spinoza, and Leibniz, and doubtless many others. Spinoza expressed it with raw courage in his first work, *The Emendation of the Intellect*, the first sentence of which is this: "After experience had taught me that all the things which regularly occur in ordinary life are empty and futile,

and I saw that all the things which were the cause of object of my fear had nothing of good or bad in themselves, except insofar as [my] mind was moved by them, I resolved at last to try to find out whether there was anything which would be the true good, capable of communicating itself, and which alone would affect the mind, all others being rejected—whether there was something which, once found and acquired, would continuously give me the greatest joy, to eternity." *The Collected Works*, ed. Curley, p. 7. The answer that Descartes, Spinoza, and Leibniz gave to this question was the intuitive understanding of reason; Spinoza's *Ethics* developed the point in existential terms. For Descartes' contextual biographical details see Desmond M. Clarke's *Descartes: A Biography*.

15. This is the whole point of Part I of the *Critique of Pure Reason*, the Transcendental Doctrine of Elements.

16. This is the point of Part II of the first *Critique*, Transcendental Doctrine of Method.

17. Peirce argued against Descartes, and by implication Spinoza and Leibniz, that all thought is hypothetical and none is intuitive, as the "light of reason" metaphor would suggest. See his essays "Questions concerning Certain Capacities Claimed for Man" and "Consequences of Certain Incapacities," in *The Essential Peirce*, volume 1. His theory of metaphysical hypotheses is found in many sources, especially "A Neglected Argument for the Reality of God" and "The Seven Systems of Metaphysics," in *The Essential Peirce*, volume 2. On Peirce's theory of metaphysics as hypothesis, see Neville, *The Highroad around Modernism,* chapter 1, and *Realism in Religion*, chapters 6-7. For its application to religious metaphysics, see Neville, *On the Scope and Truth of Theology*, especially chapter 6.

18. See his extraordinary argument in "A Neglected Argument for the Reality of God," which is really about hypothesis construction and testing.

19. Peirce's mathematical account of induction is idiosyncratic and controversial.

20. See Kant's *Critique of Pure Reasoni*, B 797–810.

21. See this argument in Neville, *The Highroad around Modernism*, pp. 138–140.

22. For example, contrary to Kant's claims that Euclidean geometry and physical determinism are synthetic a priori, there are non-Euclidean geometries and probabilistic causal patterns.

23. See his *Existence and Being*, p. 328.

24. See *Process and Reality*, e.g., pp. xiii, 22.

25. On the critical relation of *Philosophical Theology* to Whitehead's metaphysics, see Neville, *The Cosmology of Freedom*, Part 1; *Creativity and God*; and *Reconstruction of Thinking*, Parts 2–3. See also the critical defense of Whitehead by David Ray Griffin in *Whitehead's Radically Different Postmodern Philosophy*, chapter 9, and the response in Neville, "A Letter of Grateful and Affectionate Response to David Ray Griffin's *Whitehead's Radically Different Postmodern Philosophy: An Argument for Its Contemporary Relevance*.

NOTES TO CHAPTER THREE

1. This paragraph states the main outlines of the pragmatism of Charles S. Peirce and John Dewey. A defense of it, far more technical than theirs, is in Neville, *Reconstruction of Thinking* and *Recovery of the Measure*.

2. See Edmund Husserl's *Cartesian Meditations*.

3. See the definitive study of this in modern philosophy by Warren G. Frisina, *The Unity of Knowledge and Action*.

4. See Exodus 11–13 in the Hebrew Bible.

5. See Leviticus 16 in the Hebrew Bible.

6. See *III, 13, i* for an interpretation of the meaning of this sacrifice symbology; see Neville, *Symbols of Jesus*, chapter 2, for an interpretation of the sacrifice themes around Jesus as atonement for blood guilt.

7. For a more complete analysis of *network meaning*, as a technical term compared with *content meaning*, see Neville, *The Tao and the Daimon*, chapter 11. The technical terms are explained as the argument progresses throughout this and the subsequent volumes of *Philosophical Theology*.

8. On the timing of the learning of religious signs, see Candace S. Alcorta, "Religion and the Life Course: Is Adolescence and 'Experience Expectant' Period for Religious Transmission?"

9. This is a version of the formula developed by Peirce in many places, for example the papers "Questions concerning Certain Faculties Claimed for Man" and "Consequences of Four Incapacities."

10. See Neville, *Ritual and Deference*, chapters 3 and 8, for the development of the connection between Confucian ritual theory and pragmatic semiotics. See also *II, 9*.

11. See Berger's *The Sacred Canopy*.

12. Review Neville, *Recovery of the Measure*.

13. See Barrett's "Skillful Engagement and the 'Effort after Value': An Axiological Theory of the Origins of Religion."

14. See John E. Smith's *The Spirit of American Philosophy* and *Purpose and Thought: The Meaning of Pragmatism*, and Bernstein's *Praxis and Action* and *The Pragmatic Turn*, among the many books published by each of them.

15. On neo-pragmatism and its variants, in addition to the works of Smith and Bernstein previously cited, see Charley D. Hardwick and Donald A. Crosby, editors, *Pragmatism, Neo-Pragmatism, and Religion: Conversations with Richard Rorty* and Sheila Greeve Davaney and Warren G. Frisina, editors, *The Pragmatic Century: Conversations with Richard J. Bernstein*. In the former, this author coined the term *Paleopragmatism* for the parallel development of metaphysical pragmatism with neo-pragmatism. In the latter, see Frankenberry's defense of Rorty against Bernstein's insistence on experience or Peircean "secondness," "Bernstein and Rorty on Justification by Faith Alone." See also Cornel West's *Keeping Faith*, which discusses many of the Neo-pragmatists. See the Library of Living Philosophers volume, *The Philosophy of Richard Rorty*, edited by Randall E. Auxier and Lewis Edwin Hahn.

16. See Whitehead, *Process and Reality*, p. 181.

17. Paul Weiss lived more than a century and published until the very end of his life. Among the most important for pragmatic themes, although seldom acknowledged as such, are his *Nature and Man, Modes of Being, The God We Seek,* and *First Considerations*. The last has responses from Rorty and from me, with answers again from Weiss. See also the Library of Living Philosophers volume, *The Philosophy of Paul Weiss*, edited by Lewis Edwin Hahn.

18. For an analysis of this connection between pragmatism of the metaphysical sort and process philosophy, see Neville, *Realism in Religion*, chapter 9, "Whitehead and Pragmatism." That chapter has bibliographical information on the authors discussed.

19. See, for example, Richard Bernstein's magisterial *The Pragmatic Turn*, which fails to deal with any of the metaphysical pragmatists.

20. See Jeremy Wanderer's *Robert Brandom* for a study of Brandom's philosophy and its particular place in the contemporary analytical philosophical scene. Brandom's major book is *Making It Explicit*, and his main discussions of pragmatism relative to analytic philosophy are in *Between Saying and Doing: Towards an Analytic Pragmatism* and *Perspectives on Pragmatism*.

21. See Wilfrid Sellars, *Empiricism and the Philosophy of Mind* for the "myth of the given." Sellars argues that things are always experienced with categories that are already implicated in inferences about the things and their contexts. This author was a student of Sellars at Yale when Richard Rorty and Richard Bernstein were also students there.

22. See Peirce's essays, "Questions concerning Certain Faculties Claimed for Man," "Some Consequences of Four Incapacities," and "Grounds of Validity of the Laws of Logic: Further Consequences of four Incapacities," in *The Collected Papers of Charles Sanders Peirce*, volume 5, and in volume 1 of the *Essential Papers*.

23. See Richard Bernstein, *The Pragmatic Turn*.

24. For *Philosophical Theology*, this work was done in Neville, *Recovery of the Measure*.

25. See Rorty's early book by that name, which anthologizes many of the important philosophers defining this limitation to philosophy's subject matter.

26. See especially part 1 of Frankenberry's *Radical Interpretation in Religion*.

27. This point has been debated carefully by Nancy Frankenberry and by me in Frankenberry and Chapman's *Interpreting Neville*, chapter 6, "On the Very Idea of Symbolic Meaning," by Frankenberry (the title is a play on Davidson's "On the Very Idea of a Conceptual Scheme) and my reply on pp. 299–304. See also Frankenberry's "Religion as a 'mobile army of metaphors'" in her *Radical Interpretation in Religion*.

28. Peirce held that there are three basic categories of things. One is the category of things that are simply in themselves, not different from other things, just themselves; he called these Firsts. The second is the category of things that are simply different from other things, resistant, not different in any respect but just different; these he called Seconds. The third is the category of things that are what they are by mediating between two or more things; he called these Thirds. Just about anything we can designate has its own internal quality, its Firstness, and also its oppositional identity, its Secondness, and also mediates among other things, its Thirdness. Peirce wrote on signs in most of his philosophical papers. Volumes 2 and 3 of the *Collected Papers* are the most concentrated writings, although not the most popular. *Peirce on Signs*, edited by James Hoopes, collects most of the well-known and influential papers. T.L. Short's *Peirce's Theory of Signs* is a good study orienting Peirce's semiotics to analytic philosophy. Robert S. Corrington's *An Introduction to C. S. Peirce: Philosopher, Semiotician, and Ecstatic Naturalist* orients Peirce's semiotics to theological concerns. Corrington's *A Semiotic Theory of Theology and Philosophy* develops a pragmatic approach rather parallel to that in this systematic philosophical theology. Michael L. Raposa's *Peirce's Philosophy of Religion* is also a fine study that draws out theological implications for Peirce's semiotic theory.

29. Terrence W. Deacon has argued, using Peirce's categories of reference, that the development of symbolic or conventional reference is what makes language possible, or, rather, is the development of language itself. See his *The Symbolic Species*, especially chapter 3, and *Incomplete Nature: How Mind Emerged from Matter*, chapters 15–17.

30. See John Brockington, "The Sanskrit Epics."
31. See, for instance, their *Philosophy in the Flesh*.
32. See Neville, *The Truth of Broken Symbols*; the phrase, "broken symbol," comes from Paul Tillich.
33. See Anthony J. Saldarini, with Joseph Kanofsky, "To Practice Together Truth and Humility, Justice and Law, Love of Merciful Kindness and Modest Behavior."

NOTES TO CHAPTER FOUR

1. See Xunzi's essay on Nature (or Heaven), *Tien*, chapter 17 in volume 3 of *Xunzi*. For an elaborate commentary, see Edward Machle's *Nature and Heaven in the Xunzi*. For an analysis of the notion in the context of orientation, see Neville, *Religion in Late Modernity*, chapter 2.
2. This is not entirely congruent with the way Eliade or other phenomenologists define the sacred, although it has much overlap. See *I*, 7 for further discussion.
3. See Roy Rappaport's *Ritual and Religion in the Making of Humanity*.
4. This was one of the more important conclusions of the Cross Cultural Comparative Religious Ideas Project. See its volume, *Ultimate Realities*, Neville, editor, especially chapter 7.
5. See Michael Witzel's "Vedas and Upanisads" in Gavin Flood's *Hinduism* for a discussion of this.
6. See Whitehead's contrast of the reason of Odysseus with the reason of Plato in his *The Function of Reason*.
7. See his *Between Heaven and Earth*.
8. See *Between Heaven and Earth*, chapter 6.
9. See Erving Goffman's *Asylums*.
10. See also the article by Alcorta referenced in the previous chapter.

NOTE TO PART I: SUMMARY IMPLICATIONS

1. See *III*, 3, 4, and also the essays by many distinguished authors in *Theology in Global Context*, edited by Amos Yong and Peter G. Heltzel.

NOTES TO PART II: PRELIMINARY REMARKS

1. Some controversy exists about whether heritability is strictly an individual matter or is a function of groups. See David Sloan Wilson, *Darwin's Cathedral*, for a defense of group evolution.
2. But see Neville, *Reconstruction of Thinking*, Part 2, and *Recovery of the Measure*. See *III*, 1.

NOTES TO CHAPTER FIVE

1. A compelling case for this point is made by Malcolm David Eckel in his "Cooking the Last Fruits of Nihilism." See also *I*, pt. 1, pr.
2. The distinction between ontological and anthropological ultimates came out of the discussions of the Comparative Religious Ideas Project and is recorded in Neville, *Ultimate Realities*. The distinction needs further elaboration than was given in that project.

3. This is a theme through nearly all of Tillich's work. But see especially *Dynamics of Faith*, chapter 1, and *Systematic Theology*, volume 1, Introduction.

4. See the review of the scientific material in Patrick McNamara's *Neuroscience of Religious Experience*.

5. The subtitle of Kierkegaard's work is *Spiritual Preparation for the Office of Confession*, indicating the enormous discipline required. On developing the capacity for desire or love, with distinctions from will and discipline, see Neville, *Soldier, Sage, Saint*, and *III, 11*. The soldier is the hero of will, the saint of the heart, symbolizing desire and love.

6. See Sung Bae Park's *Buddhist Faith and Sudden Enlightenment* on the meaning of the vows of the bodhisattva; Park's analysis is discussed in *III, 6*.

7. See Kierkegaard's *Fear and Trembling*. See also Neville, *Soldier, Sage, Saint*, the passages on the soldier, and *III, 11, ii*.

8. See Tu's *Humanity and Self-Cultivation*, chapter 6, p. 89.

9. On the "renouncer" traditions in South Asian religions, see Patrick Olivelle's "The Renouncer Tradition."

10. Chapter 5 of the Daodejing begins: "Heaven and Earth are not Humane (*Jen*). They regard all things as straw dogs. The sage is not humane. He regards all people as straw dogs." The straw dogs in question were dolls used in a ritual after which they were burned.

NOTES TO CHAPTER SIX

1. On this distinction, see Robert Bellah's *Religion in Human Evolution*.

2. See Jonathan Goldstein's *Peoples of an Almighty God*.

3. See Jon D. Levenson's *Creation and the Persistence of Evil* for a careful comparison of the Marduk and Yahweh creation stories, citing both similarities and significant differences.

4. See Kant's *Critique of Judgment*, the "Analytic of the Sublime." The remark about the starry heavens and the moral law begins the Conclusion of his *Critique of Practical Reason* and is inscribed on Kant's tombstone.

5. On Perennial Philosophy see Huston Smith's *Forgotten Truth: The Primordial Tradition* and Frithjof Schuon's *The Transcendent Unity of Religions*. Perhaps the most creative and influential contemporary Perennial Philosophers is Seyyed Hossein Nasr; see his *Knowledge and the Sacred*. *The Philosophy of Seyyed Hossein Nasr*, edited by Hahn, Auxier, and Stone, contains a fascinating discussion of Perennial Philosophy from many perspectives, along with responses to various critics by Nasr.

NOTES TO CHAPTER SEVEN

1. See Wesley J. Wildman's theological anthropology of microbes in his *Science and Religious Anthropology*, chapter 8. Only at first does it make your skin crawl!

2. See the Christological significance of road rage in Neville, *Symbols of Jesus*, chapter 2.

3. See his *The Idea of the Holy*.

4. In noting the lack of much empirical scientific knowledge, we should take care to allow that such "savage" cultures might have a significant store of nonscientific empirical knowledge, such as the medicinal properties of herbs, that exceeds scien-

tific knowledge (because modern science tends to deny or overlook empirical claims whose causal structure cannot be imagined in modern paradigms, as in the medical dismissal of acupuncture).

5. See Robert S. Corrington's analysis of "sacred folds" in *Nature's Religion* and related material in *Nature's Self* and *Nature and Spirit*.

6. See Kant's *Critique of Pure Reason*, the chapter on "Schematism."

7. See Ricoeur's *Symbolism of Evil*, chapter 1 and following.

NOTES TO CHAPTER EIGHT

1. A phrase descriptive of Barth attributed to David Kelsey.

2. See Eliade's The *Sacred and the Mundane*, chapter 2.

3. See, for instance, the introductory material in Frankenberry's *Radical Interpretation in Religion*.

4. For a fascinating account of this metaphysics, see Francis H. Cook's *Hua-yen Buddhism: The Jewel Net of Indra* and Steve Odin's *Process Metaphysics and Hua-Yen Buddhism*. One of the most astonishing classical texts is the Lotus Sutra.

5. See Tu Weiming's *Centrality and Commonality* and *Humanity and Self-Cultivation*. See also Neville, *Boston Confucianism*.

6. See James E. Miller's *Daoism: A Short Introduction*.

7. Perhaps the most important positive interpretation of narratives at a fundamental if not ultimate level is by Paul Ricoeur who coined the distinction between first and second naiveté.

8. I owe this point to Bert Harrell in conversation.

NOTES TO PART III: PRELIMINARY REMARKS

1. The phrase is developed in Dewey's major metaphysical work, *Experience and Nature*. See the discussion of metaphysics in *I, 6, iii*.

2. Martin Heidegger is noteworthy for raising the question of being in distinction from the being of beings. See his *Being and Time*, especially the introduction. See also his *The Question of Being* and *What Is a Thing?*

3. The subtitle of Whitehead's *Process and Reality* is *An Essay in Cosmology*.

4. As Whitehead argued in *Science and the Modern World*.

5. See his *Summa Theologiae*, especially Part I, questions 2–3. For a classic discussion, see Etienne Gilson's *The Christian Philosophy of St. Thomas Aquinas*.

NOTES TO CHAPTER NINE

1. See, for instance, his *Pluralistic Universe*. See also Robert D. Richardson's biography, *William James: In the Maelstrom of American Modernism*, for a sensitive account of the emotional and existential reasons for James' brand of pluralism and anti-monism.

2. See his discussions of the "Category of the Ultimate" in *Process and Reality*, part I, chapter 2.

3. Whitehead's technical way of saying this was to claim that God has no negative prehensions.

4. Weiss taught at Yale University as Sterling Professor for many years and was the teacher of this author in the late 1950s and early 1960s; after retirement from

Yale he taught for many years at The Catholic University of America until his nineties. Weiss was the founder of *The Review of Metaphysics* and also of The Metaphysical Society of America.

5. A more elaborate version of this discussion of Weiss is in Neville, *God the Creator*, pp. 51–59.

6. *Modes of Being*, p. 512.

7. *Ibid.*

8. *Ibid.*, p. 513.

9. Weiss used the term *nonessential components* rather than *conditional components*, which is my term. But I adopted the theory of essential and conditional components from Weiss in the argument under discussion, and changed the term because the "nonessential" components are just as necessary as the essential components to things. Weiss first distinguished essential from conditional components in *Nature and Man*. He usually calls the components "features." In many of my own writings, I have used "features" rather than "components," following Weiss.

10. This argument is a summary of the longer version in Neville, *God the Creator*, pp. 16–22.

11. Keith Ward, *Religion and Creation*, especially part 2.

12. The medievals used "formal reality" to indicate the reality things have in themselves or on their own; "objective reality" is the reality things have for knowers insofar as they are objects of knowledge.

13. On these points, see Thomas' *Summa Theologiae*, I. 14, "Of God's Knowledge."

14. Aquinas, *Metaphysics*, IV, lect. 1, no. 535, in Anderson, James F., p. 37.

15. Aquinas, *De Veritate*, Q. 2,a.ii, in Anderson, James F., p. 41.

16. Loc. Cit.

17. Loc. Cit.

18. Scotus, John Duns, *Philosophical Writings*, edited by Wolter, p. 15. Thomas actually accepted this point. See his Summa Theologiae, Pt. I. Q. 13, a. 2.

NOTES TO CHAPTER TEN

1. See Whitehead's *Process and Reality*, pp. 190, 219 ff.

2. See F.H. Bradley's *Appearance and Reality: A Metaphysical Essay*.

3. These four senses of the experience of value are the principal topics of Neville, *Axiology of Thinking*, a trilogy consisting of *Reconstruction of Thinking* (for imagination), *Recovery of the Measure* (for interpretation), and *Normative Cultures* (for theorizing and the pursuit of responsibility).

4. See Neville, *Recovery of the Measure*, divisions 2–3.

5. Plato said:

> In like manner, then, you are to say that the objects of knowledge not only receive from the presence of the good their being known, but their very existence and essence is derived to them from it, though the good itself is not essence but still transcends essence in dignity and surpassing power. Republic book 6, 509b. Shorey translation, in Hamilton and Cairns, *Plato: Collected Dialogues*.

6. For a more detailed analysis, systematically connected to this one, see also Neville, *Eternity and Time's Flow*.

7. Its main antecedents are Plato, Scotus, Dewey, and Whitehead. For discussions of those antecedents and their contributions, see Neville, *The Cosmology of Freedom*, chapter 3 and *Realism in Religion*, chapter 8.

8. This is the overall point of Neville, *Axiology of Thinking*. *Reconstruction of Thinking*, part 1, analyzes the fact-value distinction in moderns science; part 2 presents a theory of imagination as perception of value. *Recovery of the Measure* provides the detailed philosophical cosmology that allows for both science and the veridical experience and criticism of value. *Normative Cultures* develops a theory of theorizing that recognizes value and a theory of culture that accounts for science and valuation. These arguments do not need to be repeated in the present volume.

9. For masterful discussions of aesthetic judgment in this generalized sense see John Dewey's *Art as Experience* and Justus Buchler's *The Main of Light*.

10. For a more extensive discussion of this complicated point about a person's essential components from the past and future as well as the present, see Neville, *The Cosmology of Freedom*, chapter 2, and *Recovery of the Measure*, division 2.

11. See Neville, *Eternity and Time's Flow*.

12. See Tillich's *The Dynamics of Faith*.

13. But see Neville, *Recovery of the Measure*, divisions 2 and 3.

14. For an analysis of the competition between formal justice and component piety, especially around the HIV/AIDS virus, see Neville, *A Theology Primer*, chapter 6, especially pp. 67–68.

15. On eternal immensity, see *Eternity and Time's Flow*, parts 3 and 4; that book focuses more on eternity than on immensity.

16. *Eternity and Time's Flow* makes this case in a careful critique of the alternative Whiteheadian account of the passage of time.

17. Discussions of value-identity in *Philosophical Theology Two* and *Three* elaborate this distinction between subjective and objective kinds of value-identity.

NOTES TO CHAPTER ELEVEN

1. For a careful explication of the physics of entanglement as well as some of its theological implications, see Kirk Wegter-McNelly, *The Entangled God: Divine Relationality and Quantum Physics*.

2. See the discussion in John J. Thatamanil's *The Imminent Divine*.

3. See the argument in his *Appearance and Reality*.

4. See Plotinus, *Enneads*, the Fifth Ennead, especially 1.6–7.

5. See the texts of Descartes and Leibniz on this in Neville, *Realism in Religion*, chapter 13. That chapter parallels the positions on intelligibility of Paul Tillich and Charles Hartshorne to Descartes and Leibniz respectively.

6. See, for instance, Seyyed Hossein Nasr's *Knowledge and the Sacred* and Huston Smith's *Forgotten Truth: The Primordial Tradition*. See also William C. Chittick's studies of this idea in Islam, for instance his *The Self-Disclosure of God*, focusing on Ibn al-'Arabi, and *The Heart of Islamic Philosophy*, focusing on Afdal al-Din Kashani. The transcultural character of this kind of Perennial Philosophy is illustrated by the Chinese Muslim scholar, Liu Zhi, who rendered the Neo-Platonic point of Islamic thought in Confucian terms. See *The Sage Learning of Liu Zhi: Islamic Thought in Confucian Terms*, by Sachiko Murata, William C. Chittick, and Tu Weiming. The Library of Living Philosophers volume, *The Philosophy of Seyyed Hossein Nasr* contains extraordinary discussions of Nasr's version of Perennial Philosophy, including

an essay by Huston Smith. It also contains my critical analysis of Nasr's version and his careful and gracious reply.

7. This thesis is defended throughout Pannenberg's three volume *Systematic Theology*.

8. See the discussion of this for early Judaism and Christianity in Daniel Boyarin's *Border Lines*.

9. See Spinoza's *Ethics*. See also Robert S. Corrington's *Ecstatic Naturalism: Signs of the World*. In the foreword to Corrington's book, John Deely traces the distinction between *natura naturans* and *natura naturata* to the Latin translations of Averroes in the first quarter of the thirteenth century; Aquinas used the distinction.

10. For an explication of Ramanuja's position, see John Braisted Carman's *The Theology of Ramanuja*.

11. See Aristotle's Metaphysics for the theory of four causes, especially book 1, in *The Basic Works of Aristotle*.

12. See *Process and Reality*, parts 3 and 4.

13. Firstness, Secondness, and Thirdness are phenomenological categories for Peirce. They are discussed mainly in the chapters in Book 2 of Volume I of *The Collected Papers of Charles Sanders Peirce*.

14. See Hartshorne's *Divine Relativity* and *The Logic of Perfection*. See also David Ray Griffin's defense of Hartshorne on this point against the criticisms made in the text here, and in Neville, *Creativity and God*, in his *Whitehead's Radically Different Postmodern Philosophy*, chapter 9. In rebuttal to Griffin, see Neville, "A Letter of Grateful and Affectionate Response to David Ray Griffin's *Whitehead's Radically Different Postmodern Philosophy: An Argument for Its Contemporary Relevance*."

15. See *Process and Reality*, p. 24 and elsewhere. See also *I, 14, iv*.

NOTES TO CHAPTER TWELVE

1. This is the beginning of Zhou Dunyi's "An Explanation of the Diagram of the Great Ultimate," as translated by Wing-tsit Chan in his *Source Book in Chinese Philosophy*, p. 463.

2. See, for instance, his argument in *The Courage to Be*, and throughout *Systematic Theology*, volume 1.

3. He did not deny differences between his conception of God as the Ground of Being and the other traditions. See, for example, his essay "Two Types of Philosophy of Religion" in *The Theology of Culture* in which he contrasts his position with Thomas's, saying that for Thomas the God of the Pure Act of To Be is still an other whom people meet as if "meeting a stranger," whereas his own view finds God in the depths of the soul, a position he likens to Augustine's Neo-Platonism. Yet he did not say that his idea of the Ground of Being entailed an ontological fullness of the sort Plotinus affirmed for the One prior to the Dyad in Neo-Platonism.

4. As in The Awakening of Mahayana Faith.

5. For a striking, if quaint and dated, treatment of eternity in modern thought, see Walter Stace's *Time and Eternity*, chapter 5.

6. "Extensive continuum" is a term developed by Whitehead in *Process and Reality*, particularly part 2, chapter 2. Some sense for the complications of the idea can be gained from the essays in David Ray Griffin, editor, *Physics and the Ultimate Significance of Time*.

7. For the details of this complex notion, and debates about interpretations, see Neville, *Creativity and God*.

8. For a related analysis of Plotinus on time and eternity, oriented to the current discussion, see Neville, *Religion in Late Modernity*, chapter 5.

9. See Kant's discussion of the Postulates of Empirical Thought in the *Critique of Pure Reason*.

10. See his discussion in *Science and the Modern World*.

11. Ashoka, the Buddhist emperor of India, sent a Buddhist mission west as far as Egypt about the time Ecclesiastes was written.

NOTES TO CHAPTER THIRTEEN

1. For a review of the scientific literature and debates about this, see Ilkka Pyysiainen, "Amazing Grace: Religion and the Evolution of the Human Mind."

2. Thomas A. James' *In Face of Reality: The Constructive Theology of Gordon D. Kaufman* is a clear exposition of recent debates in Protestant theology about whether any conception of God as an agent with personal intentions is compatible with modern science.

3. The main texts are in Wingtsit Chan's *A Source Book in Chinese Philosophy*, chapter 26.

4. On Shanqing Daoism, see James Miller's *The Way of Highest Clarity*.

5. See the account of the self in Confucian terms in Neville, *Boston Confucianism*.

6. For a more elaborate defense of this interpretation of the Daodijing, see Neville, *Ritual and Deference*, chapter 4.

7. See Francis X. Clooney, S.J., *Thinking Ritually*.

8. See, most perspicuously, his *The Courage to Be* and *Dynamics of Faith*. The point pervades his *Systematic Theology*.

9. See Thomas' *Summa Theologiae*, I, q.3, a. 5.

10. See Daniel Boyarin's discussion of logos in early Christianity and its contemporary Judaism in *Border Lines*.

11. See Neville, *Symbols of Jesus*.

12. See *Process and Reality*, Part 3.

13. See the Zhuangzi, chapter 1.

14. Zhangzai, the opening words of *The Western Inscription*, in Wing-tsit Chan, *A Source Book in Chinese Philosophy*, p. 497.

NOTES TO CHAPTER FOURTEEN

1. See the final chapter of *Process and Reality*.

2. For a systematic presentation of this, see Marjorie Suchocki's *God-Christ-Church*.

3. See Whitehead's *Symbolism*, and *Process and Reality* of course, especially part 2, chapter 2, "The Extensive Continuum."

4. See the brilliant studies of "body-thinking" by Kuang-Ming Wu, *On Chinese Body Thinking* and *On the "Logic" of Togetherness*.

5. For this discussion of Hartshorne, see the references in chapter 11, note 14.

6. See *Process and Reality*, pp. 19, 24.

NOTES TO CHAPTER FIFTEEN

1. Peirce said that arguments should be like ropes rather than chains that are only as strong as their weakest link.

2. Neville, *On the Scope and Truth of Theology: Theology as Symbolic Engagement*, develops that theory in much greater detail.

3. More particularly, the carryover of value in a true symbolic interpretive engagement is a function in part of biological and cultural characteristics of the interpreter. This physical-causation theory of truth is detailed in Neville, *Recovery of the Measure*, Part 1, and Neville, *The Truth of Broken Symbols*.

4. Peirce went so far as to say that "man is a sign," pure and simple. See his paper, "Some Consequences of Four Incapacities," in *The Collected Papers of Charles Sanders Peirce*, volume 5, pp. 156 ff., and in many collections.

5. That was the approximate time also of the composition of the opposite tending Hebrew Bible books of Ruth, which demonstrated that King David's grandmother was a Moabite, not an Israelite, Jonah, which demonstrated God's concern for the Assyrians (Israel's most vicious oppressors), and Job, whose hero was not a Jew.

6. Second Samuel 12:15b–23.

NOTES TO CHAPTER SIXTEEN

1. On the diversity of yogic meditation as spread through many intellectual traditions, see Christopher Key Chapple, *Yoga and the Luminous*.

2. See Michael Raposa's *Meditation and the Martial Arts*.

3. The anonymous writer is a philosophical theologian, whom I know.

4. See McNamara, *Neuroscience of Religious Experience*.

5. See Tillich's *The Courage to Be*, Berdyaev's *The Beginning and the End*, and Meister Eckhart's *Selected Writings*. An extraordinary expression of this is in Pavel Florensky's *The Pillar and Ground of the Truth*, which explicitly argues that full humanization requires full friendship with at least one other and that the condition for this is continuous union with God as ground.

6. See Tu Weiming's *Centrality and Commonality*.

Bibliography

Alcorta, Candace S. "Religion and the Life Course: Is Adolescence an 'Experience Expectant' Period for Religious Transmission." In Patrick McNamara, editor, *Where God and Science Meet*, volume 2, chapter 4.

Almond, Gabriel A., R. Scott Appleby, and Emmanuel Sivan. *Strong Religion: The Rise of Fundamentalisms around the World*. Chicago, IL: University of Chicago Press, 2003.

Anderson, James F., translator and editor. *An Introduction to the Metaphysics of St. Thomas Aquinas*. Chicago, IL: Henry Regnery Co., 1953.

Anderson, Victor. *Beyond Ontological Blackness: An Essay in African American Religious and Cultural Criticism*. New York, NY: Continuum Press, 1995.

———. *Pragmatic Theology: Negotiating the Intersections of an American Philosophy of Religion and Public Theology*. Albany, NY: State University of New York Press, 1998.

Aquinas, Thomas. *Summa Theologiae*. Latin-English edition. Volume 1, *Prima Pars*, Q. 1–64; Volume 2, *Prima Pars*, Q. 65–119. Scotts Valley, CA: Createspace, NovAntiqua, 2008.

———. *An Introduction to the Metaphysics of St. Thomas Aquinas*. Translated and edited by James F. Anderson. Chicago, IL: Henry Regnery Co., 1953.

Aristotle. *The Basic Works of Aristotle*. Edited by Richard McKeon. New York, NY: Random House, 1941. Various translators.

Armstrong, Karen. *The Great Transformation: The Beginning of Our Religious Traditions*. New York, NY: Random House, 2006.

———. *The Case for God*. New York, NY: Random House, 2009.

Asad, Talal. *Genealogies of Religion: Discipline and Reasons of Power in Christianity and Islam*. Baltimore, MD: Johns Hopkins Press, 1993.

———. *Formation of the Secular: Christianity, Islam, and Modernity*. Stanford, CA: Stanford University Press, 2003.

Auxier, Randall, and Lewis Edwin Hahn, editors. *The Philosophy of Richard Rorty*. The Library of Living Philosophers, volume 32. Chicago and LaSalle, Il: Open Court, 2010.

Barrett, Nathaniel. "Skillful Engagement and the 'Effort after Value': An Axiological Theory of the Origins of Religion." In Fraser Watts and Léon Turner (Eds.), *The Evolution of Religion: Critical Perspectives and New Directions*, 2012.

Bartel, T. W. Editor. *Comparative Theology: Essays for Keith Ward*. London, UK: SPCK Press, 2003.

Barth, Karl. *Church Dogmatics I.I.* Translated by G. T. Thomson. Edinburgh, UK: T. & T. Clark, 1936.

———. *On Religion: The Revelation of God as the Sublimation of Religion*. Translated with an introduction by Garrett Green. London, UK: T. & T. Clark, 2006. Paragraph 17 of the *Church Dogmatics*, 1.2.

———. *Dogmatics in Outline*. With a new Foreword by the author. Translated by G. T. Thomson. New York, NY: Harper Torchbook, 1959.

Bellah, Robert N. *Religion in Human Evolution: From the Paleolithic to the Axial Age*. Cambridge, MA: Harvard University Press, 2011.

Berdyaev, Nicolas. *The Beginning and the End*. Translated from the Russian by R. M. French. New York, NY: YMCA Press, 1952; New York, NY: Harper Torchbook, 1957.

Berger, Peter L. *The Sacred Canopy: Elements of a Sociological Theory of Religion*. Garden City, NY: Doubleday, 1967.

———. With Thomas Luckmann. *The Social Construction of Reality: A Treatise in the Sociology of Knowledge*. Garden City, NY: Doubleday, 1966.

———. *A Far Glory: The Quest for Faith in an Age of Credulity*. New York, NY: Doubleday, 1992.

Bernstein, Richard. *Praxis and Action: Contemporary Philosophies of Human Activity*. Philadelphia, PA: University of Pennsylvania Press, 1971.

———. *The Pragmatic Turn*. Malden, MA and Cambridge, UK: Polity Press, 2010.

Berry, Thomas. *The Dream of the Earth*. San Francisco, CA: Sierra Club Books, 1988.

———. *The Great Work: Our Way into the Future*. New York, NY: Bell Tower/Crown, 1999.

Boyarin, Daniel. *A Radical Jew: Paul and the Politics of Identity*. Berkeley, CA: University of California Press, 1994.

———. *Border Lines: The Partition of Judaeo-Christianity*. Philadelphia, PA: University of Pennsylvania Press, 2004.

———. *Socrates and the Fat Rabbis*. Chicago, IL: University of Chicago Press, 2009.

Bradley, F. H. *Appearance and Reality: A Metaphysical Essay*. Oxford, UK: Clarendon Press, 1893.

Brandom, Robert B. *Making It Explicit: Reasoning, Representing, and Discursive Commitment*. Cambridge, MA: Harvard University Press, 1994.

———. *Tales of the Mighty Dead: Historical Essays in the Metaphysics of Intentionality*. Cambridge, MA: Harvard University Press, 2002.

———. *Between Saying and Doing: Towards an Analytic Pragmatism*. Oxford, UK: Oxford University Press, 2008.

———. *Perspectives on Pragmatism: Classical, recent, and Contemporary*. Cambridge, MA: Harvard University Press, 2011.

Brockington, John. "The Sanskrit Epics." In Gavin Flood, *The Blackwell Companion to Hinduism*, chapter 5.

Buchler, Justus. *Nature and Judgment*. New York: Columbia University Press, 1955.

———. *The Main of Light: On the Concept of Poetry.* New York: Oxford University Press, 1974.
Capps, Walter H. *Religious Studies: The Making of a Discipline.* Minneapolis, MN: Fortress, 1995.
Carman, John Braisted. *The Theology of Ramanuja: An Essay iin Interreligious Understanding.* New Haven, CT: Yale University Press, 1974.
Chapman, J. Harley. Editor, with Nancy K. Frankenberry. *Interpreting Neville.* Albany, NY: State University of New York Press, 1999.
Chapple, Christopher Key. *Yoga and the Luminous: Patanjali's Spiritual Path to Freedom.* Albany, NY: State University of New York Press, 2008.
Chittick, William C. *The Sufi Path of Love: The Spiritual Teachings of Rumi.* Albany, NY: State University of New York Press, 1983.
———. *The Sufi Path of Knowledge: Ibn al-'Arabi's Metaphysics of Imagination.* Albany, NY: State University of New York Press, 1989.
———. *Faith and Practice of Islam: Three Thirteenth Century Sufi Texts.* Albany, NY: State University of New York Press, 1992.
———. *Imaginal Worlds: Ibn al-'Arabi and the Problem of Religious Diversity.* Albany, NY: State University of New York Press, 1994.
———. *The Self-Disclosure of God: Principles of Ibn al-'Arabi's Cosmology.* Lahore, Pakistan: Suhail Academy, 2000.
———. *The Heart of Islamic Philosophy: The Quest for Self-knowledge in the Teachings of Afdal al-Din Kashani.* Lahore, Pakistan: Suhail Academy, 2004.
———. *Ibn 'Arabi: Heir to the Prophets.* Lahore, Pakistan: Suhail Academy, 2007.
———. With Sachiko Murata and Tu Weiming, and a foreword by Seyyed Hossein Nasr. *The Sage Learning of Liu Zhi: Islamic Thought in Confucian Terms.* Cambridge, MA: Harvard University Press, 2009.
Clarke, Desmond M. *Descartes: A Biography.* Cambridge, UK: Cambridge University Press, 2006.
Clooney, Francis X., S.J. *Thinking Ritually: Rediscovering the Purva Mimamsa of Jaimini* Vienna, AU: Samlung de Nobile, 1990.
———. *Comparative Theology: Deep Learning Across Religious Borders.* Oxford, UK: Wiley-Blackwell, 2009.
Collins, Randall. *The Sociology of Philosophies: A Global Theory of Intellectual Change.* Cambridge, MA, and London, UK: Harvard University Press, 1998.
Cook, Francis H. *Hua-yen Buddhism: The Jewel Net of Indra.* University Park, PA: Pennsylvania State University Press, 1977.
Corrington, Robert S. *Nature and Spirit: An Essay in Ecstatic Naturalism.* New York, NY: Fordham University Press, 1992.
———. *An Introduction to C. S. Peirce: Philosophers, Semiotician, and Ecstatic Naturalist.* Lanham, MD: Rowman & Littlefield, 1993.
———. *A Semiotic Theory of Theology and Philosophy.* Cambridge, UK: Cambridge University Press, 2000.
———. *Ecstatic Naturalism: Signs of the World.* Bloomington, IN: Indiana University Press, 1994.
———. *Nature's Self: Our Journey from Origin to Spirit.* Lanham, MD: Rowman & Littlefield, 1996.
———. *Nature's Religion.* With a Foreword by Robert Cummings Neville. Lanham, MD: Rowman & Littlefield, 1997.

Crisp, Oliver D. Editor. *A Reader in Contemporary Philosophical Theology.* New York, NY: Continuum, 2009.

———. Editor, with Michael C. Rea. *Analytic Theology: New Essays in the Philosophy of Theology.* New York, NY: Oxford University Press, 2009.

Crosby, Donald A. Editor, with Charley D. Hardwick. *Pragmatism, Neo-Pragmatism, and Religion: Conversations with Richard Rorty.* New York, NY: Peter Lang, 1997.

Cush, Denise, Catherine Robinson, and Michael York. Editors. *Encyclopedia of Hinduism.* London, UK: Routledge, 2008.

Daveney, Sheila Greeve. Editor, with Warren G. Frisina. *The Pragmatic Century: Conversations with Richard J. Bernstein.* Albany, NY: State University of New York Press, 2006.

Dawkins, Richard. *The God Delusion.* Boston, MA: Mariner/Houghton Mifflin, 2006; paperback edition with a new preface, 2008.

Deacon, Terrence W. *The Symbolic Species: The Co-evolution of Language and the Brain.* New York, NY: W. W. Norton, 1997.

———. *Incomplete Nature: How Mind Emerged from Matter.* New York, NY: Norton, 2012.

De Lange, Nicholas, and Miri Freud-Kandel, editors. *Modern Judaism.* Oxford, UK: Oxford University Press, 2005.

Dennett, Daniel C. *Breaking the Spell: Religion as a Natural Phenomenon.* New York, NY: Viking, 2006.

Dewey, John. *Experience and Nature.* Volume 1 in *John Dewey: The Later Works: 1925–1953.* Edited by Jo Ann Boydston, with an introduction by Sidney Hook. Carbondale, IL: Southern Illinois University Press, 1981. Original first edition, 1925, second edition, 1929.

———. *Art as Experience.* Volume 10 in *John Dewey: The Later Works: 1925–1953.* Edited by Jo Ann Boydston, with an introduction by Abraham Kaplan. Carbondale, IL: Southern Illinois University Press, 1987. Original, 1934.

Durkheim, Emile. *The Elementary Forms of the Religious Life.* Translated from the French by Joseph Ward Swain. New York, NY: The Free Press, 1965; original edition, George Allen & Unwin, Ltd., 1915.

———. *The Division of Labor in Society.* Translated by W. D. Halls with an introduction by Lewis A. Coser. New York, NY: The Free Press, 1984.

Eckel, Malcolm David, with John J. Thatamanil. "Cooking the Last Fruit of Nihilism: Buddhist Approaches to Ultimate Reality." Chapter 6 in Neville, editor, *Ultimate Realities.*

———. With John J. Thatamanil. "Beginningless Ignorance: A Buddhist View of the Human Condition." Chapter 3 in Neville, editor, *The Human Condition.*

———. With John J. Thatamanil." "With Great Noise and Mighty Whirlpools the Ganges Flowed Backwards." Chapter 3 in Neville, editor, *Religious Truth.*

Eckhart, Meister. *Selected Writings.* Selected and translated by Oliver Davies. London, UK: Penguin, 1994.

Edelglass, William, and Jay L. Garfield, editors. *Buddhist Philosophy: Essential Readings.* Oxford, UK: Oxford University Press, 2009.

Eliade, Mircea. Eliade, Mircea. *The Sacred and the Profane: The Nature of Religion.* Translated by Willard R. Trask. New York, NY: Harcourt Brace, 1959. Original edition, 1957.

———. *A History of Religious Ideas*. In three volumes. Volume 1, 1978, translated by Willard R. Trask, *From the Stone Age to the Eleusinian Mysteries*; Volume 2, 1982, translated by Willard R. Trask, *From Gautama Buddha to the Triumph of Christianity*; Volume 3, 1985, translated by Alf Hiltebeitel and Diane Apostolos-Cappadona, *From Muhammad to the Age of Reforms*. Chicago, IL: University of Chicago Press.

Fakhry, Majid. *A History of Islamic Philosophy*. Third edition; New York, NY: Columbia University Press, 2004.

Flint, Thomas P., and Michael C. Rea, editors. *The Oxford Handbook of Philosophical Theology*. New York: Oxford University Press, 2009.

Flood, Gavin. *Beyond Phenomenology: Rethinking the Study of Religion*. London, UK: Cassell, 1999.

———. Editor. *The Blackwell Companion to Hinduism*. Oxford, UK: Blackwell, 2003.

Florensky, Pavel. *The Pillar and Ground of the Truth: An Essay in Orthodox Theodicy in Twelve Letters*. Translated by Boris Jakim with an introduction by Richard F. Gustafson. Princeton, NJ: Princeton University Press, 1997.

Ford, Lewis. *The Lure of God: A Biblical Background for Process Theism*. Philadelphia, PA: Fortress, 1978.

———. *The Emergence of Whitehead's Metaphysics 1925–1929*. Albany, NY: State University of New York Press, 1984.

Frankenberry, Nancy K. Editor, with J. Harley Chapman. *Interpreting Neville*. Albany, NY: State University of New York Press, 1999.

———. Editor. *Radical Interpretation in Religion*. Cambridge, UK: Cambridge University Press, 2002.

Frei, Hans W. *Types of Christian Theology*. Edited by George Hunsinger and William C. Placher. New Haven, CT: Yale University Press, 1992.

Frisina, Warren G. *The Unity of Knowledge and Action: Toward a Nonrepresentational Theory of Knowledge*. Albany, NY: State University of New York Press, 2002.

———. Editor, with Sheila Greeve Davaney. *The Pragmatic Century: Conversations with Richard J. Bernstein*. Albany, NY: State University of New York Press, 2006.

Gilson, Etienne. *The Christian Philosophy of St. Thomas Aquinas*. Translated by L. K. Shook, C.S.B. New York, NY: Random House, 1956.

Goffman, Erving. *Asylums: Essays on the Social Situation of Mental Patients and Other Inmates*. New York, NY: Doubleday, 1961.

Griffin, David Ray. Editor. *Physics and the Ultimate Significance of Time: Bohm, Prigogine, and Process Philosophy*. Albany, NY: State University of New York Press, 1986.

———. *Reenchantment without Supernaturalism: A Process Philosophy of Religion*. Ithaca, NY: Cornell University Press, 2001.

———. *Whitehead's Radically Different Postmodern Philosophy: An Argument for Its Contemporary Relevance*. Albany, NY: State University of New York Press, 2007.

Hardwick, Charley. Editor, with Donald Crosby. *Pragmatism, Neo-Pragmatism, and Religion: Conversations with Richard Rorty*. New York, NY: Peter Lang, 1997.

Harper, Charles L. Jr. Editor. *Spiritual Information: 100 Perspectives on Science and Religion: Essays in Honor of Sir John Templeton's 90th Birthday*. Philadelphia, PA: Templeton Foundation Press, 2005.

Hartshorne, Charles. *The Divine Relativity: A Social Conception of God*. New Haven, CT: Yale University Press, 1948.

———. *The Logic of Perfection and Other Essays in Neoclassical Metaphysics*. LaSalle, IL: Open Court, 1962.

———. *Creative Synthesis and Philosophic Method*. La Salle, IL: Open Court, 1970.

———. "Three Responses to Neville's *Creativity and God*." With John B. Cobb Jr., and Lewis S. Ford. *Process Studies* 10/3-4 (Fall-Winter 1980), pp. 93–109.

———. *Creativity in American Philosophy*. Albany, NY: State University of New York Press, 1984.

Harvey, Van A. *The Historian and the Believer: The Morality of Historical Knowledge and Christian Belief*. New York, NY: Macmillan, 1966.

Hegel, Georg Wilhelm Friedrich. *Lectures on the Philosophy of Religion, Together with a Work on the Proofs of the Existence of God*. In three volumes. Translated from the second German edition by E. B. Speirs and J. Burdon Sanderson. New York, NY: Humanities Press edition, 1962.

Heidegger, Martin. *Being and Time*. Translated by John Macquarrie and Edward Robinson. London, UK: SCM Press, 1962; original German edition, 1927.

———. *Existence and Being*. Translated with an introduction by Werner Brock. Chicago, IL: Henry Regnery Company, 1949.

———. *An Introduction to Metaphysics*. Translated by Ralph Manheim. New Haven, CT: Yale University Press, 1959.

———. *What Is a Thing?*. Translated by W. B. Barton Jr., and Vera Deutsch. Chicago, IL: Henry Regnery, 1967.

Heltzel, Peter G. And Amos Yong, editors. *Theology in Global Context: Essays in Honor of Robert Cummings Neville*. New York, NY, and London, UK: T & T Clark International, 2004.

Hoopes, James. Editor. *Peirce on Signs: Writings on Semiotic by Charles Sanders Peirce*. Chapel Hill, NC: The University of North Carolina Press, 1991.

Husserl, Edmund. *Ideas: General Introduction to Pure Phenomenology*. Translated by W. R. Boyce Gibson. New York, NY: Collier Books, 1962; original French edition 1913.

———. *Cartesian Meditations: An Introduction to Phenomenology*. Translated by Dorion Cairns. The Hague: Martinus Nijhoff, 1960; from the French edition, 1950.

———. *The Crisis of European Sciences and Transcendental Phenomenology*. Translated with an Introduction by David Carr. Evanston, IL: Northwestern University Press, 1970; original French edition 1954.

Jackelen, Antje. *Time and Eternity: The Question of Time in Church, Science, and Theology*. Translated from the German by Barbara Harshaw. Philadelphia, PA: Templeton Foundation Press, 2005.

James, Thomas A. *In Face of Reality: The Constructive Theology of Gordon D. Kaufman*. Eugene, OR: Pickwick Publications/Wipf and Stock, 2011.

James, William. *The Principles of Psychology*. New York: Henry Holt and Company, 1890. Two volumes bound as one. Dover reprint edition in two volumes; New York: Dover, 1950.

———. "Preface" to Edwin Diller Starbuck's *Psychology of Religion*, which see.

———. *The Varieties of Religious Experience: A Study of Human Nature*. The Gifford Lectures on Natural Religion Delivered at Edinburgh in 1901–1902. New York, NY: Longmans Green & Co., 1902.

———. *Essays in Radical Empiricism* and *A Pluralistic Universe*. Edited by Ralph Barton Perry. New York, NY: Longmans Green, 1942; original edition of *Essays in Radical Empiricism*, 1912; original edition of *A Pluralistic Universe*, 1909.

Jaspers, Karl. *The Origin and Goal of History.* Translated by Michael Bullock. London, UK: Routledge and Keegan Paul, 1953. Original German edition, 1949

Johnson, Mark. With George Lakoff. *Metaphors We Live By.* Chicago, IL: University of Chicago Press, 1980.

———. *The Body in the Mind: The Bodily Basis of Meaning, Imagination, and Reason.* Chicago, IL: University of Chicago Press, 1987.

———. With George Lakoff. *Philosophy in the Flesh: The Embodied Mind and Its Challenge to Western Thought.* New York, NY: Basic Books, 1999.

Lakoff, George. With Mark Johnson. *Metaphors We Live By.* Chicago, IL: University of Chicago Press, 1980.

———. *Women, Fire, and Dangerous Things: What Categories Reveal about the Mind.* Chicago, IL: University of Chicago Press, 1987

———. With Mark Johnson. *Philosophy in the Flesh: The Embodied Mind and Its Challenge to Western Thought.* New York, NY: Basic Books, 1999.

Leibniz, Gottfried. *Leibniz: Discourse on Metaphysics, Correspondence with Arnauld, Monodology.* Translated by George R. Montgomery. LaSalle, IL: Open Court, 1953.

Leuba, James. "Studies in the Psychology of Religious Phenomena," in American Journal of Psychology, vii 309 (1896).

———. *The Psychological Origin and Nature of Religion.* Reprint edition; India: Bradley Press, 2009. Also in Wikisource. Original 1909.

———. *The Psychological Study of Religion: Its Origins, Function, and Future.* New York, NY: Macmillan, 1912.

———. *The Belief in God and Immortality.* Boston, MA: Sherman, French, 1916.

———. *The Psychology of Religious Mysticism.* New York, NY: Harcourt, Brace, 1925.

Kakol, Peter Paul. *Emptiness and Becoming: Integrating Madhyamika Buddhism and Process Philosophy.* With a Foreword by Robert C. Neville and a Preamble by Purushottama Bilimoria. New Delhi, India: D. K. Printworld, Ltd., 2009.

Kant, Immanuel. *Critique of Pure Reason.* Translated by Norman Kemp Smith. London, UK: Macmillan, 1929. Original German first edition Riga: Johann Friedrich Hartknoch, 1781; second edition, 1787.

———. *Critique of Practical Reason.* Translated with an introduction by Lewis White Beck. New York, NY: The Liberal Arts Press, 1956. Original German edition, 1788.

———. *Critique of Judgment.* Translated by James Creed Meredith. Oxford, UK: Clarendon Press, 1928. Original German edition, 1790.

———. *Religion within the Limits of Reason Alone.* Translated with an introduction and notes by Theodore M. Greene and Hoyt H. Hudson, and an essay by John R. Silber. New York, NY: Harper & Brothers, 1960.

Keller, Catherine. *Face of the Deep: A Theology of Becoming.* New York, NY: Routledge, 2003.

Keown, Damien, and Charles S. Prebish. Editors. *Encyclopedia of Buddhism.* London, UK: Routledge, 2007.

Kierkegaard, Soren. *Purity of Heart Is to Will One Thing: Spiritual Preparation for the Office of Confession.* Translated by Douglas V. Steere. New York, NY: Harper & Brothers, 1938.

Kirkpatrick, Lee A. "Religion Is Not an Adaptation." In Patrick McNamara, editor. *Where God and Science Meet: Volume 1: Evolution, Genes, and the Religious Brain,* chapter 8.

Kohn, Livia. *Taoism Mystical Philosophy: The Scripture of the Western Ascension*. Albany, NY: State University of New York Press, 1991.

———. *Early Chinese Mysticism: Philosophy and Soteriology in the Taoist Tradition*. Princeton, NJ: Princeton University Press, 1992.

Kuehn, Manfred. *Kant: A Biography*. Cambridge, UK: Cambridge University Press, 2001.

Levenson, Jon D. *Sinai and Zion: An Entry into the Jewish Bible*. San Francisco, CA: Harper and Row, 1985.

———. *Creation and the Persistence of Evil: The Jewish Drama of Divine Omnipotence*. San Francisco, CA: Harper & Row, 1988.

Lindbeck, George. *The Nature of Doctrine*. Philadelphia, PA: Westminster, 1984.

Machle, Edward J. *Nature and Heaven in the Xunzi: A Study of the* Tien Lun. Albany, NY: State University of New York Press, 1993.

McNamara, Patrick. *Where God and Science Meet: How Brain and Evolutionary Studies Alter Our Understanding of Religion*. Volume 1: *Evolution, Genes, and the Religious Brain*. Volume 2: *The Neurology of Religious Experience*. Volume 3: *The Psychology of Religious Experience*. Westport, CT, London, UK: Praeger, 2006.

———. *Neuroscience of Religious Experience*. New York, NY and Cambridge, UK: Cambridge University Press, 2009.

Masuzawa, Tomoko. *The Invention of World Religions: Or, How European Universalism Was Preserved in the Language of Pluralism*. Chicago, IL: University of Chicago Press, 2005.

Miller, James E. *The Way of Highest Clarity: Nature, Vision and Revelation in Medieval China*. Magdalena, NM: Three Pines Press, 2008.

Moores, D. J. Editor. *Wild Poets of Ecstasy: An Anthology of Ecstatic Verse*. Nevada City, CA: Pelican Pond Publishing, 2011.

Morse, Christopher. *Not Every Spirit: A Dogmatics of Christian Disbelief*. Second edition; New York, NY: Continuum, 2009.

Murata, Sachiko. *The Dao of Islam: A Sourcebook on Gender Relationships in Islamic Thought*. Foreword by Annemarie Schimmel. Lahore, Pakistan: Suhail Academy, 2001.

———. *The Sage Learning of Liu Zhi: Islamic Thought in Confucian Terms*. With William C. Chittick and Tu Weiming, and a foreword by Seyyed Hossein Nasr. Cambridge, MA: Harvard University Press, 2009.

Nasr, Seyyed Hossein. *Knowledge and the Sacred*. Albany, NY: State University of New York Press, 1989.

———. *The Philosophy of Seyyed Hossein Nasr*. Edited by Lewis Edwin Hahn, Randall E. Auxier, and Lucian W. Stone Jr. The Library of Living Philosophers, volume 28. Chicago and LaSalle, IL: Open Court, 2001.

Netton, Ian Richard. Editor. *Encyclopedia of Islamic Civilization and Religion*. London, UK: Routledge, 2008.

Neville, Robert Cummings. *God the Creator: On the Transcendence and Presence of God*. Chicago, IL: University of Chicago Press, 1968; reprint with a new introduction, Albany, NY: State University of New York Press, 1992.

———. *The Cosmology of Freedom*. New Haven, CT: Yale University Press, 1974. New edition; Albany, NY: State University of New York Press, 1995.

———. *Soldier, Sage, Saint*. New York, NY: Fordham University Press, 1978.

———. *Creativity and God: A Challenge to Process Theology*. New York, NY: The Seabury Press/Crossroad, 1980. New edition with a new preface; Albany, NY: State University of New York Press, 1995.

———. *Reconstruction of Thinking*. Volume 1 of *Axiology of Thinking*. Albany, NY: State University of New York Press, 1981.

———. "Concerning *Creativity and God*: A Response." In *Process Studies* 11/1(Spring, 1981) pp. 1–10.

———. *The Tao and the Daimon: Segments of a Religious Inquiry*. Albany, NY: State University of New York Press, 1982.

———. *The Puritan Smile: A Look toward Moral Reflection*. Albany, NY: State University of New York Press, 1987.

———. *Recovery of the Measure*. Volume 2 of *Axiology of Thinking*. Albany, NY: State University of New York Press, 1989.

———. *Behind the Masks of God: An Essay toward Comparative Theology*. Albany, NY: State University of New York Press, 1991.

———. *A Theology Primer*. Albany, NY: State University of New York Press, 1991

———. *The Highroad around Modernism*. Albany, NY: State University of New York Press, 1992.

———. *Eternity and Time's Flow*. Albany, NY: State University of New York Press, 1993.

———. *Normative Cultures*. Volume 3 of *Axiology of Thinking*. Albany, NY: State University of New York Press, 1995.

———. *The Truth of Broken Symbols*. Albany, NY: State University of New York Press, 1996.

———. *Boston Confucianism: Portable tradition in the Late-Modern World*. Albany, NY: State University of New York Press, 2000.

———. *Symbols of Jesus: A Christology of Symbolic Engagement*. Cambridge, UK: Cambridge University Press, 2001.

———. *Religion in Late Modernity*. Albany, NY: State University of New York Press, 2002.

———. *On the Scope and Truth of Theology: Theology as Symbolic Engagement*. New York and London: T & T Clark, 2006.

———. *Ritual and Deference: Extending Chinese Philosophy in a Comparative Context*. Albany, NY: State University of New York Press, 2008.

———. "A Letter of Grateful and Affectionate Response to David Ray Griffin's *Whitehead's Radically Different Postmodern Philosophy: An Argument for Its Contemporary Relevance*." In *Process Studies* 37/1 (Spring-Summer 2008), pp. 7–38.

———. *Realism in Religion: A Pragmatist's Perspective*. Albany, NY: State University of New York Press, 2009.

———. "Pragmatism, Metaphysics, Comparison, and Realism." In *The Philosophy of Richard Rorty*, edited by Auxier and Hahn, pp. 139–54.

———. Editor. *New Essays in Metaphysics*. Albany, NY: State University of New York Press, 1987.

———. Editor. *The Human Condition: A Volume in the Comparative Religious Ideas Project*. With a Foreword by Peter L. Berger. Albany, NY: State University of New York Press, 2001.

———. Editor. *Ultimate Realities: A Volume in the Comparative Religious Ideas Project*. With a Foreword by Tu Weiming. Albany, NY: State University of New York Press, 2001.

———. Editor. *Religious Truth: A Volume in the Comparative Religious Ideas Project*. With a Foreword by Jonathan Z. Smith. Albany, NY: State University of New York Press, 2001.

Nicholson, Hugh, "The Reunification of Theology and Comparison in the New Comparative Theology." In *Journal of the American Academy of Religion*, 77/3 (September 2009), pp. 609–46.

———. "The Return of Comparative Theology." In *Journal of the American Academy of Religion*, 78/2 (June 2010), pp. 477–514.

Odin, Steve. *Process Metaphysics and Hua-Yen Buddhism: A Critical Study of Cumulative Penetration vs. Interpenetration*. Albany, NY: State University of New York Press, 1982.

Olivelle, Patrick. "The Renouncer Tradition." In Gavin Flood, editor, *The Blackwell Companion to Hinduism*.

Orsi, Robert A. *Between Heaven and Earth: The Religious Worlds People Make and the Scholars Who Study Them*. Princeton, NJ: Princeton University Press, 2005.

Otto, Rudolf. *The Idea of the Holy*. Translated by John Harvey. New York: Oxford University Press, 1926. Original edition 1917.

Pannenberg, Wolfhart. *Systematic Theology*. In three volumes. Translated by Geoffrey W. Bromily. Grand Rapids, MI: William B. Eerdmans, 1991, 1994, and 1998 respectively.

Park, Sung Bae. *Buddhist Faith and Sudden Enlightenment*. Albany, NY: State University of New York Press, 1983.

Peirce, Charles Sanders. *The Collected Papers of Charles Sanders Peirce*. Edited by Charles Hartshorne and Paul Weiss, volumes 1-6, and by Arthur Burks, volumes 7–8. Cambridge, MA: Harvard University Press, 1931, 1932, 1933, 1933, 1934, 1935, 1958, 1958 respectively.

———. *The Essential Peirce: Selected Philosophical Writings: Volume 1 (1867-1893) and Volume 2 (1893–1913)*. Edited by Nathan Houser and Christian Kloesel, Volume 1, and by the Peirce Edition Project, Volume 1. Bloomington, IN: Indiana University Press, 1992 and 1998 respectively.

Pinker, Steven. "The Evolutionary Psychology of Religion." In Patrick McNamara, editor, *Where God and Science Meet, Volume 1, Evolution, Genes, and the Religious Brain*, chapter 1.

Plantinga, Alvin. *Warranted Christian Belief*. Oxford, UK: Oxford University Press, 2000.

Plato. *Collected Dialogues*. Edited by Edith Hamilton and Huntington Cairns. New York, NY: Pantheon Books, 1961. Various translators.

Plotinus. *Enneads*. Translated by Stephen MacKenna and revised by B. S. Page. Third edition; London, UK: Faber and Faber, 1962.

Prebish, Charles S., and Damien Keown. Editors. *Encyclopedia of Buddhism*. London, UK: Routledge, 2007.

Prochnik, George. *Putnam Camp: Sigmund Freud, James Jackson Putnam, and The Purpose of American Psychology*. New York, NY: Other Press, 2006.

Pyysiainen, Ilkka. "Amazing Grace: Religion and the Evolution of the Human Mind," in Patrick McNamara, *Where God and Science Meet*, volume 1, *Evolution, Genes, and the Religious Brain*, chapter 10.

Raposa, Michael L. *Peirce's Philosophy of Religion*. Peirce Studies Number 5. Bloomington, IN: Indiana University Press, 1989.

———. *Meditation and the Martial Arts*. Charlottesville, VA: University of Virginia Press, 2003.

Rappaport, Roy A. *Ritual and Religion in the Making of Humanity*. Cambridge, UK: Cambridge University Press, 1999.

Rea, Michael C. *Oxford Readings in Philosophical Theology. Volume 1: Trinity, Incarnation, Atonement. Volume 2: Providence, Scripture, and Resurrection.* New York: Oxford University Press, 2009. 384 pages and 448 pages respectively.

Ricoeur, Paul. *Freedom and Nature: The Voluntary and the Involuntary.* Translated with an introduction by Erazim V. Kohak. Evanston, IL: Northwestern University Press, 1966.

———. *The Symbolism of Evil.* Translated by Emerson Buchanan. Boston, MA: Beacon Press, 1967.

———. *Freud and Philosophy: An Essay on Interpretation.* Translated by Denis Savage. New Haven, CT: Yale University Press, 1970.

———. *The Conflict of Interpretations: Essays in Hermeneutics.* Edited by Don Ihde. Evanston, IL: Northwestern University Press, 1974.

———. *Time and Narrative*, volume 1. Translated by Kathleen McLaughlin and David Pellauer. Chicago, IL: University of Chicago Press, 1984.

———. *Fallible Man.* Revised Translation by Charles A. Kelbley; introduction by Walter J. Lowe. New York, NY: Fordham University Press, 1986.

Richardson, Robert D. *William James: In the Maelstrom of American Modernism.* Boston, MA: Houghton Mifflin, 2006.

Rippin, Andrew. *Muslims: Their Religious Beliefs and Practices.* Third edition; London, UK: Routledge, 2005.

Robinson, Catherine, Denise Cush, and Michael York. Editors. *Encyclopedia of Hinduism.* London, UK: Routledge, 2008.

Rorty, Richard. *The Linguistic Turn: Recent Essays in Philosophical Method.* Chicago, IL: The University of Chicago Press, 1967.

———. *Philosophy and the Mirror of Nature.* Princeton, NJ: Princeton University Press, 1979.

———. *The Philosophy of Richard Rorty.* Edited by Randall E. Auxier and Lewis Edwin Hahn. The Library of Living Philosophers volume 32. Chicago and LaSalle, IL: Open Court, 2010.

Ross, James F. *Philosophical Theology.* New York, NY: Bobbs-Merrill, 1969.

Said, Edward W. *Beginnings: Intention and Method.* New York, NY: Basic Books, 1975.

———. *Orientalism.* New York, NY: Random House, 1978.

———. *Culture and Imperialism.* New York, NY: Alfred A. Knopf, 1993.

Saldarini, Anthony J. With Joseph Kanofsky. "To Practice Together Truth and Humility, Justice and Law, Love of Merciful Kindness and Modest Behavior," in Neville, editor, *Religious Truth*, chapter 4.

Schuon, Frithjof. *The Transcendent Unity of Religions.* Wheaton, IL: The Theosophical Publishing House, 1984.

Scotus, John Duns. *Philosophical Writings.* Translated and edited by Allan Wolter, O.F.M. New York, NY: Thomas Nelson & Sons, 1962.

Sellars, Wilfrid. *Empiricism and the Philosophy of Mind.* With an introduction by Richard Rorty and a study guide by Robert Brandom. Cambridge, MA: Harvard University Press, 1997. The original version of this work appeared as chapter 5 in *Science, Perception, and Reality.*

———. *Science, Perception, and Reality.* London, UK: Routledge and Kegan Paul, 1963.

———. *Science and Metaphysics: Variations on Kantian Themes.* London, UK: Routledge and Kegan Paul, 1968.

Short, T. L. *Peirce's Theory of Signs.* Cambridge, UK: Cambridge University Press, 2007.

Sizgorich, Thomas. *Violence and Belief in Late Antiquity*. Philadelphia, PA: University of Pennsylvania Press, 2009.

Smid, Robert W. *Methodologies of Comparative Philosophy: The Pragmatist and Process Traditions*. Albany, NY: State University of New York Press, 2009.

Smith, Huston. *Forgotten Truth: The Primordial Tradition*. New York, NY: Harper & Row, 1976.

Smith, John E. *The Spirit of American Philosophy*. New York, NY: Oxford University Press, 1963.

———. *Purpose and Thought: The Meaning of Pragmatism*. New Haven, CT: Yale University Press, 1978.

———. *Quasi-Religions: Humanism, Marxism and Nationalism*. New York, NY: St. Martin's Press, 1994.

Spinoza, Benedict de. *Works of Spinoza*. In two volumes: volume 1: *On the Improvement of the Understanding, The Ethics, and Correspondence*; volume 2: *A Theologico-Political Treatise, A Political Treatise*. Translated by R. H. M. Elwes. (Place unknown): G. Bell & Son, 1883. Dover edition; New York, NY: Dover, 1951.

———. *The Collected Works of Spinoza*, volume 1. Edited and Translated by Edwin Curley. Princeton, NJ: Princeton University Press, 1985.

Stace, Walter. *Time and Eternity*. Princeton, NJ: Princeton University Press, 1952.

Stout, Jeffrey. *Ethics After Babel: The Language of Morals and Their Discontents*. Boston, MA: Beacon Press, 1988.

———. *Democracy and Tradition*. Princeton, NJ: Princeton University Press, 2004.

Suchocki, Marjorie. *God-Christ-Church: A Practical Guide to Process Theology*. New Revised Edition; New York, NY: Crossroad, 1995.

Tanner, Kathryn. *Theories of Culture: A New Agenda for Theology*. Minneapolis, MN: Fortress Press, 1997.

Taylor, Mark C. *After God*. Chicago, IL: University of Chicago Press, 2007.

Thatamanil, John J. *The Immanent Divine: God, Creation, and the Human Predicament*. Minneapolis, MN: Fortress Press, 2006.

Tillich, Paul. *The Religious Situation*. Translated by H. Richard Niebuhr. New York, NY: Henry Holt, 1932.

———. *The Courage to Be*. New Haven, CT: Yale University Press, 1952.

———. *Dynamics of Faith*. New York, NY: Harper & Brothers, 1957.

———. *Systematic Theology*. Volume 1, Volume 2, Volume 3. Chicago, IL: University of Chicago Press, 1951, 1957, 1963 respectively.

———. *Theology of Culture*. Edited by Robert C. Kimball. New York, NY: Oxford University Press, 1959.

Toulmin, Stephen. *The Uses of Argument*. Cambridge, UK: Cambridge University Press, 1958.

———. *Human Understanding: The Collective Use and Evolution of Concepts*. Princeton, NJ: Princeton University Press, 1972.

Tu Weiming. *Humanity and Self-Cultivation: Essays in Confucian Thought*. Reprint edition with a new foreword by Robert Cummings Neville. Boston, MA: Cheng & Tsui, 1998.

———. *The Sage Learning of Liu Zhi: Islamic Thought in Confucian Terms*. With Sachiko Murata and Willliam C. Chittick, and a foresord by Seyyed Hossein Nasr. Cambridge, MA: Harvard University Press, 2009.

Tylor, Edward Burnett. *Primitive Culture*. Reprinted in two volumes: Volume I, *The Origins of Culture;* Volume II, *Religion in Primitive Culture*. New York, NY: Harper Torchbooks, 1958. Original edition 1872.

Van der Leeuw, G. *Religion in Essence and Manifestation.* Translated by J. E. Turner with appendices to the Torchbook edition, incorporating the additios of the second German edition, edited by Hans H. Penner. New York: Harper and Row, 1963. Original edition, 1933.

Vaught, Carl G. *The Journey toward God in Augustine's* Confessions: *Books I-VI.* Albany, NY: State University of New York Press, 2003.

———. *Encounters with God in Augustine's* Confessions: *Books VII-IX.* Albany, NY: State University of New York Press, 2004.

Wanderer, Jeremy. *Robert Brandom.* Montreal and Kingston, CAN: McGill-Queen's University Press, 2008.

Ward, Keith. *Religion and Revelation: A Theology of Revelation in the World's Religions.* Oxford, UK: Oxford University Press, 1994.

———. *Religion and Creation.* Oxford, UK: Oxford University Press, 1996.

———. *Religion and Human Nature.* Oxford, UK: Oxford University Press, 1998.

Weber, Max. *From Max Weber: Essays in Sociology.* Edited and translated, with an introduction, by H. H. Gerth and C. Wright Mills. New York, NY: Oxford University Press, 1946.

———. *The Theory of Social and Economic Organization.* Edited and translated by A. J. Henderson and Talcott Parsons, with an introduction by Parsons. New York, NY: The Free Press (as a division of Simon and Schuster), 1947.

———. *The Religion of China.* Translated and edited by Hans H. Gerth, with an Introduction by C. K. Yang. New York, NY: Free Press, 1951.

———. *The Protestant Ethic and the "Spirit" of Capitalism and Other Writings.* Edited, translated, and with an introduction by Peter Baehr and Gordon C. Wells. New York, NY: Penguin Books, 2002; original edition of *The Protestant Ethic and the "Spirit" of Capitalism,* 1905.

Wegter-McNelly, Kirk. *The Entangled God: Divine Relationality and Quantum Physics.* New York, NY: Routledge, 2011.

Weiss, Paul. *Nature and Man.* New York, NY: Henry Holt, 1947.

———. *Modes of Being.* Carbondale, IL: Southern Illinois University Press, 1958.

———. *The God We Seek.* Carbondale, IL: Southern Illinois University Press, 1964.

———. *First Considerations: An Examination of Philosophical Evidence.* With comments by Abner Shimony, Richard T. DeGeorge, Richard Rorty, Robert Neville, Andrew J. Reck, and R. M. Martin. Carbondale, IL: Southern Illinois University Press, 1977.

———. *The Philosophy of Paul Weiss.* The Library of Living Philosophers, volume 23. Edited by Lewis Edwin Hahn. Chicago and LaSalle, IL: Open Court, 1995.

West, Cornel. *The American Evasion of Philosophy: A Genealogy of Pragmatism.* Madison, WI: The University of Wisconsin Press, 1989.

———. *Keeping Faith: Philosophy and Race in America.* New York, NY: Routledge, 1993.

Whitehead, Alfred North. *The Concept of Nature.* Cambridge, UK: Cambridge University Press, 1920. Reprint edition; Ann Arbor, MI: The University of Michigan Press, 1957.

———. *Science and the Modern World.* New York, NY: Macmillan, 1925.

———. *Religion in the Making.* New York, NY: Macmillan, 1926

———. *Symbolism: Its Meaning and Effect.* New York, NY: Macmillan. 1927. Reprint edition; New York, NY: Fordham University Press, 1985.

———. *The Function of Reason.* Princeton, NJ: Princeton University Press, 1929; reprint edition, Boston, MA: Beacon, 1958.

———. *Process and Reality: An Essay in Cosmology*. Corrected edition edited by David Ray Griffin and Donald W. Sherburne. New York: The Free Press, 1978. Original edition, New York: Macmillan, 1929.

———. *Adventures of Ideas*. New York, NY: Macmillan, 1933.

———. *Modes of Thought*. New York, NY: Macmillan, 1938.

Wildman, Wesley J. "Theological Literacy: Problem and Promise" In Rodney L. Petersen with Nancy M. Rourke, editors. *Theological Literacy for the Twenty-First Century*, Grand Rapids, MI: Eerdmans, 2002, pp. 335–51.

———. "Global Spiritual Confusion and the Neglected Problem of Excess Spiritual Information. In Harper, Charles L., Jr., 2005.

———. "The Significance of the Evolution of Religious Belief and Behavior for Religious Studies and Theology." In Patrick McNamara. *Where God and Science Meet*, volume 1, chapter 11, pp. 227–72.

———. *Religious Philosophy as Multidisciplinary Inquiry: Envisioning a Future for the Philosophy of Religion*. Albany, NY: State University of New York Press, 2009.

———. *Science and Religious Anthropology: A Spiritually Evocative Naturalist Interpretation of Human Life*. With a Foreword by Philip Clayton. Farnham, UK: Ashgate, 2009

———. *Religious and Spiritual Experiences: A Multidisciplinary Inquiry into their Nature, Functions, and Value*. Cambridge, UK: Cambridge University Press, 2010.

Wilson, David Sloan. *Darwin's Cathedral: Evolution, Religion, and the Nature of Society*. Chicago, IL: University of Chicago Press, 2002.

———. *Evolution for Everyone: How Darwin's Theory Can Change the Way We Think about Our Lives*. New York, NY: Bantam Dell, 2007.

———. and Elliott Sober. *Unto Others: The Evolution of Psychology of Unselfish Behavior*. Cambridge, MA: Harvard University Press, 1998.

———. Editor, with Jonathan Gottschall. *The Literary Animal: Evolution and the Nature of Narrative*. Evanston, IL: Northwestern University Press, 2005.

Wilson, Edward O. *Human Nature*. With a new preface. Cambridge, MA: Harvard University Press, 2004; originally published 1978.

———. *Consilience: The Unity of Knowledge*. New York, NY: Random House, 1998; Vintage Books, 1999.

Wolter, Allan, O.F.M., translator and editor. *Duns Scotus: Philosophical Writings*. New York, NY: Thomas Nelson & Sons, 1962.

Wood, William. "On the New Analytic Theology, or: The Road Less Traveled." In *Journal of the American Academy of Religion*, 77/4 (December 2009), pp. 941–60.

Wu, Kuang-Ming. *On Chinese Body Thinking: A Cultural Hermeneutic*. With a foreword by Robert Cummings Neville. Leiden/New York/ Cologne: Brill, 1997.

———. *On the "Logic" of Togetherness: A Cultural Hermeneutic*. With a foreword by Robert Cummings Neville. Leiden/Boston/Cologne: Brill, 1998.

Xunzi. *Xunzi: A Translation and Study of the Complete Works*. Three volumes. Translated and edited by John Knoblock. Stanford, CA: Stanford University Press. Volume 1, books 1–6 (1988). Volume 2, books 7–16 (1990). Volume 3, books 17–32 (1994).

Yong, Amos, and Peter G. Heltzel, editors. *Theology in Global Context: Essays in Honor of Robert Cummings Neville*. New York, NY, and London, UK: T & T Clark International, 2004.

York, Michael, Denise Cush, and Catherine Robinson, editors. *Encyclopedia of Hinduism*. London, UK: Routledge, 2008.

Index

Abandonment, of self, 113–18
Abduction, xxi, 56
Abhinavagupta, 327
Abraham, 147, 154
Abrahamic religions, 125
Absolute, 195; Absolute Spirit, 188–89
Abstraction, and concreteness in philosophy, 128–29, 174–76; metaphysical versus reductionist, 130
Abstractness, of determinateness per se, 193
Abyss, 20, 222–25; mystical, 303, 309–12; mystical path of, 323–24
Accountability, in theology 16
Act of To Be, 26, 118, 181–84, 217–21, 258, 275, 292–93, 340
Act, of creation, 309
Actual occasions, 13, 176–66, 195
Actuality/potentiality, 181–82
Actualization, 3–4, 36–42, 197–99, 235–41
Adam, 274
Adaptive advantage, 101–02. See also Evolution
Adepts, 251
Adepts. See virtuosity
Adequacy, of metaphysics, xxi–xxii, 44, 331
Advaita Vedanta, 42, 107, 160, 231, 234, 260, 303
Aesthetic judgment, 196

Aesthetic judgment, 200
Aesthetic, new for our age, 165–66
Aesthetics, 183–86
Affirmation, 45
Affordances, 68
Afterlife, 242–44
Age, of persons in heaven, 242–43
Agency, 101–02; universal attribution in childhood, 254
Agents, supernatural, xix. See also Supernaturalism
Alcorta, Candace S., 333
Alexander the Great, 55
Alienation, 25
Alive, 305
All under Heaven, 128
Allah, 10
Allan, George, 68
Almond, Gabriel A., 328
American Theological Society, xxv
Analogy, 71–73, 321; of being, 118, 171, 180–84, 245–46; of human creativity, 217–18; of proportion and proper proportionality, 182–84; in Thomas Aquinas, 118
Analytic philosophy, xix, 14–15, 68, 326
Analytic pragmatism, 326
Anatman, 308
Anderson, Victor, 68
Angels, 274
Anger, 38

Annales School, 156
Annihilation, 304–06, 311
Anselm, 113, 180
Anthropological ultimacy, 5, 107–08, 244
Anthropology, 7, 25, 110, 139; and colonialism 50–51; cultural, 82–83
Anthropomorphism, 27, 85108, 110–11, 119, 141, 147, 292, 296, 320
Anti-Semitism, 155
Apologetics, xviii–xix
Apophatic theology, 2, 19–20, 33, 103, 108–09, 251, 303, 324
Appleby, R. Scott, 328
Applicability, 331
Applicability, 44
Applicability, xxi–xxii
Appreciation, 241
Apsu, 126
Aquinas, Thomas, xxi, 5, 26, 34, 77, 86, 118, 130, 170, 180–84, 191, 217–21, 245–46, 258–62, 292–93, 326, 337–38, 340–41; intentionality in God, 181; Thomism, 130, 230
Arbitrariness, 17, 38, 222–23, 258, 260–62, 267–68, 276–79, 311, 323
Archeology, 7
Argument, xv–xvii, xxi; vs. argumentation, 56–57, like rope, not chain, 58, 287
Aristotelian tradition, 185
Aristotelianism, 55
Aristotle, 14–15, 34, 113, 170, 174, 182, 193, 196, 222, 234, 282, 306, 340
Arjuna, 116–19
Armentrout, Kenneth, xxv
Armstrong, Karen, 330
Art (arts), vi, 5–6, 25, 58, 82, 87, 130, 200
Aryan traditions, 55
Asad, Talal, 4, 327, 329
Asceticism, 106–07
Aseity, divine, 274–75
Asherites, 291–92
Ashoka, 341
Assumptions, background and foreground, 46–47
Asymmetry, in ontological creative act, 222–25

Athleticism, 304–06
Atman, 39, 85–86, 115, 173–74, 256
Atomism, 194–95
Attachment, 47, 65, 70–71
Attention, in thinking ultimacy, 106, 299–300, 302
Augustine, 47, 243, 331, 340
Authenticity, xvii, 10, 20
Author of this book, described, 325
Authority, xv, xx, 31, 79
Auxier, Randall E., 333, 336
Avatars, 19116, 255, 315
Averroes, 340
Avicenna, 326
Awe, 17, 38, 284
Axial Age, 4, 16, 32–33, 55, 315, 330; religions, 41, 74, 79, 84–87, 113, 127, 1161–61, 145–48, 150–51, 294, 327

Babylonian religion, 126–27
Banana, 136, 142–43
Barrett, Nathaniel, 68, 333
Bartel, T. W., 326
Barth, Karl, xx–xxi, 17, 32, 149–50, 152, 157, 325, 327–28, 330, 337
Beauty, xv, 93, 108, 122, 131, 175, 280; glimpst from the corner of the eye, 12
Becoming, 235–41
Being (being-itself, *ipsum esse*), 21, 61, 77, 173–91, 245–47, 297, 321; analogical or univocal, 176, 180–84; as common to beings, 179–80, 184–86, 246; density of, as value, 199–201; determinate or indeterminate, 171–72, 176, 184–91, 246–47; dialectic of, 176; as dynamic dialectic, 188–91; as first object of intellect, 180; one or many, 176–80; power of, 311; as property, 184–85; question of, 169–72; as totality, 186–91, 246; and unity, 174
Belief, 6; costliness of, 46; meaning of, 45–48; reasons for, 101–02; religious, xix, 6, 70, 45–48, 165–66; unconscious, 46
Bell, Catherine M., xix
Bellah, Robert, 32, 330, 336

Benjamin, tribe of, and the Levite, 126–27
Berdyaev, Nicolas, 309, 342
Berger, Peter L., 29–33, 42, 48, 67, 109, 112, 329–30, 333
Bernstein, Richard, 68, 333–334
Berthrong, John H., xxv
Bhagavad Gita, 117–18, 315
Bhakti religion, 111, 118, 312
Bias, xvii, 6
Bible, 77, 149–50. *See also* Hebrew Bible, New Testament
Big Bang, 124, 149–50, 153, 155, 204, 220, 238, 241
Bigotry, 159
Biochemistry, 19
Biology, evolutionary, xx. *See also* Evolution
Birthdays, 92
Bliss, 109, 284
Bloch, Ernst, 327
Bodhisattva, 106, 312, 226
Body, in knowing, 283; as material quality of symbols, 304; as metaphor, 75
Bondage, spiritual, 20. *See also* Spirituality
Bosnians, 8
Boston Theological Society, xxv
Boundaries, of disciplines, xviii; policing, 8; of religious communities, 48
Boundary conditions, 3–4, 31–33, 109–13, 164; for human life, 243; as world defining, 97–98, 102–93
Boyarin, Daniel, 8, 328, 340–41
Bracketing the truth question, 20–21
Bradley, F.H., 195, 338
Brahma, 147, 116
Brahman, xxii, 1, 19, 26, 39, 109, 115, 117–18, 121, 124, 173–75, 220,–21, 229, 231, 234, 255–56, 259–60, 266, 288; Nirguna and Saguna, 85–86, 132, 273, 291, 308; *see also* Nirguna
Brahmanism, 2, 106, 115, 17, 132
Brandom, Robert, xix, 68–69, 328, 326, 334
Brockington, John, 335

Broken symbols, 19–20, 148, 159–61, 280, 324, 327. *See also* Symbols
Buchler, Justus, 68, 327
Buddha, 16, 113–14, 147, 151, 157, 231, 307, 231; Buddha-Mind, 1, 19, 220; teachings of, 77
Buddhism (or Buddhists), xvii, 2, 4–5, 7, 8, 10, 18, 26–27, 38, 40, 78, 86–96, 105–07, 111, 119, 127, 129, 137–38, 145, 150, 14–55, 194, 229–32, 234, 242, 303, 308, 329–30, 31; concepts of self, 113–15; ultimate cognitive frame, 151. *See also* Chan, Madhyamaka, Yogacara, Pure Land Buddhism
Buddhist-Confucian cultures, 91–92
Bultmann, Rudolf, xx
Bureaucracy, heavenly, 296

Cabbala, 86
Cairns, Huntington, 338
Cannibalism, 146
Capps, Walter H., 327
Care, 11
Carman, John Braisted, 340
Categories, xvi, xxi, 26–27, 60–61, 129; in Peirce, 334; of *Philosophical Theology*, and theism, 258–62; religious, 35–42
Category of the Ultimate, in Whitehead, 285–86, 337
Causation, 129, 246–47; final and efficient, 50–52; in indexical reference, 71–72, 288–89; mechanical models of, 140–41
Celibacy, 302
Chan Buddhism, 256
Chan, Wing-tsit, 220, 340–41
Change, 912, 233–34, 243, 257–58
Chaos, 31, 126, 273; needs no explanation, 225
Chapman, J. Harley, 325, 334
Chapple, Christopher Key, 342
China, 122; and Buddhism, 55
Chittick, William C., 339
Choice, 3–4, 39, 41, 201–02, 277–79
Chosen People, 78, 84, 122, 147
Christ, 19

Christendom, 91
Christianity (or Christians), xvii–xviii, 4–5, 8, 11, 18, 26, 31, 50, 46–47, 50–51, 55, 65, 77, 83–84, 86–98, 106, 118, 123, 129, 152, 154–55, 159–60, 170, 174, 230–32, 234, 255, 262–63, 274, 312, 325–26, 330; concepts of self, 114–18; evangelical, 9, 46–48, 111, and gay rights, 295
Chrysostom, 8
Citation, in *Philosophical Theology*, xxii
Civilization, 136–37; damaged by scientific reductionism, 53–54
Clarke, Desmond M., 332
Clooney, Francis X., S.J., xix–xx, 326, 341
Cobb, John B., Jr., 279
Cognitive error, 164
Cognitive science, 18, 52. See also Science
Coherence, xxi–xxii, 44, 331; in sacred canopies, 31–32
Collins, Randall, 55
Colonialism, 165–66
Colossians, 255, 274
Commentary, 25, 42
Commitment, religious, 43–44
Common natures, 198
Communities, 41, 47; boundaries of, 15–17; and liturgies, 89; religious, 18
Comparative Religious Ideas Project, 335
Comparative theology, xix–xx, 21, 21, 129, 152
Compassion, 231
Complexity, 199–201, 236, 268–69, 271; needing explanation, 130–31
Components, xi, 3–4, 10, 33–34, 97, 197–202, 227, 262–66, 312, 321; conditional and essential, 35–42, 171–72, 178–80, 193–99, 219–21, 227, 146–47, 284–85, 310, of temporal modes, 235–41, 263–66, from Paul Weiss, 338; as formed, 137; of harmonies, 36–42, 201–02; as ultimate, 243 and value, 206–07
Comportment, toward the real, 43–44
Comprehensiveness, xxi
Comprehensiveness continuum, 43–44, 91–93, 107, 131–32, 320

Computer models of interpretation, 65–66
Concern continuum, 106–07, 119
Concrescence, in Whitehead, 223, 235, 268
Conditions, for existence, 35–42; for determinateness, 3–4; for ultimacy, 173–76; as unconditioned, 131
Confessionalism, in theology, xvi–xvii, xx, 2, 17, 78–79, 175, 325. See also Theology
Conflict, among valuable things, 271, 280
Confucianism (or Confucians), xvii, xix, 4–5, 12, 63, 75, 77, 82–84, 87, 106, 119, 127, 145, 147, 150–52, 154–55, 171, 228–29, 234, 255, 257, 312–13, 315, 239–30; on ancestors, 137. See also Neo-Confucianism
Confucius, 79, 147
Consciousness, 26, 64, 106, 114, 128, 147, 173–74, 228–32, 303, 308, 327; double, 45–47; indeterminate if pure, 85–86, 256; metaphors for ultimacy, 1–2, 172, 253–62, 282
Consent to being in general, 38
Conservatism, 9
Consistency, xxi–xxii, 44, 331
Contemplation, 302–03, 312; and components of harmony, 306–09; path of, 323–24
Context, 190–91; of interpretation, 290, 298–300; of mystical interpretations, 302, 312; of religious belief, 48; transcendence of, 128
Continental philosophy, 64, 68–69. See also Philosophy
Contingency, radical, 3–4, 12, 16–17, 33–34, 37–38, 74–75, 93, 97–98, 101–03, 113, 116, 122–23, 135, 137, 225, 309–12
Continua, in worldviews, 28, 98, 118–19, 131–32. See also Concern continuum, Comprehensiveness continuum, Intensity continuum, Sacred/Mundane continuum, Sharing continuum, Sophisticated/popular religion continuum, Transcendence/intimacy continuum
Continuity of thought and body, 203

Contradictions, human, 3
Contrast terms, 186–91
Contrasts, 33–34, 199–200
Control, 201
Conventional reference, 70–73, 288–90. *See also* Reference
Conversion, 47
Cook, Francis H., 337
Correction, 135; of life, 103; of meaning-symbols, 146–48. *See also* Vulnerability to correction
Corrington, Robert S., xxv, 140, 334, 337, 340
Cosmic epoch, 278
Cosmological ultimates, 3–4. *See also* Ultimate reality, Ontological ultimate reality
Cosmology, philosophical, vi, xix, 2, 60, 112–13, 170; embracing value and fact, 200; as metaphysics, 169. *See also* Philosophy
Cosmos, 29–30; conceptions of, 123, 310
Counterculture, 140–41
Counter-factuals, 34, 237, 311
Courage, 147, 208
Covenant, 78, 152
Created world, experience of, 303–06
Creation, 11; act of, vi; of everything determinate, 1–4; *ex nihilo*, 118, 172, 284; story of, 150; of the world, 115–16; unintelligibility of, 311; *See also* God as creator, Ontological creative act, Ontological ultimate reality
Creativity, 236–41, 264, 284–85
Creator, 37; character of, 155–56; not intentional, 124; *See also* God, Ontological Act of Creation, Ontological ultimate reality
Crises, 295; and ultimate concern, 107; for worldviews, 143
Crisp, Oliver D., 326
Crosby, Donald A., 333
Cultivation, of religious virtuosity, 301–17
Culture, 13, 71, 101, 110; evolution of, 102–03; habits of changed, 63–64; and linguistic systems, 48; resisted in the name of religion, 54; and scientific reductionism, 49–52

Cumulative value-identity, 207
Curiosity, 142
Curley, Edward, 332

Damnation, 68
Dao, xxii, 1–2, 19, 25, 33, 42, 75, 83084, 86, 102, 115, 121, 123–24, 128–30, 132, 138, 151, 155, 170, 173, 175, 191, 205, 220, 228–29, 255, 257–62, 267, 296; as river, 159; transcendent and embodied, 257
Daodejing, 124, 228, 257, 336
Daoism (or Daoists), xvii, 4–5, 37, 77–78, 87, 115, 119, 125, 127, 137–38, 145, 147, 151, 154–55, 160–61, 171, 173, 228–29, 233–34, 255–57, 291, 296, 315, 339
Darfur, 88
Dates, in time, 239–41, 265, 277–79
Davaney, Sheila Greeve, 333
David, King, 127, 147, 342; and Bathsheba, 295–96
Davidson, Donald, xix, 70, 334
Dawkins, Richard, 328
De facto character of world, 227–28
Deacon, Terrence, 334
Death, 12, 38, 65, 74, 107, 119, 131–32, 311; and life after, 144
Decentering, 113
Decision points, and intelligibility, 278, 285–86
Decisions, 198–99, 247, 284–85
Deconstruction, of self, 308–09
Deduction, in Peirce, 57
Deely, John, 340
Deep grammar, 48
Deer Park Sermon, 113
Definiteness, 268
Deism, xviii
Delighting in, as love, 314
Demonic, in symbols, 90, 293–96
Demons, 255
Demonstration, in Peirce, 57
Denial, 10, 38, 203
Dennett, Daniel, 328
Density, of being, 199–201
Dependent co-origination (*pratitya samutpada*), xxii, 86, 194

Depth, 268, 279; infinite, 321; of intension in nature, 135–38; of nature, 103; in Tillich, 270
Descartes, 53, 55–56, 59, 63–68, 193, 219, 327, 331–32, 339
Destiny, 147, 229–30
Determinate distance, in analogy, 182–83
Determinateness, vi, 1–4, 112–13, 121, 184–91, 275–76, 278–79; in God, 96; and indeterminateness, 133, 177–80; and modeling, 254–62; in ontological creative act, 259–60; presupposed universally, 58, 60–61; respects of, 35; theory of, 21, 35–42, 171, 193–209, 246–47, 321; traits of, vi; in ultimacy, 2, 243–44; of world, 227–31, 309
Determinations of being, 170–72
Determinism, 49–52
Development, in worldviews, 93
Devotion, 314
Dewey, John, 68, 169, 327, 332, 337, 339
Dharmas, 114, 138, 151, 194
Dialectic, 85–86, 130, 151, 166, 169–72, 232, 256, 273, 284–87, 289, 329; of being, 174; defined, 112–13; in metaphysics, 57–61; of one and many, 224–25; of ultimate reality, 245–47
Dialectical illusion, 56
Dialogue, interreligious, 48
Diaspora, 154
Dickens, Charles, 72, 253
Diet, 292, 294, 302
Dignity, 41
Discipline, spiritual, 118
Discrimination, through signs, 65
Disgust, 73
Disharmony, 146. *See also* Harmony
Dispensationalism, 96
Distraction, in meditation and contemplation, 307
Diversity, religious, 7, 199–200, 263
Divine intentionality, not indicated by known world, 124
Divine life, 266–69
DNA, 136–37
Doctrine of the Mean, 151
Doctrine, 15–17, 77, 165

Domains, within worldviews, 82–84, 107, 142
Doubt, 111
Dravidian traditions, 55
Dream worlds, 139
Dualism, 115
Durkheim, Emile, 54, 331
Dyad, 218, 224, 234, 340. *See also* One
Dynamism, 234; of eternity, 241–44; of existential field, 265; in sacred canopies, 131; of temporal modes, 238–41, 322

Ea, 126
Earth, 135, 155
Earth, cosmic center, 123
Ecclesiastes, 242, 341
Eckel, Malcolm David, 47, 330–31, 335
Eckhart, Meister, 309, 342
Ecology, 19
Economics, 25, 50
Ecstatic fulfillments, xv–xvi, 12, 20–21, 58, 107, 133, 148
Education, 160
Edwards, Jonathan, 38
Ego, 308–09
Egypt's narrative, 156
Egyptian religion, 229
Eightfold Noble Path, 114
Ein Sof, 124
Einstein, Albert, 53, 204
Eliade, Mircea, 32, 40, 138, 150–51, 165, 335
Elwes, R.H.M., 331
Emanation, 193
Embodiedness, 39–40
Emergence, double meaning of, 257–62; spontaneous, 1–2, 151–52, 228–32; as metaphor for ultimacy, 253–62, 282
Emotional tone, of symbolic engagements, 312
Empires, and Axial Age religions, 122
Empirical reality, 49–50
Empiricism, and intelligibility, 285–86; in *Philosophical Theology*, 6–7; in religious truth, 42–44
Emptiness, 48, 84, 116–18, 231, 288, 291

Enemies, 115
Engagement, xix, 4, 6, 15–17, 69–72, 107; versus belief; defined, 67; with existential field, 203; versus truth, 67–68; of ultimates, 131–33, 287–90
Enlightenment, European, 25, 140–41; spiritual, 146
Enuma Elish, 126
Environment, 265; social, 136–37
Epistemology, 21, 54, 68, 309; pragmatic, 320; of symbolic engagements, 297
Essential components, 178–80, 291; of modes of time, 235–41. See also Components, Conditional Components, Harmony
Esthetics, 68
Eternity, 21, 133, 144, 205, 247, 322, 339; hostility to, 235; of ontological creative act, 172, 219–20, 232–35, 262, 266–69, 277–79; of a person's life, 239–40; as togetherness of modes of time, 238–41; as ultimate, 243
Ethics, 58, 68
Eucharist, 146
Europe, 55
Evangelical Christianity. See Christianity, evangelical
Evidence, 7
Evil, 42, 152
Evolution, 10, 20, 153, 308; biological and cultural, 101–03; in the human body, 135–38; as mechanism of creation, 124
Evolutionary biology, 7, 18, 41, 52, 139
Excellences, in God, 275–76
Exclusivism, religious, 7, 10
Exhibition, in philosophy, xxi–xx
Exile, 127
Existential continua, 91–93. See also Worldviews
Existential decisions, 294–95
Existential definition of the self, 27, 105, 108, 153–55
Existential field, vi, 3–4, 11–12, 40–41, 202–09, 237–41, 327; and intelligibility, 283; non-spatiotemporal, 202–03

Existential location, 3–4, 36–42, 97, 115, 137, 147, 202–09, 227, 237–41, 262–66, 312, 321; of human body in evolution, 135–38; relative to ontological creative act, 269–71; as ultimate, 243
Existential location value, 207
Existentialism, 5
Exodus, 19, 154, 333
Experience, 4, 18, 28, 69, 135, 148; of ontological act of creation, 298–99; and pressure for transcendence, 131; religious, xv, 139, 247, adaptive in evolution, 308, through theological theory, 284; of ultimacy, 5, 300
Explanation, 102–03, 112, 135, 139, 164, 284, 323; as complex or simple, 130; of ontological creative act, 223–25; in philosophy, 127–31
Explication of the hypothesis, 57
Extension, of cosmos, 19, 64, 135, 138, 155–58, 233, 265, 279; of interpretation, 71–72; ultimate in, 269–71
Extensive continuum, 232, 340
Ezra, 294

Fact/value distinction, 13–14
Facticity, 227
Faith, 46, 203, 262
Fall, 311
Fallibilism, in metaphysics, 58–61, 324
Falsity, 10
Families, 40, 93m 118–19, 206; for learning love, 313
Fantasy, 72–73
Feeling, 305
Feminism, 295
Feng shui, 140
Ferre, Fredrick, 68
Feuerbach, L. 327
Fiction (literary), 202–03
Filial piety, xxii, 313
Film, 88
Final Dissipation, 241
Finite/infinite contrasts, 33–40, 73–79, 83, 93, 97–98, 107–08, 111, 113,

Finite/infinite contrasts *(continued)* 115–18, 132–33, 173–76, 234, 304, 311–12, 319; and ultimate mystery, 44
First object of intellect, 184
First Person, of Trinity, 261–62
First principles, 284, 323
First Samuel, 127
Firstness, 15, 70, 224, 334, 340
First-order, claims, 6; issues defining theology, xv–xxi, 79, 251; ultimate realities, 16–17
First-person, 146–48
Fitting together, 195–99, 246
Flint, Thomas P., 326
Flood, Gavin, 329
Florensky, Pavel, 342
Flow, temporal, 197–99, 235–41, 266–69, 276–79
Folk, culture, 88, 159; religion, 108, on life after death, 144; science versus university science, 87–90; symbols, 44
Form of the Good, 86, 112, 130, 197, 235; creating the world, 273
Form, vi, 3–4, 13, 36–42, 97, 116, 197–202, 205–09, 227, 236–41, 262–66, 312, 321; as future possibilities, 246; and intelligibility, 283–83; as ultimate 243; with value, 206–07, 271
Formal reality, 338
Founders, of religions, 91
Four causes (in Aristotle), 222Four Noble Truths, 151
Fourfold Noble Truths, 114, 151, 307
Framing theology, 149–61
Frankenberry, Nancy K., xix, 325–26, 333, 332, 337
Freedom, 111, 133, 221–22, 260–62, 323, 326
Frege, 14–15
Frei, Hans, 48, 331
Freud, Sigmund, 51, 327
Friendship, same-sex, 83–84
Frisina, Warren G., 333
Fullness of being, 275–76
Fundamental dilemma of ontology, 184–91
Fundamentalism, 9–11, 147
Funerals, 92

Future, 3–4, 197–99, 207, 235–41, 247, 263–66, 277–79, 322. *See also* Temporal modes, Time, Past, Present

Galaxies, in collision, 123
Ganesh, 116
Gays, 11, 295
Genealogy, 4
Generic traits of existence, 169
Genetic division, 13
Genius, 16–17, 51, 79
Gentiles, 154, 158
Genus/species, 14
Geomancy, 140
Gilson, Etienne, 337
Glory, 284
God, 1–2, 5, 37, 40, 48, 75, 84, 86–88, 116, 124, 132, 141, 152–53, 170, 191, 208, 220–21, 269–71, 279–86, 288, 291, 295; as agent, 269–70, 341; backside of, 255; beyond gods, 230; blessing from, 132; as boundary condition, 123; as creator, 115, 123, 260, of non-human nature, 126; as determinate or not, 175, 233, 260–62; and evil, 42; as father, 20 118, 300; as fellow sufferer, 279; as free, 260–62 (*see also* Freedom); not in genus, 259–62; as good, 118; as Ground of Being, 5, 150, 340; High, 310; image of the invisible, 274; infinite in contrast to finite things, 180–84; as intelligent, 219; as king, 123, 125; as Lord, 125; as malleable or unchangeable, 234; and metaphors for ultimacy, 256–62; name of, 290; nature of, 118, 322–23; and ontological creative act, 229–32; as partisan, 125; personal, 38, 161; present to, 232–35; as a player in human narrative, 155–58; purposes of, 9; referred to as common noun and proper name, 260–61; revelatory, 16–17; as rock of salvation, 61, 124, 159; as shepherd, 255; as simple, 183; as temporal or eternal, 232–35; for Whitehead, 177; will of for retribution, 296
Godhead, 309

Gods, 1–2, 33, 39, 121–24, 292; household, 73, 146; personal, 34, 137–38
Goffman, Erving, 335
Golden Egg (Hiranyagarbha), 19, 22, 153, 310
Goldstein, Jonathan, 336
Good, 175; and evil, 146; Plato's lecture on, 14
Goodness, of harmonies, 263–64, 280
Grace, 17
Grange, Joseph, 68
Gratitude, 11–12, 17, 38, 75, 169, 314
Gratuitousness, 38
Great Ultimate, (taiji), 25, 37, 130, 151, 173–74, 228–89, 234, 258–60, 267, 273, 309
Greece, 55; philosophy of, 127; religion of, 229
Green, Garrett, 328
Grief, over Christendom, 165–66
Griffin, 340
Griffin, David Ray, 332
Ground of Being. *See* God, as Ground of Being
Groundedness, 111, 116, 205–07, 270–71; in components, 39–42, 201–02; and intelligibility, 282–83
Guanilo, 180
Guanyin, 230
Guanyin, 312
Guidance, from metaphysics, 247
Gurus, 84, 303–04

Habits, interpretive, 63–68
Haecceity, 198–99, 264–65
Hahn, Lewis Edwin, 333, 336
Hall, David L., 68
Hamilton, Edith, 338
Han Dynasty, 86
Hardwick, Charley D., 333
Harmony, 3–4, 21, 33–34, 97–98, 106, 137–38, 146–48, 171–72, 176, 78, 231, 246–47, 262–66, 278–79, 311–12; de facto, 266; defined, 35–42; discursive, 36, 266; not always good, 197–98; in nature, 160–61; in Plato, 14; synchronic and diachronic, 200–01; theory of, 193–209, 321; transcendental traits of, 197–209
Harrell, Bert, 337
Hartshorne, Charles, 68, 224–25, 233, 284, 339–41
Harvey, Van A., 328
Hasler, Joshua, xxv
Hassidism, 312
Heaven, 65, 74–75, 82, 141, 175, 242–44, 260, 288; bureaucracy in, 125; and Earth, 25, 37, 83–84, 86, 115, 129–30, 255; is my father, 269–70; and straw dogs, 124, 336
Heavenly Principle, 191
Hebrew Bible, xxii, 61, 122, 124–27, 152, 156–58, 242, 255, 274, 342
Hegel, G. W. F., xviii, 15, 59, 112–13, 188–91, 193, 246; Hegelianism, 69
Heidegger, Martin, 59, 61, 149, 170, 174, 337
Hell, 65
Hellenism, 122
Heltzel, Peter G., 325, 335
Hermeneutics, 2
Hierarchy, in form and value, 199–201
Highlands Institute for American Religious and Theological Thought, xxv
Hillman, Anne, xxv
Hinduism, xvii, 4–5, 10, 18, 40, 86–87, 115–16, 127, 145, 147, 154–55, 234, 273, 291, 330
Historicism, 17–19
History, 25; of religions, 6
HIV/Aids, 206–07
Hobbes, 193
Hobbes, Thomas, 50, 193
Hocking, William Ernest, 68
Holiness Code, 294
Holocaust, 147
Holocaust, 329
Holy One of Israel, 84
Holy Spirit, 20, 95, 152, 263
Hoopes, James, 334
Hope, 262
Human Condition, xvi
Humaneness (*ren*), 312–13

Humanism, 11–12, 328
Humanity, 128
Hume, David, xviii, 193
Humility, 38, 324
Husserl, Edmund, 332
Hutagalong, Toar, xxv
Hwa Yen Buddhism, 151
Hyperactive agency detection, universal in children, 139. *See also* Supernaturalism
Hypothesis, xxi, 6, 282–86, 332; about determinateness, 278–79 (*see also* Determinateness, theory of); metaphysical, xxi, 56–61, 76, 169–72; about ontological creative act, 222–25, 319–24; of *Philosophical Theology*, 1–4; about ultimacy, 245–47, 287–90, 297–300

I Jing, 218
Iconic reference, 15, 70–73, 144, 282–86, 288–90; in metaphysical theories, 293–96; in narratives, 157–58
Ideal language, 326
Ideal types, 50, 142
Idealism, 71; absolute, 186; German, 81, 105–06
Identity, in Barth's theology, 150; individual, 41–42; religious, 8, 10, 153, 324; ultimate, 4
Idolatry, 85, 135, 164; as pressure for transcendent symbols, 124–27
Ignorance, harmful, 146
Illusion, 132
Imagination, 101–02, 329
Immediacy, in material signs, 306; of ontological creative act, 223
Immensity, 135, 207, 232–35, 270, 339; of ontological creative act, 172, 219–20
Imperialism, in the study of religion, 18
Implosion, of sacred worldviews, 19–20, 146–47
Importance, in object of interpretation, 72; ultimate, 73
Impurity, 146
Incarnation, 19, 274
Inclusivism, religious, 7

Incommensurability of values, 208–09
Indeterminateness, 33–34, 44, 184–91, 263; of being; in Brahman, 117; in ontological creative act, 1–4; in pure consciousness, 256; in temporal flow, 277–79
Indexical reference, 70–73, 144–45, 159–60, 253, 282–86, 288–92, 317; in narratives, 157–58
Individuality, of ontological creative act, 259–60
Individuals versus kinship groups, 55; versus societies, 32
Individuation, of worldviews, 91–93
Indra, 86
Induction, in Peirce, 57–58
Inferentialism, 69
Infinite, bad, 188–89
Infinitesimals, in ontological creative act, 223–24, 280
Infinity, 44. *See also* Finite/infinite contrasts
In-groups, and out-groups, 11, 41, 158, 164
Innocence, 145
Inquiry, xxii, 43–44, 56–61
Insiders, 52
Instrumentation, 53
Integration, 235–41, 265, 267
Integration, and contemplation, 307
Intellect, 180–84
Intelligent design, 130, 132, 280–81
Intelligibility, 222, 278, 322; with antecedent potentials and future possibilities, 284–85; as created, 218–21; and decision points, 285–86; four dimensions of, 282–86; of ontological creative act, 323–24
Intending the ultimates, 302
Intension, of cosmos, 19, 135–38, 148, 155–58, 164–65, 279; ultimate in, 269–71
Intensity continuum, 91–93, 98, 107, 131–32, 320
Intention, of interpretation, 71–72
Intentional fulfillments, 303
Intentionality, 139, 268, 316, 330; attribution of, 254–56; divine, 175,

280–86; in interpretations, 66–67, 74–75; and reductionism, 49–50; for engaging ultimacy, 309–12; in thinking ultimacy, 298–300
Interests, human, 275
Interpretation, 15–17, 33–34, 63–68, 288, 293–96
Interpretation, always in context, 160–61; as act, 66; defined, 66; theory of, 28, 97–98; and orientations, 81–84
Interpreters, 288–90
Intimacy, 84–87, 97–98, 102; in symbols of ultimacy, 135–48, 164–65, 281–82; 297, 320–21
Intimacy/transcendence continuum. *See* Transcendence/intimacy continuum
Intuition, 332; and intelligibility, 285–86
Iran, 9
Ishvara, 116, 132, 231, 309
Islam (or Muslims), xvii 4–5, 7–8, 10–11, 18, 55, 77, 86–87, 123, 129, 145, 150, 154–55, 170, 174, 230, 234, 260, 273–74, 290, 330
Isomorphism, 1, 253
Israel, 150, 154, 156
Israelites, 122

Jack Frost, 159
Jainism, 107, 127, 154–55
James, Thomas A., 341
James, William, 32, 45, 51, 68, 331, 337; on metaphysical pluralism, 175–76
Jang, Jaehu, xxv
Jaspers, Karl, 330
Jerusalem, 40
Jesus Christ, 118
Jesus Christ, 20, 46, 70–71, 115, 118, 124–25, 147, 152, 243, 255, 262, 274, 293, 315, 328, 333; historical, 262; as sacrifice, 65
Jnana yoga, 118
Job, 123, 154, 342
Johnson, Mark, 75
Jonah, 39
Jones, Judith, 68
Joseph, 157
Joshua, 126

Journalism, on religion, xvii
Joy, 111
Joy, 20
Judah, 154
Judaism (or Jews), xvii, xxii, 4–5, 8, 11, 18 40, 55, 77, 83–84, 86, 123, 129, 145, 147, 150, 154–55, 158, 170, 174, 230, 234, 255, 273, 312, 329–30
Judges, 126
Judgments, 208; divine, 205
Justice, 11, 41, 206, 242, 281; universal, 84

Kabala, 234
Kali, the Goddess, 72, 76
Kanofsky, Joseph, 335
Kant, 49–52, 58–60, 70, 145, 193, 235, 327, 330–32, 336–37, 341; causation in, 222; on concepts as rules, 33; failed critique of metaphysics, 55–57, 174–75; on the sublime, 131
Kantian Captivity of the religious imagination, 17–19
Karma, 26, 74, 123, 143, 243, 254; Yoga, 118
Kataphatic theology, 19–20
Kaufman, Gordon D., 341
Kelsey, David, 337
Kierkegaard, Soren, 106, 336
Kim, Chanhong, xxv
Kim, Sungrae, xxv
Kindness, 281
Kinship, 128
Knight of faith, 106
Knowledge, as form, 282; of ontological creative act, 322–23; for its own sake, 308
Kohn, Livia, 78
Krishna, 116–19, 147, 255, 315
Kuehn, Manfred, 331
Kurtz, 328

Lakoff, George, 75
Lamont, Corliss, 328
Language, 334; of philosophy, 127–29; and semiotics, 64–65
Laozi, 147
Leaving, 208

Legends, 293
Legitimation, 31
Leibniz, Gottfried, xviii, 13, 56, 194–95, 204, 219, 280, 331–32, 339
Lesbians, 11
Leuba, James H., 51, 331
Levenson, Jon D., 336
Leviticus, 333
Lewis, C. I., 68
Liberalism, 9
Life, 311; as symbol for the ontological creative act, 266–67
Lindbeck, George, 48
Linguistic turn, 70
Lisbon earthquake, 42
Literacy, 88; theological, 329
Literalism, 10, 293
Literature, 18, 25, 72; as iconic, 253–54
Liturgy, xx, 73; Christian, 88–89; world of 293
Liu Zhi, 339
Liu, Xinjun, xxv
Location, 3–4; in existential field, vi (*see also* Existential location); historical and social, xvii; religious, xv–xvi
Locke, John, xviii, 50
Locklin, Reid B., 326
Log, in rapids, xxi
Logic, 14, 68
Logo-centrism, 51–52, 59–61
Logos (Wisdom), 220, 255, 262–62, 274, 279–80
Lotus Sutra, 137, 310
Love, 17, 109, 115, 133; of enemies, 315; of God and neighbor, 314; mystical path of, 303, 312–17, 323–24; universal, 84
Loving God and God loving, 324; virtuoso, 314–15
Luckman, Thomas, 29

Machle, Edward, 335
Madhyamaka Buddhism, 26–27, 47, 105, 114, 231, 208
Mahabharata, 19, 74, 125, 154, 156–57
Mahayana Buddhism, 84, 106, 114
Maimonides, Moses, 78
Maitreya, 151

Making, sheer, 216–21, 227–32, 281
Mammalian humor, primordial, 64
Mandate of Heaven, 87147, 151, 255
Maps, 72
Marduk, 86, 126, 157, 336
Marginalization, 59–61; in sociology of religion, 30–33
Marriage, 294
Martial traditions in religion, 106, 304
Martyrdom, 10
Marx, 51, 54; Marxism, 11–12, 327–28
Masuzawa, Tomoko, 327, 329
Material force (qi), 310
Material quality, of signs, 65–66, 289–90, 300–03, 309, 323–24
Mathematics, 129, 140–41, 200, 203, 263; as iconic, 253–54; as interpreting world, 13–15; and scientific reductionism, 50–52
Matter, 196
Maturation, in worldviews, 93
McNamara, Patrick, 308, 329, 331, 336, 342
Mead, George Herbert, 68
Meaning, 3–5, 11, 31–33, 68, 71, 103, 107, 142, 203, 231; network and content, 299–03
Meaningfulness, 141–46, 164–65
Meaninglessness, 109
Meat brains, 65, 298
Mediation, of carryover in truth, 298–99
Meditation, 35, 302, 209, 312; path of, 323–24; and unity, 303–06
Medium, between world and creative act, 220–21, 274
Membership, in communities, 92, 154
Mencius, 79
Mental health, 5
Mercy, 230, 281
Messiah, 46
Metaphor, 71–75, 148, 293
Metaphysics, as a function of civilization, 169
Metaphysics, xix, xxi, 7, 18–19, 32, 44, 54–61, 68, 76–79, 113, 128–31, 145, 242, 270, 319, 325; apriori, 58–59; empirical, 97–98; foundational, 58; hypothetical, 174–75; of

ontological ultimacy, 173–91, 244–27, 251, 260–66, 287–90; pluralism in, 171; as rhetorical frame, 149–53; the control on symbols, 169; as system, 61; tested, 58–61; as theological frame, 157–58; and universal adequacy, 130
Methodology, in religious studies, xx, 21
Michelangelo, 76
Microbes, 136, 156
Microscopes as signs, 65
Microstudies, 52
Miller, James E. 78, 337, 341
Mind, 1, 64
Miracle, 140
Models, of ontological creative act, 1–3, 253–62
Modern science, and metaphysics, 60; reconciling with personifying religion, 255–56; *see also* Science
Modernity, 140–41
Modes of being, for Paul Weiss, 177–80; of time, essential and conditional components, 247; *see also* Temporality, modes of.
Moments, 277–29
Monads, 13, 194
Monasticism, 114, 304–05
Monotheism, xxii, 2, 17, 42, 51, 83–84, 110–11, 116, 125, 127, 147, 160–61, 255, 260, 273, 291, 322; and consciousness, 256
Montgomery, 331
Moore, G. E., 184
Moral character, none in God, 280–86
Moral identity, 277–79
Morality, 201
Morphological division, in Whitehead, 13
Morse, Christopher, xx–xxi
Moses, 78, 122, 147, 154–57, 255
Motivation, in creation, 323
Multidisciplinary studies, xx, 54
Mundane, the, in worldviews, 83–84, 90, 244, 287
Mungre, Divine, xxv
Murata, Sachiko, 339
Musement, xxi, 56–57
Mutazilites, 291–92

Mutuality, 196–99, 204–08, 215–21, 233–34, 275–76; as ultimate, 243–44
Mysterium tremendum et fascinans, 32, 68, 139
Mystery, 44, 132
Mysticism, 1, 20, 133, 225, 251, 301–17, 323–24; and the abyss, 315–16; immediacy in, 256
Myth, of reference, 47, 334

Nagarjuna, 151
Naiveté, 145, 159–60
Narayana, 116, 147
Narrative, 19, 31–32, 34, 38–39, 96; broken, 159–61; comparative, 158; and conflict, 8, 156; all symbolically false, 155–58; and intimacy, 153–55; as rhetorical frame, 149–53; truth in, 157
Narrowness, 13
Nasr, Seyyed Hossein, 336, 339–40
Nationalism, 11–12, 328
Natura naturans and *natura naturata*, 221
Natural history, 137
Natural science, 19
Naturalism, 69; in anthropology, 54; in pragmatic epistemology, 64–68; in religion, 328
Nature, depths of, 156–58, 164–65; not always harmonious, 42–43; of ontological creative act, 321–22. *See also* Extension *and* Intension
Nazis, 8, 42, 84, 123, 328
Negation, 132, 276
Nehemiah, 294
Neo-Confucianism, 130, 151, 173, 228, 255–57, 273, 291, 303
Neo-Platonism, 26, 34, 37, 55, 74, 102, 118, 130, 133, 170, 193, 219, 230, 234, 258, 275
Neo-pragmatism, 68–70
Network meaning, 65–66, 309, 312
Networks, of signs, 70–79, 163
Neuroscience, 52
Neville, Beth, vi, xxv
New Age spirituality, 141
New Haven Theological Discussion Group, xxv

New Testament, xxii, 125–27, 152, 274
Newton, Isaac, 53
Nicholson, Hugh, 326
Nine/eleven, 9
Nineveh, 39
Nirguna Brahman, 26, 102, 117. *See also* Brahman *and* Saguna Brahman
Nirvana, 41
Noah, 126, 154
Nominalism, 19
Nomos, 29–31
Non-action (*wu-wei*), 233–34
Non-being (wuji), 131, 151, 173–75, 268, 311; equivalent to being, 171. *See also*, Ultimate of Non-Being, Great Ultimate
Non-dualism, 42, 115, 193, 260
Normative measure, 273
Norse gods, 157
Nothingness, 222–23, 227–28
Novelty, 217–25, 236, 275–76, 279, 323; creation of, 285–86
Numinous, the, 32, 68, 139
Nygren, Anders, 327

Obedience, 125
Objectification, 29–30
Objective reality, 338
Objectivity, in science, 49–52
Obligation, 3–4, 10–11, 39, 68, 107, 201, 231, 241–42, 277–79
Odin, Steve, 337
Odysseus, 88
Oil on the ocean, 137
Old Testament, xxii. *See also* Hebrew Bible
Olivelle, Patrick, 336
One and many, 21, 28, 56, 170–91, 245–47, 285–91, 297–98, 321; not a theological problem, 175–76
One, the, 26, 34, 86–87, 102, 118, 235, 275, 340
Ontological act of creation. *See* Ontological creative act
Ontological context of mutual relevance, 37–38, 171–72, 179–80, 190–91, 207–09, 227–28, 233–25, 246–47, 258–62, 266, 284–86, 291, 297–98, 310–13, 316–17, 321–24; containing the modes of time, 240–41
Ontological creative act, 1–4, 17, 21, 33–34, 159–61; 246–47, 256, 258–62, 291, 298, 301, 309, 311–12, 315, 321–22; argument for summarized, 170–72;eternal and dynamic, 242–44 as free, 276–69; as God, 229–32; as good, 263–66; hypothesis about proved, 218; intelligibility of, 284–86; as loving, 313–17; cannot be modeled, 225; nature of created, 225–32, 322–24; personified, 76; singular, 230–31; no stages of, 280; theory of as symbol for engaging ultimates, 288–300; as ultimate, 243–44
Ontological principle, in Whitehead, 225, 285–86
Ontological status, of properties, 184–86
Ontological ultimate reality, 3–5, 27, 36–37, 153, 227–44; no nature apart from creation, 273–76; not a person, 279–86, predicting, 275–76
Ontology, vi, 21, 58, 60, 149–52; in metaphysics, 169; as rhetorical frame, 149–53
Order, 176; created, 281; needs explanation, 225; intentional, 309; pockets of, 69
Organism and environment, 63, 69
Orientalism, 51
Orientation, 5, 81–93, 106, 123, 139–40, 142–46, 289, 292–96
Orsi, Robert A., 89
Orthodoxies, 92
Others (or Otherness), 3–4, 41, 68, 121–24, 190; love of, 314–17
Otto, Rudolf, 32, 139, 327
Own-being, 47, 186, 193
Ozone layer, bone of my bone, 136

Paganism, 2, 123, 170, 234, 291, 330
Paleogalactic Age, 254
Paleolithic Age, 254
Pannenberg, 340
Pannenberg, Wolfhart, 220, 340
Pantheons, comparative, 25
Park, Sung Bae, 336

Paschal lamb, 70–71
Past, 197–99, 207, 235–41, 277–79, 322. See also Modes of time, Temporal modes
Paths, of mystical engagement, 303–17
Patience, in love, 314–15
Pattern, 33, 197–201
Paul, 150, 152; on eating meat sacrificed to idols, 159–60
Peace, 8; that passes understanding, 20
Peer pressure, 46
Peirce, Charles, xxi, 15, 59, 68–70, 72, 194, 224, 283, 327, 329, 332–34, 340, 342; on metaphysics as hypothetical, 56–57
Perennial Philosophy, 37, 74, 133, 234, 336
Persian religion, 55, 86, 229. See also Zoroastrianism
Personhood, 40–41, 153, 228, 277–79, 323; divine, 155–58; as metaphoric system, 172, 254–62; as model of ontological creative act, 1–2
Personification, 26, 102–03, 159–61, 229–32, 257–58, 274–75
Peters, Richard, xxv
Pharaoh, manipulated by God, 156–57
Phenomenology, 15, 32–33, 59–61, 165; normative, 151
Phenomenon, religion as, 6
Philebus, 14, 196
Phillips, D. Z., xviii
Philosophical cosmology, 68, 112–13, 170
Philosophical Theology (this three-volume project), xvii–xviii, 2, 4–6, 17–21, 31, 69, 112–38, 152, 189, 230, 244, 242, 254, 310
Philosophical theology, xv–xxi; defined for this project, xx–xxii; three layers of, 251
Philosophy of nature. See Philosophical cosmology
Philosophy, xv, 12–15, 20, 25, 86, 325; as critic of worldviews, 294; Confucian, xix; and contemplation, 308; controlling for reductionism, 52–54; defining religion, 5–11; Indian, 12; origin of, 127–28; in *Philosophical Theology*, xvi–xvii; of religion, xviii–xx; and religious symbols, 166; of science, 170; seduced by science, 53–54; systematic, 68; see also Analytic Philosophy, Continental Philosophy, Process Philosophy, Cosmology (philosophical)
Physics, 232; and reductionism, 53
Piety, 40, 206–07, 262
Place, 40–41
Plantinga, Alvin, xviii
Plato, 14–15, 75, 86, 106, 113, 120, 170, 174, 193, 196–97, 206, 235, 273, 228–39
Platonism, xix, 55
Plausibility, 42, 46, 287–88
Plotinus, 170, 174, 218, 224, 234, 339, 341
Pluralism, 32, 96, 152; metaphysical, 175081; religious, 7
Poetry, 16
Poise, xxi
Politics, 58, 125
Polke, Christian, xxv
Popular culture, 87–90
Positivity, of all things, 311
Possibilities, 3–4, 10, 36–42, 73, 97–98 147, 205–09, 235–44, 263–66, 276–79
Possible worlds, 276–79
Postmodernism, xvi, 17–18, 51–52, 59–61, 165–66
Posture, 302
Potentialities, 26, 215–21
Power, 139; dynamics, 51
Practice, religious, xix, 20, 25
Pragmatism, xix, 43, 45–48, 63–70, 320, 326; analytical, xix, 69–70; in Berger's sociology, 30, metaphysical, 12–15;and the self, 106–09
Prakriti, 303
Pratitya samutpada. See Dependent co-origination 194
Prayer, 35, 292, 302; at meals, 84, 87, 109; employing metaphysical theory, 290
Pre-Axial Age religions, 41, 74, 121–24, 158, 165

Predicaments, xv, 11–12, 20–21, 58, 103, 133, 146–48; first person, 147–48
Predication, 182–83
Premises, xvii
Presence to consciousness, 184
Present, 197–99, 207, 235–41, 247, 277–79, 322. *See also* Past, Future, Modes of time
Pre-Socratics, 128
Presuppositions, 112–13; metaphysical, 58
Pride, 115
Principle of the ontological equality of reciprocal determinations, 187–91, 196, 246
Principle of the ontological ground of differences, 185–91, 246
Principles, first, 222, 224–25
Priorities, 107–10, 117, 164, 299, 301, 320
Probation, in Peirce, 57
Problematics of ultimacy, 34–42
Process philosophy, xix, 68–69, 170, 284–85
Process theology, 191
Prochnik, George, 331
Proofs for God's existence, 326
Prophet, 19
Propositional functions, 14–15, 328
Propositions, 70–73
Protestantism, 9, 78–79
Psalms, 61
Psychology, physiological, hermeneutical, and empirical, 51
Psychology, 25
Public, xxii, 15–18; multicultural for philosophy, 55
Pure Land Buddhism, 87, 111, 312. *See also* Buddhism
Purification, 147; of consciousness, 117
Purity, 146; of heart, 106
Purpose, and context of interpretation, 299–300; divine, 38, 41, and interpretation, 66–67, 81–82
Purusha, 303
Pyysiainen, Ilkka, 341

Quantities vs. qualities, 14
Quarks, 53
Quest, spiritual, 305–06

Qur'an, 19, 77, 127, 274

Racism, 11
Rahab, 126
Ramanuja, 221, 340
Ramayana, 19, 125, 154, 157
Raposa, Michael, 334, 342
Rappaport, Roy A., 53–54, 331, 335
Rationalism, 284–85
Rationality, of world, 263–64
Rea, Michael, C., 326
Realism, in worldviews, 139–40
Reality, corrects theory, 297; as disruptive, 5–6; existential, 12; formal 181–82; as phenomena in experience, 59–60; universal structures of, 101
Receptacle, 194
Reductionism, 6, 45–54, 66, 320; price of, 53–54; in identifying religion, 90; in sciences of religion, 97–98
Reference, 20, 43–44, 66, 70–73, 90, 97–98, 144–46, 160–61, 288–89; direct and indirect, 71; iconic, indexical, and conventional, 28, 320 (*see also* Iconic reference, Indexical reference, *and* Conventional reference); literal, 2; in narratives, 157–58; of religious symbols, 27–28
Reformed epistemology, xviii
Regularities, 130
Rehman, Adnan, xxv
Reincarnation, 132, 243
Religion, xv–xvi, 58, 68, 244, 251; approaches to, xviii; authentic, 9–11; as belief in supernatural agents, 6; as cultural, 4, 102–03; as defined, 4–9, 18–19, 84, 95–98, in the popular press, 9; distorted, 9–11; origins of, 52; quasi-, 9–12; versus religions, 17–19; scientific study of, 49–52; as dimension of society, 9–10; theories of, xviii, 21, 29–30, 79, 297, 326; as engaging ultimacy, 20–21; as universal, 4, 17–19, 35–36, 165; as worship of gods, 25
Religions, Abrahamic, 40; diverse, 101–03; symbolized, 102–03; world, xviii, 42–44

Religious philosophy, xx
Religious situation, 7
Religious studies, 20
Remedies, 146
Renouncer traditions, 106–07. 111. 336
Rents, in sacred canopies, 31–33
Renunciation, of proximate concerns, 107
Representationalism, 63–64
Representations, 300; subjective and objective, 49–50
Republic, Plato's, 206
Resentment, 38
Resonance, of symbols, 71
Resources, religious, 9
Respect, of comparison, 26; of interpretation, 43
Responsibility, 145, 276–87
Revelation, xv, xx, 16–17, 77–79, 95, 110–11, 152, 326, 328
Revelatory frame, 149
Rhetoric, 2, 103; center of gravity of, 86–87, 146–47
Richardson, Robert D., 331
Ricoeur, Paul, 145–46, 337
Righteousness, 39, 201, 241, 262
Ritschl, Albrecht, 327
Rituals, 25, 46, 82–83, 132; and interpretation, 66–67; and sacrifice, 257
Road rage, 336
Roman Catholics, 8–9, 89, 146
Romanticism, 13, 140–41
Rome, 55
Roots, religious, 92
Rorty, Richard, xix, 68–70, 326, 333–34
Rose thorns, 137
Rosenthal, Sandra, 68
Ross, James F., 326
Rower, 304–06
Royce, Josiah, 68
Ruth, Book of, 342

Sacred canopies, 19–20, 27–33, 34, 36–48, 54, 67, 73–79, 96–98, 107–09, 119, 131–33, 138–39, 146, 153, 159–60, 160–64, 231–32, 242–44, 287–90, 292–94, 297, 319–20, 329–30; as domains within worldviews, 83–84

Sacred folds, 140
Sacred history, 145
Sacred, the, and the uncanny, 138–39
Sacred/mundane continuum, 28, 81–84, 98, 119, 131–32, 139, 143–44, 320–23
Sacredness, xix, 30–33; in worldviews, 83–84
Sacrifice, 40, 146, 257–58; Jesus Christ as, 70–71
Sagehood, 106, 151
Saguna Brahman, 117. *See also* Brahman, Nirguna Brahman
Saints, 118, 146
Saldarini, Anthony J., 335
Salvation, 46–47, 152
Samkhya, 231–32, 256, 303
Sample-size, of knowledge of creation, 281
Samsara, 74, 114
Sanctification, 20
Santa Claus, 159
Saul, King, 127
Scale, 135; of cosmos, 121–24, 164–65
Scapegoat, 70–71
Schematism, 145
Schleiermacher, F., 327
Schulkin, Jay, xxv
Schuon, Frithjof, 336
Science, 13–15
Science, 6, 31, 40, 42, 58, 87, 153, 170, 269, 336; ancient, 310; cognitive, xx; and contemplation, 308; and fact/value distinction, 200–01; and meaning, 142–43; modern, 137; studying religion, 27–28; and value, 129
Scientific study of religion, xvi
Scotus, John Duns, 183, 191, 198, 338–39
Scriptures, xx, 25, 42
Seasons, in orientation, 82
Second Isaiah, 127
Second Person, of Trinity 118, 261–62, 293. *See also* Jesus Christ
Second Samuel, 342
Secondness, 15, 69–70, 224, 283, 334, 340
Sectarianism, 154–55
Secularism, 8–9, 92, 257

Self, 10, 105–09, 113–18, 243, 301, 208; deconstructing, 306–09; losing, 266; -love, 315
Selfishness, 12
Sellars, Wilfrid, 69, 334
Semantics, 70–71, 101–02
Semiotics, 4, 16, 70–73, 101–02, 270, 301–03, 312; in nature, 64–68; pragmatic, 43–44
Serbia, 8
Sex, 302; birthing and ejaculation as symbols of divine love, 316–17; images for ontological creative act, 314
Shaivism (or Shaivites), 109, 111, 263; Kashmir, 8
Shakespeare, William, 238
Shamanism, in Christianity, 89; and philosophy, 86
Shangdi, 86, 254–55
Shankara, 107, 303
Shanqing Daoism, 256–57, 341. *See also* Daoism
Sharia, xxii
Sharing continuum, 91–93, 98, 131–32, 320
Shiva, 1, 26, 124, 175, 229, 242, 255, 263, 266, 279, 327; Shiva/Shakti, 116, 147
Shock, ontological, 17, 144
Short, T. L., 334
Signifier/signified, 71
Signs, 73–79, 101–03; in interpretation, 64–68; material quality of, 65–66; in Peirce, 334; physical, intellectual, and emotional, for unity, 306; not true or false in themselves, 66; for wholeness of world, 310–12; in worldviews, 81–84
Silk Road, 55
Simple location, 236
Simples, 36, 196
Simplicity, 236, 268–69, 271, 199–201
Simultaneity, 233–34
Sin, 147
Sincerity, 115
Singularity, vi, 38, 259–62, 279, 315–16, 322; of ontological creative act, 230–24

Sisera, 126
Sivan, Emmanuel, 328
Sizgorich, Thomas, 8, 328
Skepticism, 111
Slavery, 159
Smith, Huston, 336, 339–40
Smith, John E., 11, 18–19, 68, 328, 333
Social class, 159
Social construction, 109–13, 112–13; of reality, 29; of religion, 17–19, 42–43
Social constructionism, in pragmatism, 69
Social contract, 50
Social order, and religion, 20, 39
Social sciences, 17–18. *See also* Science
Socialization, 45
Sociology, 25, 51, 110; of knowledge, 29–33
Sophistication, in intellectual life, 87–90
Sophistication/popular culture continuum, 87–90, 98, 119, 131–32, 144, 291–93, 295, 320, 323
Soul, 206
Source, 261–62
South Asia, 55
Space-time, 194–95, 219–21, 232–41, 264–65; created, 322
Spinoza, Baruch, xviii, 56, 193, 221, 331–32, 340
Spirit world, 138–41
Spiritual paths, 21
Spiritual practices, 47
Spirituality, cultivation of virtuosity, 290, 299–317
Spontaneity throughout cosmos, 277
Spontaneity, 235–41, 275, 279
Spontaneous emergence. *See* Emergence
Stability, vi
Stace, Walter, 340
Stain, 146
Starbuck, Edwin Diller, 51, 331
Starry skies above and the moral law within, 131
State of nature, 50
Stone, 336
Stout, Jeffrey, 68, 326
Straw dogs. *See* Heaven, and straw dogs
Structuralism, 51

Subject/object, 148
Subjectivism, in postmodernism, 51–52
Subjectivity, divine, 124
Substance, 195–96; in Descartes, 63–64; as model of creation, 275
Suchness, 117–18, 138
Suchocki, Marjorie, 279, 341
Suffering, 42, 47, 107, 140, 146, 264; in Buddhism, 27
Sufism, 111, 312
Supernatural agents, 102, 139
Supernaturalism, xix, 2, 25, 139, 254
Superstition, 73, 160
Surprisingness, 38, 311; in orientation, 82
Swallows, 306
Symbol systems, 147, 294–95. *See also* Semiotics, Network meaning
Symbolic engagement, 4–5, 15–17, 59–60, 72–73, 79, 97–98, 160–61, 165, 251, 301–03, 316; defined, 63–68; through metaphysical theories, 287–300; of ultimates, 18–19, 319–20
Symbolic reference, 70, 136–38, 282–86
Symbols, vi, 32, 43, 122–24; broken, 1–2, 9–10, 76–79, 137, 228, 230; engaging and/or true, 67–68, 288; engaging transcendence, 131–33; of eternity, 242–44; higher and lower levels, 299–300; metaphysical, 19; religious, 61, 65, 329, iconically false and indexically true, 72–73; theory of, 287–300 (*see also* Semiotics); of ultimacy, 11, 125, 245, 253–62, under pressure from reality, 251
Symmetry, in concept of ontological creative act, 222–25, 280–81, 289
Syntax, 70–71
System, xvi; testing of, xxii; in *Philosophical Theology*, xxi–xxii; in theology, 44, 111–12, 153

Taiji, *see* Great Ultimate
Tanner, Kathryn, 54, 331
Taste, in theology, 175–76
Taylor, Mark C., 5–6, 328, 330
Teleological argument, 130
Telos, 196

Temporality, 172, 232–35, 246, 259–62, 276–79; modes of, 219–21, 322, essential and conditional components of, 263–66, eternal togetherness of, 267–69; real only in eternity, 241–44; theory of, 235–41; as ultimate, 243
Terminus, of ontological act of creation, 1, 218–22, 231, 261–62, 268
Terror, 29, 68
Thangaraj, M. Thomas, xxv
Thatamanil, John J., 47, 330–31, 339
Theism, 2, 117–18, 138, 279; personal, 2, 123. *See also* Monotheism
Theodicy, 31, 110, 123
Theological aesthetic, 172
Theological circle, xx
Theology, xv–xxi, 44; and the metaphysics of being, 174–75; biblical, xx; breaking symbols, 160–61; comparative, xix–xx, 42, 96; as creation and critiques, 77; as deep grammar, 48; disinterest in certain questions, 190–91; as engagement of ultimacy, 251; practical, 295–96; framing rhetoric of, 103; secular, xx; as a sign, 287–300; sophisticated, 90; systematic, 90, 78–79, 90, 95, 293–96. *See also* Confessionalism
Theravada Buddhism, 114
Thinking the ultimate through thinking theory of ultimacy, 290–300
Third Person, of Trinity, 261–62
Third term, 186–87
Thirdness, in Peirce, 15, 70, 224, 334, 340
Thomas Aquinas. *See* Aquinas
Tiamat, 126, 157
Tillich, Paul, xx, 5, 26–28, 32, 77, 93, 96, 102, 105–06, 108, 111, 149–50, 152, 203, 230, 258, 270, 309, 311, 325, 327–28, 330, 336, 339–40, 342
Timaeas, 14
Time, 21, 133, 197–99; created, 322; flow of 235–41; modes of, 235–41. *See also* Temporality
Togetherness, 177–80, 215–21, 237, 247, 267–71; de facto, 284; ontological and cosmological, 286

Torah, 77–78, 149–50, 154–55, 273. See also Hebrew Bible
Toulmin, Stephen, 328
Traditions, xv–xvi, 5, 7, 18–19, 21, 25, 32, 86–87, 109, 152, 157, 284, 319; with differing symbol systems, 288–300; membership in, 165–66
Transcendence, 84–87, 97–98, 102; signals of, 330; in symbols of ultimacy, 121–33, 163–65, 282–82, 297, 320
Transcendence/intimacy continuum, 84–87, 98, 119, 131–32, 290–92, 320–23
Transcendental conditions of mind, 56–57
Transcendental ideality, 49–50
Transcendental philosophy, 235
Transcendental traits of determinateness (or of Harmony; see also Harmony), 2–3, 36–42, 169, 175, 197–209, 231, 261–69, 312, 321; as logos, 220; as ultimate, 243–44
Transfiguration, 117
Transformation, 118
Transgenders, 11
Translation, 66, 302
Triadic structure of interpretation, 66
Tribes, 121–22, 155
Trinity, 118, 261–62; and shamanism, 88–89
Triviality, 13
True believers, 10
Truth, xv, xvii–xviii, 97–98, 122, 175; as carryover of value, 43–44, 144, 293–96, 342; in religious engagement, 20, 28, 42–44, 90; in folk religion, 89; in indexical reference, 159–61; and intimacy, 141; in narratives, 157; ontological, 47; and reference, 45–54; in symbols, 288, 293–96, 319–24; in theology, 15–17, 67–68; in worldviews, 138–39
Tu Weiming, 106, 336–37, 339, 342
Twenty-third Psalm, 255
Two truths, in Buddhism, 111, 114
Tylor, E. B., 32, 138

Ultimacy, 4–9, 42–44, 5, 84, 149–50; anthropological, 75; bearing on human life, 21; conceptualizing, 21, 95–98, 149–53; as conditioned and unconditioned, 131; cosmological defined, 193–209; defined, 109–13, 297; domesticated, 132; and explanation, 128; heuristic definitions of, 297; as knowable and unknowable, 21, 251; metaphysics of, 21, 70; in mundane things, 83084, 119; as mystery, 273–86; orientation to, 75–76; and pressure on symbols, 319; and possible worlds, 276–79; in supernatural agents, 2; in the sacred, 33–34; symbols of, 65, 90, 101–03, 159–61; true, 113–18; in uncanny things, 141
Ultimate concern, 5, 11, 105–19, 294–95, 301–03, 327; defined, 27; individual and social, 118–19; as normative, 110; versus proximate concerns, 105–06
Ultimate concern continuum, 163–64, 320
Ultimate of Non-Being (wuji), 25, 220, 228–29, 234, 257–58, 260, 273, 291, 309
Ultimate realities, xi, 1–4, 9–12, 20–21, 44, 72–73, 84–87, 131–33, 269–71, 287–90, 319–24; closer to me than I am to myself, 138; defining, 25–28; interpreted as finite/infinite contrasts, 33–34, 72–79 (see Finite/infinite contrasts); good or just, 275–76; ontological 173–91, 253–62, and anthropological, 102–06, and cosmological 3–4; receding from grasp, 108–09; the unconditioned conditions, 173–76. See also Ultimacy, Ultimates
Ultimates, 9–10, 16–17; anthropomorphic, 85–87; five in number, 4, 169–72; as objects of metaphysical inquiry, 169–72; ontological, 85–86; ontological and anthropological, 153–66; ontological and cosmological, 169–70; positive knowledge of, 253–71; see also Ultimacy, Ultimate realities

Uncanny, the, 32, 103, 135, 138–41, 148, 321
Understanding, xxii
Undeservedness, 38
Uniqueness, 264
Unity, 175, 197–201, 235–41, 262–67, 280; and being, 174; of body and intentionality, 305–06; de facto, 176, 178–80; underlying diversity and change, 256; with God, 342; of ontological creative act, 259–60, 303–06; with the ultimate, 302
Universality, 129; of ultimate concern, 105–06
Univocity of being, 171; demonstrated, 182–84
Upanishads, 256

Vagueness, xxi, 13, 194, 198, 258, 329; defined, 26–27; of religious categories, 42, 96
Value, xvii, 3–4, 11–15, 26–27, 38, 41–42, 75, 122, 129, 137, 147, 184, 202, 235–42, 146–47, 262, 276–79; in depth, 271; in form, 198–201; of harmonies, defined, 205–07; and intelligibility, 283; and interpretation, 81–84; modalities of, 206–08; in nature, 170; of persons, 265–66; in ultimacy, 68
Value-identity, xi, 36–42, 97, 106, 111, 116, 148, 204–09, 227, 241, 262–66, 312, 321; of persons, 313; subjective and objective, 3–4, 49–52, 09, 339; as ultimate, 243
Van der Leeuw, Gerardus, 32, 138
Vasubandhu, 151
Vaught, Carl G., 331
Vedas, 77, 147
Verstehen, xxii
Virgin Mary, 292–93
Virtues, of traits of harmony, 208
Virtuosity, religious, 84, 133, 251, 301–17, 323–24
Vishnu, 26, 116–18, 147, 229, 255, 279, 315
Visualization, 309
Vulnerability, to correction, xvi–xvii, 58–59, 113, 324

Waltemyer, Seth, xxv
Wanderer, Jeremy, 334
Wang Yangming, 106
Wangbi, 173, 228
War, 84
Ward, Keith, xviii, 181, 326, 228
Watchmaker, 130
Watson, Lancelot, xxv
Weber, Max, 50
Wegter-McNelly, Kirk, 339
Weiss, Paul, 68, 171, 177–80, 245, 333, 337–38
Weissman, David, 68West, Cornel, 333
West, Cornel, 68, 333
Whitehead, Alfred North, xxi, 13, 33–34, 59–61, 68, 96, 140–41, 170, 193, 195, 199, 204, 223, 225, 232–36, 263, 268, 278–79, 282, 285, 328, 330–32, 335, 337–41; on metaphysical pluralism, 176–77
Whitney, Lawrence, xxv
Wholeness, 3–4, 10, 68, 97–98, 107, 231, 141; of world, 310
Width, 13
Wildman, Wesley J., v, xx, xxv, 139, 326, 328–29, 331, 336
Wildness, in divine life, 261 267, 271, 281
Will, 130
Wilson, David Sloan, 335
Wisdom, 280; Wisdom literature, 154
Wittgenstein, Ludwig, 18, 326
Witzel, Michael, 335
Wood, William, 326
Word, divine, 110–11
Works righteousness, 46–47
World religions, xxii
World Soul, 234
World, 16
World, 2–3, 16; conceptions of in Axial Age religions, 122–24; defining, 33–34, 43–44, 74107, 109–13, 116 132; as determinate, 284–85; as kingdom, 125; images of, 121–24;other possible, 276–79; religions, 96; as terminus of ontological creative act, 218–21, 322; transcendentally defined, 59; within worlds, 19, 137

Worldviews, 19, 31, 97–98, 103, 107, 109, 131–32, 138–39, 141–46, 163–64, 244, 257–58, 283, 287, 290–92, 294–96, 320; comprehensiveness of orientation, 92–93; continua intersecting, 87–88; defined, 28, 81–93; minimalist, 143; as shared, 91–93
Worship, 18, 132
Wu, Kuang-Ming, 341

Xunzi, 79, 141, 335; on orientation, 82–83

Yahweh, 86, 122, 126, 150, 254–55, 261, 336; among other gods, 127
Yale School, 4

Yin/yang, 1, 10, 38, 12, 131, 151, 171, 193, 218–19, 233–35, 258, 260, 267; vibratory patterns, 228–29
Yoga, 118, 231–32, 303–06
Yogacara Buddhism, 114, 231
Yong, Amos, 325, 335
Yugoslavia, 8

Zanetti, Nikolas, xxv
Zazen, 73
Zeus, 86
Zhangzai, 341
Zhou Dunyi, 37, 130, 173, 228–29, 234, 257–60, 273, 309, 327, 340
Zhuangzi, 269, 341
Zoroastrianism, 86, 123, 127, 255, 330